South-Western Accounting

with Peachtree Complete® 2005

• • •

Carol Yacht

• • •

THOMSON
SOUTH-WESTERN

Australia · Brazil · Canada · Mexico · Singapore · Spain · United Kingdom · United States

South-Western Accounting with Peachtree Complete 2005
Carol Yacht

VP/Editorial Director:
Jack W. Calhoun

VP/Editor-in-Chief:
Karen Schmohe

Acquisitions Editor:
Marilyn Hornsby

Project Manager:
Carol Sturzenberger

VP/Director of Marketing:
Carol Volz

Channel Manager:
Courtney Schulz

Marketing Coordinator:
Angela Russo

Production Editor:
Diane Bowdler
Amy A. Simms

Production Manager:
Patricia Matthews Boies

Manufacturing Coordinator:
Kevin Kluck

Compositor:
Peter Lippincott

Printer:
Globus Printing
Minster, OH

Internal Designer:
settingPace, LLC

Art Director:
Bethany Casey

Cover Designer:
Ann Small, a small design studio

Cover Illustration:
Philip Brooker

Table of Contents

Preface

South-Western Accounting with Peachtree Complete 2005 shows you how to use Peachtree software with first year and second year accounting textbooks. You will complete selected end-of-chapter problems with Peachtree Complete Accounting 2005 (PCA) software. For more than 25 years, Peachtree Software has produced award-winning accounting software for use by individuals, businesses, and accountants.

All problem material is included in *South-Western Accounting with Peachtree Complete 2005*. This includes numerous screen illustrations, detailed steps, and transactions for problem completion. The problem material used in this book is from *Century 21 Accounting* textbooks—First Year and Advanced.

SYSTEM REQUIREMENTS

- IBM PC compatible 300 MHz Pentium II computer minimum; 450 MHz Pentium II or higher recommended.
- Windows XP/2000/ME/98 SE or Windows NT 4.0 with Service Pack 6a. Multi-user optimized for Windows XP/2000/98/Windows NT 4.0 (peer-to-peer network), Windows 2000 Server, Windows Server 2003, Windows Small Business Server 2003, Windows NT server or Novell Netware Network 5.1, 6.0 or 6.5.
- Microsoft Internet Explorer 6.0 required. Internet Explorer 6.0 is included on the Peachtree CD. Requires 70 MB for installation.
- 64MB of RAM (minimum); 128MB of RAM recommended.
- Display settings of at least High Color (16 bit). SVGA video. 800 X 600 resolution with small fonts.
- 110-250MB of free hard disk space.
- CD-ROM drive.
- Printer supported by Windows XP/2000/Me/98/NT 4.0.
- Mouse or compatible pointing device.
- *External media for backups*: One Zip™ drive disk; one CD-R; DVD-R, USB drive. If you have a CD-RW or DVD-RW drive you can use a CD-R or DVD-R to make the backups. *Or*, five blank, formatted disks. The author suggests that you reformat floppy disks.

The Problem Files and software, Peachtree Complete Accounting 2005, Educational Version, are included with this book. The steps that follow show you how to install the Peachtree CD.

This section gives you instructions for installing Peachtree Complete Accounting 2005, Educational version, on an IBM-PC or compatible computer. *You may need to check with your teacher to see if Peachtree has already been installed in the classroom or computer lab.*

Follow these steps to install PCA 2005 on an individual computer (non-networked).

1. Turn on your computer. Exit all programs and disable virus-protection and screen saver programs on your computer. This frees up memory and avoids interference with the Peachtree Complete Accounting setup process. Insert the Peachtree Complete Accounting 2005 CD that came with this book.

2. After a few moments, the Welcome to the Peachtree Accounting Educational Version 2005 window appears. Click on Peachtree Accounting, and continue with the next step. If the Welcome window does not appear automatically, click on Start, then Run. Type **x:\setup** and select OK. (Substitute the appropriate CD drive letter for x.)

3. At the Peachtree Complete Accounting Educational Version 2005 Welcome window, click Next >. Read the Licensing Agreement, then click on the radio button next to I accept the terms in the License Agreement. Click Next >.

4. The Peachtree Accounting Setup Options window appears. Click on the Standard Setup radio button to select it. Click Next >. If necessary, click on the radio button next to Yes, install the Peachtree shortcuts to my desktop. Click Next >. Peachtree starts to install.

5. When the Finish window appears, accept the default for Yes, I would like to start Peachtree Complete Accounting Educational Version by clicking on Finish. After a few moments, the startup menu appears.

6. To exit the program, select Close this window. Then, click on File, Exit.

7. Remove the CD from your drive.

NETWORK INSTALLATION

Peachtree Software's Knowledge Center includes information about network installation. To use the Knowledge Center, you need to create a Peachtree Passport account. Follow these instructions to create a Peachtree Passport account.

1. Go to this website http://www.peachtree.com/login/newusersignup.cfm to create a Peachtree Passport account. Complete the e-mail address, password (8 to 20 characters), and confirm fields. Complete the contact information. You will be sent a confirmation email.

2. To activate Peachtree Passport, go to your email account. Link to the email from Peachtree Online Subscriptions, Welcome to Peachtree Passport, to activate your account. When the Account Activation page appears, type your password.

3. The Peachtree Passport Login Page appears. Type your E-Mail Address and Password, then click **Log In**.

4. The Welcome to Peachtree Passport page appears. Link to Get online support via the Peachtree Knowledge Center. From the Peachtree Knowledge Center page, link to LOG IN TO THE KNOWLEDGE CENTER, then link to PROCEED TO THE KNOWLEDGE CENTER.

5. The Peachtree Knowledge Center screen appears showing your name in the Logged in as field. Link to Find Answers. From the Answers page you can do Peachtree Knowledge Center searches.

Once you have a Peachtree Passport account, the website for logging in to the Peachtree Knowledge Center is https://www.peachtree.com/passportsecurity/login.cfm?PassThrough=/passport/ welcome.cfm

PEACHTREE'S GLOBAL OPTIONS

Follow these steps to set global options for Peachtree. These options will be in effect for all Peachtree companies.

1. Start Peachtree.

2. Open any company. For example, see pages 3–9 for detailed steps to open the Peachtree Problem file for the 4-5 Mastery Problem.

3. From Peachtree's menu bar, select Options, Global. If necessary, select the <u>A</u>ccounting tab. Make sure your Maintain Global Options window matches the one shown. (*Hint:* In the Decimal Entry area, Manual and 2 decimal places should be selected; the boxes in the Hide General Ledger Accounts area *must* be unchecked; Warn if a record was changed but not saved and Recalculate cash balance automatically in Receipts, Payments, and Payroll Entry should be checked.)

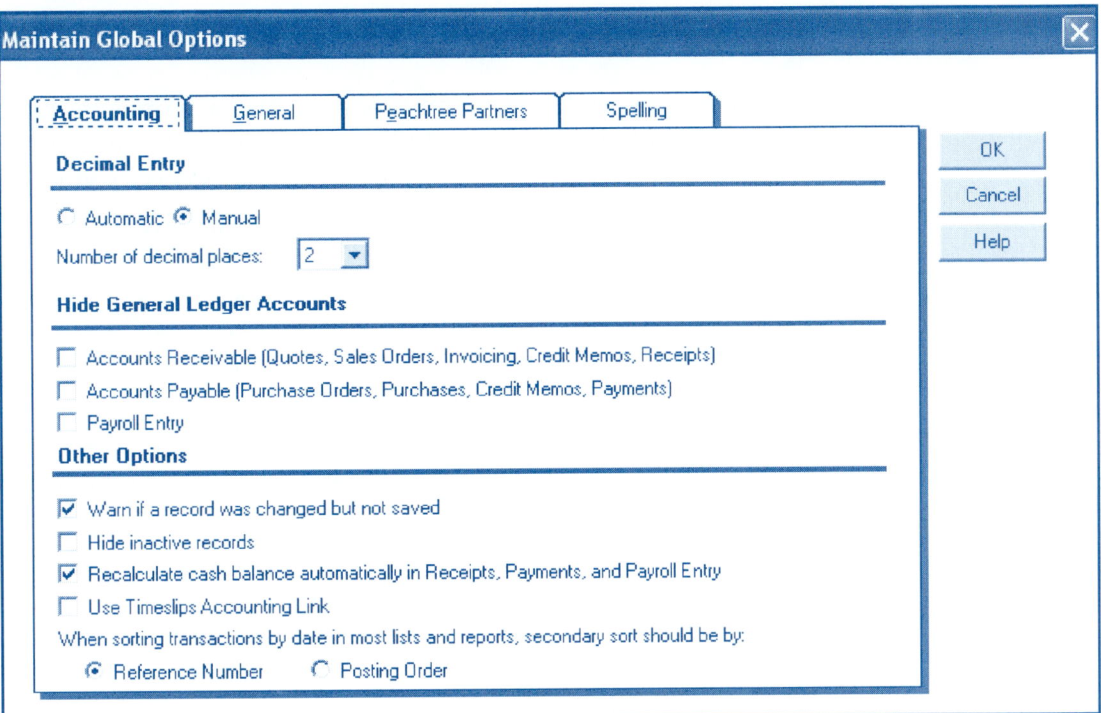

4. Click the <u>G</u>eneral tab. Make sure your screen matches the one below.

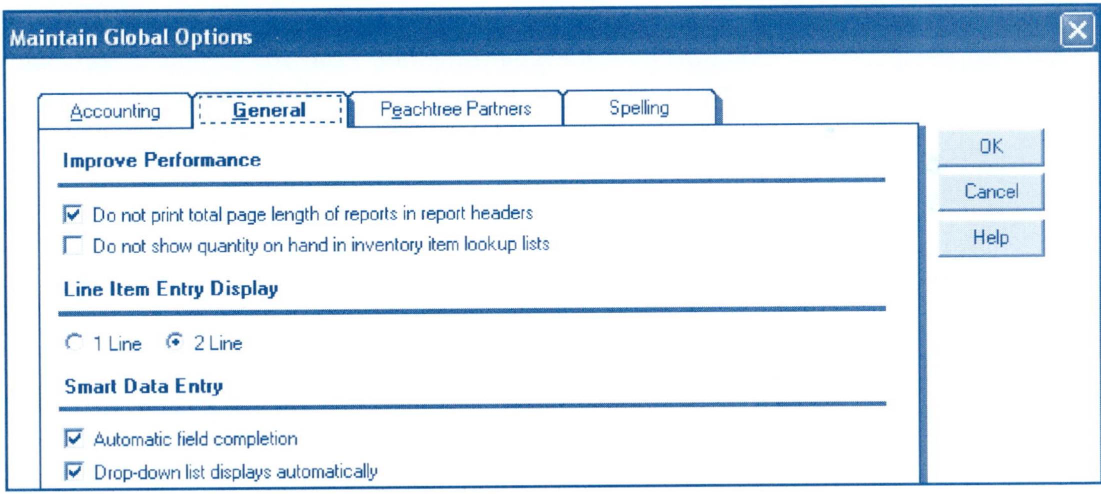

5. Click OK. The selections made in global options are now set for each company that you use in Peachtree.

As you work through the problems and activities in this book, you will be expected to read and follow the step-by-step instructions. Numerous screen illustrations allow you to check your work.

The following conventions are used in this text:

1. Information that you are to type appears in a different font..

   Examples: **MP04-5XX**

   Cash

   4-5 Mastery Problem

2. Keys on the keyboard that should be pressed appear in a keyboard font.

   Example: Enter

3. Names of buttons appear in **bold**.

4. Unnamed buttons and picture icons are shown as they actually appear on the screen.

   Examples: Next >

PROBLEM CORRELATION WITH TEXTBOOKS

South-Western Accounting with Peachtree Complete 2005 shows students how to use Peachtree software with first and second year accounting textbooks. The chart on pages xiii to xvi specifies which problems are used.

The Peachtree data file uses a zero before a single digit number; for example, 04-5MP.ptb is the 4-5 Mastery Problem, O'Kalla Lawn and Garden.

Century 21 Accounting Multicolumn Journal and General Journal Problem List

Unit 1: Identifies problems used with first-year accounting textbooks.

Problem Number	Company	Peachtree Files-Unit 1	Backup File[1]
4-5 Mastery Problem 4-4 Mastery Problem in the General Journal Version	O'Kalla Lawn and Garden	04-5MP.ptb	4-5 Mastery Problem.ptb
5-5 Mastery Problem	LawnMow	05-5MP.ptb	5-5 Mastery Problem.ptb
5-6 Challenge Problem	GolfPro	05-6MP.ptb	5-6 Challenge Problem.ptb
Reinforcement Activity 1—Part A	Extreme Adventures	RA01A.ptb	Reinforcement Activity 1—Part A.ptb
6-5 Mastery Problem	Bonita Bubbles	06-5MP.ptb	6-5 Mastery Problem.ptb
7-3 Mastery Problem	Rolstad Repair Service	07-3MP.ptb	7-3 Mastery Problem.ptb
7-4 Challenge Problem	LawnWork[2]	07-4.ptb	7-4 Challenge Problem.ptb
8-4 Mastery Problem	Rolstad Repair Service	08-4MP.ptb	8-4 Mastery Problem.ptb
8-5 Challenge Problem	LawnWork[3]	085CP.ptb	8-5 Challenge Problem.ptb
Reinforcement Activity 1—Part B	Extreme Adventures	For starting data, use the Reinforcement Activity 1—Part A.ptb back up file	Reinforcement Activity 1—Part B.ptb
9-6 Mastery Problem	Mercury Computers	09-6MP.ptb	9-6 Mastery Problem.ptb
9-7 Challenge Problem	Fitness Connection	09-7CP.ptb	9-7 Challenge Problem.ptb
10-4 Mastery Problem	Aqua Center	10-4MP.ptb	10-4 Mastery Problem.ptb
10-5 Challenge Problem	Zone 6	10-5CP.ptb	10-5 Challenge Problem.ptb
11-6 Mastery Problem	Auto Restoration, Inc.	11-6MP.ptb	11-6 Mastery Problem.ptb
11-7 Challenge Problem	Custom Golf Land	11-7CP.ptb	11-7 Challenge Problem.ptb
12-5 Application Problem	Royal Appliances	12-5AP.ptb	12-5 Application Problem.ptb
12-6 Mastery Problem	Arrow Company	12-6MP.ptb	12-6 Mastery Problem.ptb
13-5 Mastery Problem	Keller Systems, Inc.	13-5MP.ptb	13-5 Mastery Problem
13-6 Challenge Problem	Golf Design, Inc.	13-6CP.ptb	13-6 Challenge Problem.ptb
Reinforcement Activity 2—Part A	Medical Services Company	RA01-2A.ptb	Reinforcement Activity 2—Part A.ptb

(continued)

[1]After completion of the problem, students back up the file using the backup file name shown.

[2]The textbook identifies this company as LawnMow. The Peachtree company name is LawnWork.

[3]Ibid.

Problem Number	Company	Peachtree Files-Unit 1	Backup File[1]
14-1 Application Problem	Drake Corporation	14-1AP.ptb	14-1 Application Problem.ptb
14-7 Mastery Problem	Carol's Closet	14-7MP.ptb	14-7 Mastery Problem.ptb
15-5 Mastery Problem	Lighting Center, Inc.	15-5MP.ptb	15-5 Mastery Problem.ptb
16-4 Application Problem	Wilson Paint, Inc.	16-4AP.ptb	16-4 Application Problem.ptb
16-5 Mastery Problem	Northern Lights	16-5MP.ptb	16-5 Mastery Problem.ptb
Reinforcement Activity 2—Part B	Medical Services Company	For starting data, use the Reinforcement Activity 2—Part A.ptb backup file	Reinforcement Activity 2—Part B.ptb
17-2 Application Problem	Waldron Company	17-2AP.ptb	17-2 Application Problem.ptb
17-3 Application Problem	Weatherly Co.	17-3AP.ptb	17-3 Application Problem.ptb
18-1 Application Problem	Umeki Food Source	18-1AP.ptb	18-1 Application Problem.ptb
18-4 Application Problem	Ester Engineering, Inc.	18-4AP.ptb	18-4 Application Problem.ptb
19-4 Mastery Problem	Fratisi Company	19-4MP.ptb	19-4 Mastery Problem.ptb
20-2 Application Problem	Webster Company	20-2AP.ptb	20-2 Application Problem.ptb
20-5 Mastery Problem	Amory Company	20-5MP.ptb	20-5 Mastery Problem.ptb
Reinforcement Activity 3—Part A	Sparkle, Inc.	RA03-A.ptb	Reinforcement Activity 3—Part A.ptb
21-4 Mastery Problem	Youngblood, Inc.	21-4MP.ptb	21-4 Mastery Problem.ptb
21-5 Challenge Problem	Blackwell Corporation	21-5CP.ptb	21-5 Challenge Problem.ptb
22-5 Mastery Problem	Benford Corporation	22-5MP.ptb	22-5 Mastery Problem.ptb
Reinforcement Activity 3—Part B	Sparkle, Inc.	RA03-B.ptb	Reinforcement Activity 3—Part B
24-3 Mastery Problem	Argo Corporation	24-3MP.ptb	24-3 Mastery Problem.ptb

(continued)

Unit 2: Identifies problems used with second-year accounting textbooks.

Problem Number	Company	Peachtree Files-Unit 2	Backup File[1]
1-2 Application Problem	Zenix Company	01-2AP.ptb	1-2 Application Problem.ptb
1-4 Mastery Problem	Outdoor Sport	01-4MP.ptb	1-4 Mastery Problem.ptb
2-1 Application Problem	Sequoia Sport Apparel	02-1AP.ptb	2-1 Application Problem.ptb
2-2 Application Problem	Colonial Furnishings	02-2AP.ptb	2-2 Application Problem.ptb
2-3 Mastery Problem	EuroFashions	02-3MP.ptb	2-3 Mastery Problem.ptb
3-5 Application Problem	John's Automotive	03-5AP.ptb	3-5 Application Problem.ptb
4-5 Application Problem	AllSports Center	04-5AP.ptb	4-5 Application Problem.ptb
Reinforcement Activity 1	BooksPlus, Inc.	RA01.ptb	Reinforcement Activity 1.unadjusted.ptb Reinforcement Activity 1.adjusted.ptb Reinforcement Activity 1.closed.ptb
6-1 Application Problem	Bowman Lawn and Garden	06-1AP.ptb	6-1 Application Problem.ptb
7-1 Application Problem	Stallworth	07-1AP.ptb	7-1 Application Problem.ptb
7-4 Application Problem	McCafferty, Inc.	07-4AP.ptb	7-4 Application Problem.ptb
8-11 Mastery Problem	Western, Inc.	08-11MP.ptb	8-11 Mastery Problem.ptb
8-12 Challenge Problem	McNeilley, Inc.	08-12CP_2005.ptb 08-12CP_2007.ptb	8-12 Challenge Problem_2005.ptb 8-12 Challenge Problem_2007.ptb
9-1 Application Problem	Raecker, Inc.	09-1AP.ptb	9-1 Application Problem.ptb
9-4 Mastery Problem		09-4MP.ptb	9-4 Mastery Problem.ptb
10-1 Application Problem	Bellingham, Inc.	10-1AP.ptb	10-1 Application Problem.ptb
10-4 Mastery Problem	Marier, Inc.	10-4MP.ptb	10-4 Mastery Problem.ptb
11-4 Application Problem	PlasticTech, Inc.	11-4AP.ptb	11-4 Application Problem.ptb
11-5 Mastery Problem	SkyPark, Inc.	11-5MP.ptb	11-5 Mastery Problem_12-31-05.ptb 11-5 Mastery Problem.ptb
12-1 Application Problem	PC Design, Inc.	12-1AP.ptb	12-1 Mastery Problem.ptb
12-4 Mastery Problem	Sentry VideoLink, Inc.	12-4MP.ptb	12-4 Mastery Problem.ptb

(continued)

Century 21 Accounting Multicolumn Journal and General Journal Problem List *(continued)*

Problem Number	Company	Peachtree Files-Unit 2	Backup File[1]
13-5 Mastery Problem	Lander, Inc.	13-5MP.ptb	13-5 Mastery Problem.adjusted.ptb 13-5 Mastery Problem.closed.ptb 13-5 Mastery Problem.Reversed.ptb
Reinforcement Activity 2	Whitehurst, Inc.	RA02.ptb	Reinforcement Activity 2.Part A.ptb Reinforcement Activity 2.Part B Adjusted.ptb Reinforcement Activity 2.Part B Closed.ptb Reinforcement Activity 2.Part B Reversed.ptb
20-1 Application Problem	Perry, Inc.	20-1AP.ptb	20-1 Application Problem.ptb
20-5 Challenge Problem	Cozart Company	20-5CP.ptb	20-5 Challenge Problem
21-1 Application Problem	Estrada and Jeter	21-1AP.ptb	21-1 Application Problem
21-6 Mastery Problem	Hatfield and Allen	21-6MP.ptb	21-6 Mastery Problem.ptb
22-5 Mastery Problem	J & L Service	22-5MP.ptb	22-5 Mastery Problem.adjusted.ptb 22-5 Mastery Problem.closed.ptb
22-6 Challenge Problem	Doran & Eden	22-6CP.ptb	22-6 Challenge Problem.ptb
23-3 Application Problem	Town of Templeton	23-3AP.ptb	23-3 Application Problem.ptb
23-4 Mastery Problem	Town of Ingalls	23-4MP.ptb	23-4 Mastery Problem.ptb
24-4 Mastery Problem	Town of Duluth	24-4MP.ptb	24-4 Mastery Problem.ptb
24-5 Challenge Problem	Town of Winnona	24-5CP.ptb	24-5 Challenge Problem.ptb

UNIT 1

South-Western Century 21 Accounting

The problem material in Unit 1 of *South-Western Accounting with Peachtree Complete 2005* is from *South-Western Century 21 Accounting General Journal* and *Multicolumn, Eighth Edition*, textbooks. The Unit 1 problems appear in Chapters 4 through 24 of the *Century 21 Accounting 8e* textbooks. The instructions and transactions for each problem are included in this book.

Journalizing Transactions and Posting to a General Ledger

The instructions that follow show you how to do the following:

- Start Peachtree Complete Accounting.
- Restore starting data from the South-Western Accounting with Peachtree CD.
- Identify the directory where O'Kalla Lawn and Garden is stored on your computer's hard drive.
- Change the company name.
- Journalize transactions in the general journal.
- Post transactions to the general ledger.
- Print the general journal and general ledger.
- Back up (save) Peachtree data.
- Complete 4-5 Mastery Problem.

Before you start the 4-5 Mastery Problem, ask your teacher if O'Kalla Lawn and Garden, the company used for the 4-5 Mastery Problem, has already been restored on your computer. The instructions that follow assume that O'Kalla Lawn and Garden is being used for the first time.

GETTING STARTED

Use the following instructions to start Peachtree and restore the starting data for O'Kalla Lawn and Garden, owned by Patrick O'Kalla.

1. If Peachtree Complete Accounting 2005 (PCA) is *not* installed on your computer, refer to page vii in this book.

2. When PCA was installed, an icon was created for Peachtree. Place the mouse pointer on the Peachtree icon, then double-click with the left mouse button to start PCA.

   Or, click on Start, All Programs, Peachtree Complete Accounting Educational Release. Then, select Peachtree Complete Accounting. (These instructions are consistent with Windows XP. If you are using a different version of Windows, these instructions will differ slightly.)

3. The startup window appears.

From the startup window, you can select Open an existing company; Create a new company; Explore a sample company; Take a guided tour of Peachtree; Convert from a QuickBooks® or One-Write Plus® company; or Exit Peachtree.

PEACHTREE DATA FILES

The South-Western Accounting with Peachtree CD includes a Peachtree data files folder. In the steps that follow you will restore the 04-5MP.ptb file. In Peachtree, when you restore data you are copying over (or over-writing) the company data.

The steps that follow assume you are starting the 4-5 Mastery Problem for the *first* time, and that O'Kalla Lawn and Garden is *not* already restored. You may need to check with your instructor before continuing.

1. The startup menu should be displayed. From the startup menu, click Close . There are three menu bar options: File; Options; and Help. Click File; Restore.

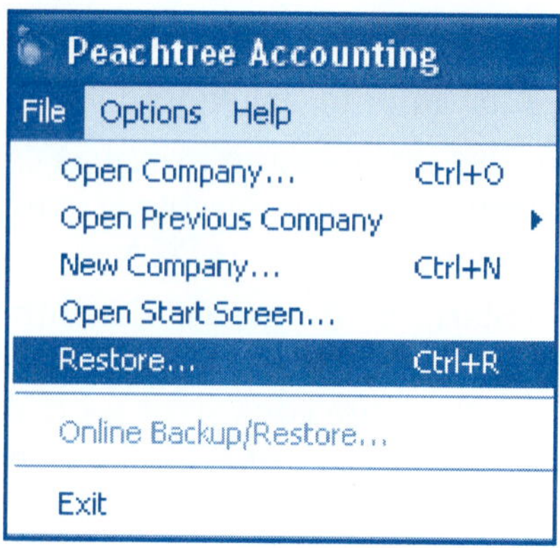

2. The Restore Wizard - Select Backup File window appears. Observe that the Location field shows where Peachtree is stored on your computer. The default location is C:\Program Files\Peachtree\Company. Your Location field may differ. The location field shown below represents Peachtree's default program and data path when the program is installed on drive C. Compare your Select Backup File window with the one shown below.

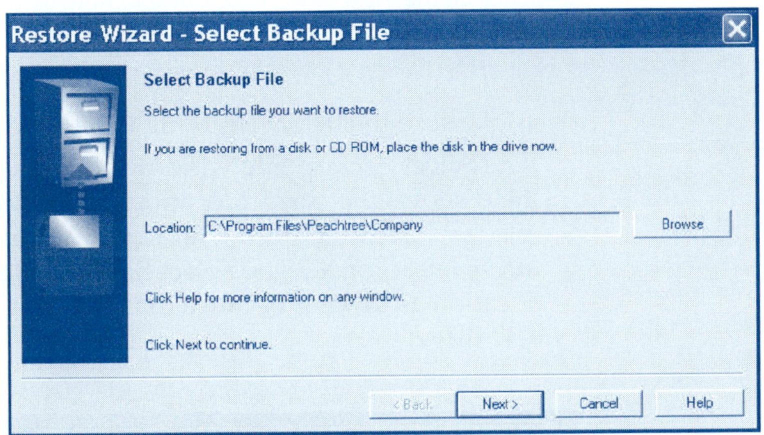

Click Browse . The Open Backup File window appears. In the Look in field, double-click on the appropriate location of the Peachtree data files. Then, click 04-5MP.ptb to select it. (If appropriate, select your CD drive then double-click the Peachtree Files-Unit 1 folder. Click 04-5MP.ptb to select it.) To identify the location of the Peachtree data files, the instructions in this book refer to a Peachtree Files folder. On your computer, the folder name may differ.

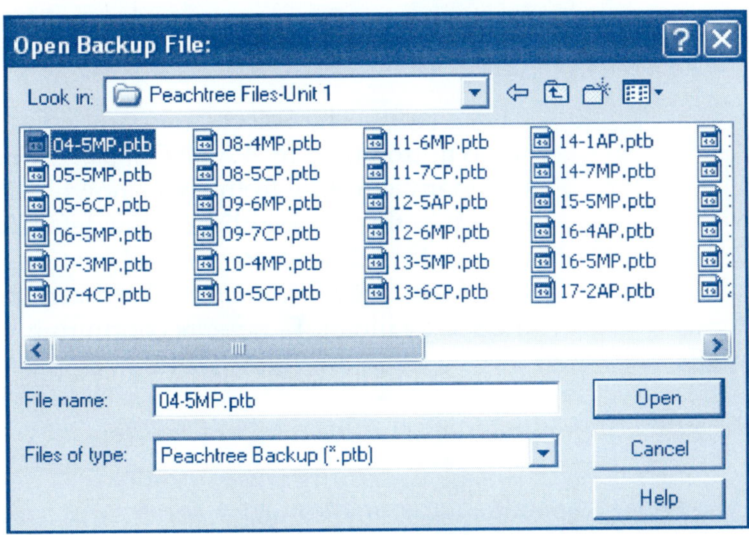

If you do *not* have a .ptb extension, follow these steps. (These steps may differ in Windows 98SE or Windows 2000):

1. Click Start, All Programs, Accessories, then Windows Explorer.

2. From the Windows Explorer menu bar, select Tools; Folder Options.

3. Click on the View tab. The box next to Hide extensions for known file types should be *unchecked*

Make sure the 04-5MP.ptb file is selected. Click Open .

The Select Backup File window appears. Make sure the Location field shows the correct location for the 04-5MP.ptb file; for example, X:\Peachtree Files-Unit 1\04-5MP.ptb. (Substitute the correct drive letter for X.) The Select Backup File window below shows the location as drive E because that is the drive letter of the author's CD drive.

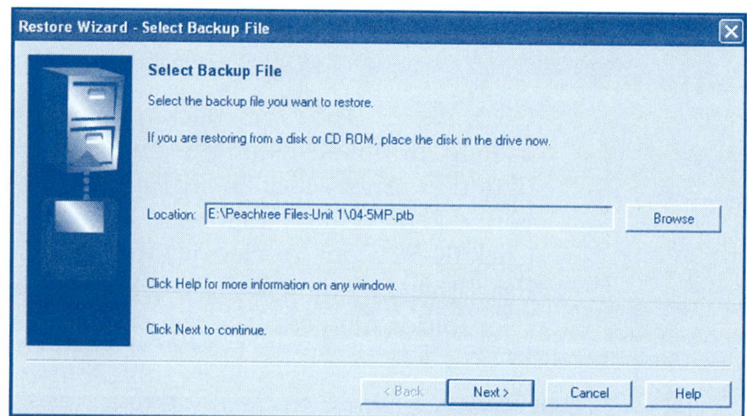

Click Next> . The Select Company window appears. Click on the radio button next to *A New Company*. Compare your Select Company window to the one shown below. The Location field shown in this book indicates the default location where drive C is used to install Peachtree. Your Location field may differ. *Make sure that the Location field ends in* **okalawan**. Read the information below the screen illustration *before* continuing with step 10.

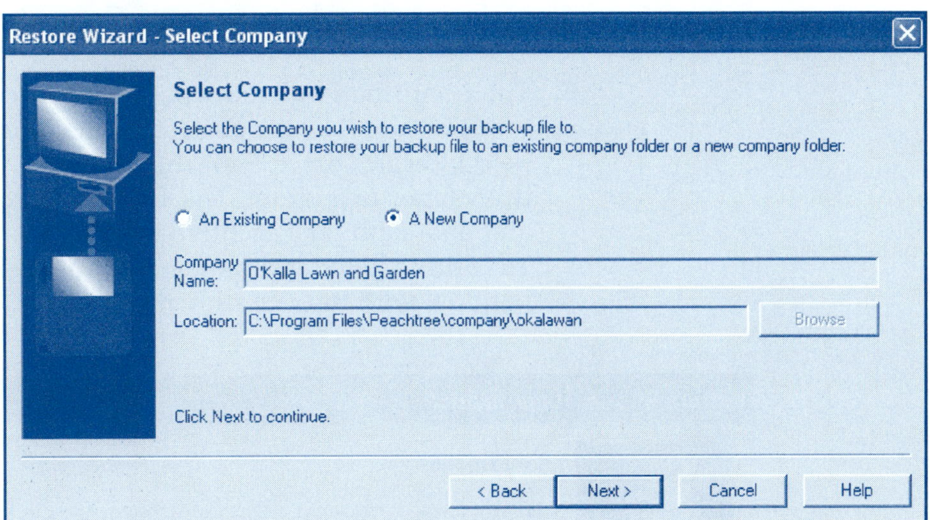

When you select *A New Company* to restore, a company folder is set up in Peachtree; and the company name is shortened. The shortened company name is added to Peachtree's program and data path. If the company has *never been restored* to the computer you are using, the shortened name is "okalawan."

If O'Kalla Lawn and Garden (the company name for the 4-5 Mastery Problem) is already set up on your computer, Peachtree changes the shortened name of the company and creates a different company name folder. For example, the company's shortened name shows "okalawam." Notice that the last letter of the shortened name is changed. This means that O'Kalla Lawn and Garden was already restored. If this is the case, select *An Existing Company*, then click Browse. Double-click O'Kalla Lawn and Garden (*or*, 04-5MPXX). An Existing Company is selected and your Location field shows the shortened company name **okalawan**. Continue with step 7.

3. Click Next >. The Restore Options window appears.

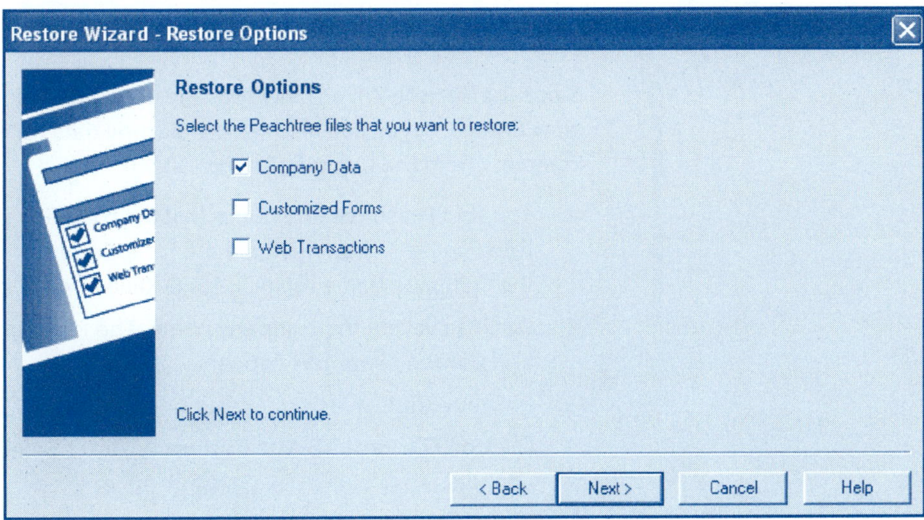

4. Make sure that the box next to Company Data is *checked*. Click Next >.

5. The Confirmation window appears. Check the From and To fields to make sure they are correct. In the illustration below the From field indicates drive E for the Peachtree Files-Unit 1 folder. Your drive letter may differ. The To field indicates the default program and data path for Peachtree when it has been installed on drive C. Your drive letter and path may differ. Compare your Confirmation window with the one shown below.

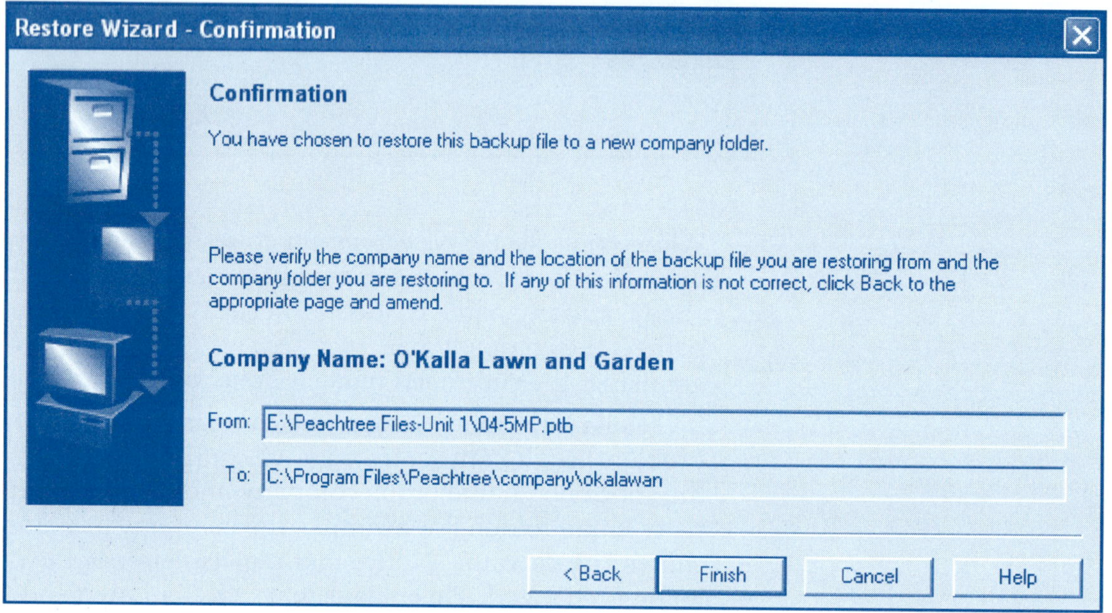

6. Click Finish. When the Restore Company scale is 100% complete, your data is restored and the Peachtree Accounting: O'Kalla Lawn and Garden menu bar appears.

7. If necessary, remove the South-Western Accounting CD.

Since the Restore Wizard includes the ability to restore An Existing Company *or* A New Company, you can also restore starting data for Peachtree by selecting that company from the Company Name list.

1. You start Peachtree and notice that the company you want to use is already listed on the Company Name list. For example, on the Open Company window, the Company Name list includes O'Kalla Lawn and Garden (*or*, 04-5MPXX).

2. Double click on the company name. The Peachtree Accounting: O'Kalla Lawn and Garden menu bar appears.

3. Put your South-Western Accounting CD into the CD drive.

4. Click on File; Restore. The Restore Wizard's Select Backup File window appears.

5. Click Browse . Open the appropriate file; for example, open the 04-5MP.ptb file. Click Next > .

6. Observe that the Select Company window defaults to An Existing Company. Accept the default for An Existing Company by clicking Next > .

7. On the Restore Options window, make sure there is a check mark next to Company Data. Click Next > .

8. At the Confirmation window, click Finish . You now have starting data for the 4-5 Mastery Problem, O'Kalla Lawn and Garden.

CHANGING THE COMPANY NAME

Before you start recording transactions for the 4-5 Mastery Problem, you should look at the company information included on the 04-5MP.ptb file. Follow these steps to look at company information.

1. The O'Kalla Lawn and Garden menu bar should be displayed. From the menu bar, click on Maintain; Company Information. The Maintain Company Information window appears. Compare your Maintain Company Information window to the one shown below.

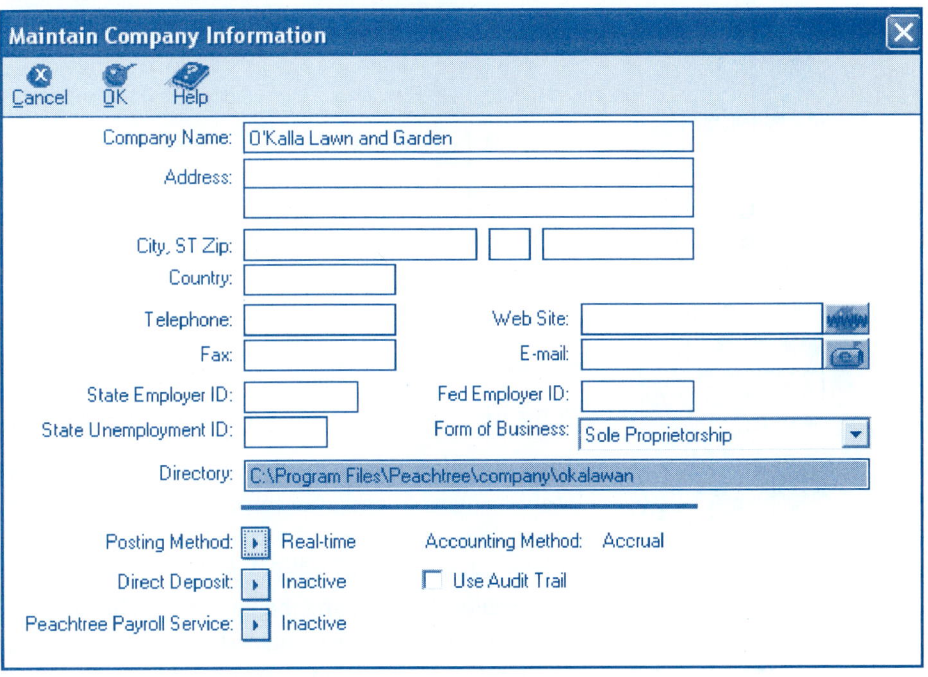

Observe that the Company Name field shows O'Kalla Lawn and Garden. The Form of Business field shows Sole Proprietorship. The Directory field shows the location on the hard drive where the company data is stored – C:\Program Files\Peachtree\company\ okalawan. When a company is created in Peachtree, the company name is shortened. The shortened company name is added to Peachtree's Program and data path. If you are working in a computer lab, Peachtree's location may differ.

2. In order to make sure that each one of your printouts shows your name and the problem number, in the Company Name field, type **04-5MPXX**. The X's are for your initials. The screen illustration shows the author's initials CY.

Maintain Company Information

Cancel   OK   Help

Company Name: 04-5MPCY
Address:
City, ST Zip:
Country:
Telephone: Web Site:
Fax: E-mail:
State Employer ID: Fed Employer ID:
State Unemployment ID: Form of Business: Sole Proprietorship
Directory: C:\Program Files\Peachtree\company\okalawan

Posting Method: ▸ Real-time   Accounting Method: Accrual
Direct Deposit: ▸ Inactive   ☐ Use Audit Trail
Peachtree Payroll Service: ▸ Inactive

Why do I have to change the company name?

The idea behind changing the company name is so that printouts will show the problem number and your initials. (Your instructor may give you different instructions.) Once you change the company name, the name of the company will also change when you start Peachtree. Remember, you can retrieve starting data for this problem by restoring the 04-5MP.ptb file from the South-Western Accounting with Peachtree CD. Once you restore the Peachtree data file (04-5MP.ptb for this problem), you have fresh, starting data.

3. When you are finished typing 04-5MPXX as the company name, click on [OK]. Once you have changed the Company Name, each one of your printouts will show the problem number and your initials.

Nothing has changed on your computer's hard drive. The Peachtree program and data path for O'Kalla Lawn and Garden is C:\Program Files\Peachtree\Company\okalawan. (You can check this by selecting Maintain; Company Information. Observe what is shown in the Directory field.) What you've done is change the company name so that your printouts will show the problem number and your initials. Remember when you restore problem data, Peachtree sets up a sub-folder with a shortened company name. In this case, the subfolder is \okalawan. Using Maintain, Company Information to rename your company does *not* change the shortened company name.

Here is what you have done so far:

- Started PCA.
- Restored the Peachtree data file from the South-Western Accounting with Peachtree CD.
- Identified the directory where Peachtree is stored on your computer's hard drive.
- Changed the company name so that your printouts will show the problem number and your initials.

These are the steps that you will follow each time you start a new problem in *South-Western Accounting with Peachtree Complete 2005*.

Each time you end a work session, you will need to back up your work. If you need to end this work session before completing the 4-5 Mastery Problem, skip ahead to the "Back Up Your Peachtree File" section and complete those steps. When you begin your next work session, you will restore the 4-5 Mastery.ptb file before continuing the problem. To Restore the back up file, refer to the "Restore Peachtree Data" section.

PEACHTREE'S CHART OF ACCOUNTS

As you know from your study of accounting, a chart of accounts is the list of accounts used by a business. Peachtree's chart of accounts is organized as follows:

Account Number: O'Kalla Lawn and Garden uses three-digit account numbers, within a division by 10s. The Account ID field shows the account number.

Account Description: Use the Description field to name the account.

Account Type: In Peachtree, you must also select the type of account you are setting up. The account type classifies the accounts for the financial statements. For example, Cash is set up as a Cash account, Accounts Receivable is set up as an Accounts Receivable account. The account type determined whether the account is a balance sheet account (an asset, liability, or owner's equity account) or an income statement account (a revenue or an expense account). Use the Account Type field for account classifications.

Another feature specific to Peachtree is how the income summary account is classified. In Peachtree, income summary is classified as Equity-Retained Earnings. In order for Peachtree to post to the general ledger, one account must be set up as Retained Earnings. The retained earnings account represents the earnings of the company.

1. From the menu bar, select Reports, then General Ledger.

2. The Select a Report window appears. Click on the Chart of Accounts to select it.

3. Click on the Preview icon.

4. The Chart of Accounts Filter window appears. Click on OK. Compare your chart of accounts to the one shown.

O'Kalla Lawn and Garden
Chart of Accounts
As of Nov 30, 2005

Filter Criteria includes: Report order is by ID. Report is printed with Accounts having Zero Amounts and in Detail Format.

Account ID	Account Description	Active?	Account Type
110	Cash	Yes	Cash
120	Accts. Rec.-Merilda Domingo	Yes	Accounts Receivable
130	Supplies	Yes	Other Current Assets
210	Accts. Pay.-Park Supplies	Yes	Accounts Payable
310	Patrick O'Kalla, Capital	Yes	Equity-doesn't close
320	Patrick O'Kalla, Drawing	Yes	Equity-gets closed
330	Income Summary	Yes	Equity-Retained Earnings
410	Sales	Yes	Income
510	Advertising Expense	Yes	Expenses
520	Miscellaneous Expense	Yes	Expenses
530	Rent Expense	Yes	Expenses

These are the accounts you will use to journalize and post the November transactions shown in the textbook.

READ ME

Notice that an Income Summary account appears on the chart of accounts. Peachtree requires that one Equity-Retained Earnings account be included for every company. This account is named Income Summary. You will *not* make any entries using this account in the 4-5 Mastery Problem.

5. Click on the close icon to return to the Select a Report window. Click on the icon again to return to the menu bar.

6. Before you start journalizing transactions, add Account No. 540, Utilities Expense to O'Kalla Lawn and Garden's Chart of Accounts. Follow these steps to add an account to the chart of accounts.

   a. From Peachtree's menu bar, select, Maintain; Chart of Accounts. The Maintain Chart of Accounts window is displayed.

<ol type="a" start="2">
<li>b. In the Account I<u>D</u> field, type 540 and press [Enter].</li>
<li>c. In the De<u>s</u>cription field, type Utilities Expense and press [Enter].</li>
<li>d. In the Account <u>T</u>ype field, select Expenses. The Account <u>T</u>ype field is important. The correct classification places the accounts correctly in the general ledger and on financial statements.</li>
</ol>

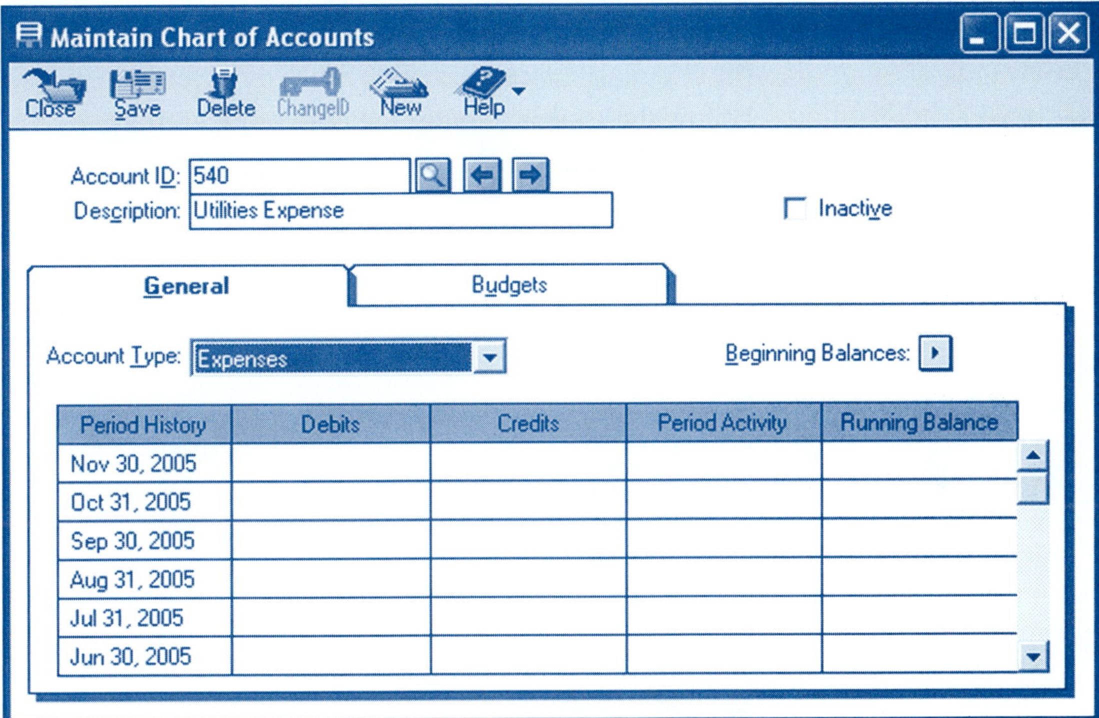

<ol type="a" start="5">
<li>e. Make sure that your Account I<u>D</u>, De<u>s</u>cription, and Account <u>T</u>ype are correct. Then click [Save].</li>
<li>f. Click [Close], to close the Maintain Chart of Accounts window.</li>
</ol>

JOURNALIZING TRANSACTIONS AND POSTING TO A GENERAL LEDGER

The data that you restored from the Peachtree data files folder contains starting data for the 4-5 Mastery Problem. Read the information that follows to learn about Peachtree's general journal and general ledger.

Peachtree's General Journal

Peachtree includes two ways to journalize general journal transactions. You can select "General Journal Entry" from the Tasks menu or you can select "General Journal Entry" from Peachtree's General Ledger Navigation Aid at the bottom of the window. (If the Navigation Aid is *not* shown, from Peachtree's menu bar select Options; click View Navigation Aid to place a checkmark next to it.) The instructions that follow show you how to make a general journal entry from Peachtree's Tasks menu.

Instructions: You are going to journalize and post the November transactions for the 4-5 Mastery Problem. The steps that follow show you how to use Peachtree's general journal to journalize and post the first transaction.

Transaction:

Nov. 1   Received cash from owner as an investment, $5,500.00. R1.

Follow these steps to enter the Nov. 1 transaction.

1. From the menu bar, select Tasks, then select General Journal Entry.

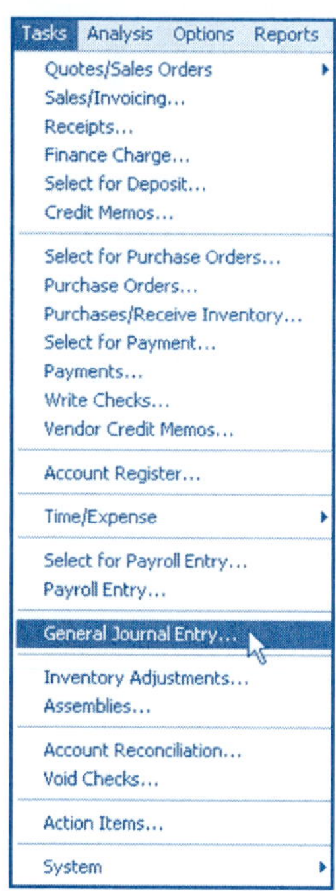

2. The "General Journal Entry" window appears. Your cursor is in the Date field. Accept the default for 11/1/05 by pressing the Enter key three times. Observe that the date changes to Nov. 1, 2005. (*Hint:* For purposes of using Peachtree, the year is 2005.)

3. Your cursor is in the GL Account field. Observe that the GL Account field has a magnifying-glass icon in it. Click on the (magnifying-glass icon) and a chart of accounts list pops up. Since you are going to debit Cash for this transaction, and Cash is highlighted, accept the default by pressing Enter or clicking on OK.

4. Type **Cash** in the Description column, then press Enter.

5. Your cursor is in the Debit column. Type **5500** in the Debit column. (If 55.00 displays instead of 5,500.00, click on Options, then Global. Make sure that "Manual" and "Number of decimal places, 2, is selected in the Decimal Entry part of the window. Click OK. Type

5500 again. Your entry should appear as 5,500.00 in the Debit column.) Press Enter three times.

6. Your cursor is in the Account No. column. Click on the magnifier, then select Account No. 310, Patrick O'Kalla, Capital.

7. Your cursor is in the Description column. Type **Patrick O'Kalla, Capital** as the description. Press the Enter key two times.

8. Your cursor is in the Credit column. Type **5500** as the credit. Observe that the Debit column shows 5,500.00, and the Credit column shows 5,500.00. The "Out of Balance" field shows 0.00. This shows that your debits equal your credits. Compare your General Journal entry screen with the one below.

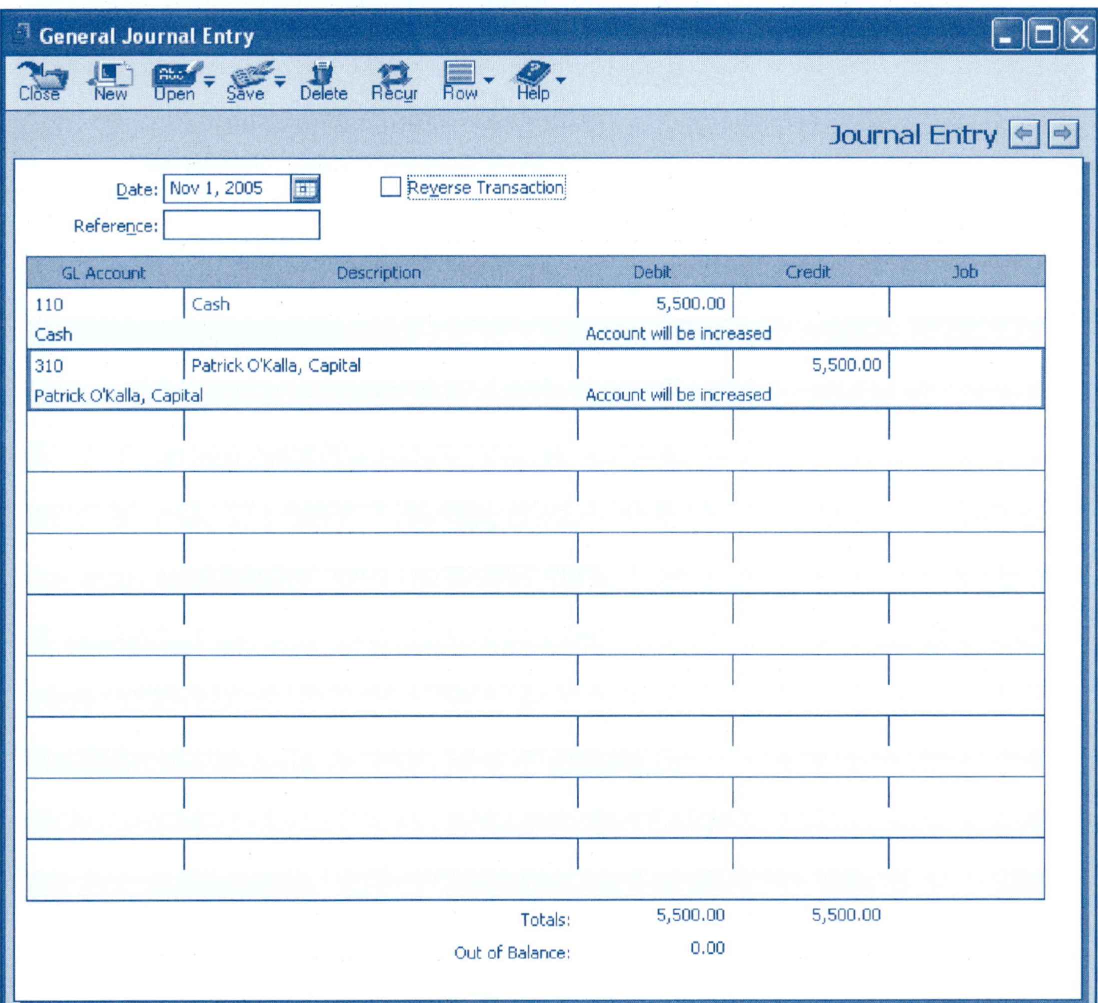

GL Account	Description	Debit	Credit	Job
110	Cash	5,500.00		
Cash		Account will be increased		
310	Patrick O'Kalla, Capital		5,500.00	
Patrick O'Kalla, Capital		Account will be increased		

Posting to the General Ledger

After you record a transaction in Peachtree, you can post to the general ledger. Observe that the General Journal Entry window has a Save icon. When you select the Save icon on Peachtree's journal window, you are also posting to the general ledger.

Follow these steps to post the Nov. 1 transaction to the general ledger.

1. The General Journal Entry window shown above should be displayed on your window. Click on the ![Save] icon.

2. Your General Journal Entry window is ready for the Nov. 3 transaction.

3. Using the transactions shown for the 4-5 Mastery Problem, journalize and post each transaction from Nov. 3 through 30. To change the date in the Date field, type the number of the date or select the calendar icon ![calendar], then select the appropriate day of the month. For the description column, type the name of the account that you are debiting and crediting. (*Hint:* Remember, you must click on the ![Save] icon after entering each transaction so that your transaction will post to the general ledger.)

Transactions:

Nov.	3	Paid cash for supplies, $400.00. C1.
	5	Received cash from sales, $900.00. T5.
	6	Sold services on account to Merilda Domingo, $280.00. S1.
	9	Paid cash for rent, $600.00. C2.
	11	Paid cash for miscellaneous expense, $50.00. C3.
	13	Bought supplies on account from Park Supplies, $240.00. M1.
	13	Received cash from sales, $430.00. T13.
	16	Paid cash for advertising, $143.00. C4.
	18	Paid cash on account to Park Supplies, $140.00. C5.
	20	Paid cash for electric bill, $230.00. C6.
	20	Received cash on account from Merilda Domingo, $150.00. R2.
	25	Paid cash for supplies, $150.00. C7.
	27	Paid cash for supplies, $80.00. C8.
	27	Received cash from sales, $2,100.00. T27.
	30	Paid cash to owner for personal use, $500.00. C9.
	30	Received cash from sales, $110.00. T30.

4. After completing the general journal transactions, click on ![Close] to return to the menu bar.

Printing the General Journal

1. From the menu bar, select Reports, then General Ledger.

2. Click on General Journal to highlight it.

3. Click on ![Print]. Make the selections to print your general journal.

Printing the General Ledger

1. From the Select a Report window, click on General Ledger to high-light it.
2. Click on Print. Make the selections to print your general journal.
3. Exit Peachtree.

BACK UP YOUR PEACHTREE FILE

Before you leave the computer lab, remember to back up your data. When you back up your Peachtree data, you are saving your work. The instructions that follow assume you are backing up to a hard drive location. You may also back up to external media; such as, a blank, formatted disk; CD-R; DVD-R; Zip disk; or USB drive.

Follow these steps to back up the 4-5 Mastery Problem.

1. If you are backing up to a floppy disk, put a floppy disk in drive A. From the menu bar, select File; Back Up. The Back Up Company window appears.

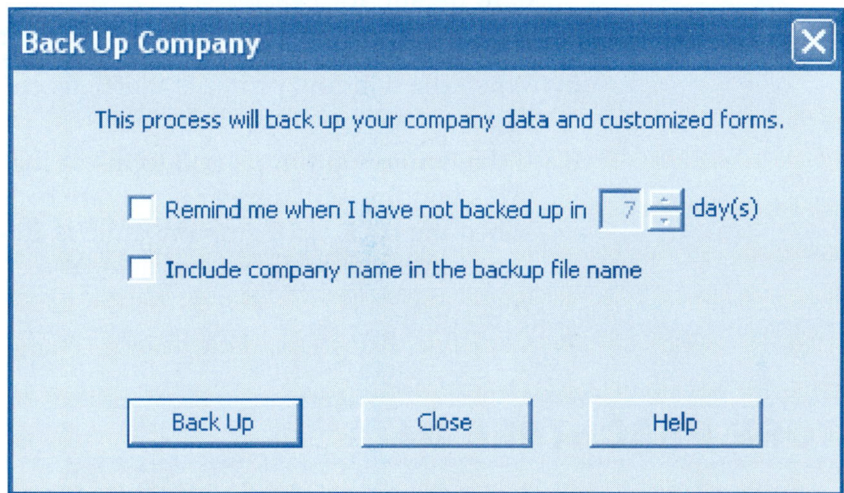

2. Click Back Up.
3. Click on the down-arrow in the Save in field. If necessary, select drive A or other location for your back up. The instructions that follow show how to back up to Peachtree's default hard-drive location: C:\Program Files\ Peachtree\Company\okalawan. Type **4-5 Mastery Problem** in the File name field.

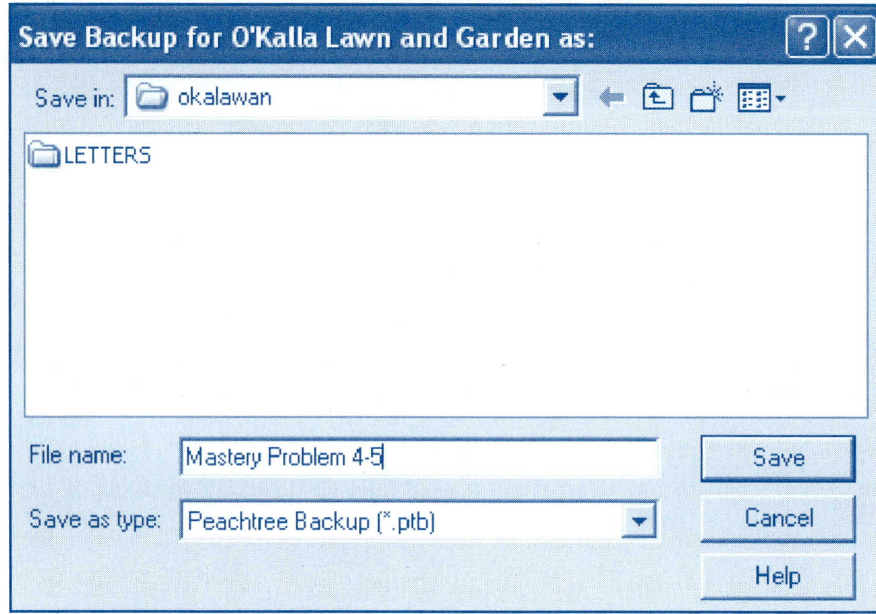

Observe that the Save as type box shows that you are making a Peachtree Backup (*.ptb), which is abbreviated ptb. This is the standard default for Peachtree backups.

4. Click Save.

5. When the window prompts that This company backup will require approximately .47MB, click OK.

6. If the window prompts you to insert the first disk, click OK. (This window will appear if you are backing up to a floppy disk.) When the Back Up Company scale is 100% complete, you have successfully backed up your data. You are returned to the menu bar.

7. Click File; Exit to exit Peachtree.

RESTORE PEACHTREE DATA

When you want to start where you left off the last time you used Peachtree, you use the Restore Wizard. Let's say you backed up, then exited Peachtree *before* completing all of the 4-5 Mastery Problem's transactions. Follow these steps to restore.

In Peachtree, when you restore data you are copying company data.

1. Start Peachtree. At the startup menu, select Open an Existing Company.

2. Open the 04-5MPXX company; *or,* if O'Kalla Lawn and Garden is shown on the Company List, double-click on it.

3. From the menu bar, click File; Restore. Once you restore, you will overwrite the company data. From the Select Backup File window, click Browse to select the appropriate location of your backup file.

4. Check the Location field to make sure you are restoring the correct file. Click Next >.

5. The Select Company window defaults to An Existing Company. The Company Name field shows O'Kalla Lawn and Garden. The Location field shows
C:\Program Files\Peachtree\company\okalawan.

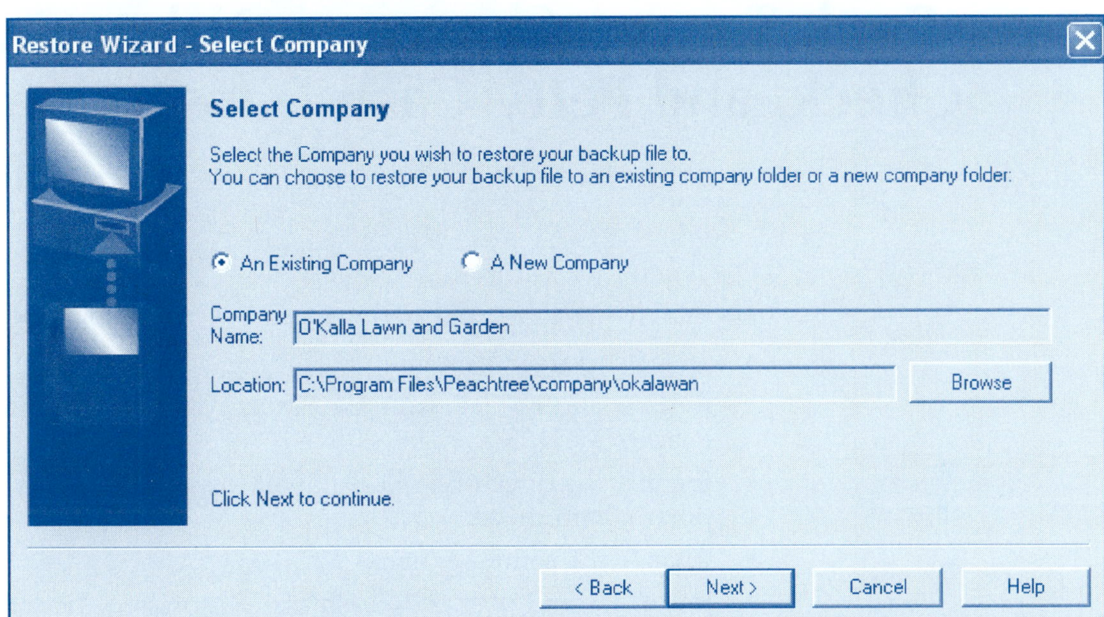

6. Click Next >.

7. The Restore Options window appears. Make sure that the box next to Company Data is *checked*. Click Next >.

8. The Confirmation window appears. Observe that the Company Name is O'Kalla Lawn and Garden. Check the From and To fields to make sure they are correct. Click Finish. When the Restore Company scale is 100% complete, your data is restored and you are returned to the menu bar.

9. If necessary, remove the external media. You can now continue with the 4-5 Mastery Problem. *Remember; always back up before exiting Peachtree and leaving the computer lab.*

You have completed the work for the 4-5 Mastery Problem: Journalizing Transactions and Posting to a General Ledger.

Reconciling a Bank Statement; Journalizing a Bank Service Charge, a Dishonored Check, and Petty Cash Transactions

The instructions that follow show you how to do the following:

- Start Peachtree Complete Accounting.
- Restore starting data from the South-Western Accounting with Peachtree CD.
- Identify the directory where LawnMow is stored on your computer's hard drive.
- Change the company name.
- Journalize and post petty cash and dishonored check transactions.
- Use Peachtree's account reconciliation feature.
- Complete 5-5 Mastery Problem.

Before you start the 5-5 Mastery Problem, ask your instructor if LawnMow, the company used for the 5-5 Mastery Problem, has already been restored. The instructions that follow assume that LawnMow has *not* been restored. If LawnMow exists as a Peachtree company, remember to restore *An Existing Company* rather than a new company.

GETTING STARTED

Use the following instructions to start Peachtree and restore the problem file for LawnMow, owned by James Astrup. The South-Western Accounting with Peachtree CD includes a Peachtree data files folder. In the steps that follow you will restore the 05-5MP file.

1. Start Peachtree. From the startup menu, select `Close`.
2. The menu bar shows three options: Files; Options; and Help. Click File; Restore.

3. The Restore Wizard - Select Backup File window appears. Observe that the Location field shows where Peachtree is stored on your computer. The default location is C:\Program Files\Peachtree\Company. Your Location field may differ. If you are restoring from a network drive, you will need to know the location of the 05-5MP.ptb file.

4. Click [Browse]. The Open Backup File window appears. In the Look in field, double-click on the appropriate location of the Peachtree data files. Then, click 05-5MP.ptb to select it. (If appropriate, select your CD drive then double-click the Peachtree Files-Unit 1 folder. Click 05-5MP.ptb to select it.)

5. Make sure the 05-5MP.ptb file is selected. Click [Open].

6. The Select Backup File window appears. Make sure the Location field shows the correct location for the 05-5MP.ptb file; for example, X:\Peachtree Files-Unit 1\05-5MP.ptb. (Substitute the correct drive letter for X.)

7. Click [Next>]. The Select Company window appears. Click on the radio button next to *A New Company*. The Location field shown in this book indicates the default location where drive C is used to install Peachtree. Your Location field may differ. *Make sure that the Location field ends in* **lawnmow**. (If your location field does not end in "w" select An Existing Company, then click [Browse]. Double-click LawnMow (*or*, 05-5MPXX). Your Location field shows the shortened company name **lawnmow**. Continue with step 8.)

8. Click [Next>]. The Restore Options window appears.

9. Make sure that the box next to Company Data is checked. Click [Next>].

10. The Confirmation window appears. Check the From and To fields to make sure they are correct. Click [Finish]. When the Restore Company scale is 100% complete, your data is restored and you are returned to the menu bar.

CHANGING THE COMPANY NAME

Before you start recording transactions for the 5-5 Mastery Problem, you should look at the company information included on the 05-5MP.ptb file. Follow these steps to look at company information.

1. The LawnMow menu bar should be displayed. From the menu bar, click on Maintain; Company Information. The Maintain Company Information window appears.

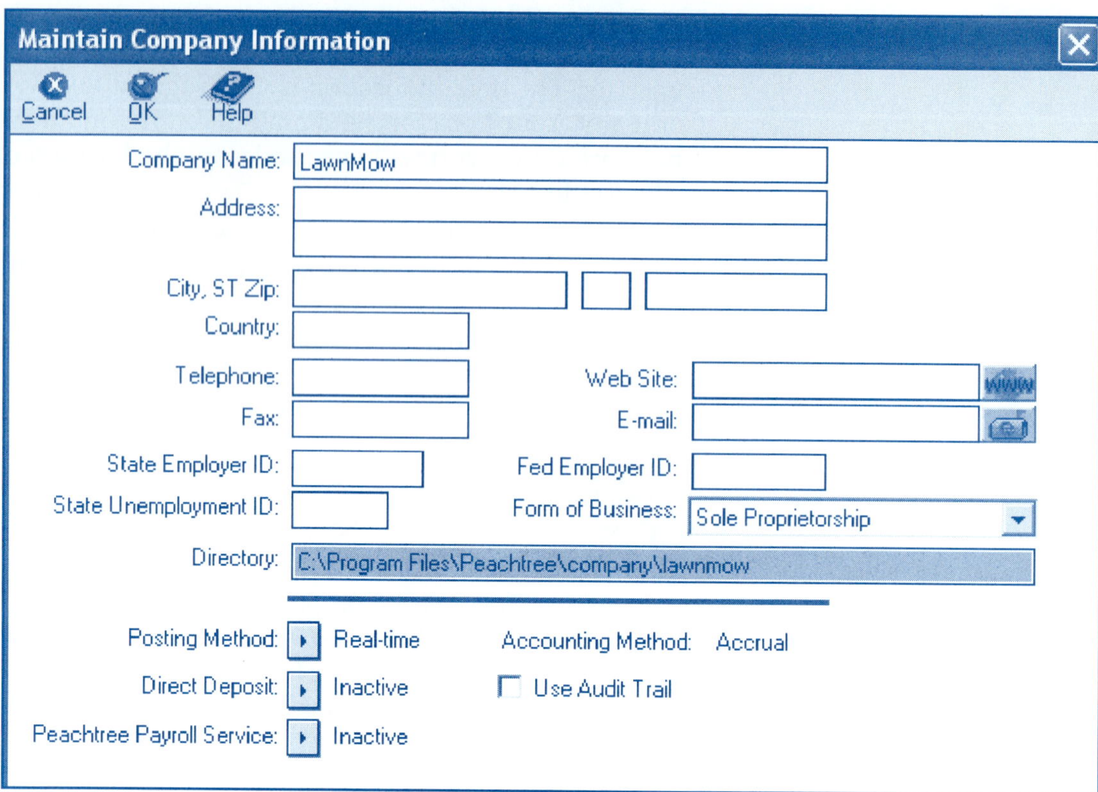

Observe that the directory field shows where your company is stored on your computer.

2. Type **05-5MPXX** in the Company Name field.

3. When you are finished typing 05-5MPXX as the company name, click on OK. Once you have changed the Company Name, each one of your printouts will show the problem number and your initials.

Nothing has changed on your computer's hard drive. The company you set up is identified in the program folder and data folder as C:\Program Files\Peachtree\Company\lawnmow. What you've done is changed the company name so that your printouts will show the problem number and your initials. Using Maintain, Company Information to rename your company does *not* change the shortened company name.

DISPLAYING THE CHART OF ACCOUNTS

The data that you restored from the Peachtree data files folder contains starting data for the 5-5 Mastery Problem. This file includes a chart of accounts for LawnMow. Follow these steps to display the chart of accounts that is included in the starting data for the 5-5 Mastery Problem.

1. From the menu bar, select Reports, then General Ledger.

2. The Select a Report window appears. In the Report List, click on Chart of Accounts to select it.

3. Click ![Preview].

4. The Chart of Accounts Filter window appears. Click [OK]. Compare your chart of accounts to the one shown.

LawnMow
Chart of Accounts
As of Aug 31, 2005

Filter Criteria includes: Report order is by ID. Report is printed with Accounts having Zero Amounts and in Detail Format.

Account ID	Account Description	Active?	Account Type
110	Cash	Yes	Cash
115	Petty Cash	Yes	Cash
120	Accts. Rec.-Bruce Kassola	Yes	Accounts Receivable
130	Supplies	Yes	Other Current Assets
140	Prepaid Insurance	Yes	Other Current Assets
310	James Astrup, Capital	Yes	Equity-doesn't close
320	James Astrup, Drawing	Yes	Equity-gets closed
330	Income Summary	Yes	Equity-Retained Earnings
520	Miscellaneous Expense	Yes	Expenses
530	Rent Expense	Yes	Expenses
535	Repair Expense	Yes	Expenses
540	Supplies Expense	Yes	Expenses
550	Utilities Expense	Yes	Expenses

These are the accounts you will use to journalize and post transactions for the 5-5 Mastery Problem.

5. Click ![Close] to return to the Select a Report window. Click ![Close] again to return to the menu bar.

JOURNALIZE AND POST TRANSACTIONS

Journalize and post the following transactions completed during August 2005. Type the check numbers (C110, etc.) and the memo number (M33) in the Reference field of the General Journal entry window. C110 is an abbreviation of Check No. 110. Remember to save after each transaction.

Transactions:

Aug. 21		Paid cash to establish a petty cash fund, $300.00, C110.
	24	Paid cash for repairs, $165.00. C111.
	26	Paid cash for supplies, $60.00. C112.
	27	Received notice from the bank of a dishonored check from Bruce Kassola, $140.00, plus $35.00 fee; total, $175.00. M33.
	28	Paid cash for miscellaneous expense, $31.00. C113.
	31	Paid cash to owner for personal use, $400.00. C114
	31	Paid cash to replenish the petty cash fund, $255.00: supplies, $125.00; miscellaneous expense, $130.00 C115.

RECONCILING THE BANK STATEMENT; JOURNALIZING A BANK SERVICE CHARGE, A DISHONORED CHECK, AND PETTY CASH TRANSACTIONS

Peachtree's account reconciliation feature allows you to reconcile the bank statement. As you know from your study of accounting, the process of bringing the balance of the bank statement and the balance of the cash account into agreement is called bank reconciliation. Peachtree calls this account reconciliation.

The textbook shows that LawnMow received a bank statement on August 31. The following information is shown:

Bank statement balance	$2,721.00
Bank service charge	15.00
Outstanding deposit, August 31	350.00
Outstanding check, No. 114	400.00
Outstanding check, No. 115	255.00
Checkbook balance on Check Stub No. 116	2,431.00

Instructions:

1. From the menu bar, select Tasks, then Account Reconciliation.
2. In the Account to Reconcile field, select Account No. 110, Cash. In the Checks and Bank Debits column, click on each check and memo that has cleared the bank. Remember, check numbers 114 and 115 are outstanding so there should be no checkmark next to them.
3. In the Deposits and Bank Credits area do *not* put a checkmark next to the deposit. The August 31 deposit is outstanding.
4. Type **15** in the Service charges field. In the Account field select Account No. 520, Miscellaneous Expense, for the service charge.
5. Type **2,721** In the Statement Ending balance field. Observe that the Unreconciled Difference shows 0.00. Observe that the GL (System) Balance is the same as the Adjusted Check Stub Balance shown on the Reconciliation of Bank Statement.
6. Click [OK].

PRINTING THE ACCOUNT RECONCILIATION REPORT AND GENERAL JOURNAL

1. From the menu bar, click on Reports, then select Account Reconciliation.
2. The Select a Report window appears. Account Reconciliation is highlighted. Click [Print].
3. Make sure that the GL Account ID field shows 110. If not, select Account No. 110 for the Cash account.

4. Click OK . Make the selections to print your account reconciliation report.

5. Close the Select a Report window to return to the menu bar.

6. Print the general journal.

BACK UP YOUR PEACHTREE FILE

Before you end your work session, remember to back up your data.
When you back up your data in Peachtree, you are saving your work
to another location.

Follow these steps to back up the 5-5 Mastery Problem.

1. If you are backing up to a floppy disk, put a floppy disk in drive
   A. From the menu bar, select File; Back Up. The Back Up Company
   window appears.

2. Click Back Up .

3. Type **5-5 Mastery Problem** in the File name field.

4. Click Save .

5. When the window prompts that This company backup will require
   approximately .47MB, click OK .

6. If the window prompts you to insert the first disk, click OK .
   (This window will appear if you are backing up to a floppy disk.)
   When the Back Up Company scale is 100% complete, you have
   successfully backed up your data. You are returned to the menu
   bar.

7. Click File; Exit to exit Peachtree.

You have completed the work for the 5-5 Mastery Problem: Reconciling
a Bank Statement; Journalizing a Bank Service Charge, a Dishonored
Check, and Petty Cash Transactions.

Reconciling a Bank Statement and Recording a Bank Service Charge

The instructions that follow show you how to do the following:

- Start Peachtree Complete Accounting.
- Restore starting data from the South-Western Accounting with Peachtree CD.
- Identify the directory where GolfPro is stored on your computer's hard drive.
- Change the company name.
- Journalize and post petty cash and dishonored check transactions.
- Use Peachtree's account reconciliation feature.
- Complete 5-6 Challenge Problem.

Before you start the 5-6 Challenge Problem, ask your instructor if GolfPro, the company used for the 5-6 Challenge Problem, has already been restored. The instructions that follow assume that Golf Pro has *not* been restored. If GolfPro exists as a Peachtree company, remember to restore *An Existing Company* rather than a new company.

GETTING STARTED

Follow these instructions to start Peachtree and restore the problem file for GolfPro, owned by John Walker. The South-Western Accounting with Peachtree CD includes a Peachtree data files folder. In the steps that follow you will restore the 05-6CP file.

1. Start Peachtree. From the startup menu, select Close .
2. The menu bar shows three options: Files; Options; and Help. Click File; Restore.
3. The Restore Wizard - Select Backup File window appears. Observe that the Location field shows where Peachtree is stored on your computer. The default location is C:\Program Files\Peachtree\Company. Your Location field may differ. If you are restoring from a network drive, you will need to know the location of the 05-6CP.ptb file.

4. Click   Browse . The Open Backup File window appears. In the Look
   in field, double-click on the appropriate location of the Peachtree
   data files. Then, click 05-6CP.ptb to select it. (If appropriate, select
   your CD drive then double-click the Peachtree Files-Unit 1 folder.
   Click 05-6CP.ptb to select it.)

5. Make sure the 05-6CP.ptb file is selected. Click   Open .

6. The Select Backup File window appears. Make sure the Location field
   shows the correct location for the 05-6CP.ptb file; for example, X:\
   Peachtree Files-Unit 1\05-6CP.ptb. (Substitute the correct drive letter
   for X.)

7. Click   Next > . The Select Company window appears. Click on the
   radio button next to *A New Company*. The Location field shown in
   this book indicates the default location where drive C is used to
   install Peachtree. Your Location field may differ. *Make sure that the
   Location field ends in* **golfpro**. (If your location field does *not* end in
   "o" select An Existing Company, then click   Browse . Double-click
   GolfPro, 05-6CPXX). Your Location field shows the shortened company name **golfpro**. Continue with step 8.)

8. Click   Next > . The Restore Options window appears.

9. Make sure that the box next to Company Data is *checked*. Click
     Next > .

10. The Confirmation window appears. Check the From and To fields
    to make sure they are correct. Click   Finish . When the Restore
    Company scale is 100% complete, your data is restored and you
    are returned to the menu bar.

CHANGING THE COMPANY NAME

Before you start recording transactions for the 5-6 Challenge Problem,
you should look at the company information included on the 05-
6CP.ptb file. Follow these steps to look at company information.

1. The GolfPro menu bar should be displayed. From the menu bar,
   click on Maintain; Company Information. The Maintain Company
   Information window appears. Observe that the directory field
   shows where your company is stored on your computer.

2. Type **05-6CPXX** in the Company Name field.

3. When you are finished typing 05-6CPXX as the company name, click
   on   OK . Once you have changed the Company Name, each one of
   your printouts will show the problem number and your initials.

DISPLAYING THE CHART OF ACCOUNTS

The data that you restored from the Peachtree data files folder contains
starting data for the 5-6 Challenge Problem. This file includes a chart
of accounts for GolfPro. Follow these steps to display the chart of
accounts that is included in the starting data for the 5-6 Challenge
Problem.

1. From the menu bar, select Reports, then General Ledger.

2. The Select a Report window appears. In the Report List, click on Chart of Accounts to select it.

3. Click ![Preview].

4. The Chart of Accounts Filter window appears. Click ![OK]. Compare your chart of accounts to the one shown.

GolfPro
Chart of Accounts
As of Aug 31, 2005

Filter Criteria includes: Report order is by ID. Report is printed with Accounts having Zero Amounts and in Detail Format.

Account ID	Account Description	Active?	Account Type
110	Cash	Yes	Cash
120	Accts. Rec.-Sheldon Martindale	Yes	Accounts Receivable
130	Supplies	Yes	Other Current Assets
210	Accts. Pay.-Patterson Supplies	Yes	Accounts Payable
215	Accts. Pay.-Dowd Company	Yes	Accounts Payable
310	John Walker, Capital	Yes	Equity-doesn't close
320	John Walker, Drawing	Yes	Equity-gets closed
330	Income Summary	Yes	Equity-Retained Earnings
515	Advertising Expense	Yes	Expenses
520	Miscellaneous Expense	Yes	Expenses
525	Insurance Expense	Yes	Expenses
530	Rent Expense	Yes	Expenses
540	Cleaning Expense	Yes	Expenses
550	Utilities Expense	Yes	Expenses

5. Click ![Close] to return to the Select a Report window. Click ![Close] again to return to the menu bar.

RECONCILING THE BANK STATEMENT AND RECORDING A BANK SERVICE CHARGE

To complete account reconciliation, use the bank statement, canceled checks, check stubs, and transactions for GolfPro shown on the following pages.

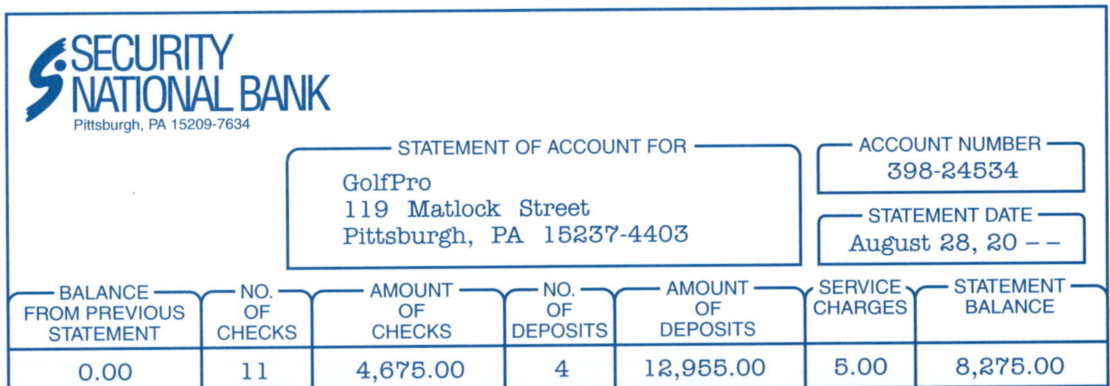

BALANCE FROM PREVIOUS STATEMENT	NO. OF CHECKS	AMOUNT OF CHECKS	NO. OF DEPOSITS	AMOUNT OF DEPOSITS	SERVICE CHARGES	STATEMENT BALANCE
0.00	11	4,675.00	4	12,955.00	5.00	8,275.00

DATE	CHECK	AMOUNT	CHECK	AMOUNT	DEPOSITS	BALANCE
08/01/– –						0.00
08/01/– –					12,000.00	12,000.00
08/04/– –	151	1,577.00				10,423.00
08/08/– –	152	200.00			125.00	10,348.00
08/13/– –	154	250.00	156	135.00		9,963.00
08/15/– –	153	1,560.00	158	75.00	260.00	8,588.00
08/17/– –	155	205.00	159	98.00		8,285.00
08/18/– –	160	140.00				8,145.00
08/20/– –	157	250.00				7,895.00
08/22/– –					570.00	8,465.00
08/25/– –	162	185.00				8,280.00
08/27/– –	SC	5.00				8,275.00

PLEASE EXAMINE AT ONCE • IF NO ERRORS ARE REPORTED WITHIN 10 DAYS THE ACCOUNT WILL BE CONSIDERED CORRECT. REFER ANY DISCREPANCY TO OUR ACCOUNTING DEPARTMENT IMMEDIATELY.

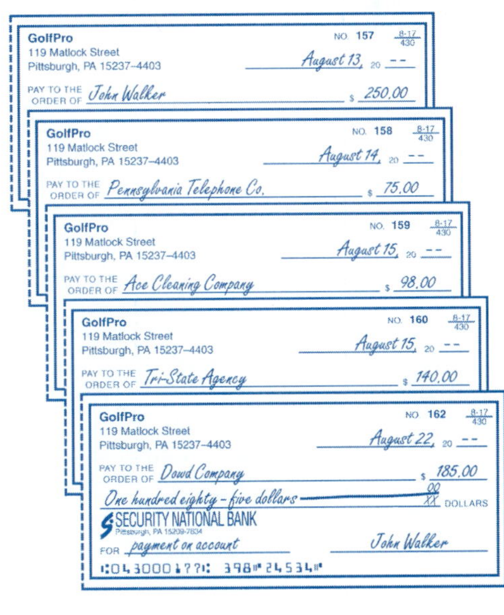

NO. 151 $ 1,577.00
Date: *August 1,*   20 - -
To: *Montag Company*
For: *Supplies*

BAL. BRO'T. FOR'D.		0	00
AMT. DEPOSITED . . . . 8 / 1 / -- Date	12,000	00
SUBTOTAL	12,000	00
OTHER:		
SUBTOTAL	12,000	00
AMT. THIS CHECK	1,577	00
BAL. CAR'D. FOR'D.	10,423	00

NO. 152 $ 200.00
Date: *August 5,*   20 - -
To: *Plain Company*
For: *Rent*

BAL. BRO'T. FOR'D.	10,423	00
AMT. DEPOSITED . . . . Date		
SUBTOTAL	10,423	00
OTHER:		
SUBTOTAL	10,423	00
AMT. THIS CHECK	200	00
BAL. CAR'D. FOR'D.	10,223	00

NO. 153 $ 1,560.00
Date: *August 8,*   20 - -
To: *Thomson Company*
For: *Supplies*

BAL. BRO'T. FOR'D.	10,223	00
AMT. DEPOSITED . . . . 8 / 8 / -- Date	125	00
SUBTOTAL	10,348	00
OTHER:		
SUBTOTAL	10,348	00
AMT. THIS CHECK	1,560	00
BAL. CAR'D. FOR'D.	8,788	00

NO. 154 $ 250.00
Date: *August 8,*   20 - -
To: *Metro Insurance Company*
For: *Insurance*

BAL. BRO'T. FOR'D.	8,788	00
AMT. DEPOSITED . . . . Date		
SUBTOTAL	8,788	00
OTHER:		
SUBTOTAL	8,788	00
AMT. THIS CHECK	250	00
BAL. CAR'D. FOR'D.	8,538	00

NO. 155 $ 205.00
Date: *August 10,*   20 - -
To: *City Electric Company*
For: *Utilities*

BAL. BRO'T. FOR'D.	8,538	00
AMT. DEPOSITED . . . . Date		
SUBTOTAL	8,538	00
OTHER:		
SUBTOTAL	8,538	00
AMT. THIS CHECK	205	00
BAL. CAR'D. FOR'D.	8,333	00

NO. 156 $ 135.00
Date: *August 10,*   20 - -
To: *Patterson Supplies*
For: *Payment on account*

BAL. BRO'T. FOR'D.	8,333	00
AMT. DEPOSITED . . . . Date		
SUBTOTAL	8,333	00
OTHER:		
SUBTOTAL	8,333	00
AMT. THIS CHECK	135	00
BAL. CAR'D. FOR'D.	8,198	00

NO. 157 $ 250.00
Date: *August 13,*   20 - -
To: *John Walker*
For: *Owner's withdrawal*

BAL. BRO'T. FOR'D.	8,198	00
AMT. DEPOSITED . . . . Date		
SUBTOTAL	8,198	00
OTHER:		
SUBTOTAL	8,198	00
AMT. THIS CHECK	250	00
BAL. CAR'D. FOR'D.	7,948	00

NO. 158 $ 75.00
Date: *August 14,*   20 - -
To: *Pennsylvania Telephone Company*
For: *Utilities*

BAL. BRO'T. FOR'D.	7,948	00
AMT. DEPOSITED . . . . Date		
SUBTOTAL	7,948	00
OTHER:		
SUBTOTAL	7,948	00
AMT. THIS CHECK	75	00
BAL. CAR'D. FOR'D.	7,873	00

NO. 159 $ 98.00
Date: *August 15,*   20 - -
To: *Ace Cleaning Company*
For: *Cleaning*

BAL. BRO'T. FOR'D.	7,873	00
AMT. DEPOSITED . . . . Date		
SUBTOTAL	7,873	00
OTHER:		
SUBTOTAL	7,873	00
AMT. THIS CHECK	98	00
BAL. CAR'D. FOR'D.	7,775	00

NO. 160 $ 140.00
Date: *August 15,*   20 - -
To: *Tri-State Agency*
For: *Miscellaneous*

BAL. BRO'T. FOR'D.	7,775	00
AMT. DEPOSITED . . . . 8 / 15 / -- Date	260	00
SUBTOTAL	8,035	00
OTHER:		
SUBTOTAL	8,035	00
AMT. THIS CHECK	140	00
BAL. CAR'D. FOR'D.	7,895	00

NO. 161 $ 375.00
Date: *August 19,*   20 - -
To: *Pittsburgh Enquirer*
For: *Advertising*

BAL. BRO'T. FOR'D.	7,895	00
AMT. DEPOSITED . . . . Date		
SUBTOTAL	7,895	00
OTHER:		
SUBTOTAL	7,895	00
AMT. THIS CHECK	375	00
BAL. CAR'D. FOR'D.	7,520	00

NO. 162 $ 185.00
Date: *August 22,*   20 - -
To: *Dowd Company*
For: *Payment on account*

BAL. BRO'T. FOR'D.	7,520	00
AMT. DEPOSITED . . . . 8 / 22 / -- Date	570	00
SUBTOTAL	8,090	00
OTHER:		
SUBTOTAL	8,090	00
AMT. THIS CHECK	185	00
BAL. CAR'D. FOR'D.	7,905	00

NO. 163 $ 17.00
Date: *August 23,*   20 - -
To: *Jason North*
For: *Miscellaneous*

BAL. BRO'T. FOR'D.	7,905	00
AMT. DEPOSITED . . . . Date		
SUBTOTAL	7,905	00
OTHER:		
SUBTOTAL	7,905	00
AMT. THIS CHECK	17	00
BAL. CAR'D. FOR'D.	7,888	00

NO. 164 $ 250.00
Date: *August 28,*   20 - -
To: *John Walker*
For: *Owner's withdrawal*

BAL. BRO'T. FOR'D.	7,888	00
AMT. DEPOSITED . . . . 8 / 28 / -- Date	430	00
SUBTOTAL	8,318	00
OTHER:		
SUBTOTAL	8,318	00
AMT. THIS CHECK	250	00
BAL. CAR'D. FOR'D.	8,068	00

NO. 165 $
Date: 20 - -
To:
For:

BAL. BRO'T. FOR'D.	8,068	00
AMT. DEPOSITED . . . . Date		
SUBTOTAL	8,068	00
OTHER:		
SUBTOTAL		
AMT. THIS CHECK		
BAL. CAR'D. FOR'D.		

__Transactions:__ For Peachtree, use August 31, 2005 as the date for the transactions.

Aug. 31 Received bank statement showing August bank service charge, $5.00.

31 Received notice from the bank of a dishonored check from Sheldon Martindale, $170.00, plus $5.00 fee; total, $175.00. M26.

Instructions:

1. Refer to the bank statement, canceled checks, and check stubs to complete account reconciliation. Review the bank statement to determine outstanding checks and deposits. Remember to record the bank service charge.
2. Print the account reconciliation report.
3. Journalize and post the dishonored check transaction.
4. Follow these steps to print the August 31, 2005 general journal.
   a. Select Reports; General Ledger.
   b. In the Report List, click General Journal; click Print.
   c. The General Journal Filter window appears. Type **8/31/05** in the From field. Press Enter. The To field shows August 31, 2005.
   d. Make the selections to print.
5. Backup. The suggested file name is **5-6 Challenge Problem**.

You have completed the work for the 5-6 Challenge Problem: Reconciling a Bank Statement and Recording a Bank Service Charge.

An Accounting Cycle for a Proprietorship: Journalizing and Posting Transactions

The instructions that follow show you how to do the following:

- Start Peachtree Complete Accounting.
- Restore the Problem File for Extreme Adventures.
- Identify the directory where Extreme Adventures is stored on your computer.
- Complete Reinforcement Activity 1—Part A.

Before you start Reinforcement Activity 1—Part A, ask your instructor if Extreme Adventures, the company used for Reinforcement Activity 1—Part A, has already been restored on your computer. The instructions that follow assume that Extreme Adventures has *not* been restored.

GETTING STARTED

The South-Western Accounting with Peachtree CD includes a Peachtree data files folder. Use the following instructions to start Peachtree and restore the service business called Extreme Adventures, owned by Brian Dawson. In the steps that follow you will restore the RA01-A.ptb file.

1. Start Peachtree. From the startup menu, select Close.
2. The menu bar shows three options: Files; Options; and Help. Click File; Restore.
3. The Restore Wizard - Select Backup File window appears. Observe that the Location field shows where Peachtree is stored on your computer. The default location is C:\Program Files\Peachtree\Company. Your Location field may differ. If you are restoring from a network drive, you will need to know the location of the RA01-A.ptb file.

4. Click `Browse`. The Open Backup File window appears. In the Look in field, double-click on the appropriate location of the Peachtree data files. Then, click RA01-A.ptb to select it. (If appropriate, select your CD drive then double-click the Peachtree Files-Unit 1 folder. Click RA01-A.ptb to select it.)

5. Make sure the RA01-A.ptb file is selected. Click `Open`.

6. The Select Backup File window appears. Make sure the Location field shows the correct location for the RA01-A.ptb file; for example, X:\Peachtree Files-Unit 1\RA01-A.ptb. (Substitute the correct drive letter for X.)

7. Click `Next >`. The Select Company window appears. Click on the radio button next to *A New Company*. The Location field shown in this book indicates the default location where drive C is used to install Peachtree. Your Location field may differ. *Make sure that the Location field ends in* **extadven**. (If your location field does not end in "n" select An Existing Company, then click `Browse`. Double-click Extreme Adventures (*or*, RA01-AXX). Your Location field shows the shortened company name **extadven**. Continue with step 8.)

8. Click `Next >`. The Restore Options window appears.

9. Make sure that the box next to Company Data is *checked*. Click `Next >`.

10. The Confirmation window appears. Check the From and To fields to make sure they are correct. Click `Finish`. When the Restore Company scale is 100% complete, your data is restored and you are returned to the menu bar.

CHANGING THE COMPANY NAME

Before you start recording transactions for Reinforcement Activity 1—Part A, you should look at the company information included on the RA01-A.ptb file. Follow these steps to look at company information.

1. The Extreme Adventures menu bar should be displayed. From the menu bar, click on Maintain; Company Information. The Maintain Company Information window appears.

Observe that the directory field shows where your company is stored on your computer: C:\Program Files\Peachtree\company\extadven.

2. Type **RA01-AXX** in the Company Name field.

3. When you are finished typing RA01-AXX as the company name, click on [OK]. Once you have changed the Company Name, each one of your printouts will show the problem number and your initials.

Nothing has changed on your computer's hard drive. The company you restored is identified in the program folder and data folder as C:\Program Files\Peachtree\Company\extadven. What you've done is changed the company name so that your printouts will show the problem number and your initials. Using Maintain, Company Information to rename your company does *not* change the shortened company name.

In May of the current year, Brian Dawson starts a service business called Extreme Adventures. The business provides adventure trips throughout the world, such as trekking in the Himalayas and helo skiing in Colorado. The business rents the facilities in which it operates, pays the utilities, and is responsible for maintenance. Extreme Adventures charges clients for each visit. Most of Extreme Adventures' sales are for cash. However, two private schools use Extreme Adventures for some physical education classes. These schools have an account with Extreme Adventures.

CHART OF ACCOUNTS

Balance Sheet Accounts

(100) ASSETS

110	Cash
120	Petty Cash
130	Accts. Rec.—Matterhorn University
140	Accts. Rec.—Midwest College
150	Supplies
160	Prepaid Insurance

(200) LIABILITIES

210	Accts. Pay.—Dunn Supplies
220	Accts. Pay.—Greenway Supplies

(300) OWNER'S EQUITY

310	Brian Dawson, Capital
320	Brian Dawson, Drawing
330	Income Summary

Income Statement Accounts

(400) REVENUE

410	Sales

(500) EXPENSES

510	Advertising Expense
520	Insurance Expense
530	Miscellaneous Expense
540	Rent Expense
550	Repair Expense
560	Supplies Expense
570	Utilities Expense

Transactions:

May	1	Received cash from owner as an investment, $15,000.00. R1.
	1	Paid cash for rent, $1,800.00. C1.
	2	Paid cash for electric bill, $105.00. C2.
	4	Paid cash for supplies, $450.00. C3.
	4	Paid cash for insurance, $1,200.00. C4.
	7	Bought supplies on account from Dunn Supplies, $900.00. M1.
	11	Paid cash to establish a petty cash fund, $250.00. C5.
	12	Received cash from sales, $475.00. T12.
	13	Paid cash for repairs, $250.00. C6.
	13	Paid cash for miscellaneous expense, $40.00. C7.
	13	Received cash from sales, $235.00. T13.
	13	Sold services on account to Midwest College, $225.00. S1.
	14	Paid cash for advertising, $300.00. C8.
	15	Paid cash to owner for personal use, $200.00. C9.
	15	Paid cash on account to Dunn Supplies, $500.00. C10.
	15	Received cash from sales, $305.00. T15.
	15	Sold services on account to Matterhorn University, $425.00. S2.
	18	Paid cash for miscellaneous expense, $95.00. C11.
	18	Received cash on account from Midwest College, $125.00. R2.
	19	Received cash from sales, $480.00. T19.
	20	Paid cash for repairs, $160.00. C12.
	20	Bought supplies on account from Greenway Supplies, $120.00. M2.
	21	Paid cash for water bill, $265.00. C13.
	21	Received cash from sales, $620.00. T21.
	25	Paid cash for supplies, $25.00. C14.
	25	Received cash from sales, $605.00. T25.

26	Paid cash for miscellaneous expense, $37.00. C15.
26	Received cash on account from Matterhorn University, $250.00. R3.
27	Received cash from sales, $715.00. T27.
28	Paid cash for telephone bill, $245.00. C16.
28	Received cash from sales, $650.00. T28.

RECORDING TRANSACTIONS

Before recording transactions, you should print or display Peachtree's chart of accounts and compare it to the one shown above. (*Hint:* From the menu bar, select Reports, General Ledger, Chart of Accounts. Then, make the selections to print.) Refer to these account numbers when recording transactions.

Instructions:

1. Using Peachtree's general journal, journalize and post the May 1 through 28 transactions. Use the appropriate check number for each transaction shown in the textbook. For example, type **C1** in the Reference field on the General Journal Entry screen.

Refer to pages 13–15 if you need help journalizing and posting transactions.

2. Using the bank statement information, complete account reconciliation. (*Hint:* The first deposit that you will check off is the $15,000 cash investment by the owner. The bank statement was received on May 29.)

Bank statement balance	$13,180.00
Bank service charge	15.00
Outstanding deposit, May 28	650.00
Outstanding checks:	
No. 14	25.00
No. 15	37.00
No. 16	245.00
Checkbook balance on Check Stub. No. 17	$13,538.00

Refer to page 24 if you need help reconciling the cash account.

3. Print the account reconciliation report.

Refer to pages 24 and 25 if you need help printing the account reconciliation report.

4. Journalize and post the following transactions for May 29 through 31.

Transactions:

May	29	Paid cash for supplies, $30.00. C17
	29	Received cash from sales, $695.00. T29.
	a.	Paid cash to replenish the petty cash fund, $165.00: miscellaneous expense, $120.00; repairs, $45.00. C18.
	b.	Paid cash to owner for personal use, $1,000.00. C19.
	c.	Received cash from sales, $660.00. T31

5. Print the general journal.

6. Print the general ledger.

7. Back up your company data. The suggested file name is **Reinforcement Activity 1—Part A.ptb**. This backup is important. Keep it in a safe place. You will use it again for Part B of this problem.

Refer to pages 17 and 18 if you need help backing up your company data.

You have completed the work for Reinforcement Activity 1—Part A: An Accounting Cycle for a Proprietorship: Journalizing and Posting Transactions. Keep your backup file in a safe place. You will use the backup made in this activity for Part B of this problem.

Completing a Work Sheet

The instructions that follow show you how to do the following:

- Start Peachtree Complete Accounting.
- Change the company name.
- Identify the directory where Bonita Bubbles is stored on your computer's hard drive.
- Restore starting data from the South-Western Accounting with Peachtree CD.
- Complete a work sheet.
- Journalize and post adjusting entries in Peachtree's general journal.
- Complete 6-5 Mastery Problem.

Before you start the 6-5 Mastery Problem, ask your instructor if Bonita Bubbles, the company used for the 6-5 Mastery Problem, has already been restored on your computer. The instructions that follow assume that Bonita Bubbles is being used for the first time.

GETTING STARTED

Use the following instructions to start Peachtree and restore the starting data for Bonita Bubbles. The South-Western Accounting with Peachtree CD includes a Peachtree data files folder. In the steps that follow you will restore the 06-5MP.ptb file.

1. Start Peachtree. From the startup menu, select Close .
2. The menu bar shows three options: Files; Options; and Help. Click File; Restore.
3. The Restore Wizard - Select Backup File window appears. Observe that the Location field shows where Peachtree is stored on your computer. The default location is C:\Program Files\Peachtree\Company. Your Location field may differ. If you are restoring from a network drive, you will need to know the location of the 06-5MP.ptb file.

4. Click Browse . The Open Backup File window appears. In the Look
    in field, double-click on the appropriate location of the Peachtree
    data files. Then, click 06-5MP.ptb to select it. (If appropriate, select
    your CD drive then double-click the Peachtree Files-Unit 1 folder.
    Click 06-5MP.ptb to select it.)

5. Make sure the 06-5MP.ptb file is selected. Click Open .

6. The Select Backup File window appears. Make sure the Location
    field shows the correct location for the 06-5MP.ptb file; for example,
    X:\Peachtree Files-Unit 1\06-5MP.ptb. (Substitute the correct drive
    letter for X.)

7. Click Next > . The Select Company window appears. Click on the
    radio button next to *A New Company*. The Location field shown in
    this book indicates the default location where drive C is used to
    install Peachtree. Your Location field may differ. *Make sure that the
    Location field ends in* **bonbubbl**. (If your location field does *not* end
    in "l" select An Existing Company, then click Browse . Double-click
    Bonita Bubbles (*or*, 06-5MPXX). Your Location field shows the
    shortened company name **bonbubbl**. Continue with step 8.)

8. Click Next > . The Restore Options window appears.

9. Make sure that the box next to Company Data is *checked*. Click
    Next > .

10. The Confirmation window appears. Check the From and To fields
    to make sure they are correct. Click Finish . When the Restore
    Company scale is 100% complete, your data is restored and you
    are returned to the menu bar.

CHANGING THE COMPANY NAME

Before you start recording transactions for the 6-5 Mastery Problem,
you should look at the company information included on the 06-
5MP.ptb file. Follow these steps to look at company information.

1. The Bonita Bubbles menu bar should be displayed. From the menu
    bar, click on Maintain; Company Information. The Maintain
    Company Information window appears.

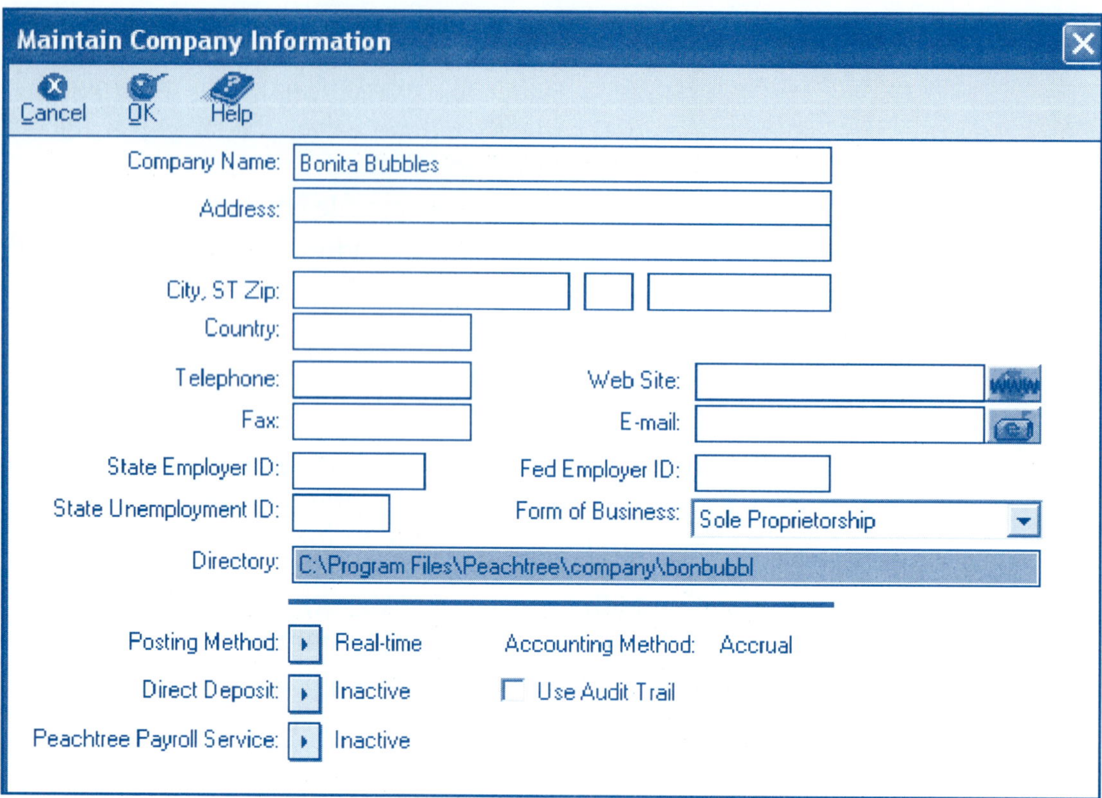

Observe that the directory field shows where your company is stored on your computer: C:\Program Files\Peachtree\company\bonbubbl.

2. Type **06-5MPXX** in the Company Name field.

3. When you are finished typing 06-5MPXX as the company name, click on [OK]. Once you have changed the Company Name, each one of your printouts will show the problem number and your initials.

Nothing has changed on your computer's hard drive. The company you restored is identified in the program folder and data folder as C:\Program Files\Peachtree\Company\bonbubbl. What you've done is changed the company name so that your printouts will show the problem number and your initials. Using Maintain, Company Information to rename your company does *not* change the shortened company name.

Account Titles	**Account Balances**	
	Debit	**Credit**
Cash	$2,829.00	
Petty Cash	150.00	
Accounts Receivable—Bernard Corbett	511.00	
Supplies	855.00	
Prepaid Insurance	1,100.00	
Accounts Payable—Spooner Supplies		$ 500.00
Paulo Gutierrez, Capital		4,500.00
Paulo Gutierrez, Drawing	440.00	
Income Summary		
Sales		2,400.00
Advertising Expense	450.00	
Insurance Expense		
Miscellaneous Expense	190.00	
Rent Expense	375.00	
Supplies Expense		
Utilities Expense	500.00	

Displaying Peachtree's Trial Balance

Follow these steps to display Peachtree's General Ledger Trial Balance.

1. From Peachtree's menu bar, select Reports; General Ledger.
2. Click on General Ledger Trial Balance to highlight it.
3. Make the selections to display or print. Compare your trial balance to the one shown below. These are the same account titles and account balances shown above.

Bonita Bubbles
General Ledger Trial Balance
As of Apr 30, 2005

Filter Criteria includes: Report order is by ID. Report is printed in Detail Format.

Account ID	Account Description	Debit Amt	Credit Amt
110	Cash	2,829.00	
120	Petty Cash	150.00	
130	Accts. Rec.-Bernard Corbett	511.00	
150	Supplies	855.00	
160	Prepaid Insurance	1,100.00	
210	Accts. Pay.-Spooner Supplies		500.00
310	Paulo Gutierrez, Capital		4,500.00
320	Paulo Gutierrez, Drawing	440.00	
410	Sales		2,400.00
510	Advertising Expense	450.00	
530	Miscellaneous Expense	190.00	
540	Rent Expense	375.00	
570	Utilities Expense	500.00	
	Total:	**7,400.00**	**7,400.00**

ACCOUNT TITLE	TRIAL BALANCE		ADJUSTMENTS		INCOME STATEMENT		BALANCE SHEET	
	1	2	3	4	5	6	7	8
	DEBIT	CREDIT	DEBIT	CREDIT	DEBIT	CREDIT	DEBIT	CREDIT

1. Complete the work sheet. Insert the appropriate column headings. (Or, you may use the work sheet shown in the *Working Papers* for the 6-5 Mastery Problem.)

2. Using information shown below, journalize and post the adjusting entries in Peachtree's general journal. Use April 30, 2005 as the date. (Or, if you completed the 6-5 Mastery Problem in the *Working Papers*, you can use the adjusting entries that you recorded in the general journal.) Type **Adjustment a** or **Adjustment b** in the Reference field.

Adjustment information, April 30

Supplies Inventory	$220.00
Value of Prepaid Insurance	$800.00

3. Print the April 30, 2005 general journal. (*Hint:* Remember to change the To field to 4/30/05. The From field shows 4/30/05).

4. Display or print Peachtree's income statement. (*Hint:* Reports; Financial Statements, <Standard> Income Statement, make the selections to display or print, uncheck Show Zero Amounts.) Compare Peachtree's income statement to the one completed on the worksheet. Observe that the net loss is shown in parenthesis.

5. Display or print Peachtree's Balance Sheet. (*Hint:* From financial statements Report List, select <Standard> Balance Sheet. Make the selections to display or print.) Compare Peachtree's balance sheet to the one completed on the worksheet. Observe that Peachtree organizes the balance sheet differently than the worksheet. The account balance on the worksheet and Peachtree's balance sheet are the same.

6. Backup your work. The suggested file name is 6-5 Mastery Problem.ptb.

You have completed the work for the 6-5 Mastery Problem: Completing a Work Sheet.

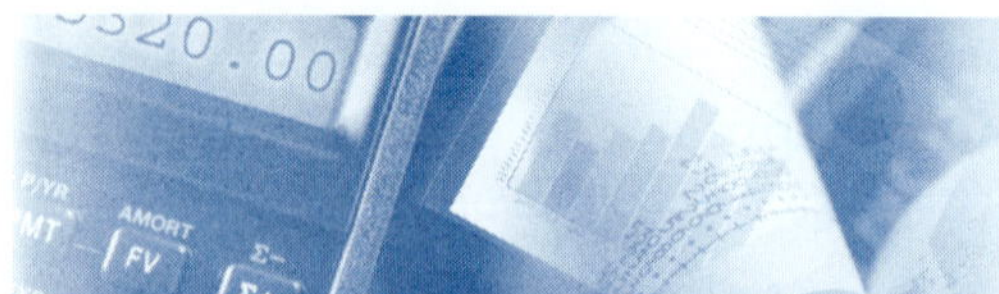

Preparing Financial Statements with a Net Loss

The instructions that follow show you how to do the following:

- Start Peachtree Complete Accounting.
- Change the company name.
- Identify the directory where Rolstad Repair Service is stored on your computer's hard drive.
- Restore starting data from the South-Western Accounting with Peachtree CD.
- Print an income statement and balance sheet.
- Complete 7-3 Mastery Problem.

Before you start the 7-3 Mastery Problem, ask your instructor if Rolstad Repair Service, the company used for the 7-3 Mastery Problem, has already been restored on your computer. The instructions that follow assume that Rolstad Repair Service is being used for the first time.

GETTING STARTED

Use the following instructions to start Peachtree and restore the starting data for Rolstad Repair Service. The South-Western Accounting with Peachtree CD includes a Peachtree data files folder. In the steps that follow you will restore the 07-3MP.ptb file.

1. Start Peachtree. From the startup menu, select Close.
2. The menu bar shows three options: Files; Options; and Help. Click File; Restore.
3. The Restore Wizard - Select Backup File window appears. Observe that the Location field shows where Peachtree is stored on your computer. The default location is C:\Program Files\Peachtree\Company. Your Location field may differ. If you are restoring from a network drive, you will need to know the location of the 07-3MP.ptb file.
4. Click Browse. The Open Backup File window appears. In the Look in field, double-click on the appropriate location of the Peachtree data files. Then, click 07-3MP.ptb to select it. (If appropriate, select

your CD drive then double-click the Peachtree Files-Unit 1 folder. Click 07-3MP.ptb to select it.)

5. Make sure the 07-3MP.ptb file is selected. Click [Open].

6. The Select Backup File window appears. Make sure the Location field shows the correct location for the 07-3MP.ptb file; for example, X:\Peachtree Files-Unit 1\07-3MP.ptb. (Substitute the correct drive letter for X.)

7. Click [Next >]. The Select Company window appears. Click on the radio button next to *A New Company*. The Location field shown in this book indicates the default location where drive C is used to install Peachtree. Your Location field may differ. *Make sure that the Location field ends in* **rolrepse**. (If your location field does not end in "e" select An Existing Company, then click [Browse]. Double-click Rolstad Repair Service (*or*, 07-3MPXX). Your Location field shows the shortened company name **rolrepse**. Continue with step 8.)

8. Click [Next >]. The Restore Options window appears.

9. Make sure that the box next to Company Data is *checked*. Click [Next >].

10. The Confirmation window appears. Check the From and To fields to make sure they are correct. Click [Finish]. When the Restore Company scale is 100% complete, your data is restored and you are returned to the menu bar.

CHANGING THE COMPANY NAME

Before you start recording transactions for the 7-3 Mastery Problem, you should look at the company information included on the 07-3MP.ptb file. Follow these steps to look at company information.

1. The Rolstad Repair Service menu bar should be displayed. From the menu bar, click on Maintain; Company Information. The Maintain Company Information window appears.

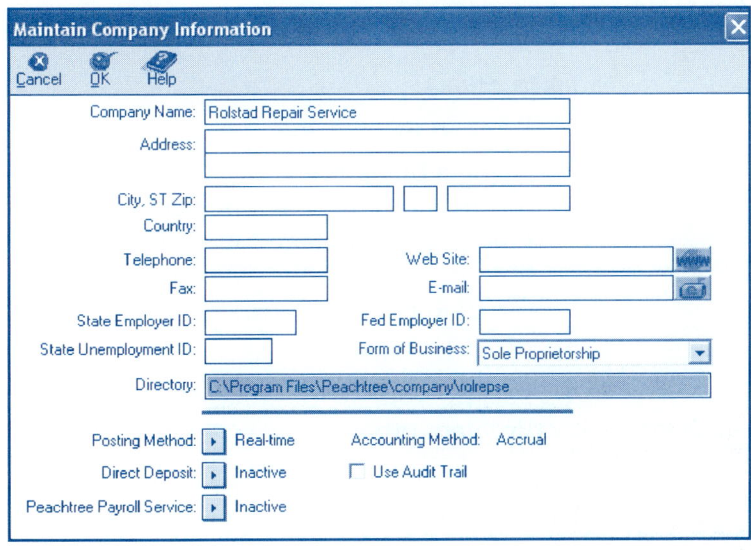

Observe that the directory field shows where your company is stored on your computer: C:\Program Files\Peachtree\company\rolrepse.

2. Type **07-3MPXX** in the Company Name field.

3. When you are finished typing 07-3MPXX as the company name, click on [OK]. Once you have changed the Company Name, each one of your printouts will show the problem number and your initials.

Nothing has changed on your computer's hard drive. The company you restored is identified in the program folder and data folder as C:\Program Files\Peachtree\Company\rolrepse. What you've done is changed the company name so that your printouts will show the problem number and your initials. Using Maintain, Company Information to rename your company does *not* change the shortened company name.

	ACCOUNT TITLE	INCOME STATEMENT		BALANCE SHEET		
		DEBIT	CREDIT	DEBIT	CREDIT	
1	Cash			6 9 5 8 00		1
2	Petty Cash			1 5 0 00		2
3	Accts. Rec.—M. Hollerud			1 9 7 00		3
4	Supplies			7 8 0 00		4
5	Prepaid Insurance			8 0 0 00		5
6	Accts. Pay.—Tampa Supply				6 1 2 00	6
7	Ron Rolstad, Capital				9 3 3 7 00	7
8	Ron Rolstad, Drawing			6 0 0 00		8
9	Income Summary					9
10	Sales		3 2 6 9 00			10
11	Advertising Expense	4 5 0 00				11
12	Insurance Expense	1 5 7 00				12
13	Miscellaneous Expense	8 5 00				13
14	Supplies Expense	1 4 0 0 00				14
15	Utilities Expense	1 6 4 1 00				15
16		3 7 3 3 00	3 2 6 9 00	9 4 8 5 00	9 9 4 9 00	16
17	Net Loss		4 6 4 00	4 6 4 00		17
18		3 7 3 3 00	3 7 3 3 00	9 9 4 9 00	9 9 4 9 00	18
19						19
20						20

Instructions:

1. Print an income statement.

2. Using a blank piece of paper or the *Working Papers*, calculate and record the component percentages for total expenses and net loss. Place the percentage for net loss in parentheses to show that it is for a net loss. Round percentage calculations to the nearest 0.1%. (*Hint:* Remember to uncheck Show Zero Amounts.)

3. Print the Balance Sheet.

4. Backup your work. The suggested file name is 7-3 Mastery Problem.ptb.

You have completed the work for 7-3 Mastery Problem: Preparing Financial Statements with a Net Loss.

Preparing Financial Statements With Two Sources of Revenue and a Net Loss

The instructions that follow show you how to do the following:

- Start Peachtree Complete Accounting.
- Change the company name.
- Identify the directory where LawnWork is stored on your computer's hard drive.
- Restore starting data from the South-Western Accounting with Peachtree CD.
- Print an income statement and balance sheet.
- Complete 7-4 Challenge Problem.

Before you start the 7-4 Challenge Problem, ask your instructor if LawnWork, the company used for the 7-4 Challenge Problem, has already been restored on your computer. The instructions that follow assume that LawnWork is being used for the first time.

GETTING STARTED

Use the following instructions to start Peachtree and restore the starting data for LawnWork. The South-Western Accounting with Peachtree CD includes a Peachtree data files folder. In the steps that follow you will restore the 07-4CP.ptb file.

1. Start Peachtree. From the startup menu, select Close .
2. The menu bar shows three options: Files; Options; and Help. Click File; Restore.
3. The Restore Wizard - Select Backup File window appears. Observe that the Location field shows where Peachtree is stored on your computer. The default location is C:\Program Files\Peachtree\ Company. Your Location field may differ. If you are restoring from a network drive, you will need to know the location of the 07-4CP.ptb file.

4. Click Browse. The Open Backup File window appears. In the Look in field, double-click on the appropriate location of the Peachtree data files. Then, click 07-4CP.ptb to select it. (If appropriate, select your CD drive then double-click the Peachtree Files-Unit 1 folder. Click 07-4CP.ptb to select it.)

5. Make sure the 07-4CP.ptb file is selected. Click Open.

6. The Select Backup File window appears. Make sure the Location field shows the correct location for the 07-4CP.ptb file; for example, X:\Peachtree Files-Unit 1\07-4CP.ptb. (Substitute the correct drive letter for X.)

7. Click Next >. The Select Company window appears. Click on the radio button next to *A New Company*. The Location field shown in this book indicates the default location where drive C is used to install Peachtree. Your Location field may differ. *Make sure that the Location field ends in* **lawnwor**. (If your location field does not end in "r" select An Existing Company, then click Browse. Double-click LawnWork (*or*, 07-4CPXX). Your Location field shows the shortened company name **lawnwor**. Continue with step 8.)

8. Click Next >. The Restore Options window appears.

9. Make sure that the box next to Company Data is *checked*. Click Next >.

10. The Confirmation window appears. Check the From and To fields to make sure they are correct. Click Finish. When the Restore Company scale is 100% complete, your data is restored and you are returned to the menu bar.

CHANGING THE COMPANY NAME

Before you start recording transactions for the 7-4 Challenge Problem, you should look at the company information included on the 07-4CP.ptb file. Follow these steps to look at company information.

1. The LawnWork menu bar should be displayed. From the menu bar, click on Maintain; Company Information. The Maintain Company Information window appears.

READ ME

For purposes of using Peachtree, the company name for the 7-4 Challenge Problem is LawnWork. The textbook identifies this company as LawnMow.

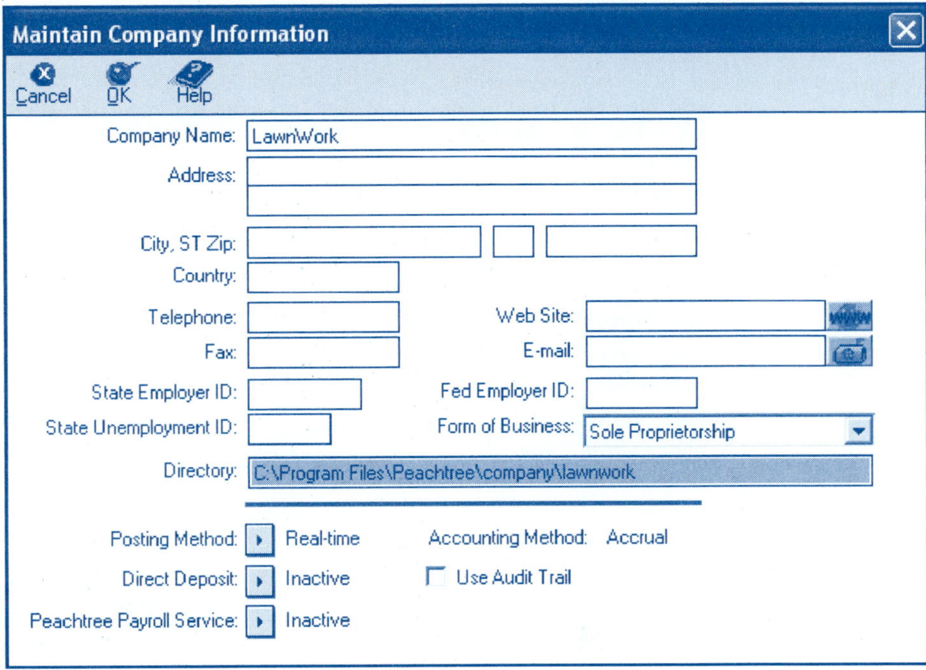

Observe that the directory field shows where your company is stored on your computer: C:\Program Files\Peachtree\company\lawnwork.

2. Type **07-4CPXX** in the Company Name field.

3. When you are finished typing 07-4CPXX as the company name, click on [OK]. Once you have changed the Company Name, each one of your printouts will show the problem number and your initials.

Nothing has changed on your computer's hard drive. The company you restored is identified in the program folder and data folder as C:\Program Files\Peachtree\Company\lawnwork. What you've done is changed the company name so that your printouts will show the problem number and your initials. Using Maintain, Company Information to rename your company does *not* change the shortened company name.

		5	6	7	8
	ACCOUNT TITLE	**INCOME STATEMENT**		**BALANCE SHEET**	
		DEBIT	**CREDIT**	**DEBIT**	**CREDIT**
1	*Cash*			1 8 9 8 00	
2	*Accts. Rec.—Sandra Rohe*			9 5 00	
3	*Supplies*			6 5 0 00	
4	*Prepaid Insurance*			1 2 0 0 00	
5	*Accts. Pay.—Corner Garage*				5 8 00
6	*Accts. Pay.—Broadway Gas*				1 1 0 00
7	*Accts. Pay.—Esko Repair*				2 1 5 00
8	*Ryo Morrison, Capital*				4 0 0 0 00
9	*Ryo Morrison, Drawing*			1 0 0 00	
10	*Income Summary*				
11	*Sales—Lawn Care*		4 9 0 0 00		
12	*Sales—Shrub Care*		2 5 0 0 00		
13	*Advertising Expense*	3 9 0 00			
14	*Insurance Expense*	4 0 0 00			
15	*Miscellaneous Expense*	5 5 0 00			
16	*Rent Expense*	3 3 0 0 00			
17	*Supplies Expense*	3 2 0 0 00			
18		7 8 4 0 00	7 4 0 0 00	3 9 4 3 00	4 3 8 3 00
19	*Net Loss*		4 4 0 00	4 4 0 00	
20		7 8 4 0 00	7 8 4 0 00	4 3 8 3 00	4 3 8 3 00
21					

Instructions:

1. Print an income statement

2. Using a blank piece of paper or the *Working Papers,* calculate and record the component percentages for total expenses and net loss. Place the percentage for net loss in parentheses to show that it is for a net loss. Round percentage calculations to the nearest 0.1%. (*Hint:* Remember to uncheck Show Zero Amounts.)

3. Print the Balance Sheet.

4. Backup your work. The suggested file name is 7-4 Challenge Problem.ptb.

You have completed the work for the 7-4 Challenge Problem: Preparing Financial Statements with Two Sources of Revenue and a Net Loss.

Journalizing and Posting Adjusting and Closing Entries with a Net Loss; Preparing a Post-Closing Trial Balance

The instructions that follow show you how to do the following:

- Start Peachtree Complete Accounting.
- Restore starting data from your South-Western Accounting with Peachtree CD.
- Journalize and post adjusting and closing entries.
- Print a post-closing trial balance.
- Complete 8-4 Mastery Problem.

Before you start the 8-4 Mastery Problem, ask your instructor if Rolstad Repair Service, the company used for the 8-4 Mastery Problem, has already been restored on your computer. The instructions that follow assume that Rolstad Repair Service is being used for the first time.

GETTING STARTED

Rolstad Repair Service's partial work sheet for the month ended October 31, 2005 is shown below. To check the general ledger accounts, you should display or print the general ledger trial balance. The Debit Amt and Credit Amt shown in each account are the account's balances before adjusting and closing entries are posted.

| | 3 | 4 | 5 | 6 | 7 | 8 | |
| ACCOUNT TITLE | ADJUSTMENTS | | INCOME STATEMENT | | BALANCE SHEET | | |
	DEBIT	CREDIT	DEBIT	CREDIT	DEBIT	CREDIT	
1 Cash					6 9 5 8 00		1
2 Petty Cash					1 5 0 00		2
3 Accts. Rec.—M. Hollerud					1 9 7 00		3
4 Supplies		(a) 1 4 0 0 00			7 8 0 00		4
5 Prepaid Insurance		(b) 1 5 7 00			8 0 0 00		5
6 Accts. Pay.—Tampa Supply						6 1 2 00	6
7 Ron Rolstad, Capital						9 3 3 7 00	7
8 Ron Rolstad, Drawing					6 0 0 00		8
9 Income Summary							9
10 Sales				3 2 6 9 00			10
11 Advertising Expense			4 5 0 00				11
12 Insurance Expense	(b) 1 5 7 00		1 5 7 00				12
13 Miscellaneous Expense			8 5 00				13
14 Supplies Expense	(a) 1 4 0 0 00		1 4 0 0 00				14
15 Utilities Expense			1 6 4 1 00				15
16	1 5 5 7 00	1 5 5 7 00	3 7 3 3 00	3 2 6 9 00	9 4 8 5 00	9 9 4 9 00	16
17 Net Loss				4 6 4 00	4 6 4 00		17
18			3 7 3 3 00	3 7 3 3 00	9 9 4 9 00	9 9 4 9 00	18
19							19

Use the following instructions to start Peachtree and restore the starting data for Rolstad Repair Service. The South-Western Accounting with Peachtree CD includes a Peachtree data files folder. In the steps that follow you will restore the 08-4MP.ptb file.

1. Start Peachtree. From the startup menu, select Close.

2. The menu bar shows three options: Files; Options; and Help. Click File; Restore.

3. The Restore Wizard - Select Backup File window appears. Observe that the Location field shows where Peachtree is stored on your computer. The default location is C:\Program Files\Peachtree\Company. Your Location field may differ. If you are restoring from a network drive, you will need to know the location of the 08-4MP.ptb file.

4. Click Browse. The Open Backup File window appears. In the Look in field, double-click on the appropriate location of the Peachtree data files. Then, click 08-4MP.ptb to select it. (If appropriate, select your CD drive then double-click the Peachtree Files-Unit 1 folder. Click 08-4MP.ptb to select it.)

5. Make sure the 08-4MP.ptb file is selected. Click Open.

6. The Select Backup File window appears. Make sure the Location field shows the correct location for the 08-4MP.ptb file; for example, X:\Peachtree Files-Unit 1\08-4MP.ptb. (Substitute the correct drive letter for X.)

7. Click Next >. The Select Company window appears. Click on the radio button next to *A New Company*. The Location field shown in this book indicates the default location where drive C is used to install Peachtree. Your Location field may differ. *Make sure that the*

Location field ends in **rolrepse**. (If your location field does not end in "e" select An Existing Company, then click [Browse]. Double-click Rolstad Repair Service (*or,* 08-4MPXX). Your Location field shows the shortened company name **rolrepse**. Continue with step 8.)

8. Click [Next >]. The Restore Options window appears.

9. Make sure that the box next to Company Data is *checked*. Click [Next >].

10. The Confirmation window appears. Check the From and To fields to make sure they are correct. Click [Finish]. When the Restore Company scale is 100% complete, your data is restored and you are returned to the menu bar.

CHANGING THE COMPANY NAME

Before you start recording transactions for the 8-4 Mastery Problem, you should look at the company information included on the 08-4MP.ptb file. Follow these steps to look at company information.

1. The Rolstad Repair Service menu bar should be displayed. From the menu bar, click on Maintain; Company Information. The Maintain Company Information window appears. Observe that the directory field shows where your company is stored on your computer: C:\Program Files\Peachtree\company\rolrepse.

2. Type **08-4MPXX** in the Company Name field.

3. When you are finished typing 08-4MPXX as the company name, click on [OK]. Once you have changed the Company Name, each one of your printouts will show the problem number and your initials.

Nothing has changed on your computer's hard drive. The company you restored is identified in the program folder and data folder as C:\Program Files\Peachtree\company\rolrepse. What you've done is changed the company name so that your printouts will show the problem number and your initials. Using Maintain, Company Information to rename your company does *not* change the shortened company name.

JOURNALIZING AND POSTING ADJUSTING ENTIRES

Instructions:

1. Using the partial worksheet shown, journalize and post the adjusting entries in Peachtree's general journal. Or, if you completed the 8-4 Mastery Problem in the *Working Papers*, you can use the adjusting entries that you recorded in the general journal. Type **Adjustment a** or **Adjustment b** in the Reference field.

2. Backup your work. The suggested file name is 8-4 Mastery Problem.adjusted.ptb.

JOURNALIZING AND POSTING CLOSING ENTRIES

Use the partial worksheet shown on page 52 to complete the closing entries. Or, if you completed the 8-4 Mastery Problem in the *Working Papers,* use the closing entries recorded in the general journal.

Instructions:

1. Journalize and post the closing entries in Peachtree's general journal. For the first closing entry, type **Closing entries** in the Reference field.

2. Follow these steps to print the October 31 general journal.

    a. From Peachtree's menu bar, select Reports, then General Ledger.

    b. Click on the General Journal to highlight it.

    c. Click ▣. Select 31 as the date in the From calendar field. The date changes to Oct 31, 2005. The To field also shows Oct 31, 2005.

    d. Make the selections to print.

3. Print the general ledger.

4. Follow these steps to print a post-closing trial balance.

    a. From Peachtree's menu bar, select Reports, then General Ledger.

    b. Click on General Ledger Trial Balance to highlight it.

    c. Click ▣. Make the selections to print.

5. Backup your data. The suggestion file name is 8-4 Mastery Problem.closed.ptb.

You have completed the work for the 8-4 Mastery Problem: Journalizing and Posting Adjusting and Closing Entries with a Net Loss; Preparing a Post-Closing Trial Balance.

Journalizing and Posting Adjusting and Closing Entries with Two Revenue Accounts and a Net Loss; Preparing a Post-Closing Trial Balance

The instructions that follow show you how to do the following:

- Start Peachtree Complete Accounting.
- Restore starting data from your South-Western Accounting with Peachtree CD.
- Journalize and post adjusting and closing entries.
- Print a post-closing trial balance.
- Complete 8-5 Challenge Problem.

Before you start the 8-5 Challenge Problem, ask your instructor if LawnWork, the company used for the 8-5 Challenge Problem, has already been restored on your computer. The instructions that follow assume that LawnWork is being used for the first time.

GETTING STARTED

For purposes of using Peachtree, the company name for the 8-5 Challenge Problem is LawnWork. The textbook identifies this company as LawnMow.

LawnWork's partial work sheet for the month ended September 30, 2005 is shown below. To check the general ledger accounts, you should display or print the general ledger trial balance. The Debit Amt and Credit Amt shown in each account are the account's balances before adjusting and closing entries are posted.

	ACCOUNT TITLE	ADJUSTMENTS		INCOME STATEMENT		BALANCE SHEET		
		3 DEBIT	**4** CREDIT	**5** DEBIT	**6** CREDIT	**7** DEBIT	**8** CREDIT	
1	Cash					1 8 9 8 00		1
2	Accts. Rec.—Sandra Rohe					9 5 00		2
3	Supplies		(a) 3 2 0 0 00			6 5 0 00		3
4	Prepaid Insurance		(b) 4 0 0 00			1 2 0 0 00		4
5	Accts. Pay.—Corner Garage						5 8 00	5
6	Accts. Pay.—Broadway Gas						1 1 0 00	6
7	Accts. Pay.—Esko Repair						2 1 5 00	7
8	Ryo Morrison, Capital						4 0 0 0 00	8
9	Ryo Morrison, Drawing					1 0 0 00		9
10	Income Summary							10
11	Sales—Lawn Care				4 9 0 0 00			11
12	Sales—Shrub Care				2 5 0 0 00			12
13	Advertising Expense			3 9 0 00				13
14	Insurance Expense	(b) 4 0 0 00		4 0 0 00				14
15	Miscellaneous Expense			5 5 0 00				15
16	Rent Expense			3 3 0 0 00				16
17	Supplies Expense	(a) 3 2 0 0 00		3 2 0 0 00				17
18		3 6 0 0 00	3 6 0 0 00	7 8 4 0 00	7 4 0 0 00	3 9 4 3 00	4 3 8 3 00	18
19	Net Loss				4 4 0 00	4 4 0 00		19
20		3 6 0 0 00	3 6 0 0 00	7 8 4 0 00	7 8 4 0 00	4 3 8 3 00	4 3 8 3 00	20
21								21

Use the following instructions to start Peachtree and restore the starting data for LawnWork. The South-Western Accounting with Peachtree CD includes a Peachtree data files folder. In the steps that follow you will restore the 08-5CP.ptb file.

1. Start Peachtree. From the startup menu, select Close.

2. The menu bar shows three options: Files; Options; and Help. Click File; Restore.

3. The Restore Wizard - Select Backup File window appears. Observe that the Location field shows where Peachtree is stored on your computer. The default location is C:\Program Files\Peachtree\ Company. Your Location field may differ. If you are restoring from a network drive, you will need to know the location of the 08-5CP.ptb file.

4. Click Browse. The Open Backup File window appears. In the Look in field, double-click on the appropriate location of the Peachtree data files. Then, click 08-5CP.ptb to select it. (If appropriate, select your CD drive then double-click the Peachtree Files-Unit 1 folder. Click 08-5CP.ptb to select it.)

5. Make sure the 08-5CP.ptb file is selected. Click Open.

6. The Select Backup File window appears. Make sure the Location field shows the correct location for the 08-5CP.ptb file; for example, X:\Peachtree Files-Unit 1\08-5CP.ptb. (Substitute the correct drive letter for X.)

7. Click Next >. The Select Company window appears. Click on the radio button next to *A New Company*. The Location field shown in this book indicates the default location where drive C is used to install Peachtree. Your Location field may differ. *Make sure that the*

Location field ends in **lawnwork**. (If your location field does not end in "k" select An Existing Company, then click [Browse]. Double-click LawnWork (*or*, 08-5CPXX). Your Location field shows the shortened company name **lawnwork**. Continue with step 8.)

8. Click [Next >]. The Restore Options window appears.

9. Make sure that the box next to Company Data is *checked*. Click [Next >].

10. The Confirmation window appears. Check the From and To fields to make sure they are correct. Click [Finish]. When the Restore Company scale is 100% complete, your data is restored and you are returned to the menu bar.

CHANGING THE COMPANY NAME

Before you start recording transactions for the 8-5 Challenge Problem, you should look at the company information included on the 08-5CP.ptb file. Follow these steps to look at company information.

1. The LawnWork menu bar should be displayed. From the menu bar, click on Maintain; Company Information. The Maintain Company Information window appears. Observe that the directory field shows where your company is stored on your computer: C:\Program Files\Peachtree\company\lawnwork.

2. Type **08-5CPXX** in the Company Name field.

3. When you are finished typing 08-5CPXX as the company name, click on [OK]. Once you have changed the Company Name, each one of your printouts will show the problem number and your initials.

Nothing has changed on your computer's hard drive. The company you restored is identified in the program folder and data folder as C:\Program Files\Peachtree\company\lawnwork. What you've done is changed the company name so that your printouts will show the problem number and your initials. Using Maintain, Company Information to rename your company does *not* change the shortened company name.

JOURNALIZING AND POSTING ADJUSTING ENTIRES

Instructions:

1. Using the partial worksheet shown, journalize and post the adjusting entries in Peachtree's general journal. Or, if you completed Challenge Problem 8-4 in the *Working Papers*, you can use the adjusting entries that you recorded in the general journal. Type **Adjustment a** or **Adjustment b** in the Reference field.

2. Backup your work. The suggested file name is 8-5 Challenge Problem.adjusted.ptb.

Use the partial worksheet on page 56 to complete the closing entries. Or, if you completed the 8-5 Challenge Problem in the *Working Papers,* use the closing entries recorded in the general journal.

Instructions:

1. Journalize and post the closing entries in Peachtree's general journal. For the first closing entry, type **Closing entries** in the Reference field.
2. Print the September 30, 2005 general journal.
3. Print the general ledger.
4. Print a post-closing trial balance.
5. Backup your data. The suggestion file name is 8-5 Challenge Problem.closed.ptb.
6. Ryo Morrison, owner of LawnWork, is disappointed that his business incurred a net loss for September. Mr. Morrison would have preferred not to have to reduce his capital by $440.00. He knows that you are studying accounting, so Mr. Morrison asks you to analyze his work sheet for September. Based on your analysis of the work sheet, what would you suggest might have caused the net loss? What steps would you suggest so that Mr. Morrison can avoid a net loss in future months? (Use the *Working Papers* or a blank piece of paper to answer this question.)

You have completed the work for the 8-5 Challenge Problem: Journalizing and Posting Adjusting and Closing Entries with Two Revenue Accounts and a Net Loss; Preparing a Post-Closing Trial Balance.

An Accounting Cycle for a Proprietorship: End-of-Fiscal-Period Work

The instructions that follow show you how to do the following:

- Start Peachtree Complete Accounting.
- Restore data from Reinforcement Activity 1—Part A, Extreme Adventures, to complete Part B.
- Complete Reinforcement Activity 1—Part B.

You *must* complete Reinforcement Activity 1—Part A, on pages 32–37 of this book, *before* starting Reinforcement Activity 1—Part B.

GETTING STARTED

Follow these instructions to restore data from Reinforcement Activity 1—Part A.

1. Start Peachtree.
2. At the startup menu, select Open an existing company. From the Open list, select Extreme Adventures. If Extreme Adventures is *not* listed, click on Browse. Select Extreme Adventures from the Company Name list.

What if Extreme Adventures is not listed on either the Open list or when I select Browse?

1. Use Windows Explorer to see if you have a program and data path identified as C:\Peachw\extadven. Close Windows Explorer.

2. From Peachtree's Open list, select Extreme Adventures. It may be identified by RA01-AXX. The X's stand for a student's initials.

3. Restore the backup file made on page 37. The suggested file name was Reinforcement Activity 1-Part A.ptb. Once you restore the backup file that you made on page 37, you will be able to start where you left off the last time you worked with Extreme Adventures.

If you have checked Windows Explorer and Extreme Adventures does *not* have a folder (\extadven), do the following.

1. Start Peachtree. At the startup menu, click `Close`.

2. The File, Options, Help menu bar appears. Select File; Restore.

3. Using the Restore Wizard, select the appropriate location of the backup file that was made on page 37 (Reinforcement Activity 1—Part A.ptb), then restore A New Company. Peachtree will restore your backup data and create the company at the same time.

3. From Peachtree's menu bar, click on File; Restore.

4. Check the Location field to make sure you are restoring the correct file. Click `Next >`.

5. The Select Company window defaults to An Existing Company. The Company Name field shows Extreme Adventures. The Location field shows C:\Program Files\Peachtree\company\extadven. Click `Next >`.

6. The Restore Options window appears. Make sure that the box next to Company Data is *checked*. Click `Next >`.

7. The Confirmation window appears. Observe that the Company Name is Extreme Adventures. Check the From and To fields to make sure they are correct. Click `Finish`. When the Restore Company scale is 100% complete, your data is restored and you are returned to the menu bar.

8. If necessary, remove the external media. You can now continue with Reinforcement Activity 1— Part B.

CHANGING THE COMPANY NAME

In order to make sure that each one of your printouts shows your name and problem number, follow these steps to change the name of the company.

1. From Peachtree's menu bar, select Maintain, then Company Information.

2. The Maintain Company Information screen appears. In the Company Name field, type **RA01-BXX**. Replace the X's with your initials.

3. When you are finished typing RA01-BXX as the company name, click `OK`. Once you have changed the Company Name, each one of your printouts will show the problem number and your initials.

Nothing has changed on your computer's hard drive. The company you restored is identified in the program folder and data folder as C:\Program Files\Peachtree\Company\extadven. What you've done is change the company name so that your printouts will show the problem number and your initials. Using Maintain, Company Information to rename your company does *not* change the file name of the company folder.

Instructions:

1. After restoring the backup that you made at the end of Reinforcement Activity 1—Part A, print a general ledger trial balance. This is your unadjusted trial balance. Compare it to the one shown below. If you completed the worksheet in your *Working Papers*, compare this trial balance to the one on your worksheet.

Extreme Adventures
General Ledger Trial Balance
As of May 31, 2005

Filter Criteria includes: Report order is by ID. Report is printed in Detail Format.

Account ID	Account Description	Debit Amt	Credit Amt
110	Cash	13,683.00	
120	Petty Cash	250.00	
130	Accts. Rec.-Matterhorn Univ.	175.00	
140	Accts. Rec.-Midwest College	100.00	
150	Supplies	1,525.00	
160	Prepaid Insurance	1,200.00	
210	Accts. Pay.-Dunn Supplies		400.00
215	Accts. Pay.-Greenway Supplies		120.00
310	Brian Dawson, Capital		15,000.00
320	Brian Dawson, Drawing	1,200.00	
410	Sales		6,090.00
510	Advertising Expense	300.00	
530	Miscellaneous Expense	307.00	
540	Rent Expense	1,800.00	
550	Repair Expense	455.00	
570	Utilities Expense	615.00	
	Total:	**21,610.00**	**21,610.00**

2. Analyze the following adjustment information into debit and credit parts.

Adjustment Information, May 31

Supplies on hand	$ 625.00
Value of prepaid insurance	1,100.00

3. Using the May 31 adjustment information, journalize and post the adjusting entries in Peachtree's general journal. Or, if you completed Reinforcement Activity 1— Part B in the *Working Papers*, you can use the adjusting entries that you recorded in the general journal. Type **Adjustment a** or **Adjustment b** in the Reference field.

4. Follow these steps to print an income statement.

    a. From Peachtree's menu bar, select Reports, then Financial Statements.

    b. Click on <Standard> Income Stmnt to highlight it.

Peachtree's standard income statement is a predefined form that is included with the software. Along with Revenues and Expenses, Peachtree's standard income statement also shows a Cost of Sales section. Cost of Sales will be covered later in your textbook and in this book. For now, observe that there are zeroes in the Cost of Sales section and that Gross Profit is the same amount as Total Revenues.

    c. Click [image]. Uncheck the boxes next to Print Page Numbers and Show Zero Amounts. Make the selections to print.

5. Follow these steps to print a balance sheet.

    a. From the Select a Report screen, click on <Standard> Balance Sheet to highlight it.

    b. Click [image]. Make the selections to print.

6. Backup your work. The suggested file name is Reinforcement Activity—Part B.adjusted.ptb.

JOURNALIZING AND POSTING CLOSING ENTRIES

Instructions:

1. Journalize and post the closing entries in Peachtree's general journal. If you completed the *Working Papers*, you can use the closing entries shown there or use your income statement (or the unadjusted trial balance) for closing entry information. Type **Closing entries** in the Reference field.

2. Follow these steps to print the May 31 general journal.

    a. From Peachtree's menu bar, select Reports, then General Ledger.

    b. Click on the General Journal to highlight it.

    c. Click [image]. Select 31 as the date in the From calendar field. The date changes to May 31, 2005. The To field also shows May 31, 2005.

    d. Make the selections to print.

READ ME

Why does my May 31 general journal show more than the adjusting and closing entries?

The general journal transactions shown for Extreme Adventures include three other May 31 transactions—a cash sale for $660.00 and the bank service charge of $15.00. Since you are printing a May 31 general journal, all the transactions journalized and posted for that date are shown. These include the adjusting and closing entries *and* the two other entries for the same date.

3. Follow these steps to print a post-closing trial balance.

    a. From the Report List, click on the General Ledger Trial Balance to highlight it.

    b. Click [image]. Make the selections to print.

4. Backup your data. The suggested file name is Reinforcement Activity 1—Part B.closed.ptb.

You have completed the work for Reinforcement Activity 1—Part B: An Accounting Cycle for a Proprietorship: End-of-Fiscal-Period Work.

Journalizing Purchases, Cash Payments, and Other Transactions

The instructions that follow show you how to do the following:

- Start Peachtree Complete Accounting.
- Restore starting data from the South-Western Accounting with Peachtree CD.
- Journalize and post Purchases Journal and Cash Disbursements Journal transactions.
- Complete 9-6 Mastery Problem.

Before you start the 9-6 Mastery Problem, ask your instructor if Mercury Computers, the company used for the 9-6 Mastery Problem, has already been restored on your computer. The instructions that follow assume that Mercury Computers is being used for the first time.

GETTING STARTED

Use the following instructions to start Peachtree and restore the starting data for Mercury Computers. The South-Western Accounting with Peachtree CD includes a Peachtree data files folder. In the steps that follow you will restore the 09-6MP.ptb file.

1. Start Peachtree. From the startup menu, select `Close`.
2. The menu bar shows three options: Files; Options; and Help. Click File; Restore.
3. The Restore Wizard - Select Backup File window appears. Observe that the Location field shows where Peachtree is stored on your computer. The default location is C:\Program Files\Peachtree\ Company. Your Location field may differ. If you are restoring from a network drive, you will need to know the location of the 09-6MP.ptb file.
4. Click `Browse`. The Open Backup File window appears. In the Look in field, double-click on the appropriate location of the Peachtree data files. Then, click 09-6MP.ptb to select it. (If appropriate, select your CD drive then double-click the Peachtree Files-Unit 1 folder. Click 09-6MP.ptb to select it.)
5. Make sure the 09-6MP.ptb file is selected. Click `Open`.

6. The Select Backup File window appears. Make sure the Location field shows the correct location for the 09-6MP.ptb file; for example, X:\Peachtree Files-Unit 1\09-6MP.ptb. (Substitute the correct drive letter for X.)

7. Click Next > . The Select Company window appears. Click on the radio button next to *A New Company*. The Location field shown in this book indicates the default location where drive C is used to install Peachtree. Your Location field may differ. *Make sure that the Location field ends in* **mercompu**. (If your location field does not end in "u" select An Existing Company, then click Browse . Double-click Mercury Computers (*or*, 09-6MPXX). Your Location field shows the shortened company name mercompu. Continue with step 8.)

8. Click Next > . The Restore Options window appears.

9. Make sure that the box next to Company Data is *checked*. Click Next > .

10. The Confirmation window appears. Check the From and To fields to make sure they are correct. Click Finish . When the Restore Company scale is 100% complete, your data is restored and you are returned to the menu bar.

CHANGING THE COMPANY NAME

Before you start recording transactions for the 9-6 Mastery Problem, you should look at the company information included on the 09-6MP.ptb file. Follow these steps to look at company information.

The Mercury Computers menu bar should be displayed. From the menu bar, click on Maintain; Company Information. The Maintain Company Information window appears. Observe that the directory field shows where your company is stored on your computer: C:\ Program Files\Peachtree\company\mercompu.

1. Type **09-6MPXX** in the Company Name field.

2. When you are finished typing 09-6MPXX as the company name, click on OK . Once you have changed the Company Name, each one of your printouts will show the problem number and your initials.

3. Nothing has changed on your computer's hard drive. The company you restored is identified in the program folder and data folder as C:\Program Files\Peachtree\company\mercompu. What you've done is changed the company name so that your printouts will show the problem number and your initials. Using Maintain, Company Information to rename your company does *not* change the shortened company name.

Instructions:

1. Mercury Computers sells computer parts and accessories.

2. Detailed steps are shown below for using Peachtree's Purchase Journal and Cash Disbursements Journal. Refer to these instructions for completing the July 2005 transactions.

Jul. 2   Purchased merchandise on account from Woodland Computers, $2,600.00. P354.

4   Paid cash on account to Pacific Industries, $1,400.00, covering P367, less 2% discount. C242.

6   Purchased merchandise on account from NewWave Electronics, $2,560.00. P355.

8   Paid cash to WCKF Radio for advertising, $750.00. C243.

8   Bought store supplies on account from Willcut & Bishop, $125.00. M39.

9   Paid cash on account to American Semiconductor, $2,690.00, covering P352. No cash discount was offered. C244.

10   Paid cash to Southern Bell for telephone bill, $136.00. C245.

11   Paid cash on account to Woodland Computers, $2,600.00, covering P354, less 2% discount. C246.

12   Returned merchandise to NewWave Electronics, $1,640.00. DM25.

12   Purchased merchandise on account from Helms Supply, $550.00. P356.

13   Paid cash to Edmondson Supply for office supplies, $126.00. C247.

14   Paid cash to Deanes Electronics for merchandise with a list price of $3,480.00, less a 60% trade discount. C248.

15   Bought office supplies on account from Office Express, $106.00. M40.

15   Purchased merchandise on account from Keel, Inc., $3,480.00. P357.

16   Paid cash on account to Farris Cable, $329.00, covering P353. No cash discount was offered. C249.

18   Purchased merchandise for cash from Columbus Industries, $429.00. C250.

20   Purchased merchandise for cash from Mena Mfg. Co., $260.00, less a 40% trade discount. C251.

22   Paid cash on account to Keel, Inc., $3,480.00, covering P357, less 2% discount. C252.

24   Paid cash to Williams Stores for store supplies, $94.00. C253.

25   Paid cash on account to NewWave Electronics, $920.00, covering P355 less DM25. C254.

27   Purchased merchandise on account from Woodland Computers, $3,200.00. P358.

30   Returned merchandise to Woodland Computers, $120.00. DM26.

31   Paid cash on account to Helms Supply, $550.00, covering P356. No discount was offered. C255.

31   Paid cash to reimburse the petty cash fund, $181.75: supplies—office, $23.45; supplies—store, $84.32; miscellaneous, $74.34; and cash over, $0.36. C256.

Use the July transactions to journalize and post to the purchase journal and cash disbursements journal. (In Peachtree, the cash payments journal is called the cash disbursements journal.) The instructions that follow show you the steps for using Peachtree's Cash Disbursements Journal and Purchase Journal.

Purchase Journal: Purchasing Merchandise on Account

Peachtree's Purchases/Receive Inventory task is used when merchandise or assets are purchased on account. Notice that the Peachtree process is different than the process described in your accounting textbook. If you completed the problem manually using the *Working Papers*, you used the general journal to record the purchase of assets and the purchases journal to record the purchase of merchandise. In Peachtree, whenever you make a purchase from a vendor (whether it is merchandise or an asset), you use the Purchases/Receive Inventory task. The Purchases/Receive Inventory task functions as the purchases journal. Another difference is the return of merchandise. In Peachtree, whenever merchandise is returned to a vendor, you use the Vendor Credit Memos task not the general journal.

Your textbook shows the following transaction for July 2.

Transaction:

Jul.　2　Purchased merchandise on account from Woodland Computers, $2,600. P354.

In Peachtree, the Purchases/Receive Inventory task functions as the Purchase Journal. Each time you record a purchase of merchandise on account, Peachtree debits Account 5110, Purchases; and credits the selected vendor and accounts payable.

Instructions:

1. The Mercury Computers menu bar should be displayed and the 09-6MP.ptb file restored. From the menu bar, select Tasks; Purchases/Receive Inventory. The Purchases/Receive Inventory screen appears.
2. Select Woodland Computers as the vendor.
3. Type or select 2 as the Date.
4. Type **P354** in the Invoice No. field.
5. Make sure the Apply to Purchases tab is selected. Type **1** in the Quantity column.
6. Type **Merchandise purchased on account** in the Description column.
7. Make sure that Account No. 5110, Purchases, is shown in the GL Account column.
8. Type **2600** as the Unit Price. (*Hint:* The Amount column should also show 2,600.00.)

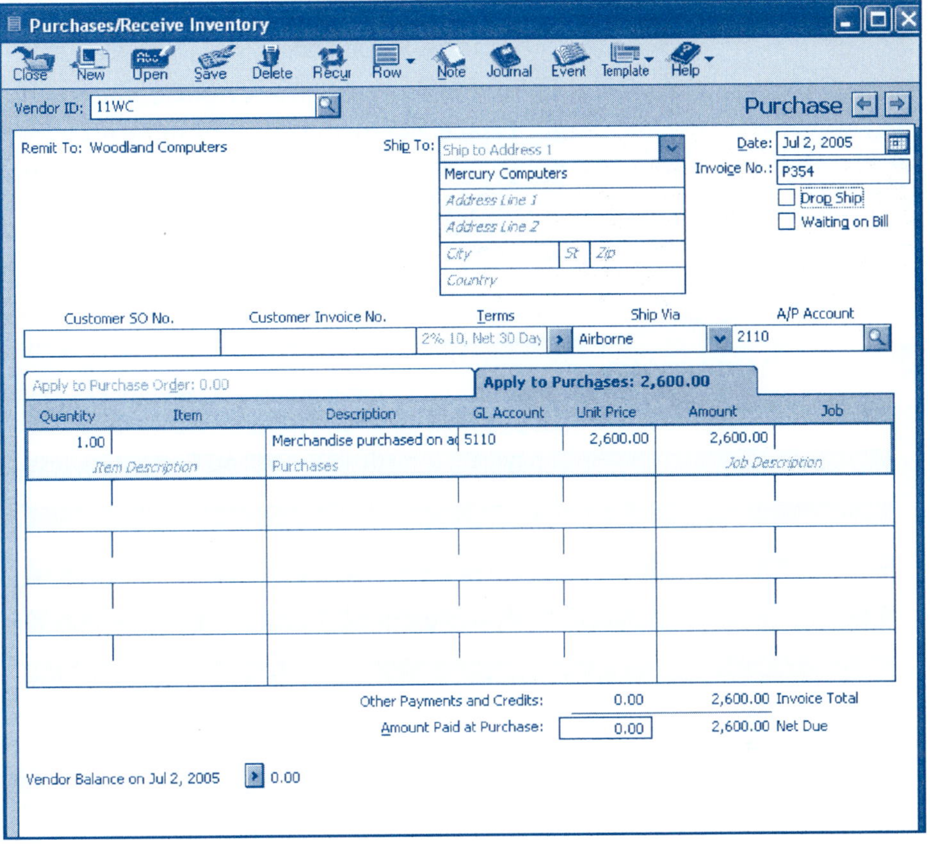

9. Post this purchase.

10. Close the Purchases/Receive Inventory screen.

Cash Disbursements Journal: Making a Vendor Payment

Use these steps to journalize and post the July 4 transaction.

Transaction:

Jul.　4　Paid cash on account to Pacific Industries, $1,400.00, covering P367, less 2% discount. C242.

Each time you pay a vendor in Peachtree, you use the Cash Disbursements Journal (this is referred to as the Cash Payments Journal in the textbook). This is done by selecting Tasks, then Payments.

1. From the menu bar, select Tasks; Payments. The Select a Cash Account window appears.

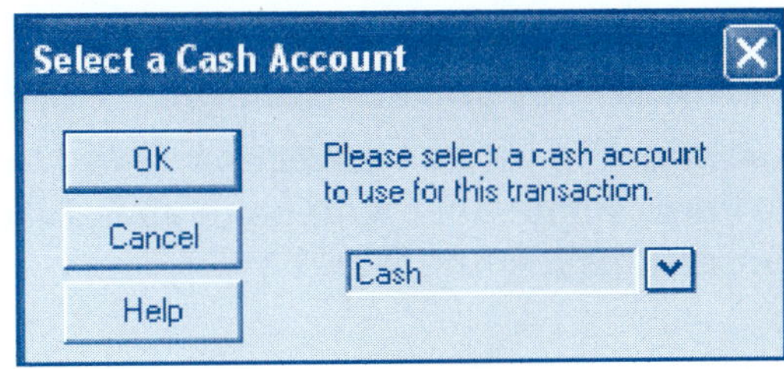

2. Make sure Cash is selected; then click OK . The Payments window appears.

3. In the Vendor ID field, select Pacific Industries.

4. Type **C242** as the Check Num<u>b</u>er.

5. Type **4** in the <u>D</u>ate field. Notice that the Apply to <u>I</u>nvoices tab is selected and that Invoice No. P367 is shown.

6. Type **28.00** in the Discount column.

Since the July 4 transaction is payment for Pacific Industries' beginning balance (invoice from June), you need to type 2% Discount ($1,400 × .2% = $28.00). On July 11 payment is made to Woodland Computers, less a 2% discount. Peachtree will automatically compute Woodland Computers' 2% discount.

7. Click on the Pay box. The upper portion of the Payments window shows a check. Notice that once you clicked the Pay box 1,372 is automatically completed in the $ field. Also, the Discount Account field shows Account No. 5120, Purchases Discounts.

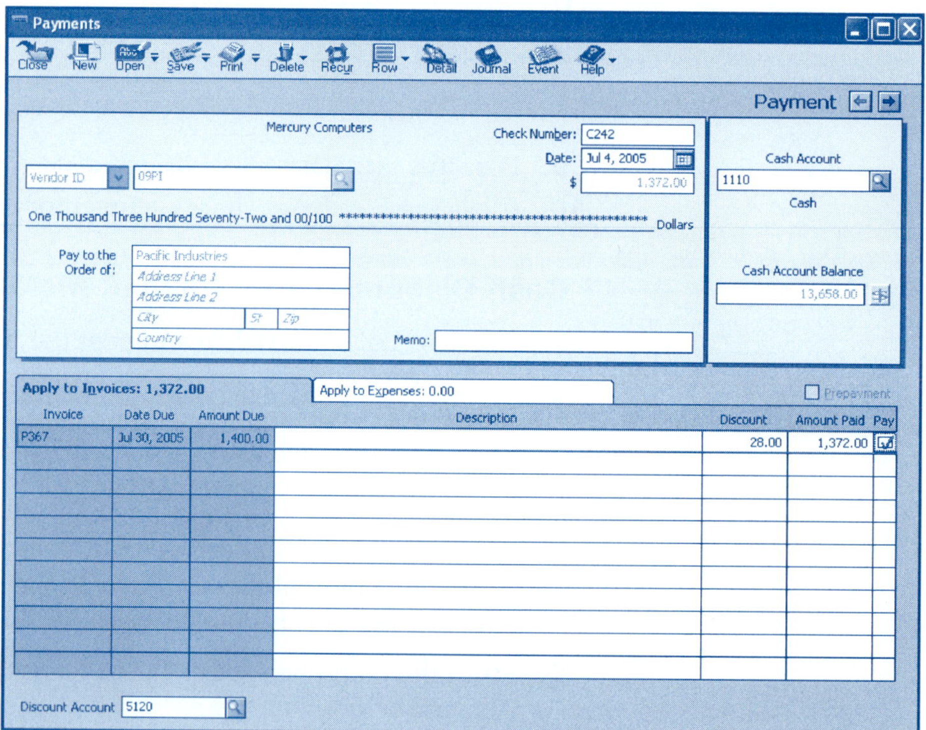

8. Post (<u>S</u>ave) this payment, and then close the Payments window.

9. Complete the July 6 transaction. Refer to the transactions shown in the book. Remember, you have already journalized and posted transactions for July 2 and 4.

Cash Disbursements Journal: Paying Cash for Expenses

In Peachtree, the Write Checks task is used to pay cash for expenses. The Write Checks task is also the cash disbursements journal. Each time you write a check for an expense, use the Write Checks task. For example, when you record a transaction to pay for advertising, you select the appropriate account to debit; then, Peachtree automatically credits cash. When you record a transaction to pay a vendor account, use the Payments task. Both the Write Checks task (used to pay expenses) and the Payments task (used to pay vendors), posts to the Cash Disbursements Journal.

Use these steps to journalize and post the July 8 transaction.

Transaction:

Jul.　8　　　Paid cash to WCKF Radio for advertising, $750.00. C243.

Instructions:

1. From the menu bar, select Tasks; Write Checks. If the select a Cash Account screen appears, make sure Cash is shown.

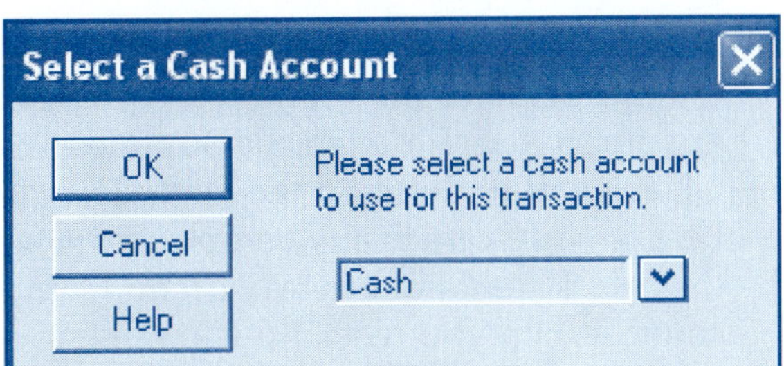

2. If necessary, click OK on the Select a Cash Account window. The Write Checks window appears.

3. Your cursor is in the Vendor ID field. Since you are going to issue a check for advertising, press the Enter key so that your cursor is in the Pay to the Order of field. Type **WCKF Radio** in the Pay to the Order of field.

4. Click on the Check Number field. Type **C243** in the Check Number field. Press Enter .

5. Type **8** in the Date field.

6. Type **750** in the $ field.

7. In the Expense Account field, select Account No. 6105, Advertising Expense. Observe that the Description field is automatically completed.

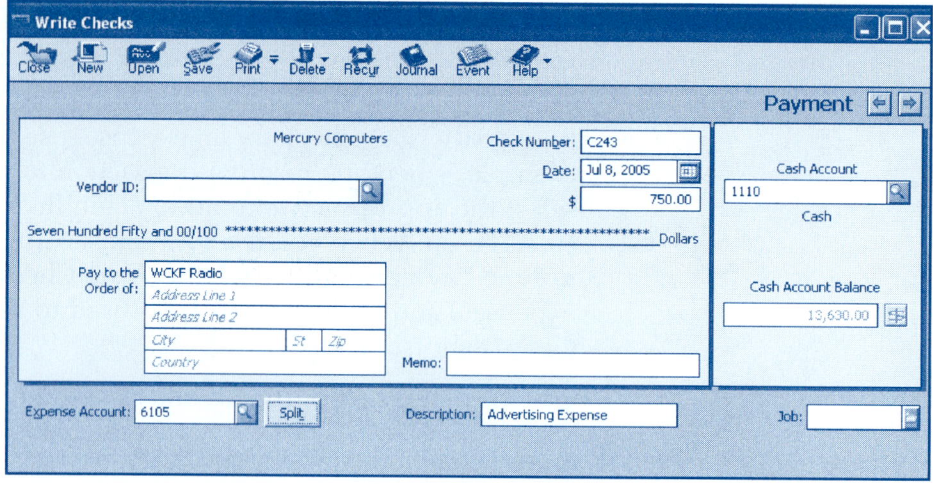

If you click , observe that this transaction is shown in the Cash Disbursements Journal as a debit to Account No. 6105, Advertising Expense; and a credit to Account No. 1110, Cash. Close the Accounting Behind the Screens window.

8. Click [icon] to post.

9. Journalize and post the July 8, 9, 10, and 11 transactions. Refer to the transactions shown in this book. (*Hint:* Remember when assets are purchased, for example Supplies—Store, select the appropriate GL account to debit on the Purchases/Receive Inventory window.) Peachtree automatically computes the vendor discount; for example, the July 11 payment to Woodland Computers includes a 2% discount. When you record this payment, observe that the Discount column is automatically completed.

Purchase Returns: Vendor Credit Memos

When entering a purchase return, it is recorded as a vendor credit memo. The following transaction is for merchandise returned to a vendor:

Transaction:

Jul.   12   Returned merchandise to NewWave Electronics, $1,640.00. DM25.

1. From the Tasks menu, select Vendor Credit Memos.

2. In the Vendor ID field, select NewWave Electronics.

3. Type **12** in the Date field.

4. Type **DM25** in the Credit No field.

5. The Apply to Invoice No. tab is selected. Click on the down-arrow to select P355.

6. Type **1** in the Returned column.

7. Type **Returned merchandise** in the Description field.

8. In the GL Account column, select Account No. 5130, Purch. Returns & Allow.

9. Type **1640** in the Unit Price field.

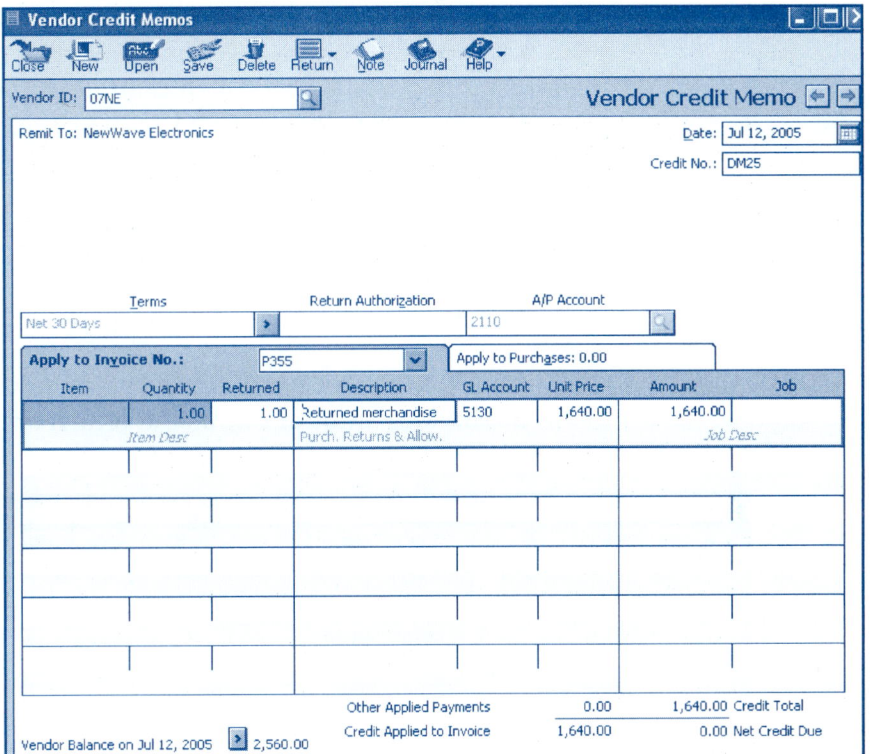

10. To see how the vendor credit memo is journalized, click ![Journal]. Notice that Account No. 5130, Purchases Returns & Allow., is credited for $1,640 and Account No. 2110, Account Payable, is debited for $1,640.00. Click ![OK] to close the Accounting Behind the Screens window.

11. Click ![Save] to post, then ![Close] the Vendor Credit Memos window.

12. Continue the journalizing and posting the July 12 through 24 transactions.

Paying a Vendor, Minus a Return of Merchandise

How does the return of merchandise affect the payment to the vendor? Follow these steps to pay Invoice less the return.

From the menu bar, select Tasks; Payments.

Transaction:

Jul.   25   Paid cash on account to NewWave Electronics, $920.00, covering P355 less DM25. C254.

1. In the Vendor ID field, select NewWave Electronics.

2. Type **C254** in the Check Number field.

3. Type **25** in the Date field. Observe that the Apply to Invoices tab is selected and that the Invoice, P355; Date Due and Amount Due columns are completed. NewWave Electronics is owed $920.00 ($2,560, original invoice amount, less the $1,640 return). Observe that the Pay box is checked.

The payment was calculated as follows:

July 6	Invoice P355	$2,560.00
July 12	Less, DM25	1,640.00
Total Paid		$920.00

4. Click on the Pay box. Peachtree automatically calculated the original invoice amount minus the return (vendor credit memo).

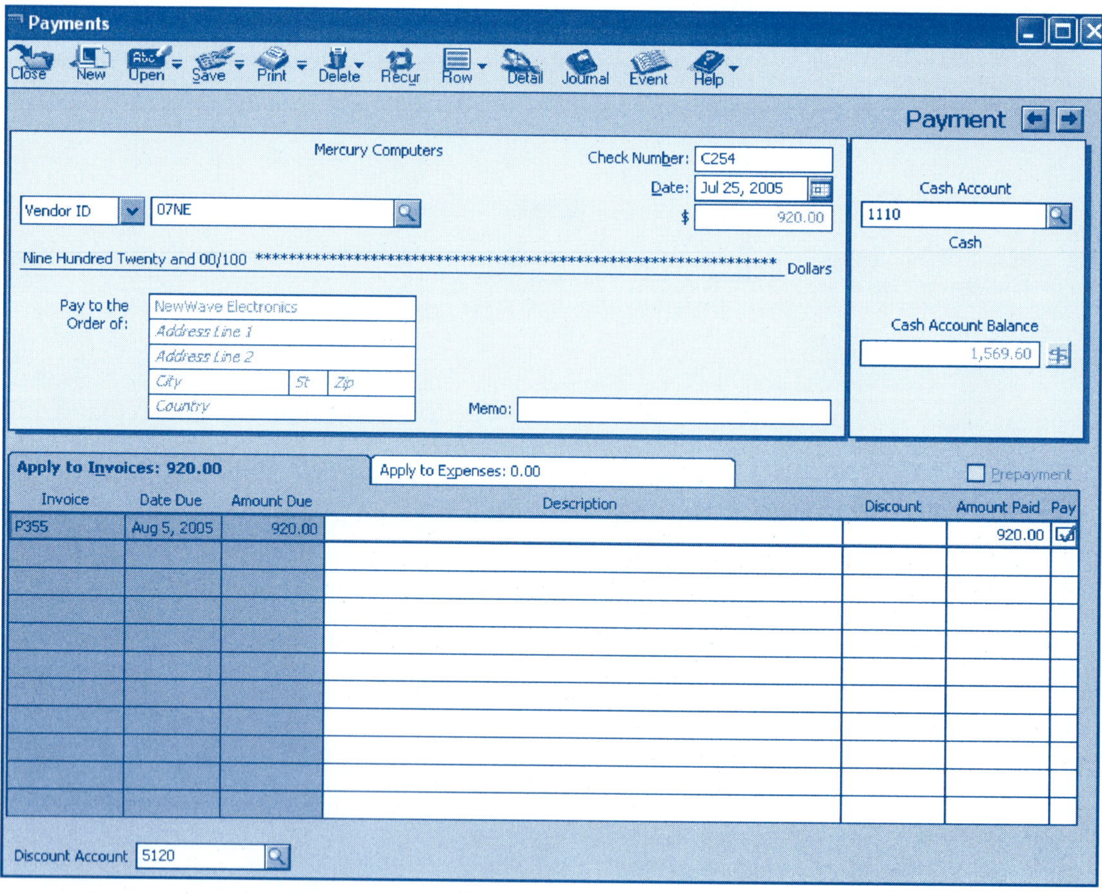

What if your Cash Account Balance field does not show an amount? Close the Payments window without saving. Then, from the menu bar, go to Options/Global. A checkmark should be placed next to Recalculate cash balance automatically in Receipts, Payments, and Payroll Entry. If necessary, click on the appropriate field, then OK. Complete the July 25 transaction.

Post the transaction.

Complete the July 27 through 31 transactions.

Split Transactions: Write Checks Task

For the second July 31 transaction to replenish the Petty Cash fund, use the Write Checks task. Follow these steps to record a compound transaction).

Transaction:

Jul. 31   Paid cash to reimburse the petty cash fund, $181.75: supplies—office, $23,45; supplies—store, $84.32; miscellaneous, $74.34; and cash over, $0.36. C256.

1. From the Tasks menu, select Write Checks.
2. Type **Petty Cash Fund** in the Pay to the Order of field.
3. Type **C256** in the Check Number field.
4. Type **31** in the Date field.
5. Type **181.75** in the $ field.
6. Click Split . The Split Transaction window appears. Complete the following fields.

Account No.	Description	Amount
1145	Supplies—Office	23.45
1150	Supplies—Store	84.32
6135	Miscellaneous Expense	74.34
6110	Cash Short and Over	−0.36

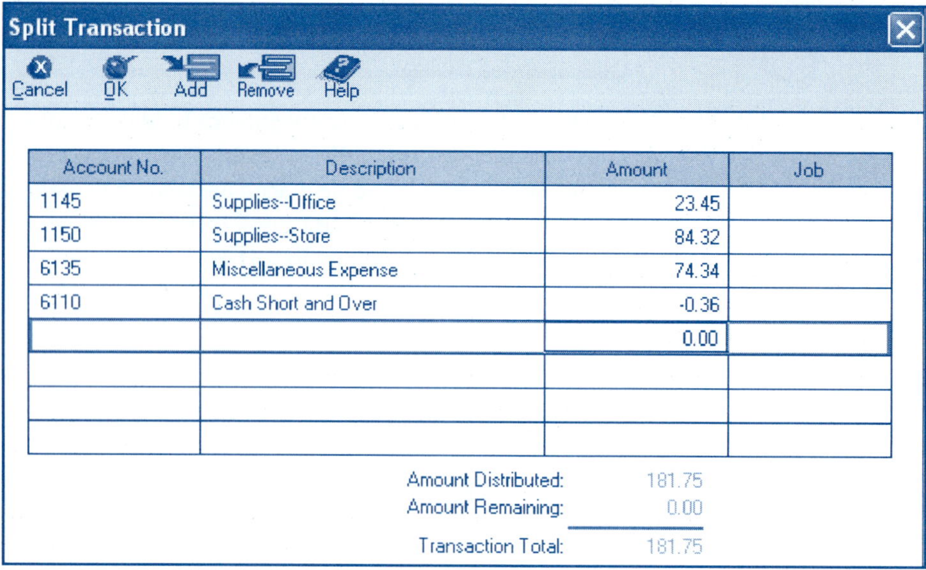

7. Click [OK]. You are returned to the Write Checks window. Observe the the Expense account field shows - Split -.

8. Post Write Checks.

9. Close the Write Checks window.

Printing the Cash Disbursements Journal

1. From the Reports menu, select Accounts Payable; Cash Disbursements Journal.

2. Make the selections to print.

Printing the Purchases Journal

1. From the Report List, select Purchase Journal.

2. Make the selections to print. Peachtree's Purchase Journal shows returns (DM25 and DM26), and purchases of assets on account (M40).

3. Back up. The suggested file name is 9-6 Mastery Problem.

You have completed the work for the 9-6 Mastery Problem: Journalizing Purchases, Cash Payments, and Other Transactions.

Journalizing Purchases, Cash Payments, and Other Transactions

The instructions that follow show you how to do the following:

- Start Peachtree Complete Accounting.
- Restore starting data from the South-Western Accounting with Peachtree CD.
- Journalize and post Purchases Journal and Cash Disbursements Journal transactions.
- Complete 9-7 Challenge Problem.

Before you start the 9-7 Challenge Problem, ask your instructor if Fitness Connection, the company used for the 9-7 Challenge Problem, has already been restored on your computer. The instructions that follow assume that Fitness Connection is being used for the first time.

GETTING STARTED

Use the following instructions to start Peachtree and restore the starting data for Fitness Connection. The South-Western Accounting with Peachtree CD includes a Peachtree data files folder. In the steps that follow you will restore the 09-7CP.ptb file.

1. Start Peachtree. From the startup menu, select Close.
2. The menu bar shows three options: Files; Options; and Help. Click File; Restore.
3. The Restore Wizard - Select Backup File window appears. Observe that the Location field shows where Peachtree is stored on your computer. The default location is C:\Program Files\Peachtree\ Company. Your Location field may differ. If you are restoring from a network drive, you will need to know the location of the 09-7CP.ptb file.
4. Click Browse. The Open Backup File window appears. In the Look in field, double-click on the appropriate location of the Peachtree data files. Then, click 09-7CP.ptb to select it. (If appropriate, select your CD drive then double-click the Peachtree Files-Unit 1 folder. Click 09-7CP.ptb to select it.)

5. Make sure the 09-7CP.ptb file is selected. Click Open .

6. The Select Backup File window appears. Make sure the Location field shows the correct location for the 09-7CP.ptb file; for example, X:\Peachtree Files-Unit 1\09-7CP.ptb. (Substitute the correct drive letter for X.)

7. Click Next> . The Select Company window appears. Click on the radio button next to *A New Company*. The Location field shown in this book indicates the default location where drive C is used to install Peachtree. Your Location field may differ. *Make sure that the Location field ends in* **fitconne**. (If your location field does not end in "e" select An Existing Company, then click Browse . Double-click Fitness Connection (*or*, 09-7CPXX). Your Location field shows the shortened company name fitconne. Continue with step 8.)

8. Click Next> . The Restore Options window appears.

9. Make sure that the box next to Company Data is *checked*. Click Next> .

10. The Confirmation window appears. Check the From and To fields to make sure they are correct. Click Finish . When the Restore Company scale is 100% complete, your data is restored and you are returned to the menu bar.

CHANGING THE COMPANY NAME

Before you start recording transactions for the 9-7 Challenge Problem, you should look at the company information included on the 09-7CP.ptb file. Follow these steps to look at company information.

1. The Fitness Connection menu bar should be displayed. From the menu bar, click on Maintain; Company Information. The Maintain Company Information window appears. Observe that the directory field shows where your company is stored on your computer: C:\Program Files\Peachtree\company\fitconne.

2. Type **09-7CPXX** in the Company Name field.

3. When you are finished typing 09-7CPXX as the company name, click on OK . Once you have changed the Company Name, each one of your printouts will show the problem number and your initials.

Nothing has changed on your computer's hard drive. The company you restored is identified in the program folder and data folder as C:\Program Files \Peachtree\ company\fitconne. What you've done is changed the company name so that your printouts will show the problem number and your initials. Using Maintain, Company Information to rename your company does *not* change the shortened company name.

Instructions:

Fitness Connection is an exercise equipment store.

Transactions:

Nov.	1	Wrote Check No. 363 for the monthly rent of $1,300.00.
	2	Bought $120.00 worth of store supplies on account from Meda Store Supplies, recorded on Memo 43, with 2/10, n/30 payment terms.
	3	Received an invoice, stamped Purchase Invoice 84, for merchandise on account from Central Fitness for $2,150.00, less a 60% trade discount.
	4	Paid $150.00 to Pitman Industries with Check No. 364 for merchandise.
	6	Wrote Check No. 365 for $1,020.00 to Pacer Equipment for Purchase Invoice 82's payment on account.
	8	Returned $260.00 of the merchandise purchased on Purchase Invoice 84 to Central Fitness, recorded on Debit Memorandum 54.
	9	Purchased $2,900.00 of merchandise on account from Trackmaster on Purchase Invoice 85, with 2/10, n/30 payment terms.
	10	Paid $52.00 to myOffice for office supplies with Check No. 366.
	11	Paid the balance of Purchase Invoice 84 less Debit Memorandum 54, to Central Fitness with Check No. 367, taking advantage of the 2/10, n/30 payment terms.
	12	Wrote Check No. 368 for $290.00 to pay the monthly insurance premium.
	16	Paid Trackmaster the amount owed on Purchase Invoice 85, writing Check No. 369.
	29	Paid Meda Store Supplies for the Nov. 2 purchase of store supplies with Check No. 370.
	30	Replenished the petty cash fund by writing Check No. 371 to the custodian for $207.00. Receipts were submitted for the following: office supplies, $48.00; store supplies, $24.00; advertising, $68.00; and miscellaneous, $66.00.

1. Journalize and post the November transactions in Peachtree's Purchase Journal and Cash Disbursements Journal. (*Hint:* When paying vendors, make sure that the Purchase Discount is calculated correctly.)

2. Print the Purchase Journal.

3. Print the Cash Disbursements Journal.

4. Back up. The suggested file name is 9-7 Challenge Problem.ptb.

You have completed the work for the 9-7 Challenge Problem: Journalizing Purchases, Cash Payments, and Other Transactions.

Journalizing Sales and Cash Receipts Transactions

The instructions that follow show you how to do the following:

- Start Peachtree Complete Accounting.
- Restore starting data from the South-Western Accounting with Peachtree CD.
- Journalize and post Sales Journal and Cash Receipts Journal transactions.
- Complete 10-4 Mastery Problem.

Before you start the 10-4 Mastery Problem, ask your instructor if Aqua Center, the company used for the 10-4 Mastery Problem, has already been set up on your computer. The instructions that follow assume that Aqua Center is being used for the first time.

GETTING STARTED

Use the following instructions to start Peachtree and restore the starting data for Aqua Center. The South-Western Accounting with Peachtree CD includes a Peachtree data files folder. In the steps that follow you will restore the 10-4MP.ptb file.

1. Start Peachtree. From the startup menu, select Close .
2. The menu bar shows three options: Files; Options; and Help. Click File; Restore.
3. The Restore Wizard - Select Backup File window appears. Observe that the Location field shows where Peachtree is stored on your computer. The default location is C:\Program Files\Peachtree\ Company. Your Location field may differ. If you are restoring from a network drive, you will need to know the location of the 10-4MP.ptb file.
4. Click Browse . The Open Backup File window appears. In the Look in field, double-click on the appropriate location of the Peachtree data files. Then, click 10-4MP.ptb to select it. (If appropriate, select your CD drive then double-click the Peachtree Files-Unit 1 folder. Click 10-4MP.ptb to select it.)
5. Make sure the 10-4MP.ptb file is selected. Click Open .

6. The Select Backup File window appears. Make sure the Location field shows the correct location for the 10-4MP.ptb file; for example, X:\Peachtree Files-Unit 1\10-4MP.ptb. (Substitute the correct drive letter for X.)

7. Click Next>. The Select Company window appears. Click on the radio button next to *A New Company*. The Location field shown in this book indicates the default location where drive C is used to install Peachtree. Your Location field may differ. *Make sure that the Location field ends in* **aqucente**. (If your location field does not end in "e" select An Existing Company, then click Browse. Double-click Aqua Center (*or*, 10-4MPXX). Your Location field shows the shortened company name aqucente. Continue with step 8.)

8. Click Next>. The Restore Options window appears.

9. Make sure that the box next to Company Data is *checked*. Click Next>.

10. The Confirmation window appears. Check the From and To fields to make sure they are correct. Click Finish. When the Restore Company scale is 100% complete, your data is restored and you are returned to the menu bar.

CHANGING THE COMPANY NAME

Before you start recording transactions for the 10-4 Mastery Problem, you should look at the company information included on the 10-4MP.ptb file. Follow these steps to look at company information.

1. The Aqua Center menu bar should be displayed. From the menu bar, click on Maintain; Company Information. The Maintain Company Information window appears. Observe that the directory field shows where your company is stored on your computer: C:\ Program Files\Peachtree company\aqucente.

2. Type **10-4MPXX** in the Company Name field.

3. When you are finished typing 10-4MPXX as the company name, click on OK. Once you have changed the Company Name, each one of your printouts will show the problem number and your initials.

Nothing has changed on your computer's hard drive. The company you restored is identified in the program folder and data folder as C:\Program Files\Peachtree\company\aqucente. What you've done is changed the company name so that your printouts will show the problem number and your initials. Using Maintain, Company Information to rename your company does *not* change the shortened company name.

Instructions:

Aqua Center installs and maintains swimming pools and spas.

Transactions:

Oct.	26	Received cash on account from Slumber Inns, covering S435 for $1,356.00, less a 2% discount. R293.
	27	Sold merchandise on account to County Hospital, $489.50, plus sales tax, $19.58; total, $509.08. S443.
	28	Recorded cash and credit card sales, $4,315.00, plus sales tax, $126.60; total, $4,441.60. TS44.
	29	Received cash on account from Summit Lodge, $467.24, covering S438. R294.
	29	Granted credit to Slumber Inns for merchandise returned, $124.00, plus sales tax, $4.96, from S293; total, $128.96. CM54.
	30	Sold merchandise on account to Southeastern University, $3,643.50. Southeastern University is exempt from sales tax. S444.
	31	Recorded cash and credit card sales, $1,232.00, plus sales tax, $42.22; total, $1,274.22. TS45.

JOURNALIZING SALES AND CASH RECEIPTS TRANSACTIONS

You will be recording transactions for Aqua Center from October 26 through October 31. You will be journalizing sales and cash receipts transactions. The instructions that follow show you the steps for using Peachtree's Cash Receipts Journal and Sales Journal.

Peachtree's Cash Receipts Journal

Transaction:

Oct. 26   Received cash on account from Slumber Inns, covering S435 for $1,356.00, less a 2% discount. $293.

In Peachtree, the Receipts task functions as the Cash Receipts Journal. Each time you enter a cash receipt, Peachtree automatically debits Cash. The offsetting credit part of the transaction goes to Sales or the account that you specify.

Instructions:

1. The Aqua Center menu bar should be displayed on your screen and the 10-4MP.ptb file restored. From the menu bar, select Tasks, then Receipts. The Select a Cash Account window appears.

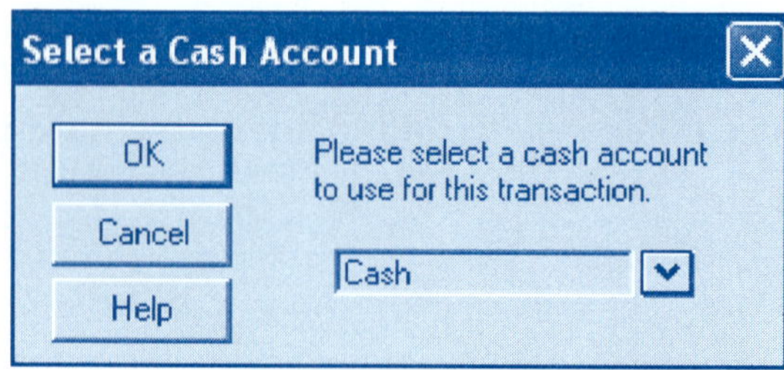

2. Make sure Cash is selected. Click OK . The Receipts window appears.

3. Your cursor is in the Deposit ID field. Type the transaction date **10/26/05** and press the Enter key.

4. In the Customer ID field, select Slumber Inns. Observe that the Apply to Invoices tab is selected.

5. Type **S435** in the Reference field. Press Enter .

6. Type **R293** in the Receipt Number field. Press Enter .

7. Type **26** in the Date field. Press Enter .

8. Verify that Account No. 1110, Cash, is displayed in the Cash Account field. Observe that the Balance field displays 40,721.78. That is the starting balance in Account No. 1110, Cash.

9. If necessary, click on the Apply to Invoices tab.

10. Type **Received cash on account** in the Description column. Press Enter .

11. Since there is a 2% discount, type **27.12** in the Discount column.

12. Click the Pay box for Invoice S435 to place a check mark in it. Observe that the Amount Paid column and the Receipt Amount fields (1,328.88) are automatically completed.

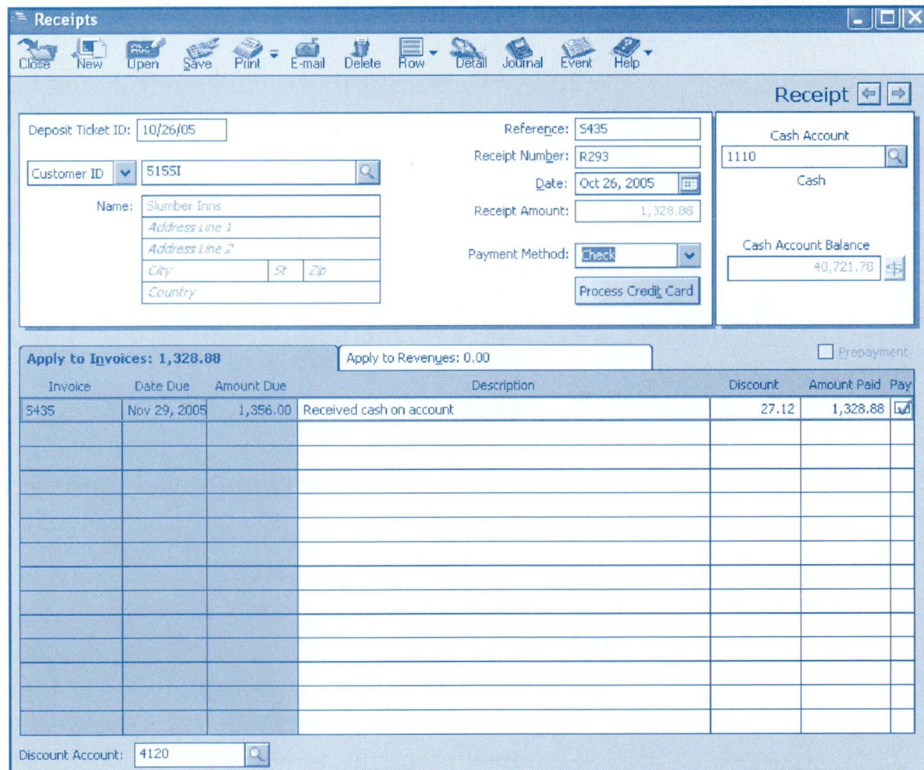

Observe that the Discount Account field shows 4120, that is the Account No. for Sales Discounts.

13. Click ![Save] to post.

14. Close the Receipts window.

Peachtree's Sales Journal

The following sales journal transaction is shown of October 27. The sales tax rate for the 10-4 Mastery Master is 4%.

Transaction:

Oct. 27   Sold merchandise on account to County Hospital, $489.50, plus sales tax, $19.58; total $509.08, S443.

In Peachtree, the Sales/Invoicing task functions as the Sales Journal. Each time you enter a credit sale, Peachtree automatically debits the customer's account and Accounts Receivable. The credit side of the transaction defaults to Account No. 4110, Sales. You can also credit account(s) that you specify.

Instructions:

1. From the menu bar, click on Tasks, Sales/Invoicing. The Sales/Invoicing screen appears. The Sales/Invoicing window appears.

2. Your cursor is in the Customer ID field. Select County Hospital as the customer.

3. Type **27** (or select 27) as the Date.

4. Type **S443** in the Invoice No. field. Press [Enter].

5. Make sure that the Apply to Sales tab is selected.

6. Type **1** in the Quantity column. Press [Enter] two times.

7. Type **Sold merchandise on account** in the Description column. Press [Enter].

8. Observe that Account No. 4110, Sales, is shown in the GL Account column. Press [Enter].

9. Type **489.50** in the Unit Price column. Press [Enter] four times.

10. Type **1** in the Quantity column. Press [Enter] two times.

11. Type **Sales Tax Payable** in the Description column.

12. Select Account No. 2145, Sales Tax Payable, in the GL Account column.

13. Type **19.58** in the Unit Price column. Observe that the Net Amount Due is 509.08. (*Hint:* This is shown at the bottom of the Sales/Invoicing window).

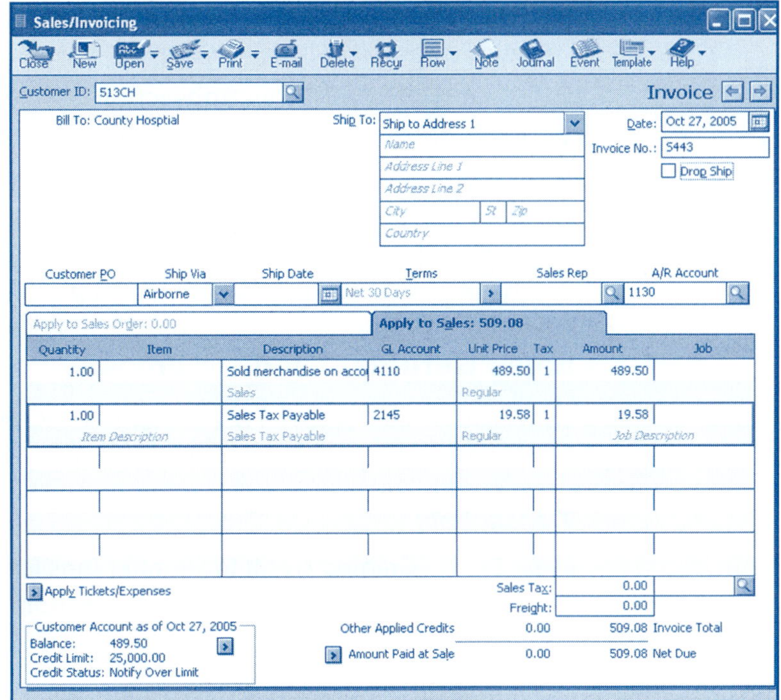

READ ME

If the GL Account column does *not* appear on the Sales/Invoicing window it is because the menu bar selection Global; Options, Accounting tab, Hide General Ledger Accounts boxes are checked. The boxes in the Hide General Ledger Accounts area *must be unchecked.* Refer to the Preface, pages x–xi, Peachtree's Global Options, for detailed steps.

Observe that Account No. 1130 is shown as the A/R Account. This is shown at the middle, right side of the window, and confirms that the accounts receivable account (Account No. 1130) is being debited.

14. You can also click on 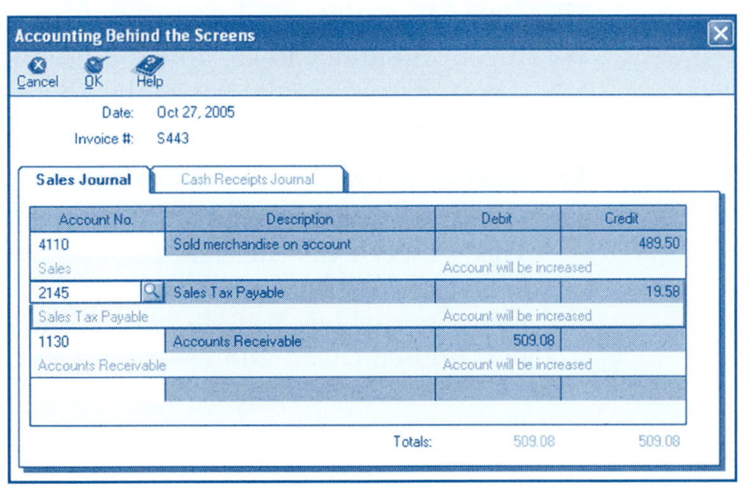 to see how this transaction is shown in the Sales Journal.

15. Click [OK] to close the Accounting Behind the Screen, Sales Journal window.

16. Click [Save] to post this transaction.

17. Close the Sales/Invoicing window.

18. Journalize and post the October 28 and 29 transactions. (*Hint:* Use the Receipts task to record cash and credit card sales. Type the terminal summary (TS) number in the Reference field. Use the transaction date for the Deposit Ticket ID.)

Sales Returns: Credit Memos

To record a sales returns use Peachtree's Credit Memos task. This transaction will post to the Sales Journal.

Transaction:

Oct. 29   Granted credit to Slumber Inns for merchandise returned, $124.00, plus sales tax, $4.96, from S293; total, $128.96. CM54.

1. From the menu bar, select Tasks; Credit Memos. The Credit Memos window appears.

2. In the Customer ID field, select Slumber Inns.

3. Type **29** in the Date field.

4. Type **CM54** in the Credit No. field. Press [Enter].

5. Make sure the Apply to Sales tab is selected.

6. Type **1** in the Quantity field. Press [Enter] two times.

7. Type **Returned merchandise** in the Description columns. Press [Enter].

8. In the GL Account column, select Account No. 4130, Sales Returns & Allowances.

9. Type **124** in the Unit Price column; press [Enter] four times.

10. Type **1** in the Quantity column.

11. Type **Sales Tax Payable** in the Description column.

12. Select 2145, Sales Tax Payable, in the GL Account column.

13. Type **4.96** in the Unit Price column.

14. If you would like to see how this transaction is journalized, click [Journal]; [OK] to close the Accounting Behind the Screens window.

15. Click [Save].

16. Journalize and post the October 30 and 31 transactions.

17. Use your *Working Papers* or a blank piece of paper to prove cash. The October 1 cash account balance in the general ledger was $4,483.25. The October 31 cash credit total in the cash disbursements journal was $39,315.22. On October 31, the balance on the next unused check stub was $8.918.50.

PRINTING THE SALES JOURNAL

Follow these steps to print the sales journal.

1. From the menu bar, click on Reports, Accounts Receivable. From the Report List, click on Sales Journal to highlight it.
2. Click [Print]. In the From calendar field, select Oct 26, 2005. The To calendar field shows Oct 31, 2005.

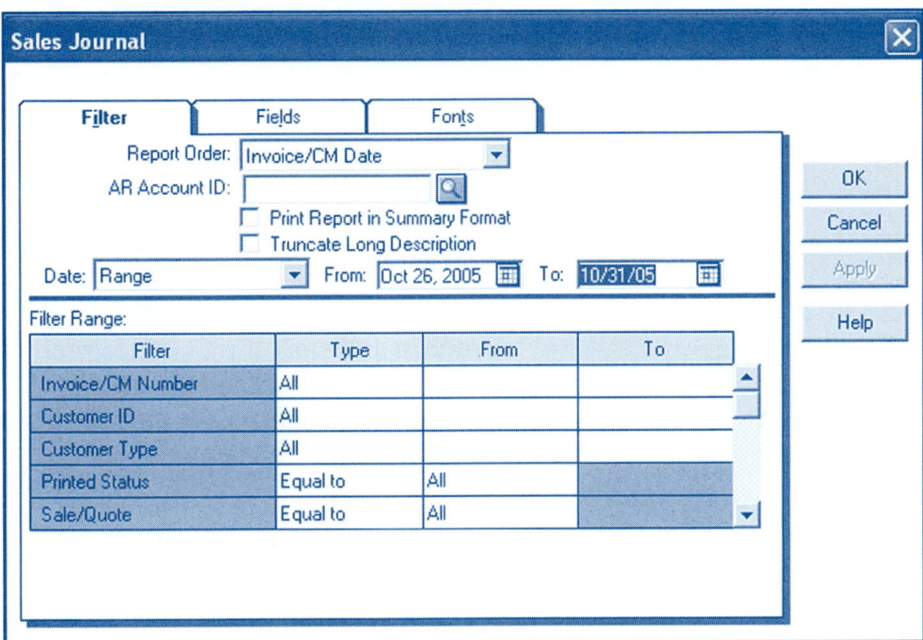

3. Make the selections to print.

PRINTING THE CASH RECEIPTS JOURNAL

1. From the Report List, click on Cash Receipts Journal to highlight it.
2. Click [Print]. Select October 26 2005 in the From calendar field. The To field shows Oct 31, 2005.
3. Make the selections to print the cash receipts journal.
4. Back up your work. The suggested file name is 10-4 Mastery Problem.

You have completed the work for the 10-4 Mastery Problem: Journalizing Sales and Cash Receipts Transactions.

Journalizing Transactions; Proving and Ruling Special Journals

The instructions that follow show you how to do the following:

- Start Peachtree Complete Accounting.
- Restore starting data from the South-Western Accounting with Peachtree CD.
- Journalize and post Purchase Journal, Cash Disbursements Journal, Sales Journal and Cash Receipts Journal transactions.
- Complete 10-5 Challenge Problem.

Before you start the 10-5 Challenge Problem, ask your instructor if Zone 6, the company used for the 10-5 Challenge Problem, has already been set up on your computer. The instructions that follow assume that Zone 6 is being used for the first time.

GETTING STARTED

Use the following instructions to start Peachtree restore the starting data for Zone 6. The South-Western Accounting with Peachtree CD includes a Peachtree data files folder. In the steps that follow you will restore the 10-5CP.ptb file.

1. Start Peachtree. From the startup menu, select Close.
2. The menu bar shows three options: Files; Options; and Help. Click File; Restore.
3. The Restore Wizard - Select Backup File window appears. Observe that the Location field shows where Peachtree is stored on your computer. The default location is C:\Program Files\Peachtree\Company. Your Location field may differ. If you are restoring from a network drive, you will need to know the location of the 10-5CP.ptb file.
4. Click Browse. The Open Backup File window appears. In the Look in field, double-click on the appropriate location of the Peachtree data files. Then, click 10-5CP.ptb to select it. (If appropriate, select your CD drive then double-click the Peachtree Files-Unit 1 folder. Click 10-5CP.ptb to select it.)

5. Make sure the 10-5CP.ptb file is selected. Click **Open**.

6. The Select Backup File window appears. Make sure the Location field shows the correct location for the 09-6MP.ptb file; for example, X:\Peachtree Files-Unit 1\10-5CP.ptb. (Substitute the correct drive letter for X.)

7. Click **Next >**. The Select Company window appears. Click on the radio button next to *A New Company*. The Location field shown in this book indicates the default location where drive C is used to install Peachtree. Your Location field may differ. *Make sure that the Location field ends in* **zone**. (If your location field does not end in "e" select An Existing Company, then click **Browse**. Double-click Zone 6 (*or*, 10-5CPXX). Your Location field shows the shortened company name zone. Continue with step 8.)

8. Click **Next >**. The Restore Options window appears.

9. Make sure that the box next to Company Data is *checked*. Click **Next >**.

10. The Confirmation window appears. Check the From and To fields to make sure they are correct. Click **Finish**. When the Restore Company scale is 100% complete, your data is restored and you are returned to the menu bar.

CHANGING THE COMPANY NAME

Before you start recording transactions for the 10-5 Challenge Problem, you should look at the company information included on the 10-5CP.ptb file. Follow these steps to look at company information.

1. The Zone 6 menu bar should be displayed. From the menu bar, click on Maintain; Company Information. The Maintain Company Information window appears. Observe that the directory field shows where your company is stored on your computer: C:\Program Files\Peachtree\company\zone.

2. Type **10-5CPXX** in the Company Name field.

3. When you are finished typing 10-5CPXX as the company name, click on **OK**. Once you have changed the Company Name, each one of your printouts will show the problem number and your initials.

Nothing has changed on your computer's hard drive. The company you restored is identified in the program folder and data folder as C:\Program Files\Peachtree\company\zone. What you've done is changed the company name so that your printouts will show the problem number and your initials. Using Maintain, Company Information to rename your company does *not* change the shortened company name.

Instructions:

Zone 6 is a lawn and garden store.

May	1	Paid cash for rent, $1,400.00. C344.
	3	Paid cash for electric bill, $186.00. C345.
	3	Granted credit to Slippery Rock Inn for merchandise returned, $235.00, plus sales tax, $18.80, from S493; total, $253.80. CM67.
	3	Purchased merchandise on account from Angelo Lawn Supplies, $1,340.00. P91.
	4	Bought $120.00 worth of store supplies on account from Mosby Store Supplies, recorded on Memo 43, with 2/10, n/30 payment terms.
	4	Paid cash on account to Northeast Nurseries, $7,632.00, covering P87. C346.
	4	Sold merchandise on account to First National Bank, $546.00, plus sales tax. S567.
	5	Bought office supplies for cash, $35.45. C347.
	5	Paid cash for some merchandise, $89.40. C348.
	6	Recorded cash and credit card sales, $3,235.00, plus sales tax of $239.40. TS23.
	7	Received an invoice, stamped Purchase Invoice 92, for merchandise on account from Forde Collectibles for $3,250.00, less a 60% trade discount.
	7	Houston Landscaping paid its $545.65 balance, less 2% discount. R490.
	8	Bought office supplies on account from Office Mart, $81.60. M44.
	10	Returned $260.00 of the merchandise purchased on Purchase Invoice 92 to Forde Collectibles, recorded on Debit Memorandum 23.
	11	Paid the remaining balance of Purchase Invoice 92, less Debit Memorandum 23, to Forde Collectibles with Check No. 349, taking advantage of the 2/10, n/30 payment terms.
	13	Cash and credit card sales for the week were $3,216.00, plus sales tax of $206.70. TS24.
	14	Jackson Public Schools bought merchandise on account for $450.00. S568.
	16	Purchased $2,900.00 of merchandise on account from Tom's Sod Farm on Purchase Invoice 93, with 2/10, n/30 payment terms.
	17	Paid cash on account to Office Mart, $81.60, covering M44. C350.
	20	Cash and credit card sales for the week were $2,554.00, plus sales tax, $184.23. TS25.
	22	First National Bank paid $589.68 cash on its account, covering S567. R491.
	23	SDR Investment Trust bought merchandise on account for $1,456.00, plus sales tax. S569.
	23	Purchased merchandise on account from LawnScapes, Inc., $4,488.00. P94.
	25	Paid $102.00 cash for advertising. C351.

27	Cash and credit card sales for the week were $2,742.00, plus sales tax, $184.25. TS25.
29	Slippery Rock Inn paid $2,345.64 on its account, covering S493. R492.
29	Granted credit to SDR Investment Trust for damaged merchandise, $45.00, plus sales tax, from S455. CM68.
31	Paid cash to replenish the petty cash fund, $361.60: office supplies, $74.40; store supplies, $85.00; advertising, $105.00; miscellaneous, $96.00. C352.
31	Recorded cash and credit card sales, $768.00, plus sales tax, $49.45. TS26.

Instructions:

1. The 10-5CP problem file should be restored and the Zone 6 menu bar displayed. Journalize and post in the appropriate journal the May 1–31 transactions. The sale tax rate is 8%. Calculate and add the appropriate sales tax amount to each sale.

2. Print the purchase journal, cash disbursements journal, sales journal, and cash receipts journal.

3. Use a blank piece of paper or the *Working Papers* to prove cash.

4. Back up your work. The suggested file name is 10-5 Challenge Problem.

You have completed the work for the 10-5 Challenge Problem: Journalizing Transactions; Proving and Ruling Special Journals.

Posting to General and Subsidiary Ledgers

The instructions that follow show you how to do the following:

- Start Peachtree Complete Accounting.
- Restore starting data from the South-Western Accounting with Peachtree CD.
- Print the purchase journal, cash disbursements journal, sales journal, cash receipts journal, general ledger, vendor ledgers, and customer ledgers.
- Complete 11-6 Mastery Problem.

Before you start the 11-6 Mastery Problem, ask your instructor if Auto Restoration, Inc., the company used for the 11-6 Mastery Problem, has already been set up on your computer. The instructions that follow assume that Auto Restoration, Inc. is being used for the first time.

GETTING STARTED

Use the following instructions to start Peachtree and restore the starting data for Auto Restoration, Inc. The South-Western Accounting with Peachtree CD includes a Peachtree data files folder. In the steps that follow you will restore the 11-6MP.ptb file.

1. Start Peachtree. From the startup menu, select Close .
2. The menu bar shows three options: Files; Options; and Help. Click File; Restore.
3. The Restore Wizard - Select Backup File window appears. Observe that the Location field shows where Peachtree is stored on your computer. The default location is C:\Program Files\Peachtree\ Company. Your Location field may differ. If you are restoring from a network drive, you will need to know the location of the 11-6MP.ptb file.
4. Click Browse . The Open Backup File window appears. In the Look in field, double-click on the appropriate location of the Peachtree data files. Then, click 11-6MP.ptb to select it. (If appropriate, select your CD drive then double-click the Peachtree Files-Unit 1 folder. Click 11-6MP.ptb to select it.)
5. Make sure the 11-6MP.ptb file is selected. Click Open .

6. The Select Backup File window appears. Make sure the Location field shows the correct location for the 11-6MP.ptb file; for example, X:\Peachtree Files-Unit 1\11-6MP.ptb. (Substitute the correct drive letter for X.)

7. Click Next >. The Select Company window appears. Click on the radio button next to *A New Company*. The Location field shown in this book indicates the default location where drive C is used to install Peachtree. Your Location field may differ. *Make sure that the Location field ends in* **autresin**. (If your location field does not end in "n" select An Existing Company, then click Browse. Double-click Auto Restoration, Inc. (*or*, 11-6MPXX). Your Location field shows the shortened company name autresin. Continue with step 8.)

8. Click Next >. The Restore Options window appears.

9. Make sure that the box next to Company Data is *checked*. Click Next >.

10. The Confirmation window appears. Check the From and To fields to make sure they are correct. Click Finish. When the Restore Company scale is 100% complete, your data is restored and you are returned to the menu bar.

CHANGING THE COMPANY NAME

Before you start recording transactions for the 11-6 Mastery Problem, you should look at the company information included on the 11-6MP.ptb file. Follow these steps to look at company information.

1. The Auto Restoration, Inc. menu bar should be displayed. From the menu bar, click on Maintain; Company Information. The Maintain Company Information window appears. Observe that the directory field shows where your company is stored on your computer: C:\Program Files\Peachtree\ company\autresin.

2. Type **11-6MPXX** in the Company Name field.

3. When you are finished typing 11-6MPXX as the company name, click on OK. Once you have changed the Company Name, each one of your printouts will show the problem number and your initials.

Nothing has changed on your computer's hard drive. The company you restored is identified in the program folder and data folder as C:\Program Files\Peachtree\company\autresin. What you've done is changed the company name so that your printouts will show the problem number and your initials. Using Maintain, Company Information to rename your company does *not* change the shortened company name.

The journals, subsidiary ledgers, and the general ledger accounts for Auto Restoration, Inc. are included in the 11-6MP.ptb file.

1. The 11-6MP problem file should be restored and the Auto Restoration, Inc. menu bar displayed.

2. Print the sales journal. Compare it to the one shown in the *Working Papers*. Remember, Peachtree posts credit memos and memos, including the account correction, to the Sales Journal.

3. Print the cash receipts journal. Compare it to the one shown in the *Working Papers*.

4. Print the purchase journal. Compare it to the one shown in the *Working Papers*. Remember, Peachtree posts vendor credit memos to the purchase journal. Purchases of assets on account are also in the purchase journal.

5. Print the cash disbursements journal. Compare it to the one shown in the *Working Papers*. There is *no* general journal in Peachtree.

6. Print the general ledger. Compare it to the one shown in the *Working Papers*. Peachtree's general ledger shows an account balance for Account No. 3110, Capital Stock.

7. Follow these instructions to print the account payable ledger. This is called the vendor ledgers by Peachtree.

   a. From the Reports menu, select Accounts Payable, Vendor Ledger.

   b. Make the selections to print.

   c. Compare it to the account payable ledger shown in the *Working Papers*.

8. Follow these instructions to print the accounts receivable ledger.

   a. From the Reports <u>A</u>rea, select Accounts Receivable; Customer Ledgers.

   b. Make the selections to print.

   c. Compare it to the accounts payable ledger shown in the *Working Papers*.

9. Back up. The suggested file name is 11-6 Mastery Problem.

You have completed the work for the 11-6 Mastery Problem: Posting to General and Subsidiary Ledgers.

Journalizing and Posting Business Transactions

The instructions that follow show you how to do the following:

- Start Peachtree Complete Accounting.
- Restore starting data from the South-Western Accounting with Peachtree CD.
- Journalize and post transactions in the sales journal, purchase journal, cash disbursements journal, and cash receipts journal.
- Complete 11-7 Challenge Problem.

Before you start the 11-7 Challenge Problem, ask your instructor if Custom Golf Land, the company used for the 11-7 Challenge Problem, has already been set up on your computer. The instructions that follow assume that Custom Golf Land is being used for the first time.

GETTING STARTED

Use the following instructions to start Peachtree and restore the starting data for Custom Golf Land. The South-Western Accounting with Peachtree CD includes a Peachtree data files folder. In the steps that follow you will restore the 11-7CP.ptb file.

1. Start Peachtree. From the startup menu, select Close .
2. The menu bar shows three options: Files; Options; and Help. Click File; Restore.
3. The Restore Wizard - Select Backup File window appears. Observe that the Location field shows where Peachtree is stored on your computer. The default location is C:\Program Files\Peachtree\ Company. Your Location field may differ. If you are restoring from a network drive, you will need to know the location of the 11-7CP.ptb file.
4. Click Browse . The Open Backup File window appears. In the Look in field, double-click on the appropriate location of the Peachtree data files. Then, click 11-7CP.ptb to select it. (If appropriate, select your CD drive then double-click the Peachtree Files-Unit 1 folder. Click 11-7CP.ptb to select it.)

5. Make sure the 11-7CP.ptb file is selected. Click Open .

6. The Select Backup File window appears. Make sure the Location field shows the correct location for the 11-7CP.ptb file; for example, X:\Peachtree Files-Unit 1\11-7CP.ptb. (Substitute the correct drive letter for X.)

7. Click Next > . The Select Company window appears. Click on the radio button next to *A New Company*. The Location field shown in this book indicates the default location where drive C is used to install Peachtree. Your Location field may differ. *Make sure that the Location field ends in* **cusgolla**. (If your location field does not end in "a" select An Existing Company, then click Browse . Double-click Custom Golf Land (*or*, 11-7CPXX). Your Location field shows the shortened company name cusgolla. Continue with step 8.)

8. Click Next > . The Restore Options window appears.

9. Make sure that the box next to Company Data is *checked*. Click Next > .

10. The Confirmation window appears. Check the From and To fields to make sure they are correct. Click Finish . When the Restore Company scale is 100% complete, your data is restored and you are returned to the menu bar.

CHANGING THE COMPANY NAME

Before you start recording transactions for the 11-7 Challenge Problem, you should look at the company information included on the 11-7CP.ptb file. Follow these steps to look at company information.

1. The Custom Golf Land menu bar should be displayed. From the menu bar, click on Maintain; Company Information. The Maintain Company Information window appears. Observe that the directory field shows where your company is stored on your computer: C:\Program Files\Peachtree\company\cusgolla.

2. Type **11-7CPXX** in the Company Name field.

3. When you are finished typing 11-7CPXX as the company name, click on OK . Once you have changed the Company Name, each one of your printouts will show the problem number and your initials.

Nothing has changed on your computer's hard drive. The company you restored is identified in the program folder and data folder as C:\Program Files\Peachtree\company\cusgolla. What you've done is changed the company name so that your printouts will show the problem number and your initials. Using Maintain, Company Information to rename your company does *not* change the shortened company name.

Instructions:

Journalize and post the following transactions completed during October 2005. Add an 8% sales tax to all sales transactions. Source documents are abbreviated as follows: check, C; memorandum, M; purchase invoice, P; receipts, R; sales invoice, S; terminal summary, TS.

Transactions:

Oct.	2	Wrote a check for rent, $1,150.00. C265.
	3	Received an invoice from Vista Golf Co. for merchandise purchased on account, $1,950.00. P71.
	4	Paid for merchandise, $142.80. C266.
	6	A check was received in payment on account from Viola Davis, $829.44, covering S45. R43.
	7	Eagle Golf Equipment was paid on account, $2,358.00, covering P67. C267.
	7	Cash and credit card sales, $5,676.00. TS31.
	11	Merchandise was sold on account to Doris McCarley, $306.00. S49.
	13	Store supplies were bought on account from Golf Source, $258.00. M34.
	14	Cash and credit card sales, $5,808.00. TS32.
	17	Wrote a check for electric bill, $220.20. C268.
	20	Wrote a check to Vista Golf Co. on account, $3,216.00, less 2% discount, covering P68. C269.
	21	Recorded cash and credit card sales, $5,376.00. TS33.
	23	Design Golf was paid on account, $2,916.00, covering P69. C270.
	24	Barry Fuller bought merchandise on account, $1,315.00. S50.
	24	Received payment on account from Leona Silva, $285.12, covering S46. R44.
	25	Merchandise was purchased on account from Pro Golf Supply, $1,542.00. P72.
	27	A check was received in payment on account from David Bench, $972.00, covering S47. R45.
	28	Received an invoice from Design Golf for merchandise purchased on account, $2,790.00. P73.
	28	Merchandise was sold on account to Leona Silva, $1,314.00. S51.
	28	Recorded cash and credit card sales, $5,556.00. TS34.
	30	Discovered that a sale on account to David Bench on October 28, S51, was incorrectly charged to the account of Leona Silva, $1,419.12. M35.
	30	Replenish the petty cash fund, $251.00: office supplies, $40.00; store supplies, $51.00; advertising, $62.00; miscellaneous, $98.00. C271.
	31	Recorded cash and credit card sales, $1,680.00. TS35.

1. The 11-7CP problem file should be restored and the Custom Golf Land menu bar displayed.

2. Journalize and post the October transactions. For Peachtree, use 2005 as the year.

3. Print the sales journal, cash receipts journal, purchase journal, and cash disbursements journal.

4. Print the vendor ledgers and customer ledgers.

5. Print the general ledger.

6. To prove cash, use a blank piece of paper or the *Working Papers*.

7. Prove the accuracy of the subsidiary ledgers by comparing the totals with the balances of the controlling accounts in the general ledger. If the totals are not the same, you can use Peachtree's drill down feature or Peachtree's editing journal entries feature to correct errors. Read the information that follows about drill down and editing journals.

DRILL DOWN

Let's say you add up the balances in the vendor ledger and it does *not* agree with the accounts payable balance in the general ledger. Follow these steps to use Peachtree's drill down-down feature.

a. Display the Vendor Ledgers.

b. Click on one of the account balances. A zoom icon appears. Double-click ☐ .

c. This takes you to the Purchases/Receive Inventory window. Make sure the transaction was entered correctly. If necessary, make any needed corrections, then post.

These instructions show you how to drill down from the vendor ledger report to the Purchases/Receive Inventory window. Use similar steps from other reports.

EDITING JOURNALS

Another way to edit transactions is to go directly to the journal. Here is how you would do that.

1. From the Tasks menu, select Purchases/Receive Inventory.

a. Click ☐ . The Select Purchase window appears.

b. Double-click one of the entries. This takes you to the Purchases/Receive Inventory window. Make any needed corrections, then post.

c. Read the paragraph about sales taxes *before* you answer.

In states that have sales taxes, businesses are required to collect taxes on their sales and submit the taxes to the state. This additional activity requires considerable extra effort: keeping a separate record of the taxes collected at the time of sale, maintaining a separate account for the sales taxes collected, Sales Taxes Payable, and recording the collection and payment of the sales taxes in the account. These additional activities place an additional administrative burden on businesses, especially small businesses with few employees.

Can you think of a procedure that would not require the separate record for collecting and accounting for sales taxes, yet comply with a state's requirement to collect and submit sales taxes based on sale of merchandise sold? Using a blank piece of paper or the *Working Papers*, write a brief response providing an alternative approach to collecting and paying sales taxes.

2. Back up. The suggested file name is 11-7 Challenge Problem.

You have completed the work for the 11-7 Challenge Problem: Journalizing and Posting Business Transactions.

Preparing Payroll Checks

The instructions that follow show you how to do the following:

- Start Peachtree Complete Accounting.
- Restore starting data from the South-Western Accounting with Peachtree CD.
- Journalize and post payroll transactions.
- Complete 12-5 Application Problem.

GETTING STARTED

Use the following instructions to start Peachtree and restore the starting data for Royal Appliance. The South-Western Accounting with Peachtree CD includes a Peachtree data files folder. In the steps that follow you will restore the 12-5AP.ptb file.

1. Start Peachtree. From the startup menu, select Close .
2. The menu bar shows three options: Files; Options; and Help. Click File; Restore.
3. The Restore Wizard - Select Backup File window appears. Observe that the Location field shows where Peachtree is stored on your computer. The default location is C:\Program Files\Peachtree\ Company. Your Location field may differ. If you are restoring from a network drive, you will need to know the location of the 12-5AP.ptb file.
4. Click Browse . The Open Backup File window appears. In the Look in field, double-click on the appropriate location of the Peachtree data files. Then, click 12-5AP.ptb to select it. (If appropriate, select your CD drive then double-click the Peachtree Files-Unit 1 folder. Click 12-5AP.ptb to select it.)
5. Make sure the 12-5AP.ptb file is selected. Click Open .
6. The Select Backup File window appears. Make sure the Location field shows the correct location for the 12-5AP.ptb file; for example, X:\Peachtree Files-Unit 1\12-5AP.ptb. (Substitute the correct drive letter for X.)
7. Click Next > . The Select Company window appears. Click on the radio button next to *A New Company*. The Location field shown in

this book indicates the default location where drive C is used to install Peachtree. Your Location field may differ. *Make sure that the Location field ends in* **royappli**. (If your location field does not end in "i" select An Existing Company, then click `Browse`. Double-click Royal Appliance (*or*, 12-5APXX). Your Location field shows the shortened company name royappli. Continue with step 8.)

8. Click `Next >`. The Restore Options window appears.

9. Make sure that the box next to Company Data is *checked*. Click `Next >`.

10. The Confirmation window appears. Check the From and To fields to make sure they are correct. Click `Finish`. When the Restore Company scale is 100% complete, your data is restored and you are returned to the menu bar.

CHANGING THE COMPANY NAME

Before you start recording transactions for the 12-5 Application Problem, you should look at the company information included on the 12-5AP.ptb file. Follow these steps to look at company information.

1. The Royal Appliance menu bar should be displayed. From the menu bar, click on Maintain; Company Information. The Maintain Company Information window appears. Observe that the directory field shows where your company is stored on your computer: C:\ Program Files\Peachtree\ company\royappli.

2. Type **12-5APXX** in the Company Name field.

3. When you are finished typing 12-5APXX as the company name, click on `OK`. Once you have changed the Company Name, each one of your printouts will show the problem number and your initials.

Nothing has changed on your computer's hard drive. The company you restored is identified in the program folder and data folder as C:\Program Files\Peachtree\company\royappli. What you've done is changed the company name so that your printouts will show the problem number and your initials. Using Maintain, Company Information to rename your company does *not* change the shortened company name

JOURNALIZING PAYROLL TRANSACTIONS

Royal Appliances' net payroll for the semimonthly pay period ended May 15, 2005, is $7,498.80. Payroll checks are prepared May 15, 2005.

Payroll information for two employees is shown below. Use this information to journalize and post transactions in the Cash Disbursements Journal (Tasks; Payments). Detailed steps are shown below for the first employee, Wanda M. Curtis.

Before you journalize and post the payroll transaction, you need to establish the payroll account. Use the following transaction information:

Transaction:

May 15   Make a check payable to the Payroll Account (Account No. 1120) for $7,498.80, Check No. 630. This is the total net pay for May 15, 2005.

1. Use Peachtree's Payments task to journalize the May 15 transaction to establish the payroll account; Check No. 630 in the amount of $7,498.80

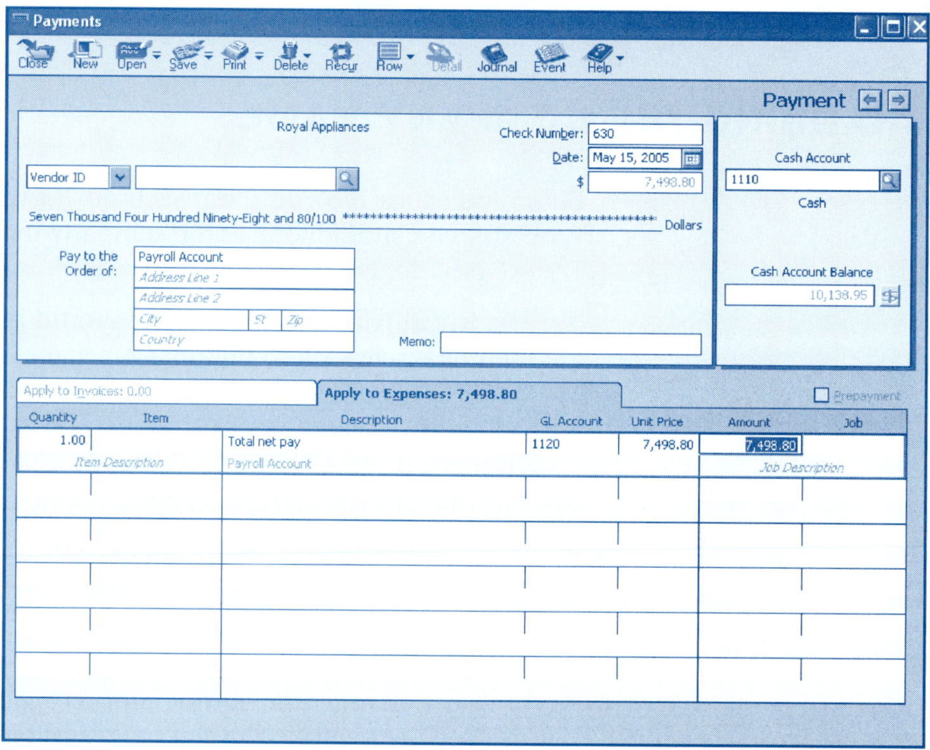

2. Post the Payments entry.

3. Use the instructions that follow to journalize the May 15 paycheck for Wanda M. Curtis, Check No. 823.

Date	Transaction	
May 15	Wanda M. Curtis	
	Check No. 823	
	Regular Earnings	$740.00
	Overtime Earnings	40.00
	Deductions:	
	Federal Income Tax	$33.00
	Social Security Tax	48.36
	Medicare Tax	11.31
	Health Insurance	35.00

4. If necessary, select Payments from the Tasks menu. When the Select a Cash Account window appears, select Payroll Account. *Or,* if the Payments window is displayed, select Account No. 1120 in the Cash Account field.

5. Make sure that Account No. 1120, Payroll is shown in the Cash Account field. Type **Wanda M. Curtis** in the Pay to the Order of field.

6. Type **823** in the Check Number field.

7. If necessary, type or select 15 as your date.

8. Type **1** for the Quantity; type **Regular earnings** for the Description; select Account No. 6150 for the GL Account; type **740** for the Unit Price. Press the Enter key three times.

9. Complete the following fields. Make sure that you put minus signs in front of each amount deducted.

Quantity	Description	GL Account	Unit Price
1	Overtime earnings	6155	40.00
1	Federal income tax	2120	−33.00
1	Social security tax	2135	−48.36
1	Medicare tax	2140	−11.31
1	Health insurance	2160	−35.00

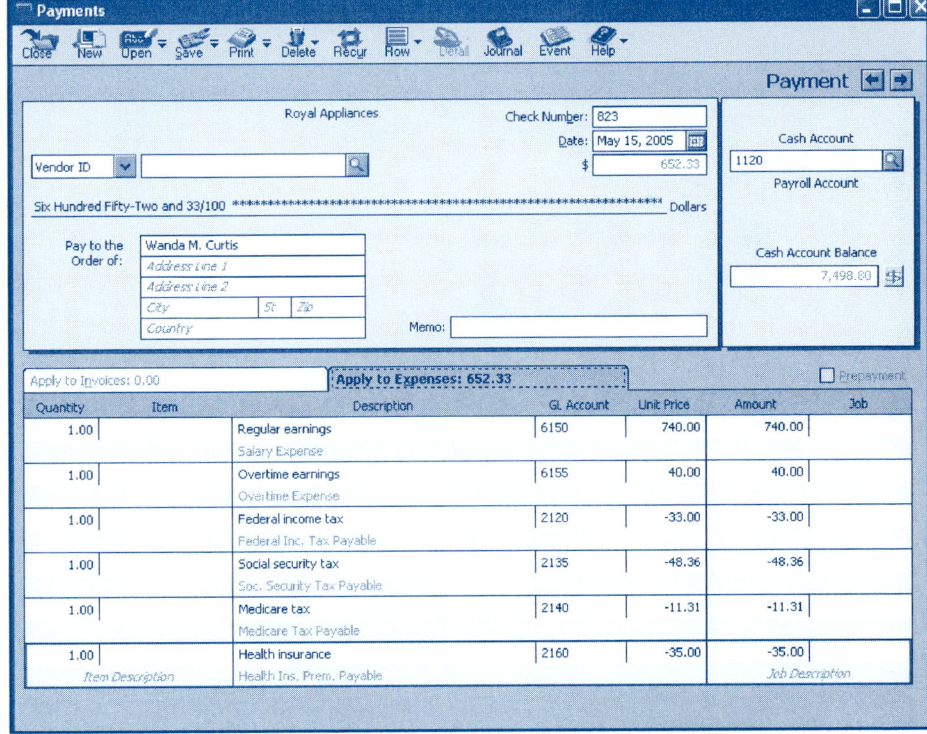

10. Post this payment.

11. Journalize and post the following transaction.

Date	**Transaction**
May 15	Kevin R. Hayes
	Check No. 824

Regular earnings	$920.00
Overtime earnings	30.00
Deductions:	
Federal income tax	$23.00
Social security tax	58.90
Medicare tax	13.78
Health insurance	60.00
Savings bond	20.00 (Account No. 2165)

12. Post this payment.

13. When you journalize the second May 15 transaction make sure that you put minus signs in front of each amount deducted.

14. Print the cash disbursements journal.

15. Back up. The suggested file name is 12-5 Application Problem.ptb.

You have completed the work for the 12-5 Application Problem: Preparing Payroll Checks.

Preparing a Semimonthly Payroll

The instructions that follow show you how to do the following:

- Start Peachtree Complete Accounting.
- Restore starting data from the South-Western Accounting with Peachtree CD.
- Journalize and post payroll transactions.
- Complete 12-6 Mastery Problem.

GETTING STARTED

Use the following instructions to start Peachtree and restore the starting data for Arrow Company. The South-Western Accounting with Peachtree CD includes a Peachtree data files folder. In the steps that follow you will restore the 12-6MP.ptb file.

1. Start Peachtree. From the startup menu, select Close.
2. The menu bar shows three options: Files; Options; and Help. Click File; Restore.
3. The Restore Wizard - Select Backup File window appears. Observe that the Location field shows where Peachtree is stored on your computer. The default location is C:\Program Files\Peachtree\Company. Your Location field may differ. If you are restoring from a network drive, you will need to know the location of the 12-6MP.ptb file.
4. Click Browse. The Open Backup File window appears. In the Look in field, double-click on the appropriate location of the Peachtree data files. Then, click 12-6MP.ptb to select it. (If appropriate, select your CD drive then double-click the Peachtree Files-Unit 1 folder. Click 12-6MP.ptb to select it.)
5. Make sure the 12-6MP.ptb file is selected. Click Open.
6. The Select Backup File window appears. Make sure the Location field shows the correct location for the 12-6MP.ptb file; for example, X:\Peachtree Files-Unit 1\12-6MP.ptb. (Substitute the correct drive letter for X.)

7. Click Next > . The Select Company window appears. Click on the
    radio button next to *A New Company*. The Location field shown in
    this book indicates the default location where drive C is used to
    install Peachtree. Your Location field may differ. *Make sure that the
    Location field ends in* **arrcompa**. (If your location field does not end
    in "a" select An Existing Company, then click Browse . Double-click
    Arrow Company (*or,* 12-6MPXX). Your Location field shows the
    shortened company name **arrcompa**. Continue with step 8.)

8. Click Next > . The Restore Options window appears.

9. Make sure that the box next to Company Data is *checked*. Click
     Next > .

10. The Confirmation window appears. Check the From and To fields
    to make sure they are correct. Click Finish . When the Restore
    Company scale is 100% complete, your data is restored and you
    are returned to the menu bar.

CHANGING THE COMPANY NAME

Before you start recording transactions for the 12-6 Mastery Problem,
you should look at the company information included on the
12-6MP.ptb file. Follow these steps to look at company information.

1. The Arrow Company menu bar should be displayed. From the
    menu bar, click on Maintain; Company Information. The Maintain
    Company Information window appears. Observe that the directory
    field shows where your company is stored on your computer:
    C:\Program Files\Peachtree\ company\arrcompa.

2. Type **12-6MPXX** in the Company Name field.

3. When you are finished typing 12-6MPXX as the company name,
    click on OK . Once you have changed the Company Name, each
    one of your printouts will show the problem number and your
    initials.

Nothing has changed on your computer's hard drive. The company
you restored is identified in the program folder and data folder as C:\
Program Files\Peachtree\company\arrcompa. What you've done is
changed the company name so that your printouts will show the problem number and your initials. Using Maintain, Company Information
to rename your company does *not* change the shortened company
name.

JOURNALIZING PAYROLL TRANSACTIONS

The following information for Arrow Company is for the semimonthly pay period August 16–31, 2005.

EMPL. NO.	EMPLOYEE'S NAME	MARITAL STATUS	NO. OF ALLOWANCES	EARNINGS		DEDUCTIONS	
				REGULAR	OVERTIME	HEALTH INSURANCE	SAVINGS BONDS
5	Acron, Peter C.	M	3	1126 40	115 20	60 00	10 00
7	Barenis, Mary P.	S	1	1155 00		25 00	
6	Epps, John P.	M	2	792 00		40 00	10 00
1	Goforth, Alice A.	S	2	1135 20	77 40	40 00	
8	Hiett, Franklin B.	M	3	1188 00		60 00	10 00
9	Land, Keith	S	1	954 60		25 00	10 00
2	Malone, Lillie L.	S	1	1083 60		25 00	
4	Rivers, Linda K.	M	2	1091 20	93 00	40 00	
10	Sowell, Jacob S.	M	2	1161 60		40 00	10 00
3	Vole, Ryan V.	M	5	1075 00		80 00	10 00

Instructions:

Use the *Working Papers* form or use a blank piece of paper to prepare a payroll register. Use the income tax withholding tables shown on the next page to find the income tax withholding for each employee. Calculate social security and Medicare tax withholdings using 6.2% and 1.45% tax rates, respectively. None of the employees has accumulated earnings greater than the social security tax base.

SINGLE Persons—SEMIMONTHLY Payroll Period

If the wages are—		And the number of withholding allowances claimed is—										
At least	But less than	0	1	2	3	4	5	6	7	8	9	10
		The amount of income tax to be withheld is—										
$0	$115	$0	$0	$0	$0	$0	$0	$0	$0	$0	$0	$0
115	120	1	0	0	0	0	0	0	0	0	0	0
120	125	1	0	0	0	0	0	0	0	0	0	0
125	130	2	0	0	0	0	0	0	0	0	0	0
130	135	2	0	0	0	0	0	0	0	0	0	0
235	240	13	0	0	0	0	0	0	0	0	0	0
240	245	13	0	0	0	0	0	0	0	0	0	0
245	250	14	1	0	0	0	0	0	0	0	0	0
250	260	14	2	0	0	0	0	0	0	0	0	0
260	270	15	3	0	0	0	0	0	0	0	0	0
540	560	51	32	18	5	0	0	0	0	0	0	0
560	580	54	35	20	7	0	0	0	0	0	0	0
580	600	57	38	22	9	0	0	0	0	0	0	0
600	620	60	41	24	11	0	0	0	0	0	0	0
620	640	63	44	26	13	0	0	0	0	0	0	0
640	660	66	47	28	15	2	0	0	0	0	0	0
660	680	69	50	31	17	4	0	0	0	0	0	0
680	700	72	53	34	19	6	0	0	0	0	0	0
700	720	75	56	37	21	8	0	0	0	0	0	0
720	740	78	59	40	23	10	0	0	0	0	0	0
740	760	81	62	43	25	12	0	0	0	0	0	0
760	780	84	65	46	27	14	1	0	0	0	0	0
780	800	87	68	49	29	16	3	0	0	0	0	0
800	820	90	71	52	32	18	5	0	0	0	0	0
820	840	93	74	55	35	20	7	0	0	0	0	0
840	860	96	77	58	38	22	9	0	0	0	0	0
860	880	99	80	61	41	24	11	0	0	0	0	0
880	900	102	83	64	44	26	13	0	0	0	0	0
900	920	105	86	67	47	28	15	2	0	0	0	0
920	940	108	89	70	50	31	17	4	0	0	0	0
940	960	111	92	73	53	34	19	6	0	0	0	0
960	980	114	95	76	56	37	21	8	0	0	0	0
980	1,000	117	98	79	59	40	23	10	0	0	0	0
1,000	1,020	120	101	82	62	43	25	12	0	0	0	0
1,020	1,040	123	104	85	65	46	27	14	2	0	0	0
1,040	1,060	126	107	88	68	49	29	16	4	0	0	0
1,060	1,080	129	110	91	71	52	32	18	6	0	0	0
1,080	1,100	132	113	94	74	55	35	20	8	0	0	0
1,100	1,120	135	116	97	77	58	38	22	10	0	0	0
1,120	1,140	138	119	100	80	61	41	24	12	0	0	0
1,140	1,160	141	122	103	83	64	44	26	14	1	0	0
1,160	1,180	144	125	106	86	67	47	28	16	3	0	0
1,180	1,200	147	128	109	89	70	50	31	18	5	0	0
1,200	1,220	150	131	112	92	73	53	34	20	7	0	0
1,220	1,240	153	134	115	95	76	56	37	22	9	0	0
1,240	1,260	156	137	118	98	79	59	40	24	11	0	0
1,260	1,280	159	140	121	101	82	62	43	26	13	0	0
1,280	1,300	163	143	124	104	85	65	46	28	15	2	0
1,300	1,320	168	146	127	107	88	68	49	30	17	4	0
1,320	1,340	173	149	130	110	91	71	52	33	19	6	0

1. On August 31, 2005, journalize and post a Check No. 0928 for the total amount of the net pay. Make the check payable to the Payroll Account. (*Hint:* Remember to select Account No. 1110 as the Cash Account.)

2. Journalize and post payroll checks for Peter C. Acron, Check No. 1692, and Franklin B. Hiett, Check No. 1696. For the "Other" deduction, use United Way Donations Payable, Account No. 2170. (*Hint:* Remember to select Account No. 1120 as the Cash Account.)

3. Print the cash disbursements journal.

4. Back up. The suggested file name is 12-6 Mastery Problem.ptb.

You have completed the work for the 12-6 Mastery Problem: Preparing a Semimonthly Payroll.

Journalizing Payroll Transactions

The instructions that follow show you how to do the following:

- Start Peachtree Complete Accounting.
- Restore starting data from the South-Western Accounting with Peachtree CD.
- Journalize and post payroll transactions.
- Complete 13-5 Mastery Problem.

GETTING STARTED

Use the following instructions to start Peachtree and restore the starting data for Keller Systems, Inc. The South-Western Accounting with Peachtree CD includes a Peachtree data files folder. In the steps that follow you will restore the 13-5MP.ptb file.

1. Start Peachtree. From the startup menu, select Close .

2. The menu bar shows three options: Files; Options; and Help. Click File; Restore.

3. The Restore Wizard - Select Backup File window appears. Observe that the Location field shows where Peachtree is stored on your computer. The default location is C:\Program Files\Peachtree\Company. Your Location field may differ. If you are restoring from a network drive, you will need to know the location of the 13-5MP.ptb file.

4. Click Browse . The Open Backup File window appears. In the Look in field, double-click on the appropriate location of the Peachtree data files. Then, click 13-5MP.ptb to select it. (If appropriate, select your CD drive then double-click the Peachtree Files-Unit 1 folder. Click 13-5MP.ptb to select it.)

5. Make sure the 13-5MP.ptb file is selected. Click Open .

6. The Select Backup File window appears. Make sure the Location field shows the correct location for the 13-5MP.ptb file; for example, X:\Peachtree Files-Unit 1\13-5MP.ptb. (Substitute the correct drive letter for X.)

7. Click Next > . The Select Company window appears. Click on the radio button next to *A New Company*. The Location field shown in

this book indicates the default location where drive C is used to install Peachtree. Your Location field may differ. *Make sure that the Location field ends in* **kelsysin**. (If your location field does not end in "n" select An Existing Company, then click Browse. Double-click Keller Systems, Inc. (*or*, 13-5MPXX). Your Location field shows the shortened company name kelsysin. Continue with step 8.)

8. Click Next >. The Restore Options window appears.

9. Make sure that the box next to Company Data is *checked*. Click Next >.

10. The Confirmation window appears. Check the From and To fields to make sure they are correct. Click Finish. When the Restore Company scale is 100% complete, your data is restored and you are returned to the menu bar.

CHANGING THE COMPANY NAME

Before you start recording transactions for the 13-5 Mastery Problem, you should look at the company information included on the 13-5MP.ptb file. Follow these steps to look at company information.

1. The Keller Systems, Inc. menu bar should be displayed. From the menu bar, click on Maintain; Company Information. The Maintain Company Information window appears. Observe that the directory field shows where your company is stored on your computer: C:\ Program Files\Peachtree\ company\kelsysin.

2. Type **13-5MPXX** in the Company Name field.

3. When you are finished typing 13-5MPXX as the company name, click on OK. Once you have changed the Company Name, each one of your printouts will show the problem number and your initials.

Nothing has changed on your computer's hard drive. The company you restored is identified in the program folder and data folder as C:\ Program Files\Peachtree\company\kelsysin. What you've done is changed the company name so that your printouts will show the problem number and your initials. Using Maintain, Company Information to rename your company does *not* change the shortened company name

JOURNALIZING PAYROLL TRANSACTIONS

Keller Systems, Inc., completed payroll transactions during the period May 1 to June 15, 2005. Payroll tax rates are as follows: social security, 6.2%; Medicare, 1.45%; federal unemployment, 0.8%; state unemployment, 5.4%. The company buys savings bonds for employees as accumulated withholdings reach the necessary amount to purchase a bond. No total earnings have exceeded the tax base for calculating unemployment taxes. Keller Systems is a monthly schedule depositor for payroll taxes.

Journalize and post the May 15 and May 31, 2005 transactions in Peachtree's cash disbursements journal. Use the general journal to record the employer payroll taxes expense for the May 15 and May 31.

Transactions:

May	15	Paid cash for April's payroll tax liability. Withheld taxes from April payrolls: employee income tax, $532.00; social security tax, $634.88; and Medicare tax, $148.48. C421.
	15	Paid cash for semimonthly payroll. Total earnings, $5,250.00; withholdings: employee income tax, $273.00; U.S. Savings Bonds, $60.00 (calculate the social security and Medicare deductions). C422.
	15	Recorded employer payroll taxes expense for the May 15 payroll. M42.
	15	Paid cash for U.S. Savings Bonds for employees, $300.00. C423.
	31	Paid cash for semimonthly payroll. Gross wages, $5,310.00; withholdings: employee income tax, $276.00; U.S. Savings Bonds, $60.00. C461.
	31	Recorded employer payroll taxes expense for the May 31 payroll. M46.
	31	Paid cash for federal unemployment tax liability for quarter ended March 31, $245.76. C462.
	31	Paid cash for state unemployment tax liability for quarter ended March 31, $1,658.88. C463.
Jun.	15	Paid cash for the May liability for employee income tax, social security tax, and Medicare tax, C487. (Calculate the social security and Medicare tax liabilities by multiplying total earnings for the period by 12.4% for social security tax and 2.9% for Medicare tax.)
	15	Paid cash for semimonthly payroll. Gross wages, $5,280.00; withholdings: employee income tax, $274.00; U.S. Savings Bonds, $75.00. C488.
	15	Recorded employer payroll taxes expense. M53.

CHANGE THE ACCOUNTING PERIOD

Before you journalize and post the June 15 transactions, you should change accounting periods. Observe that the Peachtree's status bar at the bottom of your screen shows Period 5 – 5/1/05 to 5/31/05. In order to change accounting period to Period 6 – 6/1/05 to 6/30/05, follow these steps.

1. From the Tasks menu, select System; Change Accounting Period.

2. Click on 06-June 01, 2005 to June 30, 2005 to highlight it.

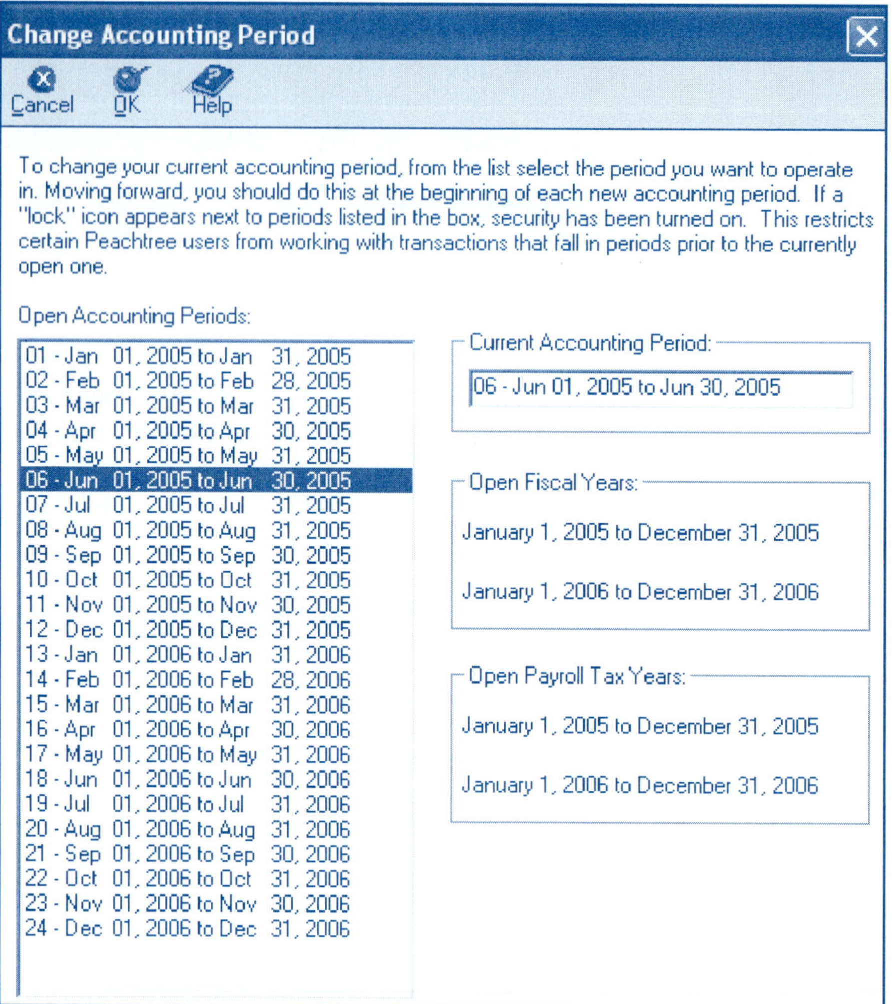

3. Make sure period 6 is selected; click [OK].

4. When the window appears asking Would you like to print your reports before continuing?, click [No]. Observe that the status bar shows Period 6 – 6/1/05 to 6/30/05.

5. Journalize and post the June 15 transactions. Use the General Journal for the payroll tax expense transactions.

6. Print the May 15 through June 15, 2005 cash disbursements journal.

7. Back up. The suggested file name is 13-5 Mastery Problem.ptb.

You have completed the work for the 13-5 Mastery Problem: Journalizing Payroll Transactions.

Journalizing and Posting Payroll Transactions

The instructions that follow show you how to do the following:

- Start Peachtree Complete Accounting.
- Restore starting data from the South-Western Accounting with Peachtree CD.
- Journalize and post payroll transactions.
- Complete 13-6 Challenge Problem.

GETTING STARTED

Use the following instructions to start Peachtree and restore the starting data for Golf Design, Inc. The South-Western Accounting with Peachtree CD includes a Peachtree data files folder. In the steps that follow you will restore the 13-6CP.ptb file.

1. Start Peachtree. From the startup menu, select Close .
2. The menu bar shows three options: Files; Options; and Help. Click File; Restore.
3. The Restore Wizard - Select Backup File window appears. Observe that the Location field shows where Peachtree is stored on your computer. The default location is C:\Program Files\Peachtree\ Company. Your Location field may differ. If you are restoring from a network drive, you will need to know the location of the 13-6CP.ptb file.
4. Click Browse . The Open Backup File window appears. In the Look in field, double-click on the appropriate location of the Peachtree data files. Then, click 13-6CP.ptb to select it. (If appropriate, select your CD drive then double-click the Peachtree Files-Unit 1 folder. Click 13-6CP.ptb to select it.)
5. Make sure the 13-6CP.ptb file is selected. Click Open .
6. The Select Backup File window appears. Make sure the Location field shows the correct location for the 13-6CP.ptb file; for example, X:\Peachtree Files-Unit 1\13-6CP.ptb. (Substitute the correct drive letter for X.)

7. Click [Next>]. The Select Company window appears. Click on the radio button next to *A New Company*. The Location field shown in this book indicates the default location where drive C is used to install Peachtree. Your Location field may differ. *Make sure that the Location field ends in* **goldesin**. (If your location field does not end in "n" select An Existing Company, then click [Browse]. Double-click Golf Design, Inc. (*or*, 13-6CPXX). Your Location field shows the shortened company name goldesin. Continue with step 8.)

8. Click [Next>]. The Restore Options window appears.

9. Make sure that the box next to Company Data is *checked*. Click [Next>].

10. The Confirmation window appears. Check the From and To fields to make sure they are correct. Click [Finish]. When the Restore Company scale is 100% complete, your data is restored and you are returned to the menu bar.

CHANGING THE COMPANY NAME

Before you start recording transactions for the 13-6 Challenge Problem, you should look at the company information included on the 13-6CP.ptb file. Follow these steps to look at company information.

1. The Golf Design, Inc. menu bar should be displayed. From the menu bar, click on Maintain; Company Information. The Maintain Company Information window appears. Observe that the directory field shows where your company is stored on your computer: C:\ Program Files\Peachtree\ company\goldesin.

2. Type **13-6CPXX** in the Company Name field.

3. When you are finished typing 13-6CPXX as the company name, click on [OK]. Once you have changed the Company Name, each one of your printouts will show the problem number and your initials.

Nothing has changed on your computer's hard drive. The company you restored is identified in the program folder and data folder as C:\Program Files\Peachtree\company\goldesin. What you've done is changed the company name so that your printouts will show the problem number and your initials. Using Maintain, Company Information to rename your company does *not* change the shortened company name

JOURNALIZING PAYROLL TRANSACTIONS

Golf Design, Inc. completed payroll transactions during the period May 1 to June 15, 2005. Payroll tax rates are as follows: social security, 6.2%; Medicare, 1.45%; federal unemployment, 0.8%; state unemployment, 5.4%. The company buys savings bonds for employees as accumulated withholdings reach the necessary amount to purchase a bond. No total earnings have exceeded the tax base for calculating unemployment taxes.

The balances in the general ledger as of January 1, 2005 are already recorded on the 13-6CP.ptb file.

Instructions:

1. Journalize and post the following transactions in Peachtree's cash disbursements journal. Use the general journal to record the employer payroll taxes expense.

Transactions:

Jan.	2	Wrote a check for 15 U.S. Savings Bonds at $25.00 each for employees. C195.
	15	Paid the December liability for employee income tax, social security tax, and Medicare tax. C204.
	31	Wrote a check for federal unemployment tax liability for quarter ended December 31. C210.
	31	Wrote a check for state unemployment tax liability for quarter ended December 31. C211.
	31	Paid January payroll (total payroll, $12,200.00, less deductions: employee income tax, $805.00; U.S. Savings Bonds, $125.00). C216.
	31	Recorded employer payroll taxes expense. M98.
Feb.	15	Wrote a check for January liability for employee income tax and for social security tax and Medicare tax. C222.
	28	Paid February payroll (total payroll, $12,360.00, less deductions: employee income tax, $816.00; U.S. Savings Bonds, $125.00). C232.
	28	Recorded employer payroll taxes expense. M107.
Mar.	15	Wrote a check for February liability for employee income tax, social security tax, and Medicare tax. C237.
	31	Paid March payroll (total payroll, $11,860.00, less deductions: employee income tax, $783.00; U.S. Savings Bonds, $125.00). C258.
	31	Recorded employer payroll taxes expense. M116.
Apr.	1	Paid cash for 15 U.S. Savings Bonds at $25.00 each for employees. C259.
	15	Wrote a check for March liability for employee income tax, social security tax, and Medicare tax. C270.
	30	Wrote a check for federal unemployment tax liability for quarter ended March 31. C276.
	30	Wrote a check for state unemployment tax liability for quarter ended March 31. C277.

Remember to change accounting periods at the end of each month. For example, at the end of January, change accounting periods to February; at the end of February, change accounting periods to March; and at the end of March, change accounting periods to April.

2. Print the January through April 2005 cash disbursements journal.

3. Print the January 2 through March 2005 general journal.

4. Print the January through April 2005 general ledger.

5. Back up. The suggested file name is 13-6 Challenge Problem.ptb.

You have completed the work for the 13-6 Challenge Problem: Journalizing and Posting Payroll Transactions.

An Accounting Cycle for a Corporation: Journalizing and Posting Transactions

The instructions that follow show you how to do the following:

- Start Peachtree Complete Accounting.
- Restore the Problem File for Medical Services Company.
- Identify the program and data path for Medical Services Company.
- Complete Reinforcement Activity 2—Part A.

Before you start Reinforcement Activity 2—Part A, ask your instructor if Medical Services Company, the company used for Reinforcement Activity 2—Part A, has already been restored on your computer. The instructions that follow assume that that Medical Services Company has *not* been restored.

GETTING STARTED

Use the following instructions to start Peachtree and restore the merchandising business called Medical Services Company.

1. Start Peachtree. From the startup menu, select Close .
2. The menu bar shows three options: Files; Options; and Help. Click File; Restore.
3. The Restore Wizard - Select Backup File window appears. Observe that the Location field shows where Peachtree is stored on your computer. The default location is C:\Program Files\Peachtree\Company. Your Location field may differ. If you are restoring from a network drive, you will need to know the location of the RA02-A.ptb file.
4. Click Browse . The Open Backup File window appears. In the Look in field, double-click on the appropriate location of the Peachtree data files. Then, click RA02-A.ptb to select it. (If appropriate, select your CD drive then double-click the Peachtree Files-Unit 1 folder. Click RA02-A.ptb to select it.)
5. Make sure the RA02-A.ptb file is selected. Click Open .
6. The Select Backup File window appears. Make sure the Location field shows the correct location; for example, X:\Peachtree Files-Unit 1\RA02-A.ptb. (Substitute the correct drive letter for X.)

7. Click [Next >]. The Select Company window appears. Click on the radio button next to *A New Company*. The Location field shown in this book indicates the default location where drive C is used to install Peachtree. Your Location field may differ. *Make sure that the Location field ends in* **medserco**. (If your location field does not end in "o" select An Existing Company, then click [Browse]. Double-click Medical Services Company (*or*, RA02-AXX). Your Location field shows the shortened company name **medserco**. Continue with step 8.)

8. Click [Next >]. The Restore Options window appears.

9. Make sure that the box next to Company Data is *checked*. Click [Next >].

10. The Confirmation window appears. Check the From and To fields to make sure they are correct. Click [Finish]. When the Restore Company scale is 100% complete, your data is restored and you are returned to the menu bar.

CHANGING THE COMPANY NAME

Before you start recording transactions for Reinforcement Activity 2 —Part A, you should look at the company information included on the RA02-A.ptb file. Follow these steps to look at company information.

1. The Medical Services Company menu bar should be displayed. From the menu bar, click on Maintain; Company Information. The Maintain Company Information window appears. Observe that the directory field shows where you company is stored on your computer: C:\Program Files\Peachtree\company\medserco.

2. Type **RA02-AXX** in the Company Name field.

3. When you are finished typing RA02-AXX as the company name, click on [OK]. Once you have changed the Company Name, each one of your printouts will show the problem number and your initials.

Nothing has changed on your computer's hard drive. The company you restored is identified in the program folder and data folder as C:\Program Files\Peachtree\Company\medserco. What you've done is changed the company name so that your printouts will show the problem number and your initials. Using Maintain, Company Information to rename your company does *not* change the shortened company name.

DISPLAYING THE MEDICAL SERVICES COMPANY CHART OF ACCOUNTS

Before recording transactions, you should print or display Peachtree's chart of accounts and compare it to the one shown on the next page. (*Hint:* From the menu bar, select Reports, General Ledger, Chart of Accounts. Then, make the selections to display or print.) Refer to these account numbers when recording transactions.

Medical Services Company
Chart of Accounts
As of Dec 31, 2005

Filter Criteria includes: Report order is by ID. Report is printed with Accounts having Zero Amounts and in Detail Format.

Account ID	Account Description	Active?	Account Type
1110	Cash	Yes	Cash
1120	Petty Cash	Yes	Cash
1130	Accounts Receivable	Yes	Accounts Receivable
1135	Allow. for Uncoll. Accts.	Yes	Accounts Receivable
1140	Merchandise Inventory	Yes	Inventory
1145	Supplies--Office	Yes	Other Current Assets
1150	Supplies--Store	Yes	Other Current Assets
1160	Prepaid Insurance	Yes	Other Current Assets
1210	Office Equipment	Yes	Fixed Assets
1220	Acc. Dep.--Office Equip.	Yes	Accumulated Depreciation
1230	Store Equipment	Yes	Fixed Assets
1240	Acc. Depr.--Store Equip.	Yes	Accumulated Depreciation
2110	Accounts Payable	Yes	Accounts Payable
2115	Federal Inc. Tax Payable	Yes	Other Current Liabilities
2120	Empl. Inc. Tax Payable	Yes	Other Current Liabilities
2130	Soc. Security Tax Payable	Yes	Other Current Liabilities
2135	Medicare Tax Payable	Yes	Other Current Liabilities
2140	Sales Tax Payable	Yes	Other Current Liabilities
2150	Unemp. Tax Pay.--Federal	Yes	Other Current Liabilities
2160	Unempl. Tax Pay.--State	Yes	Other Current Liabilities
2170	Health Ins. Prem. Payable	Yes	Other Current Liabilities
2180	U.S. Sav. Bonds Payable	Yes	Other Current Liabilities
2190	United Way Don. Payable	Yes	Other Current Liabilities
2195	Dividends Payable	Yes	Other Current Liabilities
3110	Capital Stock	Yes	Equity-doesn't close
3120	Retained Earnings	Yes	Equity-Retained Earnings
3130	Dividends	Yes	Equity-gets closed
3140	Income Summary	Yes	Equity-gets closed
4110	Sales	Yes	Income
4120	Sales Discount	Yes	Income
4130	Sales Returns & Allow.	Yes	Income
5110	Purchases	Yes	Cost of Sales
5120	Purchases Discount	Yes	Cost of Sales
5130	Purch. Returns & Allow.	Yes	Cost of Sales
6110	Advertising Expense	Yes	Expenses
6115	Cash Short and Over	Yes	Expenses
6120	Credit Card Fee Expense	Yes	Expenses
6125	Depr. Exp.--Office Equip.	Yes	Expenses
6130	Depr. Exp.--Store Equip.	Yes	Expenses
6135	Insurance Expense	Yes	Expenses
6140	Miscellaneous Expense	Yes	Expenses
6150	Payroll Taxes Expense	Yes	Expenses
6160	Rent Expense	Yes	Expenses
6165	Repairs Expense	Yes	Expenses
6170	Salary Expense	Yes	Expenses
6175	Supplies Exp.--Office	Yes	Expenses
6180	Supplies Exp.--Store	Yes	Expenses
6185	Uncoll. Accts. Expense	Yes	Expenses
6190	Utilities Expense	Yes	Expenses
7105	Federal Inc. Tax Expense	Yes	Expenses

RECORDING TRANSACTIONS

The accounting work of a single merchandising business for the last month of a yearly fiscal period is used in this reinforcement activity. The records kept and reports prepared illustrate the application of accounting concepts for all merchandising businesses.

Medical Services Company (MSC), a merchandising business, is organized as a corporation. The business sells a complete line of medical accessories, from crutches to lift chairs. MSC is located in a medical office plaza adjacent to the hospital and is open for business Monday through Saturday. A monthly rent is paid for the building. MSC accept credit cards from customers.

The December 1, 2005 account balances for the general ledger a subsidiary ledgers are included on the RA02-A.ptb file.

Instructions:

1. Journalize and post the following transactions completed during December 2005. Use the sales journal, purchase journal, general journal, cash receipts journal, and cash disbursements journal. The sales tax rate is 6%. Source documents are abbreviated as follows: check, C; memorandum, M; purchase invoice, P; receipt, R; sales invoice, S; terminal summary, TS; debit memorandum, DM; credit memorandum, CM.

Transactions:

Dec.	1	Paid cash for rent, $1,200.00. C372.
	2	Paid cash for electric bill, $346.20. C373.
	2	Received cash on account from Clegg Medical Center, covering S64 for $413.40, less 2% sales discount. R92.
	3	Paid cash for miscellaneous expense, $72.00. C374.
	3	Paid cash on account to Spencer Industries, covering P73 for $580.00, less 2% discount. C375.
	4	Sold merchandise on account to Bratton Clinic, $450.00, plus sales tax, $27.00; total, $477.00. S67.
	5	Recorded cash and credit card sales, $5,796.00, plus sales tax, $347.76; total, $6,143.76. TS45.
	7	Sold merchandise on account to Glenmore School, $462.00. Glenmore School is exempt from sales tax. S68.
	7	Received cash on account from Treet Retirement Home, $432.48, covering S65. R93.
	8	Bought office supplies on account from Cross Office Supply, $351.60. M43.
	9	Purchased merchandise on account from Ogden Instruments, $2,250, less a 40% trade discount. P77.
	9	Bought store supplies on account from Ziegler, Inc., $330.00. M44.
	10	Paid cash for office supplies, $174.00. C376.
	11	Paid cash on account to Evans Supply, $1,170.00, covering P74. C377.
	11	Purchased merchandise on account from Spencer Industries, $1,032.00. P78.
	12	Paid cash for store supplies, $264.00. C378.

12	Recorded cash and credit card sales, $7,125.00, plus sales tax, $427.50; total, $7,552.50. TS46.
14	Purchased merchandise on account from Evans Supply, $3,276.00. P79.
14	Sold merchandise on account to Odom Daycare, $170.00, plus sales tax, $10.20; total, $180.20. S69.
14	Paid cash for advertising, $415.00. C379.
15	Returned $226.00 of merchandise to Evans Supply from P79, $226.00. DM4.
15	Paid cash on account to Armstrong Medical, $1,272.00, covering P75. C380.
15	Received cash on account from Jamacus Clinic, $821.50, covering S66. R94.
15	Sold merchandise on account to Clegg Medical Center, $490.00, plus sales tax, $29.40; total, $519.40. S70.
15	Paid cash for liability for employee income tax, $342.00, social security tax, $767.00, and Medicare tax, $179.38; total, $1,288.38. C381.
15	Paid cash for semimonthly payroll, $2,313.85 (total payroll, $2,930.00, less deductions: employee income tax, $162.00; social security tax, $181.66; Medicare tax, $42.49; health insurance, $170.00; U.S. Savings Bonds, $30.00; United Way donations, $30.00). C382.
15	Recorded employer payroll taxes, $248.95, for the semimonthly pay period ended December 15. Taxes owed are: social security tax, $181.66; Medicare tax, $42.49; federal unemployment tax, $3.20; and state unemployment tax, $21.60. M45.
19	Recorded cash and credit card sales, $6,925.00, plus sales tax, $415.50; total, $7,340.50. TS47.
23	Paid cash on account to Ogden Instruments, $2,200.00, covering P76. C383.
24	Received cash on account from Odom Daycare, covering S69 for $180.20, less 2% discount. R95.
24	Granted credit to Clegg Medical Center for merchandise returned, $120.00, plus sales tax, $7.20, from S70; total, $127.20. CM5.
26	Recorded cash and credit card sales, $6,980.00, plus sales tax, $418.80; total, $7,398.80. TS48.
28	Recorded credit card fee expense, $342.00. M46. (Debit Credit Card Fee Expense; credit Cash.)
30	Purchased merchandise on account from Armstrong Medical, $1,940.00. P80.
31	Paid cash to replenish the petty cash fund, $145.20: office supplies, $35.00; store supplies, $19.00; advertising, $64.00; miscellaneous, $26.00; cash short, $1.20. C384.

31   Paid cash for semimonthly payroll, $2,462.32 (total payroll, $3,120.00, less deductions: employee income tax, $189.00; social security tax, $193.44; Medicare tax, $45.24; health insurance, $170.00; U.S. Savings Bonds, $30.00; United Way donations, $30.00). C385.

31   Recorded employer payroll taxes, $263.48, for the semimonthly pay period ended December 31. Taxes owed are: social security tax, $193.44: Medicare tax, $45.24; federal unemployment tax, $3.20; and state unemployment tax, $21.60. M47.

31   Recorded cash and credit card sales, $3,890.00, plus sales tax, $233.40; total, $4,123.40. TS49.

2. Print the sales journal, purchase journal, general journal, cash receipts journal, and cash disbursements journal.

3. Print the customer ledgers and vendor ledgers.

4. Print the December 1–31, 2005 general ledger.

5. Use the *Working Papers* or a blank piece of paper to prove cash.

6. Back up your company data. The suggested file name is Reinforcement Activity 2-Part A.ptb. This backup is important. Keep it in a safe place. You will use it again for Part B of this problem.

You have completed the work for Reinforcement Activity 2—Part A: An Accounting Cycle for a Corporation: Journalizing and Posting Transactions. Keep your backup file in a safe place. You will use the backup made in this activity for Part B of this problem.

Journalizing Dividends

The instructions that follow show you how to do the following:

- Start Peachtree Complete Accounting.
- Restore starting data from the South-Western Accounting with Peachtree CD.
- Journalize and post transactions.
- Complete 14-1 Application Problem.

GETTING STARTED

Use the following instructions to start Peachtree and restore the starting data for Drake Corporation. The South-Western Accounting with Peachtree CD includes a Peachtree data files folder. In the steps that follow you will restore the 14-1AP.ptb file.

1. Start Peachtree. From the startup menu, select **Close**.
2. The menu bar shows three options: Files; Options; and Help. Click File; Restore.
3. The Restore Wizard - Select Backup File window appears. Observe that the Location field shows where Peachtree is stored on your computer. The default location is C:\Program Files\Peachtree\Company. Your Location field may differ. If you are restoring from a network drive, you will need to know the location of the 14-1AP.ptb file.
4. Click **Browse**. The Open Backup File window appears. In the Look in field, double-click on the appropriate location of the Peachtree data files. Then, click 14-1AP.ptb to select it. (If appropriate, select your CD drive then double-click the Peachtree Files-Unit 1 folder. Click 14-1AP.ptb to select it.)
5. Make sure the 14-1AP.ptb file is selected. Click **Open**.
6. The Select Backup File window appears. Make sure the Location field shows the correct location for the 14-1AP.ptb file; for example, X:\Peachtree Files-Unit 1\14-1AP.ptb. (Substitute the correct drive letter for X.)

7. Click [Next >]. The Select Company window appears. Click on the radio button next to *A New Company*. The Location field shown in this book indicates the default location where drive C is used to install Peachtree. Your Location field may differ. *Make sure that the Location field ends in* **dracorpo**. (If your location field does not end in "o" select An Existing Company, then click [Browse]. Double-click Drake Corporation (*or*, 14-1APXX). Your Location field shows the shortened company name dracorpo. Continue with step 8.)

8. Click [Next >]. The Restore Options window appears.

9. Make sure that the box next to Company Data is *checked*. Click [Next >].

10. The Confirmation window appears. Check the From and To fields to make sure they are correct. Click [Finish]. When the Restore Company scale is 100% complete, your data is restored and you are returned to the menu bar.

CHANGING THE COMPANY NAME

Before you start recording transactions for the 14-1 Application Problem, you should look at the company information included on the 14-1AP.ptb file. Follow these steps to look at company information.

1. The Drake Corporation menu bar should be displayed. From the menu bar, click on Maintain; Company Information. The Maintain Company Information window appears. Observe that the directory field shows where your company is stored on your computer: C:\Program Files\Peachtree\ company\dracorpo.

2. Type **14-1APXX** in the Company Name field.

3. When you are finished typing 14-1APXX as the company name, click on [OK]. Once you have changed the Company Name, each one of your printouts will show the problem number and your initials.

Nothing has changed on your computer's hard drive. The company you restored is identified in the program folder and data folder as C:\Program Files\Peachtree\company\dracorpo. What you've done is changed the company name so that your printouts will show the problem number and your initials. Using Maintain, Company Information to rename your company does *not* change the shortened company name

JOURNALIZING TRANSACTIONS

Drake Corporation completed the following transactions during December 2005 and January 2006.

1. Journalize and post the dividend declared on Decmeber 15, 2005 in the general journal.
2. Change accounting periods from Period 12, Dec 1–31, 2005; to Period 13, January 1–31, 2006.
3. Using the Write Checks task, journalize and post the payment of the dividend on January 15, 2006.

Transactions:

2005

Dec. 15   The board of directors declared a dividend of $1.50 per share; capital stock issued is 2,100 shares. M258.

2006

Jan. 15   Paid cash for dividend declared December 15, C271.

1. Print the December 15, 2005 general journal.
2. Print the January 15, 2006 cash disbursements journal.
3. Back up. The suggested file name is 14-1 Application Problem.ptb.

You have completed the work for the 14-1 Application Problem: Journalizing Dividends.

Preparing an 8-Column Work Sheet for a Merchandising Business

The instructions that follow show you how to do the following:

- Start Peachtree Complete Accounting.
- Restore starting data from the South-Western Accounting with Peachtree CD.
- Journalize and post adjusting entries.
- Complete 14-7 Mastery Problem.

GETTING STARTED

Use the following instructions to start Peachtree and restore the starting data for Carol's Closet. The South-Western Accounting with Peachtree CD includes a Peachtree data files folder. In the steps that follow you will restore the 14-7MP.ptb file.

1. Start Peachtree. From the startup menu, select [Close].
2. The menu bar shows three options: Files; Options; and Help. Click File; Restore.
3. The Restore Wizard - Select Backup File window appears. Observe that the Location field shows where Peachtree is stored on your computer. The default location is C:\Program Files\Peachtree\Company. Your Location field may differ. If you are restoring from a network drive, you will need to know the location of the 14-7MP.ptb file.
4. Click [Browse]. The Open Backup File window appears. In the Look in field, double-click on the appropriate location of the Peachtree data files. Then, click 14-7MP.ptb to select it. (If appropriate, select your CD drive then double-click the Peachtree Files-Unit 1 folder. Click 14-7MP.ptb to select it.)
5. Make sure the 14-7MP.ptb file is selected. Click [Open].
6. The Select Backup File window appears. Make sure the Location field shows the correct location for the 14-7MP.ptb file; for example, X:\Peachtree Files-Unit 1\14-7MP.ptb. (Substitute the correct drive letter for X.)

7. Click Next >. The Select Company window appears. Click on the radio button next to *A New Company*. The Location field shown in this book indicates the default location where drive C is used to install Peachtree. Your Location field may differ. *Make sure that the Location field ends in* **carclose**. (If your location field does not end in "e" select An Existing Company, then click Browse. Double-click Carol's Closet (*or*, 14-7MPXX). Your Location field shows the shortened company name carclose. Continue with step 8.)

8. Click Next >. The Restore Options window appears.

9. Make sure that the box next to Company Data is *checked*. Click Next >.

10. The Confirmation window appears. Check the From and To fields to make sure they are correct. Click Finish. When the Restore Company scale is 100% complete, your data is restored and you are returned to the menu bar.

CHANGING THE COMPANY NAME

Before you start recording transactions for the 14-7 Mastery Problem, you should look at the company information included on the 14-7MP.ptb file. Follow these steps to look at company information.

1. The Carol's Closet menu bar should be displayed. From the menu bar, click on Maintain; Company Information. The Maintain Company Information window appears. Observe that the directory field shows where your company is stored on your computer: C:\Program Files\Peachtree\ company\carclose.

2. Type **14-7MPXX** in the Company Name field.

3. When you are finished typing 14-7MPXX as the company name, click on OK. Once you have changed the Company Name, each one of your printouts will show the problem number and your initials.

Nothing has changed on your computer's hard drive. The company you restored is identified in the program folder and data folder as C:\Program Files\Peachtree\company\carclose. What you've done is changed the company name so that your printouts will show the problem number and your initials. Using Maintain, Company Information to rename your company does *not* change the shortened company name

DISPLAYING THE TRIAL BALANCE

To trial balance for Carol's Closet as of December 31, 2005 is included on the 14-7MP.ptb file. You should display or print Peachtree's general ledger trial balance to see the account balances. Compare the trial balance with the one shown below. This trial balance is also shown on the work sheet included in the *Working Papers*.

Carol's Closet
General Ledger Trial Balance
As of Dec 31, 2005

Filter Criteria includes: Report order is by ID. Report is printed in Detail Format.

Account ID	Account Description	Debit Amt	Credit Amt
1110	Cash	28,548.25	
1120	Petty Cash	500.00	
1130	Accounts Receivable	32,518.28	
1135	Allow. for Uncoll. Accts.		155.25
1140	Merchandise Inventory	229,282.36	
1145	Supplies--Office	6,128.25	
1150	Supplies--Store	4,218.36	
1160	Prepaid Insurance	12,000.00	
1205	Office Equipment	28,187.25	
1210	Acc. Dep.--Office Equip.		5,158.25
1215	Store Equipment	42,841.05	
1220	Acc. Depr.--Store Equip.		12,483.25
2110	Accounts Payable		21,543.20
2130	Empl. Inc. Tax Payable		1,248.25
2135	Soc. Security Tax Payable		822.00
2140	Medicare Tax Payable		192.24
2145	Sales Tax Payable		2,415.25
2150	Unemp. Tax Pay.--Federal		33.60
2155	Unempl. Tax Pay.--State		226.80
2160	Health Ins. Prem. Payable		960.00
2165	U.S. Sav. Bonds Payable		75.00
2170	United Way Don. Payable		100.00
2180	Dividends Payable		11,000.00
3110	Capital Stock		55,000.00
3120	Retained Earnings		172,980.13
3130	Dividends	44,000.00	
4110	Sales		948,484.25
4120	Sales Discount	3,154.15	
4130	Sales Returns & Allow.	7,148.15	
5110	Purchases	489,335.54	
5120	Purchases Discount		5,015.25
5130	Purch. Returns & Allow.		7,058.05
6105	Advertising Expense	16,025.00	
6110	Cash Short and Over	7.25	
6115	Credit Card Fee Expense	7,015.95	
6135	Miscellaneous Expense	5,098.00	
6140	Payroll Taxes Expense	18,152.25	
6145	Rent Expense	28,000.00	
6150	Salary Expense	193,971.80	
6170	Utilities Expense	4,818.88	
9205	Federal Inc. Tax Expense	44,000.00	
	Total:	**1,244,950.77**	**1,244,950.77**

JOURNALIZING ADJUSTING ENTRIES

Carol's Closet completed the following transactions during December 2005 and January 2006.

Instructions:

1. Analyze the following adjustment information collected on December 31, 2005. Journalize and post the adjustments in the general journal. Type Adjustment a. through h. in the Reference column.

a.	Office supplies inventory	$1,407.00
b.	Store supplies inventory	570.11
c.	Merchandise inventory	238,830.61
d.	Uncollectible accounts are 1.2% of credit sales of:	458,200.00
e.	Value of prepaid insurance	2,000.00
f.	Estimate of office equipment depreciation	5,216.00
g.	Estimate of store equipment depreciation	4,820.00
h.	Federal income tax expense	3,005.22

2. Print the December 31, 2005 general journal.

3. Print the income statement and balance sheet. If you have completed the work sheet in the *Working Papers* for the 14-7 Mastery Problem, compare Peachtree's income statement account balances and the balance sheet's account balances to the work sheet's columns.

4. Back up. The suggested file name is 14-7 Mastery Problem.ptb.

You have completed the work for the 14-7 Mastery Problem: Preparing an 8-column Work Sheet for a Merchandising Business.

Preparing Financial Statements

The instructions that follow show you how to do the following:

- Start Peachtree Complete Accounting.
- Restore starting data from the South-Western Accounting with Peachtree CD.
- Print financial statements.
- Complete 15-5 Mastery Problem.

GETTING STARTED

Use the following instructions to start Peachtree and restore the starting data for Lighting Center, Inc. The South-Western Accounting with Peachtree CD includes a Peachtree data files folder. In the steps that follow you will restore the 15-5MP.ptb file.

1. Start Peachtree. From the startup menu, select Close.
2. The menu bar shows three options: Files; Options; and Help. Click File; Restore.
3. The Restore Wizard - Select Backup File window appears. Observe that the Location field shows where Peachtree is stored on your computer. The default location is C:\Program Files\Peachtree\Company. Your Location field may differ. If you are restoring from a network drive, you will need to know the location of the 15-5MP.ptb file.
4. Click Browse. The Open Backup File window appears. In the Look in field, double-click on the appropriate location of the Peachtree data files. Then, click 15-5MP.ptb to select it. (If appropriate, select your CD drive then double-click the Peachtree Files-Unit 1 folder. Click 15-5MP.ptb to select it.)
5. Make sure the 15-5MP.ptb file is selected. Click Open.
6. The Select Backup File window appears. Make sure the Location field shows the correct location for the 15-5MP.ptb file; for example, X:\Peachtree Files-Unit 1\15-5MP.ptb. (Substitute the correct drive letter for X.)

7. Click Next> . The Select Company window appears. Click on the
    radio button next to *A New Company*. The Location field shown in
    this book indicates the default location where drive C is used to
    install Peachtree. Your Location field may differ. *Make sure that the
    Location field ends in* **ligcenin**. (If your location field does not end in
    "n" select An Existing Company, then click Browse . Double-click
    Lighting Center, Inc. (*or*, 15-5MPXX). Your Location field shows the
    shortened company name ligcenin. Continue with step 8.)

8. Click Next> . The Restore Options window appears.

9. Make sure that the box next to Company Data is *checked*. Click
    Next> .

10. The Confirmation window appears. Check the From and To fields
    to make sure they are correct. Click Finish . When the Restore
    Company scale is 100% complete, your data is restored and you
    are returned to the menu bar.

CHANGING THE COMPANY NAME

Before you start recording transactions for the 15-5 Mastery Problem,
you should look at the company information included on the 15-
5MP.ptb file. Follow these steps to look at company information.

1. The Lighting Center, Inc. menu bar should be displayed. From the
    menu bar, click on Maintain; Company Information. The Maintain
    Company Information window appears. Observe that the directory
    field shows where your company is stored on your computer: C:\
    Program Files\Peachtree\ company\ligcenin.

2. Type **15-5MPXX** in the Company Name field.

3. When you are finished typing 15-5MPXX as the company name,
    click on OK . Once you have changed the Company Name, each one
    of your printouts will show the problem number and your initials.

Nothing has changed on your computer's hard drive. The company you
restored is identified in the program folder and data folder as
C:\Program Files\Peachtree\company\ligcenin. What you've done is
changed the company name so that your printouts will show the problem number and your initials. Using Maintain, Company Information to
rename your company does *not* change the shortened company name

The work sheet for Lighting Center, Inc. for the year ended December
31 is shown.

Lighting Center, Inc.

Work Sheet

For Year Ended December 31, 20 – –

	ACCOUNT TITLE	TRIAL BALANCE		ADJUSTMENTS		INCOME STATEMENT		BALANCE SHEET		
		DEBIT	CREDIT	DEBIT	CREDIT	DEBIT	CREDIT	DEBIT	CREDIT	
1	Cash	14 258 00						14 258 00		1
2	Petty Cash	500 00						500 00		2
3	Accounts Receivable	22 318 25						22 318 25		3
4	Allow. for Uncoll. Accts.		1 088 80		(e) 1 525 00				2 613 80	4
5	Merchandise Inventory	219 248 25			(d) 2 154 25			217 094 00		5
6	Supplies—Office	3 510 15			(a) 3 015 12			495 03		6
7	Supplies—Store	4 828 19			(b) 3 815 32			1 012 87		7
8	Prepaid Insurance	12 000 00			(c) 10 000 00			2 000 00		8
9	Office Equipment	23 185 00						23 185 00		9
10	Acc. Depr.—Office Equip.		8 450 00		(f) 4 050 00				12 500 00	10
11	Store Equipment	46 184 00						46 184 00		11
12	Acc. Depr.—Store Equip.		12 280 00		(g) 6 025 00				18 305 00	12
13	Accounts Payable		24 158 20						24 158 20	13
14	Federal Income Tax Payable				(h) 52 86				52 86	14
15	Emp. Income Tax Payable		1 055 00						1 055 00	15
16	Social Security Tax Payable		747 60						747 60	16
17	Medicare Tax Payable		174 84						174 84	17
18	Sales Tax Payable		2 248 25						2 248 25	18
19	Unemploy. Tax Payable—Fed.		25 60						25 60	19
20	Unemploy. Tax Payable—State		172 80						172 80	20
21	Health Insur. Premiums Payable		750 00						750 00	21
22	U.S. Savings Bonds Payable		100 00						100 00	22
23	United Way Donations Payable		70 00						70 00	23
24	Dividends Payable		10 000 00						10 000 00	24
25	Capital Stock		100 000 00						100 000 00	25
26	Retained Earnings		107 246 92						107 246 92	26

(continued on next page.)

Lighting Center, Inc.
Work Sheet
For Year Ended December 31, 20 – –

	ACCOUNT TITLE	TRIAL BALANCE		ADJUSTMENTS		INCOME STATEMENT		BALANCE SHEET		
		DEBIT	CREDIT	DEBIT	CREDIT	DEBIT	CREDIT	DEBIT	CREDIT	
27	Dividends	40 0 0 0 00						40 0 0 0 00		27
28	Income Summary			(d) 2 1 5 4 25		2 1 5 4 25				28
29	Sales		745 8 2 4 50				745 8 2 4 50			29
30	Sales Discount	1 1 5 4 25				1 1 5 4 25				30
31	Sales Returns and Allowances	3 4 8 1 25				3 4 8 1 25				31
32	Purchases	368 4 8 2 22				368 4 8 2 22				32
33	Purchases Discount		1 5 4 8 00				1 5 4 8 00			33
34	Purch. Returns and Allowances		3 8 4 8 77				3 8 4 8 77			34
35	Advertising Expense	12 5 1 0 00				12 5 1 0 00				35
36	Cash Short and Over		1 4 02				1 4 02			36
37	Credit Card Fee Expense	9 1 8 2 22				9 1 8 2 22				37
38	Depr. Exp.—Office Equipment			(f) 4 0 5 0 00		4 0 5 0 00				38
39	Depr. Exp.—Store Equipment			(g) 6 0 2 5 00		6 0 2 5 00				39
40	Insurance Expense			(c) 10 0 0 0 00		10 0 0 0 00				40
41	Miscellaneous Expense	12 1 4 0 00				12 1 4 0 00				41
42	Payroll Taxes Expense	15 4 8 2 98				15 4 8 2 98				42
43	Rent Expense	36 0 0 0 00				36 0 0 0 00				43
44	Salary Expense	139 1 5 8 47				139 1 5 8 47				44
45	Supplies Expense—Office			(a) 3 0 1 5 12		3 0 1 5 12				45
46	Supplies Expense—Store			(b) 3 8 1 5 32		3 8 1 5 32				46
47	Uncollectible Accounts Expense			(e) 1 5 2 5 00		1 5 2 5 00				47
48	Utilities Expense	8 1 5 2 03				8 1 5 2 03				48
49	Federal Income Tax Expense	28 0 0 0 00		(h) 5 2 86		28 0 5 2 86				49
50		1019 7 8 9 28	1019 7 8 9 28	30 6 3 7 55	30 6 3 7 55	664 3 9 4 99	751 2 2 1 27	367 0 4 7 15	280 2 2 0 87	50
51	Net Income after Fed. Income Tax					86 8 2 6 28			86 8 2 6 28	51
52						751 2 2 1 27	751 2 2 1 27	367 0 4 7 15	367 0 4 7 15	52

1. Print an income statement. On a blank piece of paper or in the *Working Papers,* calculate the following component percentages: (a) cost of merchandise sold, (b) gross profit on sales, (c) total expenses, and (d) net income or loss before federal income tax. Round percentage calculations to the nearest 0.1%.

Merchandise Inventory does *not* appear on Peachtree's income statement. Peachtree organizes their financial statements according to how each account is classified on the chart of accounts. Merchandise Inventory is classified as an asset (inventory); therefore, it appears on Peachtree's balance sheet. If you are preparing the income statement manually in the *Working Papers,* please note that this difference affects the component percentages and the income statement results. The account balances on Peachtree's income statement are the same as the manually completed income statement. Peachtree's income statement lists all accounts classified as revenue and expense accounts.

2. Print a balance sheet. Observe that the information necessary for the statement of stockholders' equity is contained in Peachtree's balance sheet. You may decide to prepare the statement of stockholders' equity manually in the *Working Papers.* Or, continue with instruction 3 to print Peachtree's statement of Retained Earnings.

Peachtree's balance sheet includes the following amounts in its Capital section related to Retained Earnings. Complete the following calculation to obtain total retained earnings:

Retained Earnings	107,246.92
Dividends	(40,000.00)
Income Summary	(2,154.25)
Net Income	88,980.53
Total Retained Earnings	$154,073.20

This amount, $154,073.20, agrees with the manually prepared balance sheet in the *Working Papers.*

3. Substitute Peachtree's statement of retained earnings for the statement of stockholders' equity. Print Peachtree's <Standard> Retained Earnings statement. Peachtree's Statement of Retained Earnings does not show the beginning Capital Stock balance of $100,000. Add that balance to the Ending Retained Earnings balance ($154,073.20 + $100,000 × $254,073.20) so that Peachtree's

statement agrees with the manually prepared statement of stockholders' equity in the *Working Papers*.

4. On a blank piece of paper or in the *Working Papers*, calculate the earnings per share and price-earnings ratio. The current market price of the stock is $28.50.

5. Back up. The suggested file name is 15-5 Mastery Problem.ptb.

You have completed the work for the 15-5 Mastery Problem: Preparing Financial Statements.

Journalizing and Posting Adjusting and Closing Entries; Preparing a Post-Closing Trial Balance

The instructions that follow show you how to do the following:

- Start Peachtree Complete Accounting.
- Restore starting data from the South-Western Accounting with Peachtree CD.
- Journalize and post adjusting and closing entries.
- Print a post-closing trial balance.
- Complete 16-4 Application Problem.

GETTING STARTED

Use the following instructions to start Peachtree and restore the starting data for Wilson Paint, Inc. The South-Western Accounting with Peachtree CD includes a Peachtree data files folder. In the steps that follow you will restore the 16-4AP.ptb file.

1. Start Peachtree. From the startup menu, select `Close`.
2. The menu bar shows three options: Files; Options; and Help. Click File; Restore.
3. The Restore Wizard - Select Backup File window appears. Observe that the Location field shows where Peachtree is stored on your computer. The default location is C:\Program Files\Peachtree\Company. Your Location field may differ. If you are restoring from a network drive, you will need to know the location of the 16-4AP.ptb file.
4. Click `Browse`. The Open Backup File window appears. In the Look in field, double-click on the appropriate location of the Peachtree data files. Then, click 16-4AP.ptb to select it. (If appropriate, select your CD drive then double-click the Peachtree Files-Unit 1 folder. Click 16-4AP.ptb to select it.)
5. Make sure the 16-4AP.ptb file is selected. Click `Open`.

6. The Select Backup File window appears. Make sure the Location field shows the correct location for the 16-4AP.ptb file; for example, X:\Peachtree Files-Unit 1\16-4AP.ptb. (Substitute the correct drive letter for X.)

7. Click _Next >_. The Select Company window appears. Click on the radio button next to *A New Company*. The Location field shown in this book indicates the default location where drive C is used to install Peachtree. Your Location field may differ. *Make sure that the Location field ends in* **wilpaiin**. (If your location field does not end in "n" select An Existing Company, then click _Browse_. Double-click Wilson Paint, Inc. (*or*, 16-4APXX). Your Location field shows the shortened company name wilpaiin. Continue with step 8.)

8. Click _Next >_. The Restore Options window appears.

9. Make sure that the box next to Company Data is *checked*. Click _Next >_.

10. The Confirmation window appears. Check the From and To fields to make sure they are correct. Click _Finish_. When the Restore Company scale is 100% complete, your data is restored and you are returned to the menu bar.

CHANGING THE COMPANY NAME

Before you start recording transactions for the 16-4 Application Problem, you should look at the company information included on the 16-4AP.ptb file. Follow these steps to look at company information.

1. The Wilson Paint, Inc. menu bar should be displayed. From the menu bar, click on Maintain; Company Information. The Maintain Company Information window appears. Observe that the directory field shows where your company is stored on your computer: C:\ Program Files\Peachtree\ company\wilpaiin.

2. Type **16-4APXX** in the Company Name field.

3. When you are finished typing 16-4APXX as the company name, click on _OK_. Once you have changed the Company Name, each one of your printouts will show the problem number and your initials.

Nothing has changed on your computer's hard drive. The company you restored is identified in the program folder and data folder as C:\ Program Files\Peachtree\company\wilpaiin. What you've done is changed the company name so that your printouts will show the problem number and your initials. Using Maintain, Company Information to rename your company does *not* change the shortened company name.

The work sheet for Wilson Paint, Inc. for the year ended December 31 is shown.

	ACCOUNT TITLE	TRIAL BALANCE DEBIT	TRIAL BALANCE CREDIT	ADJUSTMENTS DEBIT	ADJUSTMENTS CREDIT	INCOME STATEMENT DEBIT	INCOME STATEMENT CREDIT
1	Cash	15 482 00					
2	Petty Cash	500 00					
3	Accounts Receivable	42 158 80					
4	Allow. for Uncoll. Accts.		684 20		(e) 3 560 00		
5	Merchandise Inventory	274 535 33		(d) 1 483 60			
6	Supplies—Office	6 158 84			(a) 5 847 10		
7	Supplies—Store	5 548 55			(b) 4 918 50		
8	Prepaid Insurance	8 000 00			(c) 7 200 00		
9	Office Equipment	22 158 66					
10	Acc. Depr.—Office Equipment		4 848 00		(f) 3 580 00		
11	Store Equipment	34 158 11					
12	Acc. Depr.—Store Equipment		12 480 00		(g) 6 140 00		
13	Accounts Payable		15 487 99				
14	Federal Income Tax Payable				(h) 1 356 14		
15	Employee Income Tax Payable		1 125 58				
16	Social Security Tax Payable		903 96				
17	Medicare Tax Payable		211 41				
18	Sales Tax Payable		2 345 99				
19	Unemployment Tax Pay.—Federal		25 60				
20	Unemployment Tax Pay.—State		172 80				
21	Health Insurance Premiums Payable		350 00				
22	U.S. Savings Bonds Payable		50 00				
23	United Way Donations Payable		60 00				
24	Dividends Payable		5 000 00				
25	Capital Stock		125 000 00				
26	Retained Earnings		136 843 68				
27	Dividends	20 000 00					
28	Income Summary			(d) 1 483 60			1 483 60
29	Sales		724 183 99				724 183 99
30	Sales Discount	1 694 48				1 694 48	
31	Sales Returns and Allowances	4 189 64				4 189 64	
32	Purchases	331 805 18				331 805 18	
33	Purchases Discount		3 418 47				3 418 47
34	Purch. Returns and Allowances		4 684 69				4 684 69
35	Advertising Expense	14 518 00				14 518 00	
36	Cash Short and Over	4 60				4 60	
37	Credit Card Fee Expense	12 180 00				12 180 00	
38	Depr. Exp.—Office Equipment			(f) 3 580 00		3 580 00	
39	Depr. Exp.—Store Equipment			(g) 6 140 00		6 140 00	
40	Insurance Expense			(c) 7 200 00		7 200 00	
41	Miscellaneous Expense	6 481 00				6 481 00	
42	Payroll Taxes Expense	14 184 60				14 184 60	
43	Rent Expense	20 150 00				20 150 00	
44	Salary Expense	168 483 60				168 483 60	
45	Supplies Expense—Office			(a) 5 847 10		5 847 10	
46	Supplies Expense—Store			(b) 4 918 50		4 918 50	
47	Uncollectible Accounts Expense			(e) 3 560 00		3 560 00	
48	Utilities Expense	5 484 97				5 484 97	
49	Federal Income Tax Expense	30 000 00		(h) 1 356 14		31 356 14	
50		1037 876 36	1037 876 36	34 085 34	34 085 34	641 777 81	733 770 75
51	Net Income after Federal Income Tax					91 992 94	
52						733 770 75	733 770 75

Print or display Peachtree's general ledger trial balance. The 16-4AP.ptb file includes general ledger account balances shown on the work sheet's trial balance columns. Compare these account balances to the ones shown on Peachtree's general ledger trial balance.

Wilson Paint, Inc.
General Ledger Trial Balance
As of Dec 31, 2005

Filter Criteria includes: Report order is by ID. Report is printed in Detail Format.

Account ID	Account Description	Debit Amt	Credit Amt
1110	Cash	15,482.00	
1120	Petty Cash	500.00	
1130	Accounts Receivable	42,158.80	
1135	Allow. for Uncoll. Accts.		684.20
1140	Merchandise Inventory	274,535.33	
1145	Supplies--Office	6,158.84	
1150	Supplies--Store	5,548.55	
1160	Prepaid Insurance	8,000.00	
1205	Office Equipment	22,158.66	
1210	Acc. Dep.--Office Equip.		4,848.00
1215	Store Equipment	34,158.11	
1220	Acc. Depr.--Store Equip.		12,480.00
2110	Accounts Payable		15,487.99
2130	Empl. Inc. Tax Payable		1,125.58
2135	Soc. Security Tax Payable		903.96
2140	Medicare Tax Payable		211.41
2145	Sales Tax Payable		2,345.99
2150	Unemp. Tax Pay.--Federal		25.60
2155	Unempl. Tax Pay.--State		172.80
2160	Health Ins. Prem. Payable		350.00
2165	U.S. Sav. Bonds Payable		50.00
2170	United Way Don. Payable		60.00
2180	Dividends Payable		5,000.00
3110	Capital Stock		125,000.00
3120	Retained Earnings		136,843.68
3130	Dividends	20,000.00	
4110	Sales		724,183.99
4120	Sales Discount	1,694.48	
4130	Sales Returns & Allow.	4,189.64	
5110	Purchases	331,805.18	
5120	Purchases Discount		3,418.47
5130	Purch. Returns & Allow.		4,684.69
6105	Advertising Expense	14,518.00	
6110	Cash Short and Over	4.60	
6115	Credit Card Fee Expense	12,180.00	
6135	Miscellaneous Expense	6,481.00	
6140	Payroll Taxes Expense	14,184.60	
6145	Rent Expense	20,150.00	
6150	Salary Expense	168,483.60	
6170	Utilities Expense	5,484.97	
7105	Federal Inc. Tax Expense	30,000.00	
	Total:	**1,037,876.36**	**1,037,876.36**

1. Journalize and post the adjusting entries.

2. Print the income statement. Compare the account balances on Peachtree's income statement to the work sheet's income statement columns. (*Hint:* You must print the income statement before journalizing and posting the closing entries. As you know from your study of accounting, after completing the closing entries revenues, cost of sales, and expense accounts have zero balances.)

Peachtree does *not* report Merchandise inventory or Income Summary on its income statement. They are asset and equity accounts, respectively; which are reported on Peachtree's balance sheet.

3. Journalize and post the closing entries.

4. Print the December 31, 2005 general journal.

5. Print the general ledger.

6. Print the post-closing trial balance.

7. Back up. The suggested file name is 16-4 Application Problem.ptb.

You have completed the work for the 16-4 Application Problem: Journalizing and Posting Adjusting and Closing Entries; Preparing a Post-Closing Trial Balance.

Journalizing and Posting Adjusting and Closing Entries; Preparing a Post-Closing Trial Balance

The instructions that follow show you how to do the following:

- Start Peachtree Complete Accounting.
- Restore starting data from the South-Western Accounting with Peachtree CD.
- Journalize and post adjusting and closing entries.
- Print a post-closing trial balance.
- Complete 16-5 Mastery Problem.

GETTING STARTED

Use the following instructions to start Peachtree and restore the starting data for Northern Lights. The South-Western Accounting with Peachtree CD includes a Peachtree data files folder. In the steps that follow you will restore the 16-5MP.ptb file.

1. Start Peachtree. From the startup menu, select Close .
2. The menu bar shows three options: Files; Options; and Help. Click File; Restore.
3. The Restore Wizard - Select Backup File window appears. Observe that the Location field shows where Peachtree is stored on your computer. The default location is C:\Program Files\Peachtree\ Company. Your Location field may differ. If you are restoring from a network drive, you will need to know the location of the 16-5MP.ptb file.
4. Click Browse . The Open Backup File window appears. In the Look in field, double-click on the appropriate location of the Peachtree data files. Then, click 16-5MP.ptb to select it. (If appropriate, select your CD drive then double-click the Peachtree Files-Unit 1 folder. Click 16-5MP.ptb to select it.)
5. Make sure the 16-5MP.ptb file is selected. Click Open .

6. The Select Backup File window appears. Make sure the Location field shows the correct location for the 16-5MP.ptb file; for example, X:\Peachtree Files-Unit 1\16-5MP.ptb. (Substitute the correct drive letter for X.)

7. Click Next >. The Select Company window appears. Click on the radio button next to *A New Company*. The Location field shown in this book indicates the default location where drive C is used to install Peachtree. Your Location field may differ. *Make sure that the Location field ends in* **norlight**. (If your location field does not end in "t" select An Existing Company, then click Browse. Double-click Northern Lights (*or*, 16-5MPXX). Your Location field shows the shortened company name norlight. Continue with step 8.)

8. Click Next >. The Restore Options window appears.

9. Make sure that the box next to Company Data is *checked*. Click Next >.

10. The Confirmation window appears. Check the From and To fields to make sure they are correct. Click Finish. When the Restore Company scale is 100% complete, your data is restored and you are returned to the menu bar.

CHANGING THE COMPANY NAME

Before you start recording transactions for the 16-5 Mastery Problem, you should look at the company information included on the 16-5MP.ptb file. Follow these steps to look at company information.

1. The Northern Lights menu bar should be displayed. From the menu bar, click on Maintain; Company Information. The Maintain Company Information window appears. Observe that the directory field shows where your company is stored on your computer: C:\ Program Files\Peachtree\ company\norlight.

2. Type **16-5MPXX** in the Company Name field.

3. When you are finished typing 16-5MPXX as the company name, click on OK. Once you have changed the Company Name, each one of your printouts will show the problem number and your initials.

Nothing has changed on your computer's hard drive. The company you restored is identified in the program folder and data folder as C:\ Program Files\Peachtree\company\norlight. What you've done is changed the company name so that your printouts will show the problem number and your initials. Using Maintain, Company Information to rename your company does *not* change the shortened company name.

The work sheet for Northern Lights for the year ended December 31 is shown.

Work Sheet

	ACCOUNT TITLE	Trial Balance Debit	Trial Balance Credit	Adjustments Debit	Adjustments Credit	Income Statement Debit	Income Statement Credit
1	Cash	5 1 2 4 12					
2	Petty Cash	2 5 0 00					
3	Accounts Receivable	14 8 4 3 30					
4	Allow. for Uncoll. Accts.		1 2 4 55		(e) 2 1 2 0 00		
5	Merchandise Inventory	154 3 1 8 22			(d) 3 4 8 8 14		
6	Supplies—Office	3 4 1 5 58			(a) 3 1 4 8 66		
7	Supplies—Store	6 1 8 4 56			(b) 5 3 4 8 84		
8	Prepaid Insurance	7 0 0 0 00			(c) 6 0 0 0 00		
9	Office Equipment	21 4 8 2 66					
10	Acc. Depr.—Office Equipment		6 4 8 0 00		(f) 3 5 8 0 00		
11	Store Equipment	40 4 8 1 66					
12	Acc. Depr.—Store Equipment		18 4 8 0 00		(g) 6 1 4 0 00		
13	Accounts Payable		8 4 1 8 36				
14	Federal Income Tax Payable				(h) 9 6 5 64		
15	Employee Income Tax Payable		4 5 8 00				
16	Social Security Tax Payable		5 2 8 24				
17	Medicare Tax Payable		1 2 3 54				
18	Sales Tax Payable		1 4 1 5 30				
19	Unemployment Tax Pay.—Federal		4 00				
20	Unemployment Tax Pay.—State		2 7 00				
21	Health Insurance Premiums Payable		2 5 0 00				
22	U.S. Savings Bonds Payable		4 0 00				
23	United Way Donations Payable		6 0 00				
24	Dividends Payable		4 0 0 0 00				
25	Capital Stock		80 0 0 0 00				
26	Retained Earnings		89 7 6 1 21				
27	Dividends	16 0 0 0 00					
28	Income Summary			(d) 3 4 8 8 14		3 4 8 8 14	
29	Sales		514 8 1 5 35				514 8 1 5 35
30	Sales Discount	2 1 5 4 94				2 1 5 4 94	
31	Sales Returns and Allowances	6 1 8 4 74				6 1 8 4 74	
32	Purchases	301 5 4 8 60				301 5 4 8 60	
33	Purchases Discount		2 1 5 4 65				
34	Purch. Returns and Allowances		2 8 8 9 41				2 1 5 4 65
35	Advertising Expense	2 4 9 1 95				2 4 9 1 95	2 8 8 9 41
36	Cash Short and Over	5 25				5 25	
37	Credit Card Fee Expense	8 1 5 4 62				8 1 5 4 62	
38	Depr. Exp.—Office Equipment			(f) 3 5 8 0 00		3 5 8 0 00	
39	Depr. Exp.—Store Equipment			(g) 6 1 4 0 00		6 1 4 0 00	
40	Insurance Expense			(c) 6 0 0 0 00		6 0 0 0 00	
41	Miscellaneous Expense	4 1 0 00				4 1 0 00	
42	Payroll Taxes Expense	14 1 8 4 60				14 1 8 4 60	
43	Rent Expense	15 4 0 0 00				15 4 0 0 00	
44	Salary Expense	102 2 4 0 30				102 2 4 0 30	
45	Supplies Expense—Office			(a) 3 1 4 8 66		3 1 4 8 66	
46	Supplies Expense—Store			(b) 5 3 4 8 84		5 3 4 8 84	
47	Uncollectible Accounts Expense			(e) 2 1 2 0 00		2 1 2 0 00	
48	Utilities Expense	4 1 5 4 51				4 1 5 4 51	
49	Federal Income Tax Expense	4 0 0 0 00		(h) 9 6 5 64		4 9 6 5 64	
50		730 0 2 9 61	730 0 2 9 61	30 7 9 1 28	30 7 9 1 28	491 7 2 0 79	
51	Net Income after Federal Income Tax					28 1 3 8 62	519 8 5 9 41
52						519 8 5 9 41	
							519 8 5 9 41

DISPLAY THE TRIAL BALANCE

Print or display Peachtree's general ledger trial balance. The 16-5MP.ptb file includes general ledger account balances shown on the work sheet's trial balance columns. Compare these account balances to the ones shown on Peachtree's general ledger trial balance.

Northern Lights
General Ledger Trial Balance
As of Dec 31, 2005

Filter Criteria includes: Report order is by ID. Report is printed in Detail Format.

Account ID	Account Description	Debit Amt	Credit Amt
1110	Cash	5,124.12	
1120	Petty Cash	250.00	
1130	Accounts Receivable	14,843.30	
1135	Allow. for Uncoll. Accts.		124.55
1140	Merchandise Inventory	154,318.22	
1145	Supplies--Office	3,415.58	
1150	Supplies--Store	6,184.56	
1160	Prepaid Insurance	7,000.00	
1205	Office Equipment	21,482.66	
1210	Acc. Dep.--Office Equip.		6,480.00
1215	Store Equipment	40,481.66	
1220	Acc. Depr.--Store Equip.		18,480.00
2110	Accounts Payable		8,418.36
2130	Empl. Inc. Tax Payable		458.00
2135	Soc. Security Tax Payable		528.24
2140	Medicare Tax Payable		123.54
2145	Sales Tax Payable		1,415.30
2150	Unemp. Tax Pay.--Federal		4.00
2155	Unempl. Tax Pay.--State		27.00
2160	Health Ins. Prem. Payable		250.00
2165	U.S. Sav. Bonds Payable		40.00
2170	United Way Don. Payable		60.00
2180	Dividends Payable		4,000.00
3110	Capital Stock		80,000.00
3120	Retained Earnings		89,761.21
3130	Dividends	16,000.00	
4110	Sales		514,815.35
4120	Sales Discount	2,154.94	
4130	Sales Returns & Allow.	6,184.74	
5110	Purchases	301,548.60	
5120	Purchases Discount		2,154.65
5130	Purch. Returns & Allow.		2,889.41
6105	Advertising Expense	2,491.95	
6110	Cash Short and Over	5.25	
6115	Credit Card Fee Expense	8,154.62	
6135	Miscellaneous Expense	410.00	
6140	Payroll Taxes Expense	14,184.60	
6145	Rent Expense	15,400.00	
6150	Salary Expense	102,240.30	
6170	Utilities Expense	4,154.51	
7105	Federal Inc. Tax Expense	4,000.00	
	Total:	**730,029.61**	**730,029.61**

Instructions:

1. Journalize and post the adjusting entries.

2. Print the income statement. Compare the account balances on Peachtree's income statement to the work sheet's income statement columns. (*Hint:* You must print the income statement *before* journalizing and posting the closing entries. As you know from your study of accounting, after completing the closing entries revenue and expense accounts have zero balances.)

Peachtree does *not* report Merchandise inventory or Income Summary on its income statement. They are asset and equity accounts, respectively; which are reported on Peachtree's balance sheet.

3. Journalize and post the closing entries.
4. Print the December 31, 2005 general journal.
5. Print the general ledger.
6. Print the post-closing trial balance.
7. Back up. The suggested file name is 16-5 Mastery Problem.ptb.

You have completed the work for the 16-5 Mastery Problem: Journalizing and Posting Adjusting and Closing Entries; Preparing a Post-Closing Trial Balance.

An Accounting Cycle for a Corporation: End-of-Fiscal-Period Work

The instructions that follow show you how to do the following:

- Start Peachtree Complete Accounting.
- Restore data from Reinforcement Activity 2—Part A, Medical Services Company, to complete Part B.
- Complete Reinforcement Activity 2—Part B.

You *must* complete Reinforcement Activity 2—Part A, on pages 115–120, *before* starting Reinforcement Activity 2—Part B.

GETTING STARTED

Follow these instructions to restore data from Reinforcement Activity 2—Part A.

1. Start Peachtree.

2. At the startup menu, select Open an existing company. From the Open list, select Medical Services Company. If Medical Services Company is *not* listed, click on Browse. Select Medical Services Company from the Company Name list.

What if Medical Services Company is not listed on either the Open list or when I select Browse?

1. Use Windows Explorer to see if you have a program and data path identified as C:\Peachw\medserco. Close Windows Explorer.

2. From Peachtree's Open list, select Medical Services Company. It may be identified by RA02-AXX. The X's stand for a student's initials.

3. Restore the backup file made on page 120. The suggested file name was Reinforcement Activity 2-Part A.ptb. Once you restore the backup file that you made on page 120, you will be able to start where you left off the last time you worked with Medical Services Company.

If you have checked Windows Explorer and Medical Services Company does *not* have a folder (\medserco), do the following.

1. Start Peachtree. At the startup menu, click `Close`.
2. The File, Options, Help menu bar appears. Select File; Restore.
3. Using the Restore Wizard, select the appropriate location of the backup file that was made on page 120 (Reinforcement Activity 2-Part A.ptb), then restore A New Company. Peachtree will restore your backup data and create the company at the same time.

3. From Peachtree's menu bar, click on File; Restore.

4. Check the Location field to make sure you are restoring the correct file. Click `Next >`.

5. The Select Company window defaults to An Existing Company. The Company Name field shows Medical Services Company. The Location field shows C:\Program Files\Peachtree\company\medserco. Click `Next >`.

6. The Restore Options window appears. Make sure that the box next to Company Data is *checked*. Click `Next >`.

7. The Confirmation window appears. Observe that the Company Name is Medical Services Company. Check the From and To fields to make sure they are correct. Click `Finish`. When the Restore Company scale is 100% complete, your data is restored and you are returned to the menu bar.

8. If necessary, remove the external media. You can now continue with Reinforcement Activity 2—Part B.

CHANGING THE COMPANY NAME

In order to make sure that each one of your printouts shows your name and problem number, follow these steps to change the name of the company.

1. From Peachtree's menu bar, select Maintain, then Company Information.

2. The Maintain Company Information screen appears. In the Company Name field, type **RA02-BXX**. Replace the X's with your initials.

3. When you are finished typing RA02-BXX as the company name, click. Once you have changed the Company Name, each one of your printouts will show the problem number and your initials.

Nothing has changed on your computer's hard drive. The company you restored is identified in the program folder and data folder as C:\Program Files\Peachtree\Company\medserco. What you've done is change the company name so that your printouts will show the problem number and your initials. Using Maintain, Company Information to rename your company does *not* change the file name of the company folder.

Instructions:

1. After restoring the backup that you made at the end of Reinforcement Activity 2—Part A, print a general ledger trial balance. This is the unadjusted trial balance. Compare it to the one shown below. If you completed the worksheet in the *Working Papers*, compare this trial balance to the one on your worksheet.

Medical Services Company
General Ledger Trial Balance
As of Dec 31, 2005

Filter Criteria includes: Report order is by ID. Report is printed in Detail Format.

Account ID	Account Description	Debit Amt	Credit Amt
1110	Cash	40,126.14	
1120	Petty Cash	250.00	
1130	Accounts Receivable	14,689.34	
1135	Allow. for Uncoll. Accts.		102.12
1140	Merchandise Inventory	34,521.56	
1145	Supplies--Office	4,316.60	
1150	Supplies--Store	4,823.00	
1160	Prepaid Insurance	8,000.00	
1210	Office Equipment	13,752.00	
1220	Acc. Dep.--Office Equip.		2,210.00
1230	Store Equipment	10,259.00	
1240	Acc. Depr.--Store Equip.		5,844.00
2110	Accounts Payable		9,696.85
2120	Empl. Inc. Tax Payable		351.00
2130	Soc. Security Tax Payable		750.20
2135	Medicare Tax Payable		175.46
2140	Sales Tax Payable		2,061.61
2150	Unemp. Tax Pay.--Federal		18.40
2160	Unempl. Tax Pay.--State		124.20
2170	Health Ins. Prem. Payable		340.00
2180	U.S. Sav. Bonds Payable		60.00
2190	United Way Don. Payable		60.00
2195	Dividends Payable		7,500.00
3110	Capital Stock		10,000.00
3120	Retained Earnings		38,718.01
3130	Dividends	30,000.00	
4110	Sales		342,447.00
4120	Sales Discount	264.87	
4130	Sales Returns & Allow.	1,680.00	
5110	Purchases	131,176.10	
5120	Purchases Discount		1,908.95
5130	Purch. Returns & Allow.		2,510.50
6110	Advertising Expense	17,002.00	
6115	Cash Short and Over	9.63	
6120	Credit Card Fee Expense	2,324.55	
6140	Miscellaneous Expense	1,636.00	
6150	Payroll Taxes Expense	7,099.86	
6160	Rent Expense	12,000.00	
6165	Repairs Expense	2,446.00	
6170	Salary Expense	69,410.00	
6190	Utilities Expense	9,091.65	
7105	Federal Inc. Tax Expense	10,000.00	
	Total:	**424,878.30**	**424,878.30**

2. Journalize and post the following adjustment information.

Adjustment Information, December 31, 2005

a.	Office supplies inventory	$476.60
b.	Store supplies inventory	817.00
c.	Merchandise inventory	33,278.01
d.	Uncollectible accounts are 2.0% of credit sales of $65,000.00	
e.	Value of prepaid insurance	500.00
f.	Estimate of office equipment depreciation	3,520.00
g.	Estimate of store equipment depreciation	2,240.00
h.	Federal Income Tax adjustment	2,269.06

3. Print an income statement. On a blank piece of paper or in the *Working Papers,* calculate the following component percentages: (a) cost of merchandise sold, (b) gross profit on sales, (c) total expenses, and (d) net income or loss before federal income tax. Round percentage calculations to the nearest 0.1%.

4. On a blank piece of paper or in the *Working Papers,* complete the following calculation. The company had 9,500 shares of $1.00 par value stock outstanding on January 1. The company issued an additional 500 shares during the year.

5. Print the statement of retained earnings. (*Hint:* Peachtree's statement of retained earnings does *not* show the capital stock balance on December 31. Once you factor that in, Peachtree's statement of retained earnings will be in agreement with the manually prepared statement of stockholders' equity in the *Working Papers.*)

6. Print the balance sheet.

7. Journalize and post the closing entries.

8. Print the December 31 general journal.

9. Print the general ledger.

10. Print the post-closing trial balance.

11. Backup your work. The suggested file name is Reinforcement Activity 2-Part B.ptb.

You have completed the work for Reinforcement Activity 2—Part B: An Accounting Cycle for a Corporation: End-of-Fiscal-Period Work.

Recording Entries Related to Uncollectible Accounts Receivable

The instructions that follow show you how to do the following:

- Start Peachtree Complete Accounting.
- Restore starting data from the South-Western Accounting with Peachtree CD.
- Journalize and post transactions.
- Print the sales journal; cash receipts journal; customer ledger; and general ledger.
- Complete 17-2 Application Problem.

GETTING STARTED

Use the following instructions to start Peachtree and restore the starting data for Waldron Company. The South-Western Accounting with Peachtree CD includes a Peachtree data files folder. In the steps that follow you will restore the 17-2AP.ptb file.

1. Start Peachtree. From the startup menu, select Close .
2. The menu bar shows three options: Files; Options; and Help. Click File; Restore.
3. The Restore Wizard - Select Backup File window appears. Observe that the Location field shows where Peachtree is stored on your computer. The default location is C:\Program Files\Peachtree\ Company. Your Location field may differ. If you are restoring from a network drive, you will need to know the location of the 17-2AP.ptb file.
4. Click Browse . The Open Backup File window appears. In the Look in field, double-click on the appropriate location of the Peachtree data files. Then, click 17-2AP.ptb to select it. (If appropriate, select your CD drive then double-click the Peachtree Files-Unit 1 folder. Click 17-2AP.ptb to select it.)
5. Make sure the 17-2AP.ptb file is selected. Click Open .

6. The Select Backup File window appears. Make sure the Location field shows the correct location for the 17-2AP.ptb file; for example, X:\Peachtree Files-Unit 1\17-2AP.ptb. (Substitute the correct drive letter for X.)

7. Click Next>. The Select Company window appears. Click on the radio button next to *A New Company*. The Location field shown in this book indicates the default location where drive C is used to install Peachtree. Your Location field may differ. *Make sure that the Location field ends in* **walcompa**. (If your location field does not end in "a" select An Existing Company, then click Browse. Double-click Waldron Company (*or*, 17-2APXX). Your Location field shows the shortened company name walcompa. Continue with step 8.)

8. Click Next>. The Restore Options window appears.

9. Make sure that the box next to Company Data is *checked*. Click Next>.

10. The Confirmation window appears. Check the From and To fields to make sure they are correct. Click Finish. When the Restore Company scale is 100% complete, your data is restored and you are returned to the menu bar.

CHANGING THE COMPANY NAME

Before you start recording transactions for the 17-2 Application Problem, you should look at the company information included on the 17-2AP.ptb file. Follow these steps to look at company information.

1. The Waldron Company menu bar should be displayed. From the menu bar, click on Maintain; Company Information. The Maintain Company Information window appears. Observe that the directory field shows where your company is stored on your computer: C:\Program Files\Peachtree\company\walcompa.

2. Type **17-2APXX** in the Company Name field.

3. When you are finished typing 17-2APXX as the company name, click on OK. Once you have changed the Company Name, each one of your printouts will show the problem number and your initials.

Nothing has changed on your computer's hard drive. The company you restored is identified in the program folder and data folder as C:\Program Files\Peachtree\company\walcompa. What you've done is changed the company name so that your printouts will show the problem number and your initials. Using Maintain, Company Information to rename your company does *not* change the shortened company name.

WRITE OFF CUSTOMER ACCOUNT

The September 5 transaction describes an account to be written off as uncollectible.

Transaction:

Sept. 5   Wrote off Jackson Company's past-due account as uncollectible,
$124.00. M234.

In Peachtree, when you write off a customer account you use the
Receipts task. Account No. 1130, Allowance for Uncollectible Accounts,
is debited and Account No. 1125, Accounts Receivable, and the customer account are credited.

Instructions:

1. From the Tasks menu, select Receipts. When the Select a Cash
    Account window appears, click OK .

2. Type **9/5/05** in the Deposit Ticket ID field.

3. In the Customer ID field, select Jackson Company.

4. Type **M234** in the Reference field.

5. Type or select 5 as the date.

6. In the Cash Account field, select Account No. 1130, Allowance for
    Uncollectible Accounts. By changing the Cash Account field, you
    are changing the account to debit.

7. Click on the Pay box. Notice that 124.00 appears in the Receipt
    Amount field. (The Cash Account Balance refers to the Allowance
    for Uncollectible Account balance. When a balance has a minus sign
    in front of it that means it is a credit balance in the general ledger.)

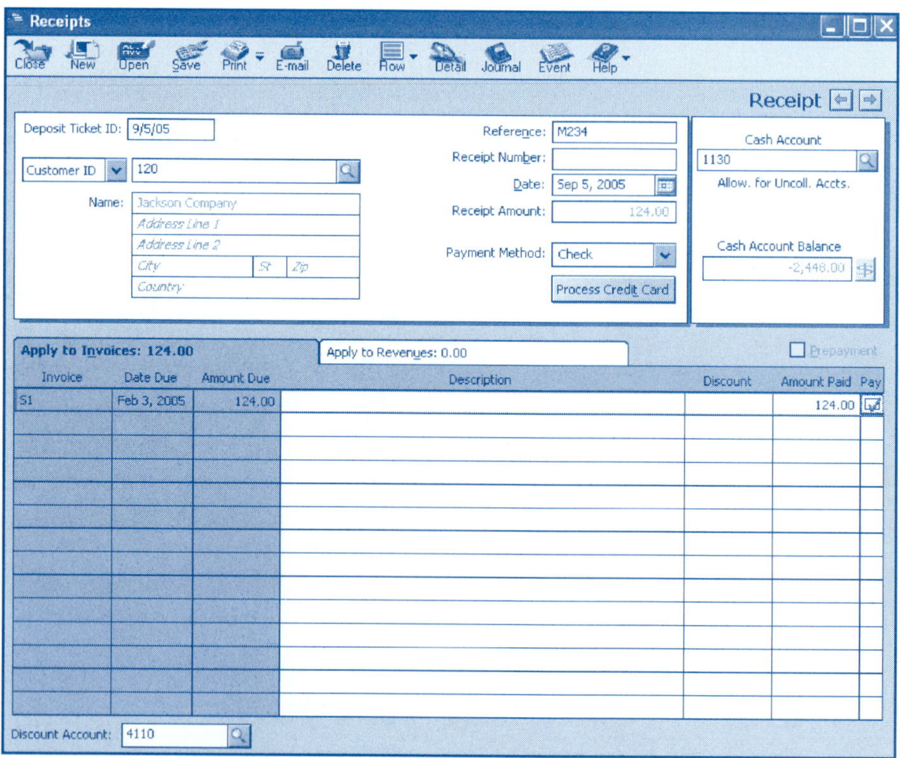

8. Post.

PAYMENT OF ACCOUNT PREVIOUSLY WRITTEN OFF

The September 7 journal entry is shown below.

Sept. 7   Received cash in full payment of Davis Industries' account, previously written off as uncollectible, $185.00. M235 and R339.

As you know from your study of accounting, there are two journal entries when a previously written off account is paid. You must first debit Accounts Receivable and the customer's account and credit Allowance for Uncollectible Accounts. Then you use the Cash Receipts Journal to debit Cash for the amount of the payment and credit Accounts Receivable and the customer's account. Use the following steps to record these two journal entries in Peachtree.

Instructions:

1. From the menu, select Tasks; Sales Invoicing.
2. Select Davis Industries as the customer.
3. Type or select 7 as the date.
4. Type **M235** in the Invoice No. field.
5. Complete the following fields:

Quantity	Description	GL Account	Unit Price
1	Reopen account	1130	185

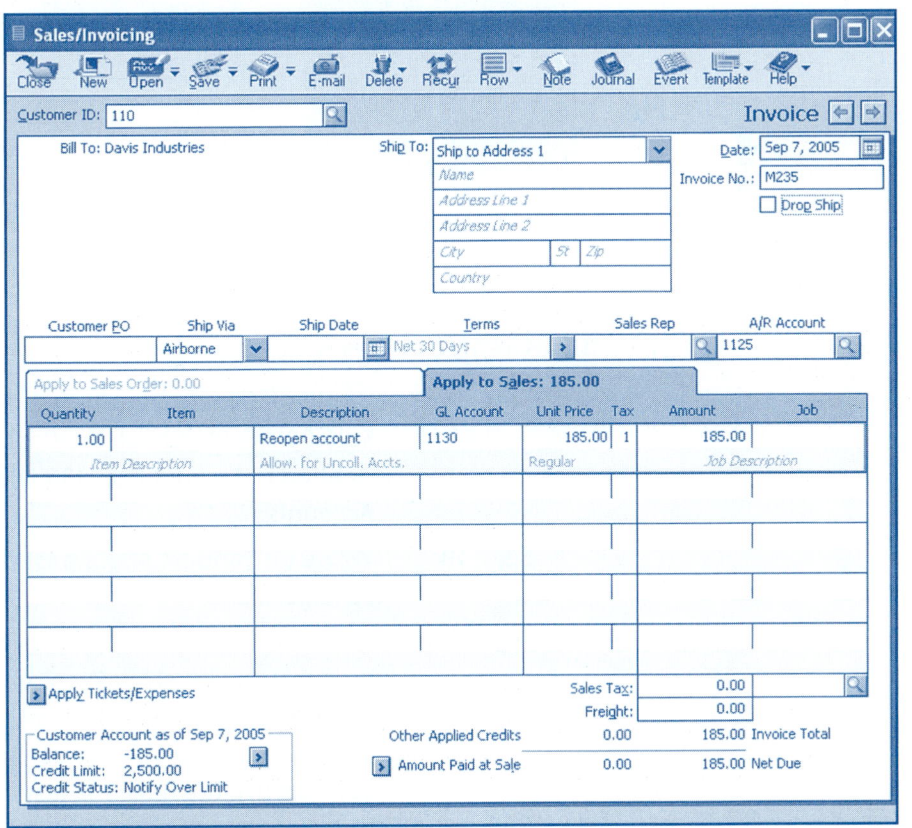

6. Post.

7. Select Tasks; Receipts.

8. Type **9/7/05** in the Deposit Ticket ID field.

9. Select Davis Industries as the customer.

10. Type **M235** as the reference.

11. Type **R339** as the Receipt.

12. Type **7** as the date.

13. Change the Cash Account field to Account No. 1105, Cash.

14. Click on the Pay box. The Receipt Amount field shows 185.00.

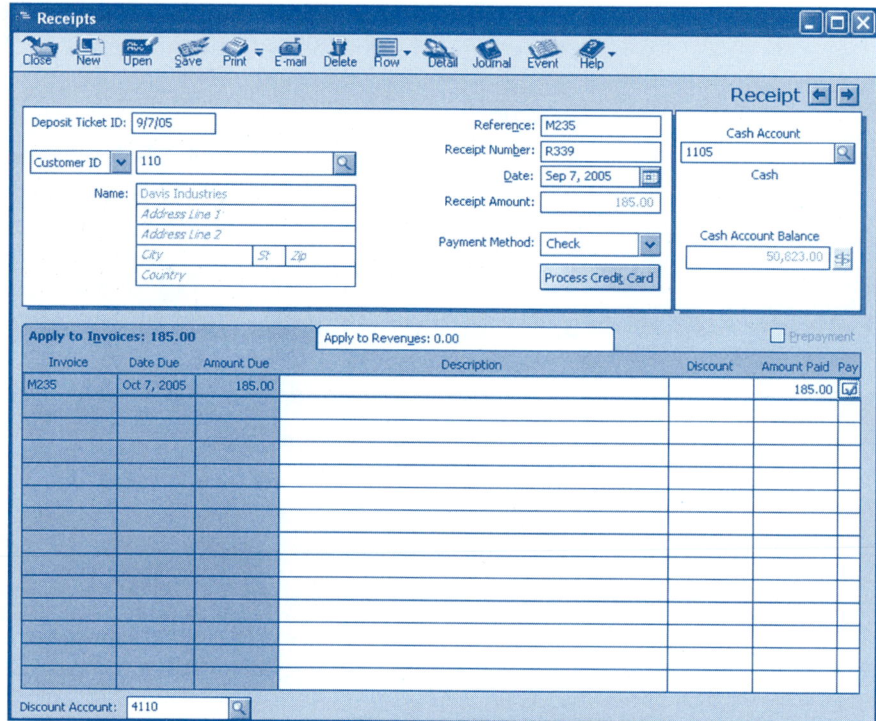

15. Post.

16. Complete these transactions:

Sept. 14	Wrote off Lancing, Inc.'s past-due account as uncollectible, $215.00. M238. (Check the Cash Account field. The account debited is Account No. 1130, Allowance for Uncollectible Accounts.)
Sept. 19	Wrote off Sanders Mfg.'s past-due account as uncollectible, $842.00. M243.
Sept. 27	Received cash in full payment of Jackson Company's account, previously written off as uncollectible, $124.00. M251 and R362. (*Hint:* This transaction requires two journal entries—use the Sales/Invoicing task to reopen the account; use the Receipts task for the payment.)

17. Print the sales journal, cash receipts journal, and customer ledger.

18. Follow these steps to print the accounts receivable and allowance for uncollectible accounts in the general ledger.

    a. From the reports menu, select General Ledger. Click (print).

    b. In the From field, select Account No. 1125; in the To field, select Account No. 1130.

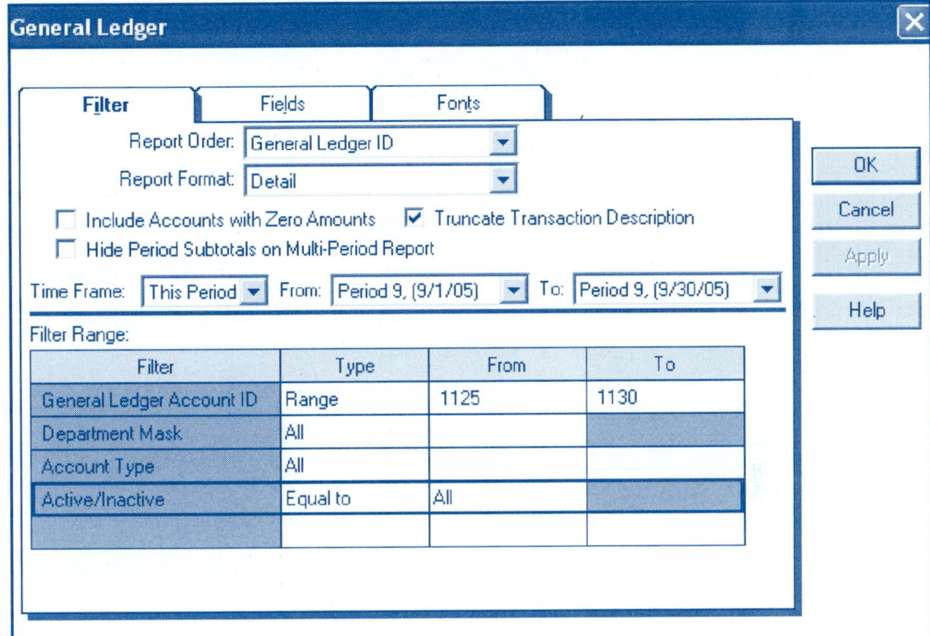

    c. Click OK. Make the selections to print.

19. Back up. The suggested file name is 17-2 Application Problem.ptb.

You have completed the work for the 17-2 Application Problem: Recording Entries Related to Uncollectible Accounts Receivable.

Recording Entries Related to Uncollectible Accounts Receivable

The instructions that follow show you how to do the following:

- Start Peachtree Complete Accounting.
- Restore starting data from the South-Western Accounting with Peachtree CD.
- Journalize and post transactions.
- Print the sales journal; cash receipts journal; customer ledger; and general ledger.
- Complete 17-3 Application Problem.

GETTING STARTED

Use the following instructions to start Peachtree and restore the starting data for Weatherly Co. The South-Western Accounting with Peachtree CD includes a Peachtree data files folder. In the steps that follow you will restore the 17-3AP.ptb file.

1. Start Peachtree. From the startup menu, select `Close`.
2. The menu bar shows three options: Files; Options; and Help. Click File; Restore.
3. The Restore Wizard - Select Backup File window appears. Observe that the Location field shows where Peachtree is stored on your computer. The default location is C:\Program Files\Peachtree\Company. Your Location field may differ. If you are restoring from a network drive, you will need to know the location of the 17-3AP.ptb file.
4. Click `Browse`. The Open Backup File window appears. In the Look in field, double-click on the appropriate location of the Peachtree data files. Then, click 17-3AP.ptb to select it. (If appropriate, select your CD drive then double-click the Peachtree Files-Unit 1 folder. Click 17-3AP.ptb to select it.)
5. Make sure the 17-3AP.ptb file is selected. Click `Open`.

6. The Select Backup File window appears. Make sure the Location
    field shows the correct location for the 17-3AP.ptb file; for example,
    X:\Peachtree Files-Unit 1\17-3AP.ptb. (Substitute the correct drive
    letter for X.)

7. Click Next >. The Select Company window appears. Click on the
    radio button next to *A New Company*. The Location field shown in
    this book indicates the default location where drive C is used to
    install Peachtree. Your Location field may differ. *Make sure that the
    Location field ends in* **weaco**. (If your location field does not end in
    "o" select An Existing Company, then click Browse. Double-click
    Weatherly Co. (*or*, 17-3APXX). Your Location field shows the
    shortened company name weaco. Continue with step 8.)

8. Click Next >. The Restore Options window appears.

9. Make sure that the box next to Company Data is *checked*. Click
    Next >.

10. The Confirmation window appears. Check the From and To fields
    to make sure they are correct. Click Finish. When the Restore
    Company scale is 100% complete, your data is restored and you
    are returned to the menu bar.

CHANGING THE COMPANY NAME

Before you start recording transactions for the 17-3 Application
Problem, you should look at the company information included on the
17-3AP.ptb file. Follow these steps to look at company information.

1. The Weatherly Co. menu bar should be displayed. From the
    menu bar, click on Maintain; Company Information. The Maintain
    Company Information window appears. Observe that the directory
    field shows where your company is stored on your computer: C:\
    Program Files\Peachtree\company\weaco.

2. Type **17-3APXX** in the Company Name field.

3. When you are finished typing 17-3APXX as the company name,
    click on OK. Once you have changed the Company Name, each one
    of your printouts will show the problem number and your initials.

Nothing has changed on your computer's hard drive. The company
you restored is identified in the program folder and data folder as C:\
Program Files\Peachtree\company\weaco. What you've done is
changed the company name so that your printouts will show the
problem number and your initials. Using Maintain, Company
Information to rename your company does *not* change the
shortened company name.

The following transactions related to accounts receivable occurred during February 2005. Journalize the transactions using the sales journal and cash receipts journal.

Transactions:

Feb. 3   Received a $1,458.00 check from Bearden Co. in full payment of its account. The account was written off in the previous month based on a newspaper story that indicated the company was about to close. M24 and R134.

    7   Monique Pearce, controller of Hampton Industries, just called, stating that the company had serious cash flow problems and would not be able to pay its $2,584.00 account balance. M25.

    10   Received a letter from Rankin Co.'s legal counsel, stating that the company was in the process of filing bankruptcy. The letter gave little hope that Weatherly would collect Rankin's $948.00 account. M28.

    12   Received a check from Camden Enterprises in full payment of its $1,784.00 account. The account was written off in January after months of efforts to collect the account. M31 and R142.

    21   A letter from Wilmont Co's receiving department supervisor, Daymon Lewis, stat that Wilmont refuses to pay for a prior year shipment of product for $548.00. The supervisor contends that the products were spoiled on arrival and were discarded. M34.

    27   Received a letter and check in the mail from Monique Pearce of Hampton Industries. Two weeks ago the company was purchased by another company and therefore has access to cash to pay its debt. M35 and R159.

1. Print the sales journal, cash receipts journal, and customer ledger.
2. Print the accounts receivable and allowance for uncollectible accounts in the general ledger.
3. Back up. The suggested file name is 17-3 Application Problem.ptb.

You have completed the work for the 17-2 Application Problem: Recording Entries Related to Uncollectible Accounts Receivable.

Journalizing Buying Plant Assets and Paying Property Tax

The instructions that follow show you how to do the following:

- Start Peachtree Complete Accounting.
- Restore starting data from the South-Western Accounting with Peachtree CD.
- Journalize and post transactions.
- Print the cash disbursements journal and selected general ledger accounts.
- Complete 18-1 Application Problem.

GETTING STARTED

Use the following instructions to start Peachtree and restore the starting data for Umeki Food Source. The South-Western Accounting with Peachtree CD includes a Peachtree data files folder. In the steps that follow you will restore the 18-1AP.ptb file.

1. Start Peachtree. From the startup menu, select Close.
2. The menu bar shows three options: Files; Options; and Help. Click File; Restore.
3. The Restore Wizard - Select Backup File window appears. Observe that the Location field shows where Peachtree is stored on your computer. The default location is C:\Program Files\Peachtree\Company. Your Location field may differ. If you are restoring from a network drive, you will need to know the location of the 18-1AP.ptb file.
4. Click Browse. The Open Backup File window appears. In the Look in field, double-click on the appropriate location of the Peachtree data files. Then, click 18-1AP.ptb to select it. (If appropriate, select your CD drive then double-click the Peachtree Files-Unit 1 folder. Click 18-1AP.ptb to select it.)
5. Make sure the 18-1AP.ptb file is selected. Click Open.

6. The Select Backup File window appears. Make sure the Location field shows the correct location for the 18-1AP.ptb file; for example, X:\Peachtree Files-Unit 1\18-1AP.ptb. (Substitute the correct drive letter for X.)

7. Click Next >. The Select Company window appears. Click on the radio button next to *A New Company*. The Location field shown in this book indicates the default location where drive C is used to install Peachtree. Your Location field may differ. *Make sure that the Location field ends in* **umefooso**. (If your location field does not end in "o" select An Existing Company, then click Browse. Double-click Umeki Food Source (*or*, 18-1APXX). Your Location field shows the shortened company name umefooso. Continue with step 8.)

8. Click Next >. The Restore Options window appears.

9. Make sure that the box next to Company Data is *checked*. Click Next >.

10. The Confirmation window appears. Check the From and To fields to make sure they are correct. Click Finish. When the Restore Company scale is 100% complete, your data is restored and you are returned to the menu bar.

CHANGING THE COMPANY NAME

Before you start recording transactions for the 18-1 Application Problem, you should look at the company information included on the 18-1AP.ptb file. Follow these steps to look at company information.

1. The Umeki Food Source menu bar should be displayed. From the menu bar, click on Maintain; Company Information. The Maintain Company Information window appears. Observe that the directory field shows where your company is stored on your computer: C:\Program Files\Peachtree\company\umefooso.

2. Type **18-1APXX** in the Company Name field.

3. When you are finished typing 18-1APXX as the company name, click on OK. Once you have changed the Company Name, each one of your printouts will show the problem number and your initials.

Nothing has changed on your computer's hard drive. The company you restored is identified in the program folder and data folder as C:\Program Files\Peachtree\company\umefooso. What you've done is changed the company name so that your printouts will show the problem number and your initials. Using Maintain, Company Information to rename your company does *not* change the shortened company name.

1. Journalize and post the following transactions. You do not have to change accounting periods to complete the transactions in the 18-1 Application Problem. Before you start the 18-1 Application Problem display or print the trial balance. The 18-1AP.ptb file includes the following account balance for Office Equipment and Store Equipment:

| 1205 | Office Equipment | $15,848.50 |
| 1215 | Store Equipment | 82,483.75 |

Transactions:

Jan.	4	Paid cash for office desk, $700.00. C334.
	5	Paid cash for a freezer, $4,200.00. C337.
Feb.	24	Paid property taxes on real property with an assessed value of $240,000.00. The tax rate in the city where the property is located is 1.4% of assessed value. C411.
May	12	Paid cash for shopping carts, $1,250. C354.

2. Journalize and post the transactions. Use the Write Checks task. You do *not* need to change accounting periods.
3. Print the cash disbursements journal from January 4, 2005 to May 12, 2005.
4. Print the office equipment and store equipment general ledger accounts from Period 1 (1/1/05) through Period 5 (5/31/05).
5. Print the Property Tax account for February, 2005.
6. Back up. The suggested file name is 18-1 Application Problem.ptb.

You have completed the work for the 18-1 Application Problem: Journalizing Buying Plant Assets and Paying Property Tax.

Journalizing Annual Depreciation Expense

The instructions that follow show you how to do the following:

- Start Peachtree Complete Accounting.
- Restore starting data from the South-Western Accounting with Peachtree CD.
- Journalize and post transactions.
- Print the general journal and selected general ledger accounts.
- Complete 18-4 Application Problem.

GETTING STARTED

Use the following instructions to start Peachtree and restore the starting data for Ester Engineering, Inc.. The South-Western Accounting with Peachtree CD includes a Peachtree data files folder. In the steps that follow you will restore the 18-4AP.ptb file.

1. Start Peachtree. From the startup menu, select `Close`.
2. The menu bar shows three options: Files; Options; and Help. Click File; Restore.
3. The Restore Wizard - Select Backup File window appears. Observe that the Location field shows where Peachtree is stored on your computer. The default location is C:\Program Files\Peachtree\Company. Your Location field may differ. If you are restoring from a network drive, you will need to know the location of the 18-4AP.ptb file.
4. Click `Browse`. The Open Backup File window appears. In the Look in field, double-click on the appropriate location of the Peachtree data files. Then, click 18-4AP.ptb to select it. (If appropriate, select your CD drive then double-click the Peachtree Files-Unit 1 folder. Click 18-4AP.ptb to select it.)
5. Make sure the 18-4AP.ptb file is selected. Click `Open`.

6. The Select Backup File window appears. Make sure the Location field shows the correct location for the 18-4AP.ptb file; for example, X:\Peachtree Files-Unit 1\18-4AP.ptb. (Substitute the correct drive letter for X.)

7. Click [Next>]. The Select Company window appears. Click on the radio button next to *A New Company*. The Location field shown in this book indicates the default location where drive C is used to install Peachtree. Your Location field may differ. *Make sure that the Location field ends in* **estengin**. (If your location field does not end in "n" select An Existing Company, then click [Browse]. Double-click Ester Engineering, Inc. (*or*, 18-4APXX). Your Location field shows the shortened company name estengin. Continue with step 8.)

8. Click [Next>]. The Restore Options window appears.

9. Make sure that the box next to Company Data is *checked*. Click [Next>].

10. The Confirmation window appears. Check the From and To fields to make sure they are correct. Click [Finish]. When the Restore Company scale is 100% complete, your data is restored and you are returned to the menu bar.

CHANGING THE COMPANY NAME

Before you start recording transactions for the 18-4 Application Problem, you should look at the company information included on the 18-4AP.ptb file. Follow these steps to look at company information.

> The Ester Engineering, Inc. menu bar should be displayed. From the menu bar, click on Maintain; Company Information. The Maintain Company Information window appears. Observe that the directory field shows where your company is stored on your computer: C:\Program Files\Peachtree\ company\estengin.
>
> Type **18-4APXX** in the Company Name field.
>
> When you are finished typing 18-4APXX as the company name, click on [OK]. Once you have changed the Company Name, each one of your printouts will show the problem number and your initials.

Nothing has changed on your computer's hard drive. The company you restored is identified in the program folder and data folder as C:\Program Files\Peachtree\ company\estengin. What you've done is changed the company name so that your printouts will show the problem number and your initials. Using Maintain, Company Information to rename your company does *not* change the shortened company name.

Instructions:

1. On December 31, Ester Engineering, Inc. determined that total depreciation expense for office equipment was $4,320.00. Record the adjusting entry in the general journal and post the transaction to the general ledger. Identify the adjusting entry as f.
2. Print the December 31, 2005 general journal.
3. Print the general ledger's Office Equipment and Accumulated Depreciation-Office Equipment accounts.
4. Print the general ledger's Depreciation Expense-Office Equipment account.
5. Back up. The suggested file name is 18-4 Application Problem.ptb.

You have completed the work for the 18-4 Application Problem: Journalizing Annual Depreciation Expense.

Determining the Cost of Inventory Using the Fifo, Lifo, and Weighted-Average Inventory Methods

The instructions that follow show you how to do the following:

- Start Peachtree Complete Accounting.
- Restore starting data from the South-Western Accounting with Peachtree CD.
- Journalize and post transactions.
- Print the purchase journal, sales journal and item costing report.
- Complete 19-4 Mastery Problem.

GETTING STARTED

Use the following instructions to start Peachtree and restore the starting data for Fratisi Company. The South-Western Accounting with Peachtree CD includes a Peachtree data files folder. In the steps that follow you will restore the 19-4MP.ptb file.

1. Start Peachtree. From the startup menu, select `Close`.
2. The menu bar shows three options: Files; Options; and Help. Click File; Restore.
3. The Restore Wizard - Select Backup File window appears. Observe that the Location field shows where Peachtree is stored on your computer. The default location is C:\Program Files\Peachtree\ Company. Your Location field may differ. If you are restoring from a network drive, you will need to know the location of the 19-4MP.ptb file.
4. Click `Browse`. The Open Backup File window appears. In the Look in field, double-click on the appropriate location of the Peachtree data files. Then, click 19-4MP.ptb to select it. (If appropriate, select your CD drive then double-click the Peachtree Files-Unit 1 folder. Click 19-4MP.ptb to select it.)
5. Make sure the 19-4MP.ptb file is selected. Click `Open`.

6. The Select Backup File window appears. Make sure the Location field shows the correct location for the 19-4MP.ptb file; for example, X:\Peachtree Files-Unit 1\19-4MP.ptb. (Substitute the correct drive letter for X.)

7. Click Next> . The Select Company window appears. Click on the radio button next to *A New Company*. The Location field shown in this book indicates the default location where drive C is used to install Peachtree. Your Location field may differ. *Make sure that the Location field ends in* **fracompa**. (If your location field does not end in "a" select An Existing Company, then click Browse . Double-click Fratisi Company (*or*, 19-4MPXX). Your Location field shows the shortened company name fracompa. Continue with step 8.)

8. Click Next> . The Restore Options window appears.

9. Make sure that the box next to Company Data is *checked*. Click Next> .

10. The Confirmation window appears. Check the From and To fields to make sure they are correct. Click Finish . When the Restore Company scale is 100% complete, your data is restored and you are returned to the menu bar.

CHANGING THE COMPANY NAME

Before you start recording transactions for the 19-4 Mastery Problem, you should look at the company information included on the 19-4MP.ptb file. Follow these steps to look at company information.

1. The Fratisi Company menu bar should be displayed. From the menu bar, click on Maintain; Company Information. The Maintain Company Information window appears. Observe that the directory field shows where your company is stored on your computer: C:\Program Files\Peachtree\ company\fracompa.

2. Type **19-4MPXX** in the Company Name field.

3. When you are finished typing 19-4MPXX as the company name, click on . Once you have changed the Company Name, each one of your printouts will show the problem number and your initials.

Nothing has changed on your computer's hard drive. The company you restored is identified in the program folder and data folder as C:\Program Files\Peachtree\company\fracompa. What you've done is changed the company name so that your printouts will show the problem number and your initials. Using Maintain, Company Information to rename your company does *not* change the shortened company name.

1. Fratisi Company began the year with 8 units of its model P-234 electronic switch in beginning inventory. East unit sells for $9.95. The sales tax is 6 percent. The following transactions involving model P-234 occurred during the year. Source documents are abbreviated as follows: purchase invoice, P; sales invoice, S. In the steps that follow you use Peachtree's fifo inventory method.

Transactions:

Jan.	6	Purchased 20 units from Master Electronics for $5.12 per unit, 2/10, n/30. P154. (*Hint:* Remember to select P-234, Electronic Switch as the item. Change the Unit Price to $5.12.)
Apr.	5	Sold 22 units to Evan Construction, n/30. S1998. (*Hint:* Remember to select P-234, Electronic Switch as the item. Sales tax is 6%.)
	14	Purchased 20 units from Master Electronics for $5.18 per unit, 2/10, n/30. P223.
Jul.	28	Sold 25 units to Pette Hardware, n/30. S2245.
Aug.	3	Purchased 20 units from Master Electronics for $5.23 per unit, 2/10, n/30. P298.
Dec	2	Sold 15 units to Century Homebuilders, n/30. S2848.
	12	Purchased 20 units from Master Electronics for $5.27 per unit, 2/10, n/30. P332.

2. Journalize and post the transactions. (*Hint:* On the Purchases/Receive Inventory window, and the Sales/Invoicing window, select P-234, Electronic Switch, in the Item column. You do *not* have to change accounting periods.)

3. Print the purchase journal from January 6, 2005 to December 12, 2005.

4. Print the sales journal from April 5, 2005 to December 2, 2005.

5. Print the Item Costing Report from January 1, 2005 to December 31, 2005. This report calculates fifo. (*Hint:* From the Reports menu, select Inventory; Item Costing Report.)

6. Use a blank piece of paper or the *Working Papers* to determine the cost of inventory using the lifo and weighted-average inventory costing methods.

7. Use a blank piece of paper or the *Working Papers* to answer this question: Which of the inventory costing methods results in the highest cost of merchandise sold? Merchandise available for sale is the total cost of beginning inventory plus all purchases during the year.

8. Back up. The suggested file name is 19-4 Mastery Problem.ptb.

You have completed the work for the 19-4 Mastery Problem: Determining the Cost of Inventory Using the Fifo, Lifo, and Weighted-Average Inventory Methods.

Journalizing Notes Payable Transactions

The instructions that follow show you how to do the following:

- Start Peachtree Complete Accounting.
- Restore starting data from the South-Western Accounting with Peachtree CD.
- Journalize and post transactions.
- Print the cash receipts journal, purchase journal, and cash disbursements journal.
- Complete 20-2 Application Problem.

GETTING STARTED

Use the following instructions to start Peachtree and restore the starting data for Webster Company. The South-Western Accounting with Peachtree CD includes a Peachtree data files folder. In the steps that follow you will restore the 20-2AP.ptb file.

1. Start Peachtree. From the startup menu, select `Close`.
2. The menu bar shows three options: Files; Options; and Help. Click File; Restore.
3. The Restore Wizard - Select Backup File window appears. Observe that the Location field shows where Peachtree is stored on your computer. The default location is C:\Program Files\Peachtree\Company. Your Location field may differ. If you are restoring from a network drive, you will need to know the location of the 20-2AP.ptb file.
4. Click `Browse`. The Open Backup File window appears. In the Look in field, double-click on the appropriate location of the Peachtree data files. Then, click 20-2AP.ptb to select it. (If appropriate, select your CD drive then double-click the Peachtree Files-Unit 1 folder. Click 20-2AP.ptb to select it.)
5. Make sure the 20-2AP.ptb file is selected. Click `Open`.
6. The Select Backup File window appears. Make sure the Location field shows the correct location for the 20-2AP.ptb file; for example, X:\Peachtree Files-Unit 1\20-2AP.ptb. (Substitute the correct drive letter for X.)

7. Click [Next >]. The Select Company window appears. Click on the radio button next to *A New Company*. The Location field shown in this book indicates the default location where drive C is used to install Peachtree. Your Location field may differ. *Make sure that the Location field ends in* **webcompa**. (If your location field does not end in "a" select An Existing Company, then click [Browse]. Double-click Webster Company (*or, 20-2APXX*). Your Location field shows the shortened company name webcompa. Continue with step 8.)

8. Click [Next >]. The Restore Options window appears.

9. Make sure that the box next to Company Data is *checked*. Click [Next >].

10. The Confirmation window appears. Check the From and To fields to make sure they are correct. Click [Finish]. When the Restore Company scale is 100% complete, your data is restored and you are returned to the menu bar.

CHANGING THE COMPANY NAME

Before you start recording transactions for the 20-2 Application Problem, you should look at the company information included on the 20-2AP.ptb file. Follow these steps to look at company information.

1. The Webster Company menu bar should be displayed. From the menu bar, click on Maintain; Company Information. The Maintain Company Information window appears. Observe that the directory field shows where your company is stored on your computer: C:\ Program Files\Peachtree\ company\webcompa.

2. Type **20-2APXX** in the Company Name field.

3. When you are finished typing 20-2APXX as the company name, click on [OK]. Once you have changed the Company Name, each one of your printouts will show the problem number and your initials.

Nothing has changed on your computer's hard drive. The company you restored is identified in the program folder and data folder as C:\ Program Files\Peachtree\company\webcompa. What you've done is changed the company name so that your printouts will show the problem number and your initials. Using Maintain, Company Information to rename your company does *not* change the shortened company name.

Instructions:

1. Using 2005, journalize and post each of the following transactions. You do not need to change accounting periods. Detailed steps are shown below for the April 6, April 12, and July 11 transaction.

Apr. 6   Signed a 180-day, 12% note, for $10,000.00 with First American Bank. R127. (*Hint:* Use the Receipts task. Remember to select Account No. 2105, Notes Payable, to credit. Account No. 1105, Cash is debited.)

12   Signed a 60-day, 9% note with Milligan Company for an extension of time on this accounts payable, $600.00. M32. (*Hint:* Use the Purchases/Receive Inventory task. The April 12, 2005 Purchases/Receive Inventory window is shown below. Notice that the A/P Account field shows 2105, Notes Payable—that is the account credited. The GL Account field shows 2115, Account Payable—that is the account debited.)

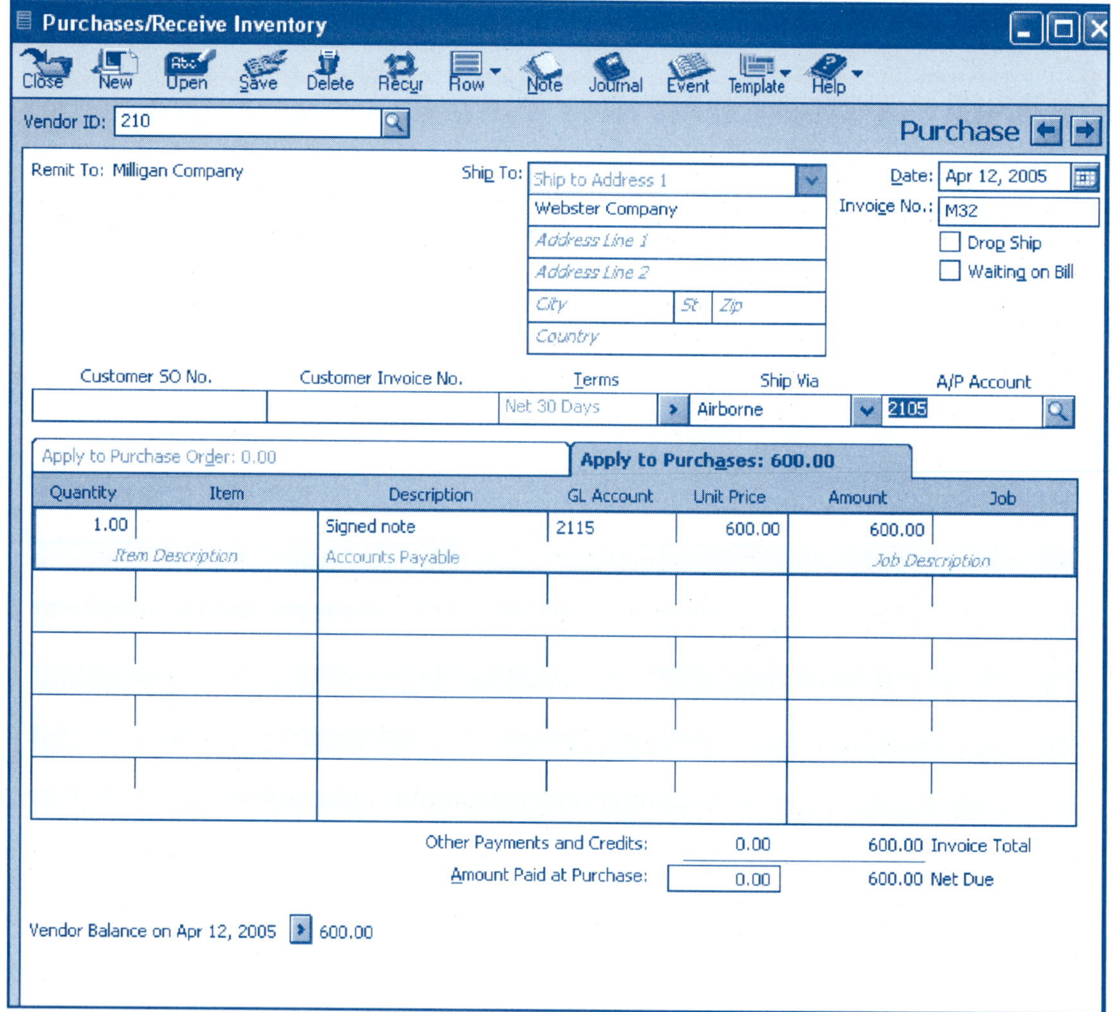

15   Signed a 90-day, 10% note, for $5,000.00 with First National Bank.

23   Signed a 60-day, 14% note with Yeatman Industries for an extension of time on this account payable, $3,000.00. M42.

2. Journalize and post the following transactions in the cash disbursements journal (use Peachtree Write Checks task).

Transactions:

Jun. 11   Paid cash for the maturity value of the $600.00 note dated April 12. C310. (*Hint:* Use the Write Checks task. Remember to debit the appropriate accounts and credit Cash. You can split the Write Checks transactions.)

     22   Paid cash for the maturity value of the $3,000.00 notes dated April 23. C318.

Jul. 14   Paid cash for the maturity value of the $5,000.00 note dated April 15. C456.

Oct. 3   Paid cash for the maturity value of the $10,000.00 note dated April 6. C645.

3. Print the April 6 to April 15, 2005 Cash Receipts journal.

4. Print the April 12 to April 23, 2005 Purchase Journal.

5. Print the June 11, 2005 to October 3, 2005 Cash Disbursements Journal.

6. Back up. The suggested file name is 20-2 Application Problem.ptb.

You have completed the work for the 20-2 Application Problem: Journalizing Notes Payable Transactions.

Journalizing Notes Payable and Notes Receivable Transactions

The instructions that follow show you how to do the following:

- Start Peachtree Complete Accounting.
- Restore starting data from the South-Western Accounting with Peachtree CD.
- Journalize and post transactions.
- Print the cash receipts journal, sales journal, purchases journal, and cash disbursements journal.
- Complete 20-5 Mastery Problem.

GETTING STARTED

Use the following instructions to start Peachtree and restore the starting data for Amory Company. The South-Western Accounting with Peachtree CD includes a Peachtree data files folder. In the steps that follow you will restore the 20-5MP.ptb file.

1. Start Peachtree. From the startup menu, select Close.
2. The menu bar shows three options: Files; Options; and Help. Click File; Restore.
3. The Restore Wizard - Select Backup File window appears. Observe that the Location field shows where Peachtree is stored on your computer. The default location is C:\Program Files\Peachtree\ Company. Your Location field may differ. If you are restoring from a network drive, you will need to know the location of the 20-5MP.ptb file.
4. Click Browse. The Open Backup File window appears. In the Look in field, double-click on the appropriate location of the Peachtree data files. Then, click 20-5MP.ptb to select it. (If appropriate, select your CD drive then double-click the Peachtree Files-Unit 1 folder. Click 20-5MP.ptb to select it.)
5. Make sure the 20-5MP.ptb file is selected. Click Open.

6. The Select Backup File window appears. Make sure the Location field shows the correct location for the 20-5MP.ptb file; for example, X:\Peachtree Files-Unit 1\20-5MP.ptb. (Substitute the correct drive letter for X.)

7. Click Next> . The Select Company window appears. Click on the radio button next to *A New Company*. The Location field shown in this book indicates the default location where drive C is used to install Peachtree. Your Location field may differ. *Make sure that the Location field ends in* **amocompa**. (If your location field does not end in "a" select An Existing Company, then click Browse . Double-click Amory Company (*or, 20-5MPXX*). Your Location field shows the shortened company name amocompa. Continue with step 8.)

8. Click Next> . The Restore Options window appears.

9. Make sure that the box next to Company Data is *checked*. Click Next> .

10. The Confirmation window appears. Check the From and To fields to make sure they are correct. Click Finish . When the Restore Company scale is 100% complete, your data is restored and you are returned to the menu bar.

CHANGING THE COMPANY NAME

Before you start recording transactions for the 20-5 Mastery Problem, you should look at the company information included on the 20-5MP.ptb file. Follow these steps to look at company information.

1. The Company menu bar should be displayed. From the menu bar, click on Maintain; Company Information. The Maintain Company Information window appears. Observe that the directory field shows where your company is stored on your computer: C:\Program Files\Peachtree\company\amocompa.

2. Type **20-5MPXX** in the Company Name field.

3. When you are finished typing 20-5MPXX as the company name, click on OK . Once you have changed the Company Name, each one of your printouts will show the problem number and your initials.

Nothing has changed on your computer's hard drive. The company you restored is identified in the program folder and data folder as C:\Program Files\Peachtree\company\amocompa. What you've done is changed the company name so that your printouts will show the problem number and your initials. Using Maintain, Company Information to rename your company does *not* change the shortened company name.

1. The following transactions related to notes payable and notes receivable were completed by Company during July 2005.

Transactions:

Jul.	2	Signed a 90-day note, for $5,000.00 with Commercial Bank. R51.
	7	Accepted a 90-day, 10% note from Nan Albert for an extension of time on her account, $1,500.00. NR9. (*Hint:* The July 7, 2005 Receipts window is shown below. Notice that the Cash Account field shows Account No. 1115, Notes Receivable—that is the account debited. The account credited is Account No. 1125, Accounts Receivable/Nan Albert. Notice that the pay box for $1,500 is checked.)

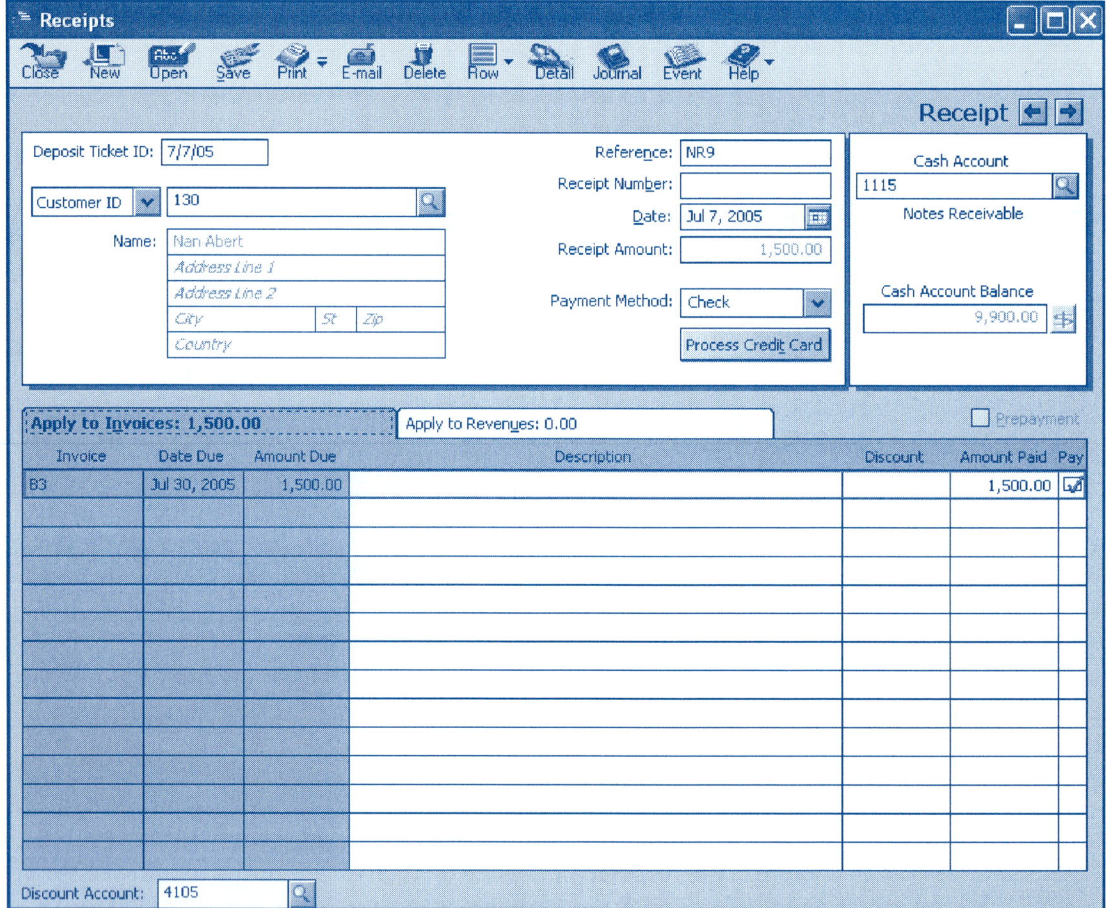

	9	Received cash for maturity value of NR4, a 60-day, 9% note for $1,600.00. R62.
	12	Accepted a 90-day, 10% note from Tom Burns for an extension of time on his account, $400.00. NR10. (*Hint:* Use the Receipts tasks. Remember to debit Account No. 1115, Notes Receivable.)

17	Received cash for the maturity value of NR5, a 60-day, 9% note for $800.00. R65.
23	Signed a 180-day, 8% note, for $8,000.00 with American National Bank. R74.
24	Gibson Co. dishonored NR2, a 90-day, 12% note, for $3,000.00. M43. (*Hint:* Use the Sales/Invoicing task. Debit Account No. 1125, Accounts Receivable/Gibson Co.; credit Account No. 1115, Notes Receivable and Account No. 4200, Interest Income.)
28	Received cash for the maturity value of NR3, a 90-day, 12% note for $4,500.00. R79.
29	Signed a 60-day, 12% note with Daily Supply for an extension of time on this account payable, $2,500.00. M44.

2. Journalize and post the following transactions in the cash disbursements journal. You do *not* need to change accounting periods. Determine the maturity date and maturity value of each note signed by the Company. Journalize the following transactions in the cash disbursements journal. Use the maturity dates and maturity values calculated in previous steps.

Transactions:

Paid cash for the maturity value of the $2,500.00 note dated July 29. C417.

Paid cash for the maturity value of the $5,000.00 note dated July 2. C610.

Paid cash for the maturity value of the $8,000.00 note dated July 23. C821.

3. Print July's cash receipts journal.

4. Print July's sales journal.

5. Print July's purchase Journal.

6. Print the cash disbursements journal from September 27, 2005 to January 19, 2006.

7. Back up. The suggested file name is 20-5 Mastery Problem.ptb.

You have completed the work for the 20-5 Mastery Problem: Journalizing Notes Payable and Notes Receivable Transactions.

An Accounting Cycle for a Corporation: Journalizing and Posting Transactions

The instructions that follow show you how to do the following:

- Start Peachtree Complete Accounting.
- Restore the Problem File for Sparkle, Inc.
- Journalize and post transactions.
- Complete Reinforcement Activity 3—Part A.

Before you start Reinforcement Activity 3—Part A, ask your instructor if Sparkle, Inc., the company used for Reinforcement Activity 3—Part A, has already been restored on your computer. The instructions that follow assume that that Sparkle, Inc. has *not* been restored.

GETTING STARTED

Use the following instructions to start Peachtree and restore the merchandising business called Sparkle, Inc.

1. Start Peachtree. From the startup menu, select Close .
2. The menu bar shows three options: Files; Options; and Help. Click File; Restore.
3. The Restore Wizard - Select Backup File window appears. Observe that the Location field shows where Peachtree is stored on your computer. The default location is C:\Program Files\Peachtree\Company. Your Location field may differ. If you are restoring from a network drive, you will need to know the location of the RA03-A.ptb file.
4. Click Browse . The Open Backup File window appears. In the Look in field, double-click on the appropriate location of the Peachtree data files. Then, click RA03-A.ptb to select it. (If appropriate, select your CD drive then double-click the Peachtree Files-Unit 1 folder. Click RA03-A.ptb to select it.)
5. Make sure the RA03-A.ptb file is selected. Click Open .
6. The Select Backup File window appears. Make sure the Location field shows the correct location; for example, X:\Peachtree Files-Unit 1\RA03-A.ptb. (Substitute the correct drive letter for X.)

7. Click [Next >]. The Select Company window appears. Click on the
   radio button next to *A New Company*. The Location field shown in
   this book indicates the default location where drive C is used to
   install Peachtree. Your Location field may differ. *Make sure that the
   Location field ends in* **spainc**. (If your location field does not end in
   "c" select An Existing Company, then click [Browse]. Double-click
   Sparkle, Inc. (*or*, RA03-AXX). Your Location field shows the shortened company name spainc. Continue with step 8.)

8. Click [Next >]. The Restore Options window appears.

9. Make sure that the box next to Company Data is *checked*. Click
   [Next >].

10. The Confirmation window appears. Check the From and To fields
    to make sure they are correct. Click [Finish]. When the Restore
    Company scale is 100% complete, your data is restored and you
    are returned to the menu bar.

CHANGING THE COMPANY NAME

Before you start recording transactions for Reinforcement Activity
3—Part A, you should look at the company information included on the
RA03-A.ptb file. Follow these steps to look at company information.

1. The Sparkle, Inc. menu bar should be displayed. From the menu
   bar, click on Maintain; Company Information. The Maintain
   Company Information window appears. Observe that the directory
   field shows where your company is stored on your computer: C:\
   Program Files\Peachtree\company\spainc.

2. Type **RA03-AXX** in the Company Name field.

3. When you are finished typing RA03-AXX as the company name,
   click on [OK]. Once you have changed the Company Name, each
   one of your printouts will show the problem number and your
   initials.

Nothing has changed on your computer's hard drive. The company
you restored is identified in the program folder and data folder as C:\
Program Files\Peachtree\spainc. What you've done is changed the
company name so that your printouts will show the problem number
and your initials. Using Maintain, Company Information to rename
your company does *not* change the shortened company name.

DISPLAYING THE SPARKLE, INC. CHART OF ACCOUNTS

Before recording transactions, you should print or display Peachtree's
chart of account and compare it to the one shown. Refer to these
account numbers when recording transactions.

Peachtree's chart of accounts classifies the following accounts as Income:

4200 Gain on Plant Assets

4210 Interest Income

Your textbook shows these accounts as "Other Revenue" and numbers them 7105 and 7110, respectively. Since there is *no* Other Revenue (or Other Income) classification in Peachtree, all revenue accounts are numbered using 4000's.

Sparkle, Inc.
Chart of Accounts
As of Dec 31, 2005

Filter Criteria includes: Report order is by ID. Report is printed with Accounts having Zero Amounts and in Detail Format.

Account ID	Account Description	Active?	Account Type
1105	Cash	Yes	Cash
1110	Petty Cash	Yes	Cash
1115	Notes Receivable	Yes	Other Current Assets
1120	Interest Receivable	Yes	Other Current Assets
1125	Accounts Receivable	Yes	Accounts Receivable
1130	Allow. for Uncoll. Accts.	Yes	Accounts Receivable
1135	Merchandise Inventory	Yes	Inventory
1140	Supplies	Yes	Other Current Assets
1145	Prepaid Insurance	Yes	Other Current Assets
1205	Office Equipment	Yes	Fixed Assets
1210	Acc. Depr.-Office Equipment	Yes	Accumulated Depreciation
1215	Warehouse Equipment	Yes	Fixed Assets
1220	Acc. Depr.-Warehouse Equipment	Yes	Accumulated Depreciation
2105	Notes Payable	Yes	Other Current Liabilities
2110	Interest Payable	Yes	Other Current Liabilities
2115	Accounts Payable	Yes	Accounts Payable
2120	Federal Income Tax Payable	Yes	Other Current Liabilities
2125	Empl. Inc. Tax Payable	Yes	Other Current Liabilities
2130	Soc. Security Tax Payable	Yes	Other Current Liabilities
2135	Medicare Tax Payable	Yes	Other Current Liabilities
2140	Sales Tax Payable	Yes	Other Current Liabilities
2145	Unempl. Tax Payable-Federal	Yes	Other Current Liabilities
2150	Unempl. Tax Payable-State	Yes	Other Current Liabilities
2155	Health Ins. Prem. Payable	Yes	Other Current Liabilities
2160	Dividends Payable	Yes	Other Current Liabilities
3105	Capital Stock	Yes	Equity-doesn't close
3110	Retained Earnings	Yes	Equity-Retained Earnings
3115	Dividends	Yes	Equity-gets closed
3120	Income Summary	Yes	Equity-gets closed
4105	Sales	Yes	Income
4110	Sales Discount	Yes	Income
4115	Sales Returns & Allow.	Yes	Income
4200	Gain on Plant Assets	Yes	Income
4210	Interest Income	Yes	Income
5105	Purchases	Yes	Cost of Sales
5110	Purchases Discount	Yes	Cost of Sales
5115	Purch. Returns & Allow.	Yes	Cost of Sales
6105	Advertising Expense	Yes	Expenses
6110	Cash Short and Over	Yes	Expenses
6115	Credit Card Fee Expense	Yes	Expenses
6120	Depr. Exp.-Office Equipment	Yes	Expenses
6125	Depr. Exp.-Warehouse Equipment	Yes	Expenses
6130	Insurance Expense	Yes	Expenses
6135	Miscellaneous Expense	Yes	Expenses
6140	Payroll Taxes Expense	Yes	Expenses
6145	Rent Expense	Yes	Expenses
6150	Repairs Expense	Yes	Expenses
6155	Salary Expense	Yes	Expenses
6160	Supplies Expense	Yes	Expenses
6165	Uncoll. Accts. Expense	Yes	Expenses
6170	Utilities Expense	Yes	Expenses
8105	Interest Expense	Yes	Expenses
8110	Loss on Plant Assets	Yes	Expenses
9105	Federal Income Tax Expense	Yes	Expenses

RECORDING TRANSACTIONS

The chart below shows which journals are used for Reinforcement Problem 3. The journals are abbreviated as follows: sales journal, SJ; cash receipts journal, CRJ; purchase journal, PJ; cash disbursements journal, CDJ; general journal, GJ.

Transactions	SJ	CRJ	PJ	CDJ	GJ
Customers - accounts receivable	√				
Cash, credit card, customer receipts		√			
Vendors – accounts payable			√		
Vendor payments				√	
Depreciation					√
Payroll taxes expense					√
Adjusting entries					√
Closing entries					√

Reinforcement Activity 3 covers a complete accounting cycle for a merchandising business organized as a corporation. Reinforcement Activity 3 is a single problem divided into two parts: Part A includes learning from Part 2 and Chapters 17 through 20 of Part 3 of the textbook. Part B includes learning from Chapters 21 and 22 of the textbook.

The accounting work of a single merchandising business for the last month of 2005 is used in this reinforcement activity. The records kept and reports prepared illustrate the application of accounting concepts for all merchandising businesses.

Sparkle, Inc., a merchandising business, is organized as a corporation. The business sells a complete line of cleaning and maintenance supply, mostly to business customers. Sparkle is located within an industrial park and is open for business Monday through Saturday. Monthly rent is paid for the building. Sparkle sells to some businesses on account and accepts cash or credit cards from small business owners.

The December 1, 2005 account balances for the general ledger and subsidiary ledgers are included on the RA03-A.ptb file.

Instructions:

Journalize and post the following transactions completed during December 2005. Use the sales journal, purchase journal, general journal, cash receipts journal, and cash disbursements journal. The sales tax rate is 6%. Source documents are abbreviated as follows: check, C; memorandum, M; purchase invoice, P; receipt, R; sales invoice, S; terminal summary, TS; debit memorandum, DM; credit memorandum, CM; Note Receivable, NR; Notes Payable, NP.

| Dec. | 1 | Paid cash for rent, $1,750.00. C578. |

Dec. 1   Paid cash for rent, $1,750.00. C578.

     2   Received cash on account from Ruocco Plastics, covering S637 for $3,250.00. R671.

     3   Paid cash on account to Walbash Manufacturing, covering P324 for $620.00, less 2% discount. C579.

     3   Paid cash for the maturity value of the NP31, a 180-day, 9% note for $10,000.00 to First American Bank. C580.

     5   Bought a printer/scanner for the office: cost, $1,200.00; estimated salvage value, $200.00; estimated useful life, 3 years; plant asset No. 998; serial number, MNT-9343. C581. Open a plant asset record for this office equipment. Sparkle Inc. uses the straight-line method of depreciation.

     5   Sold merchandise on account to Horton Company, $500.00, plus sales tax. S657.

     6   Recorded cash and credit card sales, $5,430.00, plus sales tax, $325.80; total, $5,755.80. TS49.

     6   Bought supplies on account from Draper Company, $362.40. M45.

     7   Accepted a 90-day, 10% note from Nelson Co. for an extension of time on its account, $3,600.00. NR34. M45.

     8   Purchased merchandise on account from Glenson Company, $4,518.00. P332.

     9   Sold merchandise on account to Ruocco Plastics, $480.00, plus sales tax. S658.

     9   Wrote off Felton Industries' past-due account as uncollectible, $2,460.00. M46.

    10   Paid cash for supplies, $223.00. C582.

    12   Received cash on account from Horton Company, covering S657 for $530.00, less 2% discount. R672.

    12   Purchased merchandise on account from Hinsdale Supply Co., $6,812.00. P333.

    13   Recorded cash and credit card sales, $5,987.00, plus sales tax, $359.22; total, $6,346.22. TS50.

    14   Received cash for sale of a hand truck, plant asset No. 432, $1,400.00. M47 and R673.

    14   Returned merchandise purchased from Glenson Company on P332, $198.00. DM34.

    15   Paid cash liability for employee income tax, $324.00; social security tax, $742.00; and Medicare tax, $162.35. C583.

    15   Paid cash for semimonthly payroll, $2,256.27 (total payroll, $2,820.00, less deductions: employee income tax, $158.00; social security tax, $174.84; Medicare tax, $40.89; health insurance, $190.00). C584.

15   Recorded employer payroll taxes, $250.45, for the semimonthly pay period ended December 15. Taxes owed are: social security tax, $174.84; Medicare tax, $40.89; federal unemployment tax, $4.48; and state unemployment tax, $30.24. M48.

16   Purchased merchandise on account from Buntin Supply Company, $4,833.00. P334.

17   Paid cash for electric bill, $346.20. C585.

17   Paid cash on account to Glenson Company, covering P332 for $4,518.00, less 2% discount. C586.

18   Received cash in full payment of Baker & Associates' account, previously written off as uncollectible, $948.00. M49 and R674.

19   Paid cash for miscellaneous expense, $72.00. C587.

20   Sold merchandise on account to Hilldale School, $1,560.00. Hilldale School is exempt from sales tax. S659.

20   Recorded cash and credit card sales, $3,554.00, plus sales tax, $213.24; total, $3,767.24. TS51.

21   Paid cash for merchandise, $357.00. C588.

22   Granted credit to Ruocco Plastics for merchandise returned, $120.00; plus sales tax, $7.20; $127.20 total. CM15.

23   Paid cash on account to Hinsdale Supply Co., covering P333 for $6,812.00. C589.

26   Received cash for the maturity value of NR32, a 90-day, 12% note for $5,800.00. R675.

27   Recorded cash and credit card sales, $2,337.00, plus sales tax, $140.22; total, $2,477.22. TS52.

28   Sold merchandise on account to Horton Company, $2,500.00, plus sales tax. S660.

28   Purchased merchandise on account from Draper Company, $6,148.00. P335.

28   Signed a 90-day, 10% note, for $6,000.00 with Commercial National Bank. NP33 and R676.

28   Received cash for sale of a computer printer, plant asset No. 667, $150.00. M50 and R677. Update the plant asset record and record the sale.

29   Paid $500.00 on the outstanding balance of the SHF Corp. account. C590.

30   Ruocco Plastics dishonored NR33, a 60-day, 12% note, for $3,000.00. M51.

30   Recorded credit card fee expense, $418.00. M52.

31   Paid cash to replenish the petty cash fund, $84.96: supplies, $12.50; advertising, $50.00; miscellaneous, $22.37; cash short, $.09. C591.

31	Paid cash for semimonthly payroll, $2,206.86 (total payroll, $2,760.00, less deductions: employee income tax, $152.00; social security tax, $171.12; Medicare tax, $40.02; health insurance, $190.00. C592.
31	Recorded employer payroll taxes, $242.14, for the semimonthly pay period ended December 31. Taxes owed are: social security tax, $171.12: Medicare tax, $40.02; federal unemployment tax, $4.00; and state unemployment tax, $27.00. M53.
31	Recorded cash and credit card sales, $465.00, plus sales tax, $27.90; total, $492.90. TS53.

1. Print the general journal from December 14 to December 31, 2005; sales journal, purchase journal, cash receipts journal, and cash disbursements journal.

2. Print the vendor ledgers and customer ledgers.

3. Print the general ledger.

4. Use the *Working Papers* or a blank piece of paper to update depreciation.

5. Back up your company data. The suggested file name is **Reinforcement Activity 3-Part A.ptb**. This backup is important. Keep it in a safe place. You will use it again for Part B of this problem.

You have completed the work for Reinforcement Activity 3—Part A: An Accounting Cycle for a Corporation: Journalizing and Posting Transactions. Keep your backup file in a safe place. You will use the backup made in this activity for Part B of this problem.

Journalizing and Posting Entries for Accrued Interest Revenue and Expense

The instructions that follow show you how to do the following:

- Start Peachtree Complete Accounting.
- Restore starting data from the South-Western Accounting with Peachtree CD.
- Journalize and post transactions.
- Print the general journal, cash receipts journal, cash disbursements journal, and general ledger.
- Complete 21-4 Mastery Problem.

GETTING STARTED

Use the following instructions to start Peachtree and restore the starting data for Youngblood, Inc. The South-Western Accounting with Peachtree CD includes a Peachtree data files folder. In the steps that follow you will restore the 21-4MP.ptb file.

1. Start Peachtree. From the startup menu, select Close.
2. The menu bar shows three options: Files; Options; and Help. Click File; Restore.
3. The Restore Wizard - Select Backup File window appears. Observe that the Location field shows where Peachtree is stored on your computer. The default location is C:\Program Files\Peachtree\ Company. Your Location field may differ. If you are restoring from a network drive, you will need to know the location of the 21-4MP.ptb file.
4. Click Browse. The Open Backup File window appears. In the Look in field, double-click on the appropriate location of the Peachtree data files. Then, click 21-4MP.ptb to select it. (If appropriate, select your CD drive then double-click the Peachtree Files-Unit 1 folder. Click 21-4MP.ptb to select it.)
5. Make sure the 21-4MP.ptb file is selected. Click Open.

6. The Select Backup File window appears. Make sure the Location field shows the correct location for the 21-4MP.ptb file; for example, X:\Peachtree Files-Unit 1\21-4MP.ptb. (Substitute the correct drive letter for X.)

7. Click **Next >**. The Select Company window appears. Click on the radio button next to *A New Company*. The Location field shown in this book indicates the default location where drive C is used to install Peachtree. Your Location field may differ. *Make sure that the Location field ends in* **youinc**. (If your location field does not end in "c" select An Existing Company, then click **Browse**. Double-click Youngblood, Inc. (*or*, 21-4MPXX). Your Location field shows the shortened company name youinc. Continue with step 8.)

8. Click **Next >**. The Restore Options window appears.

9. Make sure that the box next to Company Data is *checked*. Click **Next >**.

10. The Confirmation window appears. Check the From and To fields to make sure they are correct. Click **Finish**. When the Restore Company scale is 100% complete, your data is restored and you are returned to the menu bar.

CHANGING THE COMPANY NAME

Before you start recording transactions for the 21-4 Mastery Problem, you should look at the company information included on the 21-4MP.ptb file. Follow these steps to look at company information.

1. The Youngblood, Inc. menu bar should be displayed. From the menu bar, click on Maintain; Company Information. The Maintain Company Information window appears. Observe that the directory field shows where your company is stored on your computer: C:\Program Files\Peachtree\ company\youinc.

2. Type **21-4MPXX** in the Company Name field.

3. When you are finished typing 21-4MPXX as the company name, click on **OK**. Once you have changed the Company Name, each one of your printouts will show the problem number and your initials.

Nothing has changed on your computer's hard drive. The company you restored is identified in the program folder and data folder as C:\Program Files\Peachtree\company\youinc. What you've done is changed the company name so that your printouts will show the problem number and your initials. Using Maintain, Company Information to rename your company does *not* change the shortened company name.

Youngblood, Inc. completed the following transactions related to notes receivable and notes payable during 2005 and 2006. The first two transactions have already been journalized and posted and are included on the 21-4MP.ptb file. One note receivable and one note payable are the only notes on hand at the end of the fiscal period. Source documents are abbreviated as follows: receipt, R; check, C; note receivable, NR.

Transactions:

2005

Nov.	11	Accepted a 90-day, 12% note from Centre Plaza for an extension of time on their account, $900.00. NR10.
Dec.	6	Signed a 120-day, 8% note, $7,200.00 with First American Bank. R336.

2006

Feb.	6	Received cash for the maturity value of NR10. R336.
Apr.	5	Paid cash for the maturity value of the First American Bank note. C612.

Instructions:

1. Journalize and post the adjusting entries for accrued interest income and accrued expense on December 31, 2005. (*Hint:* To plan the adjustments, you may want to use a blank piece of paper or the work sheet in the *Working Papers.*)
2. Journalize and post the closing entries for interest income and interest expense.
3. Journalize and post the reversing entries for accrued interest income and accrued interest expense.
4. Journalize and post the receipt of cash for the maturity value of NR10.
5. Journalize the cash payment for the maturity value of the note payable.
6. Print the December 31, 2005 to January 1, 2006 general journal.
7. Print the February 9, 2006 cash receipts journal.
8. Print the April 5, 2006 cash disbursements journal.
9. Print the general ledger from December 1, 2005 to April 30, 2006.
10. Back up. The suggested file name is 21-4 Mastery Problem.ptb.

You have completed the work for the 21-4 Mastery Problem: Journalizing and Posting Entries for Accrued Interest Revenue and Expense.

Journalizing and Posting Entries for Accrued Interest Revenue and Expenses

The instructions that follow show you how to do the following:

- Start Peachtree Complete Accounting.
- Restore starting data from the South-Western Accounting with Peachtree CD.
- Journalize and post transactions.
- Print the general journal, cash receipts journal, cash disbursements journal, and general ledger.
- Complete 21-5 Challenge Problem.

GETTING STARTED

Use the following instructions to start Peachtree and restore the starting data for Blackwell Corporation. The South-Western Accounting with Peachtree CD includes a Peachtree data files folder. In the steps that follow you will restore the 21-5CP.ptb file.

1. Start Peachtree. From the startup menu, select Close.
2. The menu bar shows three options: Files; Options; and Help. Click File; Restore.
3. The Restore Wizard - Select Backup File window appears. Observe that the Location field shows where Peachtree is stored on your computer. The default location is C:\Program Files\Peachtree\Company. Your Location field may differ. If you are restoring from a network drive, you will need to know the location of the 21-5CP.ptb file.
4. Click Browse. The Open Backup File window appears. In the Look in field, double-click on the appropriate location of the Peachtree data files. Then, click 21-5CP.ptb to select it. (If appropriate, select your CD drive then double-click the Peachtree Files-Unit 1 folder. Click 21-5CP.ptb to select it.)
5. Make sure the 21-5CP.ptb file is selected. Click Open.

6. The Select Backup File window appears. Make sure the Location field shows the correct location for the 21-5CP.ptb file; for example, X:\Peachtree Files-Unit 1\21-5CP.ptb. (Substitute the correct drive letter for X.)

7. Click [Next >]. The Select Company window appears. Click on the radio button next to *A New Company*. The Location field shown in this book indicates the default location where drive C is used to install Peachtree. Your Location field may differ. *Make sure that the Location field ends in* **blacorpo**. (If your location field does not end in "o" select An Existing Company, then click [Browse]. Double-click Blackwell Corporation (*or*, 21-5CPXX). Your Location field shows the shortened company name blacorpo. Continue with step 8.)

8. Click [Next >]. The Restore Options window appears.

9. Make sure that the box next to Company Data is *checked*. Click [Next >].

10. The Confirmation window appears. Check the From and To fields to make sure they are correct. Click [Finish]. When the Restore Company scale is 100% complete, your data is restored and you are returned to the menu bar.

CHANGING THE COMPANY NAME

Before you start recording transactions for the 21-5 Challenge Problem, you should look at the company information included on the 21-5CP.ptb file. Follow these steps to look at company information.

1. The Blackwell Corporation menu bar should be displayed. From the menu bar, click on Maintain; Company Information. The Maintain Company Information window appears. Observe that the directory field shows where your company is stored on your computer: C:\Program Files\Peachtree\ company\blacorpo.

2. Type **21-5CPXX** in the Company Name field.

3. When you are finished typing 21-5CPXX as the company name, click on [OK]. Once you have changed the Company Name, each one of your printouts will show the problem number and your initials.

Nothing has changed on your computer's hard drive. The company you restored is identified in the program folder and data folder as C:\Program Files\Peachtree\company\blacorpo. What you've done is changed the company name so that your printouts will show the problem number and your initials. Using Maintain, Company Information to rename your company does *not* change the shortened company name.

Blackwell Corporation completed the following transactions related to notes receivable and notes payable during the 2005 and 2006. The first two transactions have already been journalized and posted and are included on the 21-5CP.ptb file. These notes are the only ones outstanding on December 31, 2005, the fiscal year-end.

Transactions:

2005

Dec.	8	Margaret Snider signed a 90-day, 18% note for an extension of time on their account, $900.00. NR56.
	15	Signed a 180-day, 12% note, with American National Bank, $10,000.00. R416.

2006

Mar.	8	Margaret Snider dishonored NR56, maturity value due today. M98.
	12	Paid off the American National Bank note ahead of the maturity date. American National charges interest only for the number of days the note is outstanding, with no early payment penalty. C645.

Instructions:

1. Journalize and post the adjusting entries for accrue, close, and reverse interest-related accounts at the fiscal year-end. (*Hint:* To plan the adjustments, you may want to use a blank piece of paper or the work sheet in the *Working Papers.*)
2. Journalize and post the 2006 transactions.
3. Print the December 31, 2005 to January 1, 2006 general journal.
4. Print the March 8, 2006 cash receipts journal.
5. Print the March 12, 2006 cash disbursements journal.
6. Print the general ledger from December 1, 2005 to March 31, 2006.
7. Back up. The suggested file name is 21-5 Challenge Problem.ptb.

You have completed the work for the 21-5 Challenge Problem: Journalizing and Posting Entries for Accrued Interest Revenue and Expenses.

Preparing a Work Sheet, Financial Statements, and End-of-Fiscal-Period Entries for a Corporation

The instructions that follow show you how to do the following:

- Start Peachtree Complete Accounting.
- Restore starting data from the South-Western Accounting with Peachtree CD.
- Journalize and post adjusting, closing, and reversing entries.
- Print the financial statements.
- Print the general journal.
- Complete 22-5 Mastery Problem.

GETTING STARTED

Use the following instructions to start Peachtree and restore the starting data for Benford Corporation. The South-Western Accounting with Peachtree CD includes a Peachtree data files folder. In the steps that follow you will restore the 22-5MP.ptb file.

1. Start Peachtree. From the startup menu, select Close.

2. The menu bar shows three options: Files; Options; and Help. Click File; Restore.

3. The Restore Wizard - Select Backup File window appears. Observe that the Location field shows where Peachtree is stored on your computer. The default location is C:\Program Files\Peachtree\Company. Your Location field may differ. If you are restoring from a network drive, you will need to know the location of the 22-5MP.ptb file.

4. Click Browse. The Open Backup File window appears. In the Look in field, double-click on the appropriate location of the Peachtree data files. Then, click 22-5MP.ptb to select it. (If appropriate, select your CD drive then double-click the Peachtree Files-Unit 1 folder. Click 22-5MP.ptb to select it.)

5. Make sure the 22-5MP.ptb file is selected. Click Open.

6. The Select Backup File window appears. Make sure the Location field shows the correct location for the 22-5MP.ptb file; for example, X:\Peachtree Files-Unit 1\22-5MP.ptb. (Substitute the correct drive letter for X.)

7. Click **Next >**. The Select Company window appears. Click on the radio button next to *A New Company*. The Location field shown in this book indicates the default location where drive C is used to install Peachtree. Your Location field may differ. *Make sure that the Location field ends in* **bencorpo**. (If your location field does not end in "o" select An Existing Company, then click **Browse**. Double-click Benford Corporation (*or*, 22-5MPXX). Your Location field shows the shortened company name bencorpo. Continue with step 8.)

8. Click **Next >**. The Restore Options window appears.

9. Make sure that the box next to Company Data is *checked*. Click **Next >**.

10. The Confirmation window appears. Check the From and To fields to make sure they are correct. Click **Finish**. When the Restore Company scale is 100% complete, your data is restored and you are returned to the menu bar.

CHANGING THE COMPANY NAME

Before you start recording transactions for the 22-5 Mastery Problem, you should look at the company information included on the 22-5MP.ptb file. Follow these steps to look at company information.

1. The Benford Corporation menu bar should be displayed. From the menu bar, click on Maintain; Company Information. The Maintain Company Information window appears. Observe that the directory field shows where your company is stored on your computer: C:\Program Files\Peachtree\company\bencorpo.

2. Type **22-5MPXX** in the Company Name field.

3. When you are finished typing 22-5MPXX as the company name, click on **OK**. Once you have changed the Company Name, each one of your printouts will show the problem number and your initials.

Nothing has changed on your computer's hard drive. The company you restored is identified in the program folder and data folder as C:\Program Files\Peachtree\company\bencorpo. What you've done is changed the company name so that your printouts will show the problem number and your initials. Using Maintain, Company Information to rename your company does *not* change the shortened company name.

Benford Corporation completed the following transactions related to notes receivable and notes payable during the December 2005 and January 2006.

Instructions:

Display Benford Corporation's general ledger trial balance. This is the unadjusted trial balance. Journalize and post adjusting entries using the following information. Label the adjusting entries a. through i.

Adjustment Information, December 31, 2005

Accrued interest income	$80.00
Uncollectible accounts expenses estimated as 0.6% of sales on account.	
Sales on account for year, $945,000.00.	
Merchandise inventory	283,028.08
Supplies inventory	998.99
Value of prepaid insurance	2,000.00
Annual depreciation expense—office equipment	5,480.00
Annual depreciation expense—store equipment	5,060.00
Accrued interest expense	312.50
Federal income tax	3,522.81

1. Journalize and post the adjusting entries.

2. Print an income statement. Use a blank piece of paper or the *Working Papers* to calculate and record the following component percentages: (a) cost of merchandise sold; (b) gross profit on operations; (c) total operating expenses; (d) income from operations; (e) net addition or deduction resulting from other revenue and expenses; and (f) net income before federal income tax. (*Hint:* Peachtree includes federal income tax as an expense account. Complete (f) manually.) Round percentages to the nearest 0.1%. Peachtree's income statement does *not* report Merchandise Inventory which is an asset account and is reported on the balance sheet.)

3. Analyze the corporation's income statement by determining if component percentages are within acceptable levels. If any component percentage is not within an acceptable level, suggest steps that the company should take. The corporation considers the following component percentages acceptable.

Cost of merchandise sold	Not more than 70.0%
Gross profit on operations	Not less than 30.0%
Total operating expenses	Not more than 25.0%
Income from operations	Not less than 5.0%
Net deduction from other revenue and expenses	Not more than 0.1%
Net income before federal income tax	Not less than 4.9%

4. Print a statement of retained earnings. Make any needed changes to Peachtree's report. Use the following additional information.

January 2 balance of capital stock account	$140,000.00
(14,000 shares issued for $10.00 per share)	
Shares issued during the year	1,000 shares

5. Print a balance sheet.

6. On a blank piece of paper or in the *Working Papers,* calculate the corporation's (a) working capital and (b) current ratio. Determine if these items are within acceptable levels. The corporation considers the following levels acceptable.

Working capital	Not less than $150,000.00
Current ratio	Between 3.0 to 1 and 4.0 to 1

7. Back up. The suggested file name is 22-5 Mastery Problem.adjusted.ptb.

8. Journalize and post the closing entries.

9. Back up. The suggested file name is 22-5 Mastery Problem.closed.ptb.

10. Journalize and post the reversing entries. (There is no need to change accounting periods.)

11. Print the December 31, 2005 to January 1, 2006 general journal.

12. Back up. The suggested file name is 22-5 Mastery Problem.ptb.

You have completed the work for the 22-5 Mastery Problem: Preparing a Work Sheet, Financial Statements, and End-of-Fiscal-Period Entries for a Corporation.

An Accounting Cycle for a Corporation: End-of-Fiscal-Period Work

The instructions that follow show you how to do the following:

- Start Peachtree Complete Accounting.
- Restore data from Reinforcement Activity 3—Part A, Sparkle, Inc., to complete Part B.
- Complete Reinforcement Activity 3—Part B.

You *must* complete Reinforcement Activity 3—Part A on pages 174–180, *before* starting Reinforcement Activity 3—Part B.

GETTING STARTED

Follow these instructions to restore data from Reinforcement Activity 3—Part B.

1. Start Peachtree.
2. At the startup menu, select <u>O</u>pen an existing company. From the Open list, select Sparkle, Inc. If Sparkle, Inc. is *not* listed, click on Browse. Select Sparkle, Inc. from the Company Name list.

What if Sparkle, Inc. is not listed on either the Open list or when I select Browse?

1. Use Windows Explorer to see if you have a program and data path identified as C:\Peachw\spainc. Close Windows Explorer.

2. From Peachtree's Open list, select Sparkle, Inc. It may be identified by RA03-AXX. The X's stand for a student's initials.

3. Restore the backup file made on page 180. The suggested file name was Reinforcement Activity 3-Part A.ptb. Once you restore the backup file that you made on page 180, you will be able to start where you left off the last time you worked with Sparkle, Inc.

If you have checked Windows Explorer and Sparkle, Inc. does *not* have a folder (\spainc), do the following.

1. Start Peachtree. At the startup menu, click Close.

2. The File, Options, Help menu bar appears. Select File; Restore.

3. Using the Restore Wizard, select the appropriate location of the backup file that was made on page 180 (Reinforcement Activity 3-Part A.ptb), then restore A New Company. Peachtree will restore your backup data and create the company at the same time.

3. From Peachtree's menu bar, click on File; Restore.

4. Check the Location field to make sure you are restoring the correct file. Click Next >.

5. The Select Company window defaults to An Existing Company. The Company Name field shows Sparkle, Inc.. The Location field shows C:\Program Files\Peachtree\company\spainc. Click Next >.

6. The Restore Options window appears. Make sure that the box next to Company Data is *checked*. Click Next >.

7. The Confirmation window appears. Observe that the Company Name is Sparkle, Inc.. Check the From and To fields to make sure they are correct. Click Finish. When the Restore Company scale is 100% complete, your data is restored and you are returned to the menu bar.

8. If necessary, remove the external media. You can now continue with Reinforcement Activity 3—Part B.

CHANGING THE COMPANY NAME

In order to make sure that each one of your printouts shows your name and problem number, follow these steps to change the name of the company.

1. From Peachtree's menu bar, select Maintain, then Company Information.

2. The Maintain Company Information screen appears. In the Company Name field, type **RA03-BXX**. Replace the X's with your initials.

3. When you are finished typing RA03-BXX as the company name, click OK. Once you have changed the Company Name, each one of your printouts will show the problem number and your initials.

Nothing has changed on your computer's hard drive. The company you restored is identified in the program folder and data folder as C:\Peachw\spainc. What you've done is change the company name so that your printouts will show the problem number and your initials. Using Maintain, Company Information to rename your company does *not* change the file name of the company folder.

Instructions:

1. After restoring the backup that you made at the end of Reinforcement Activity 3—Part A, print the general ledger trial balance. This is the unadjusted trial balance. Compare it to the one shown below. If you completed the worksheet in the *Working Papers*, compare this trial balance to the one on your worksheet.

Sparkle, Inc.
General Ledger Trial Balance
As of Dec 31, 2005

Filter Criteria includes: Report order is by ID. Report is printed in Detail Format.

Account ID	Account Description	Debit Amt	Credit Amt
1105	Cash	8,100.70	
1110	Petty Cash	200.00	
1115	Notes Receivable	3,600.00	
1125	Accounts Receivable	7,894.60	
1130	Allow. for Uncoll. Accts.	1,469.40	
1135	Merchandise Inventory	74,176.95	
1140	Supplies	3,099.05	
1145	Prepaid Insurance	8,600.00	
1205	Office Equipment	23,830.00	
1210	Acc. Depr.-Office Equipment		7,160.00
1215	Warehouse Equipment	26,110.00	
1220	Acc. Depr.-Warehouse Equipment		7,040.00
2105	Notes Payable		16,000.00
2115	Accounts Payable		14,112.65
2125	Empl. Inc. Tax Payable		310.00
2130	Soc. Security Tax Payable		691.92
2135	Medicare Tax Payable		161.82
2140	Sales Tax Payable		6,210.66
2145	Unempl. Tax Payable-Federal		21.53
2150	Unempl. Tax Payable-State		145.29
2155	Health Ins. Prem. Payable		1,105.00
2160	Dividends Payable		5,000.00
3105	Capital Stock		30,000.00
3110	Retained Earnings		23,889.20
3115	Dividends	20,000.00	
4105	Sales		779,210.90
4110	Sales Discount	1,889.20	
4115	Sales Returns & Allow.	6,174.80	
4200	Gain on Plant Assets		745.00
4210	Interest Income		414.00
5105	Purchases	529,022.40	
5110	Purchases Discount		3,596.08
5115	Purch. Returns & Allow.		3,236.00
6105	Advertising Expense	9,606.70	
6110	Cash Short and Over	20.09	
6115	Credit Card Fee Expense	14,529.40	
6120	Depr. Exp.-Office Equipment	240.00	
6125	Depr. Exp.-Warehouse Equipment	440.00	
6135	Miscellaneous Expense	5,828.32	
6140	Payroll Taxes Expense	10,669.44	
6145	Rent Expense	21,000.00	
6150	Repairs Expense	1,394.80	
6155	Salary Expense	104,878.00	
6170	Utilities Expense	7,236.20	
8105	Interest Expense	2,750.00	
8110	Loss on Plant Assets	290.00	
9105	Federal Income Tax Expense	6,000.00	
	Total:	**899,050.05**	**899,050.05**

2. On a blank piece of paper or in the *Working Papers,* record the 2005 depreciation on the plan asset record of plant asset no. 998.

3. Journalize and post the following adjustment information.

Adjustment Information, December 31, 2005

a.	Outstanding notes receivable consist of NR34, a 90-day, 10% note accepted from Nelson Co. on December 7, 2005, for an extension of time on its account, $3,600.	
b.	Uncollectible account expense is estimated as 4.0% of sales on account. Sales on account for the year, $90,000.	
c.	Merchandise inventory	$80,491.95
d.	Supplies inventory	425.05
e.	Value of prepaid insurance	600.00
f.	Estimate of office equipment depreciation	6,520.00
g.	Estimate of warehouse equipment depreciation	4,210.00
h.	Outstanding notes payable consist of (1) NP32, a 90-day, 12% note for $10,000.00 signed on November 16, 2005, and (2) NP33, a 90-day, 10% note for $6,000.00 signed on December 28, 2005.	
i.	Federal income tax	2,103.16

4. Print the income statement. On a blank piece of paper or in the *Working Papers,* calculate the following component percentages: (a) cost of merchandise sold, (b) gross profit on operations, (c) total operating expenses; and (d) net income from operations; (3) net additional or deduction resulting from other revenue and expenses; and (f) net income before federal income tax. Round percentage calculations to the nearest 0.1%.

Use the information on Peachtree's income statement, and the adjustment information above, to determine the component percentages. You will need to rework Peachtree's income statement to match the income statement prepared in the *Working Papers.* Remember, Peachtree does *not* include the merchandise inventory adjustment on the income statement nor does it separately report Other Revenue, Other Expenses, and Net Income before Federal Income Tax.

5. On a blank piece of paper or in the *Working Papers,* analyze the corporation's income statement by determining if the component percentages are within acceptable levels. If any component percentage is not within an acceptable level, suggest steps that the company should take. The corporation considers the following component percentages acceptable:

Cost of merchandise sold: Not more than 62.0%
Gross profit on operations: Not less than 38.0%
Total operating expenses: Not more than 28.0%
Income from operations: Not less than 10.0%
Net deduction from other revenue and expenses: Not more than 0.5%
Net income before federal income tax: Not less than 9.5%

6. On a blank piece of paper or in the *Working Papers*, calculate the earnings per share and price-earnings ratio. Current market price is $225.00.

7. Print the statement of retained earnings. The company had 3,000 shares of $10.00 par value stock outstanding on January 1. The company did not issue any additional shares during the year. (*Hint:* Peachtree's statement of retained earnings does *not* show the capital stock balance on December 31. Once you factor that in, Peachtree's statement of retained earnings will be in agreement with the manually prepared statement of stockholders' equity in the *Working Papers*.)

8. Print the balance sheet.

9. Back up. The suggested file name is Reinforcement Problem 3-Part B.adjusted.ptb.

10. Journalize and post the closing entries.

11. Print the post-closing trial balance.

12. Back up. The suggested file name is Reinforcement Problem 3-Part B.closed.ptb.

13. Journalize and post the reversing entries. (*Hint:* There is no need to change accounting periods.)

14. Print the December 31, 2005 to January 1, 2006 general journal.

15. Print the December 1 to January 31, 2006 general ledger.

16. Backup your work. The suggested file name is Reinforcement Activity 3-Part B.reversed.ptb.

You have completed the work for Reinforcement Activity 3—Part B: An Accounting Cycle for a Corporation: End-of-Fiscal-Period Work.

Recording International and Internet Sales

The instructions that follow show you how to do the following:

- Start Peachtree Complete Accounting.
- Restore starting data from the South-Western Accounting with Peachtree CD.
- Journalize and post transactions.
- Print the general journal and cash receipts journal.
- Complete the 24-3 Mastery Problem.

GETTING STARTED

Use the following instructions to start Peachtree and restore the starting data for Argo Corporation. The South-Western Accounting with Peachtree CD includes a Peachtree data files folder. In the steps that follow you will restore the 24-3MP.ptb file.

1. Start Peachtree. From the startup menu, select **Close**.
2. The menu bar shows three options: Files; Options; and Help. Click File; Restore.
3. The Restore Wizard - Select Backup File window appears. Observe that the Location field shows where Peachtree is stored on your computer. The default location is C:\Program Files\Peachtree\ Company. Your Location field may differ. If you are restoring from a network drive, you will need to know the location of the 24-3MP.ptb file.
4. Click **Browse**. The Open Backup File window appears. In the Look in field, double-click on the appropriate location of the Peachtree data files. Then, click 24-3MP.ptb to select it. (If appropriate, select your CD drive then double-click the Peachtree Files-Unit 1 folder. Click 24-3MP.ptb to select it.)
5. Make sure the 24-3MP.ptb file is selected. Click **Open**.

6. The Select Backup File window appears. Make sure the Location field shows the correct location for the 24-3MP.ptb file; for example, X:\Peachtree Files-Unit 1\24-3MP.ptb. (Substitute the correct drive letter for X.)

7. Click Next> . The Select Company window appears. Click on the radio button next to *A New Company*. The Location field shown in this book indicates the default location where drive C is used to install Peachtree. Your Location field may differ. *Make sure that the Location field ends in* **argcorpo**. (If your location field does not end in "o" select An Existing Company, then click Browse . Double-click Argo Corporation (*or*, 24-3MPXX). Your Location field shows the shortened company name argcorpo. Continue with step 8.)

8. Click Next> . The Restore Options window appears.

9. Make sure that the box next to Company Data is *checked*. Click Next> .

10. The Confirmation window appears. Check the From and To fields to make sure they are correct. Click Finish . When the Restore Company scale is 100% complete, your data is restored and you are returned to the menu bar.

CHANGING THE COMPANY NAME

Before you start recording transactions for the 24-3 Mastery Problem, you should look at the company information included on the 24-3MP.ptb file. Follow these steps to look at company information.

1. The Argo Corporation menu bar should be displayed. From the menu bar, click on Maintain; Company Information. The Maintain Company Information window appears. Observe that the directory field shows where your company is stored on your computer: C:\Program Files\Peachtree\company\argcorpo.

2. Type **24-3MPXX** in the Company Name field.

3. When you are finished typing 24-3MPXX as the company name, click on OK . Once you have changed the Company Name, each one of your printouts will show the problem number and your initials.

Nothing has changed on your computer's hard drive. The company you restored is identified in the program folder and data folder as C:\Program Files\Peachtree\company\argcorpo. What you've done is changed the company name so that your printouts will show the problem number and your initials. Using Maintain, Company Information to rename your company does *not* change the shortened company name.

Argo Corporation has both international and Internet sales.

Instructions:

Journalize and post the following transactions affecting sales and cash receipts completed during February 2005. Use the general journal and cash receipts journal for recording transactions. (*Hint:* Cash receipts journal transactions involve cash.)

Transactions:

Feb.	5	Received a 30-day time draft from Akeo Doi for an internation sales, $5,000.00. TD10.
	8	Recorded Internet credit card sales, $12,300.00. TS23.
	12	Recorded an international cash sale, $10,500.00. M8.
	14	Received cash for the value of Time Draft No. 4, $23,000.00. R35.
	18	Recorded Internet credit card sales, $18,400.00. TS24.
	21	Received cash for the value of Time Draft No. 7, $8,000.00. R37.
	24	Recorded an internal cash sale, $13,500.00. M12.
	27	Recorded Internet credit card sales, $9,200.00. TS25.
	28	Received a 30-day time draft from Sachi Nozaki for international sale of merchandise, $6,000.00. TD11.

1. Journalize and post the transactions in the appropriate journal.
2. Print the general journal and cash receipts journal.
3. Back up. The suggested file name is 24-3 Mastery Problem.ptb.

You have completed the work for the 24-3 Mastery Problem: Recording International and Internet Sales.

UNIT 2

South-Western Century 21
Accounting Advanced

The problem material in Unit 2 of *South-Western Accounting with Peachtree Complete 2005* is from the *Advanced South-Western Century 21 Accounting, Eighth Edition*, textbook. The Unit 2 problems cover Chapters 1 through 4; 6 through 13; and 20 through 24 of the *Advanced Century 21 Accounting 8e* textbook. The instructions and transactions for each problem are included in this book.

Journalizing and Posting Departmental Purchases on Account and Purchases Returns and Allowances

The instructions that follow show you how to do the following:

- Start Peachtree Complete Accounting.
- Restore starting data from the South-Western Accounting with Peachtree CD.
- Complete journal entries for October 2005.
- Print the purchase journal, general ledger, and vendor ledgers.
- Complete the 1-2 Application Problem.

Before you start the 1-2 Application Problem, ask your instructor if Zenix Communications, the company used for the 1-2 Application Problem has already been restored on your computer. The instructions that follow assume that Zenix Communications is being used for the first time.

GETTING STARTED

Use the following instructions to start Peachtree and restore the starting data for the 1-2 Application Problem. The South-Western Accounting with Peachtree CD includes a folder called Peachtree Files-Unit 2. In the steps that follow you will restore the 01-2AP.ptb file.

1. Start Peachtree. From the startup menu, select `Close`.
2. The menu bar shows three options: Files; Options; and Help. Click File; Restore.
3. The Restore Wizard - Select Backup File window appears. Observe that the Location field shows where Peachtree is stored on your computer. The default location is C:\Program Files\Peachtree\Company. Your Location field may differ. If you are restoring from

a network drive, you will need to know the location of the 01-2AP.ptb file.

4. Click [Browse]. The Open Backup File window appears. In the Look in field, double-click on the appropriate location of the Peachtree Files-Unit 2 folder. Then, click 01-2AP.ptb to select it. (If appropriate, select your CD drive then double-click the Peachtree Files-Unit 2 folder. Click 01-2AP.ptb to select it.)

5. Make sure the 01-2AP.ptb file is selected. (*Hint:* Starting data for the 1-2 Application Problem is in the Peachtree Files-Unit 2 folder.) Click [Open].

6. The Select Backup File window appears. Make sure the Location field shows the correct location for the 01-2AP.ptb file; for example, X:\Peachtree Files-Unit 2\01-2AP.ptb. (Substitute the correct drive letter for X.)

7. Click [Next >]. The Select Company window appears. Click on the radio button next to *A New Company*. The Location field shown in this book indicates the default location where drive C is used to install Peachtree. Your Location field may differ. *Make sure that the Location field ends in* **zencommu**. (If your location field does not end in "u," select An Existing Company, then click [Browse]. Double-click Zenix Communications (*or*, 01-2APXX). Your Location field shows the shortened company name zencommu. Continue with step 8.)

8. Click [Next >]. The Restore Options window appears.

9. Make sure that the box next to Company Data is *checked*. Click [Next >].

10. The Confirmation window appears. Check the From and To fields to make sure they are correct. Click [Finish]. When the Restore Company scale is 100% complete, your data is restored and you are returned to the menu bar.

CHANGING THE COMPANY NAME

Before you start recording transactions for the 1-2 Application Problem, you should look at the company information included on the 01-2AP.ptb file. Follow these steps to look at company information.

1. The Zenix Communications menu bar should be displayed. From the menu bar, click on Maintain; Company Information. The Maintain Company Information window appears. Observe that the directory field shows where your company is stored on your computer: C:\Program Files\Peachtree\company\zencommu.

2. Type **01-2APXX** in the Company Name field.

3. When you are finished typing 01-2APXX as the company name, click on [OK]. Once you have changed the Company Name, each one of your printouts will show the activity number and your initials.

Nothing has changed on your computer's hard drive. The company you restored is identified in the program folder and data folder as C:\Program Files\Peachtree\company\zencommu. What you've done is change the company name so that your printouts will show the activity number and your initials. Using Maintain, Company Information to rename your company does *not* change the shortened company name.

Transactions:

Zenix Communications has two departments: Cellular Phones and Pagers. The vendor ledgers and accounts payable account is shown below. This data is included on the 01-2AP.ptb file. Source documents are abbreviated as follows: debit memorandum, DM; purchase invoice, P.

To see vendor account balances, display Peachtree's vendor ledgers (Reports; Accounts Payable, Vendor Ledgers). Then, display the accounts payable account (Reports; General Ledger, General Ledger, Preview Account No. 2105).

Vendor Ledgers

Zenix Communications
Vendor Ledgers
For the Period From Oct 1, 2005 to Oct 31, 2005

Filter Criteria includes: Report order is by ID.

Vendor ID Vendor	Date	Trans No	Type	Paid	Debit Amt	Credit Amt	Balance
210 Car Phone Wholesalers	10/1/05	Balance Fwd					650.00
220 Cell Advantage, Inc.							0.00
230 ComSystems	10/1/05	Balance Fwd					430.00
240 ExecuPhone							0.00
250 PageMax, Inc.							0.00
260 Phone Solutions	10/1/05	Balance Fwd					850.00
270 Telecom Corporation							0.00
280 Western Distributers	10/1/05	Balance Fwd					705.00

The total of the vendor balances agrees with the ending balance in Account No. 2105, Accounts Payable: $650 + 430 + 850 + 705 = $2,635.

General Ledger Account No. 2105, Accounts Payable

Zenix Communications
General Ledger
For the Period From Oct 1, 2005 to Oct 31, 2005

Filter Criteria includes: 1) IDs from 2105 to 2105. Report order is by ID. Report is printed with Truncated Transaction Descriptions and in Detail Format.

Account ID Account Description	Date	Reference	Jrnl	Trans Description	Debit Amt	Credit Amt	Balance
2105	10/1/05			Beginning Balance			
Accounts Payable	10/1/05	BEGBAL	GEN			2,635.00	
				Current Period Cha		2,635.00	-2,635.00
	10/31/05			**Ending Balance**			**-2,635.00**

Transactions:

Oct.	1	Purchased phones on account from CarPhone Wholesalers, $1,270.00. P183.
	2	Purchased pagers on account from PageMax, Inc., $970.00. P184.
	5	Purchased phones on account from ExecuPhone, $2,100.00. P185.
	6	The order from Western Distributors contained 5 defective pagers. Returned pagers, $205.00, from P180. DM40.
	9	Purchased pagers on account from Cell Advantage, Inc., $945.00. P186.
	13	Purchased pagers on account from ComSystems, $2,240.00. P187.
	17	Returned phones to CarPhone Wholesalers, $120.00, from P183. DM41.
	19	Purchased phones on account from Telecom Corporation, $450.00. P188.
	20	Returned pagers to PageMax, Inc., $90.00, from P184. DM42.
	23	Issued P189 to purchase phones on account from ExecuPhone, $1,003.00.
	30	Returned $75.00 of phones to Phone Solution, from P181. DM43.

Instructions:

1. Journalize and post the transactions completed during October 2005. (*Hint:* Use Peachtree's Purchases/Receive Inventory task for *both* purchase transactions and returns. For purchase returns, refer to the 9-6 Mastery Problem, pages 70 and 71, Purchase Returns: Vendor Credit Memos.)
2. Print the purchase journal.

3. Print the following general ledger accounts: accounts payable, pur-
   chases-cellular phone; purchases returns and allowances-cellular
   phones; purchases-pagers; purchases returns and allowances-
   pagers.
4. Print the vendor ledgers.
5. Back up. The suggested file name is 1-2 Application Problem.ptb.

Journalizing Departmental Purchases and Cash Payments

The instructions that follow show you how to do the following:

- Start Peachtree Complete Accounting.
- Restore starting data from the South-Western Accounting with Peachtree CD.
- Complete journal entries for April 2005.
- Print the purchase journal, cash disbursements journal and general journal.
- Complete the 1-4 Mastery Problem.

Before you start the 1-4 Mastery Problem, ask your instructor if Outdoor Sport, the company used for the 1-4 Mastery Problem has already been restored on your computer. The instructions that follow assume that Outdoor Sport is being used for the first time.

GETTING STARTED

Use the following instructions to start Peachtree and restore the starting data for the 1-4 Mastery Problem. The South-Western Accounting with Peachtree CD includes a folder called Peachtree Files-Unit 2. In the steps that follow you will restore the 01-4MP.ptb file.

1. Start Peachtree. From the startup menu, select Close .
2. The menu bar shows three options: Files; Options; and Help. Click File; Restore.
3. The Restore Wizard - Select Backup File window appears. Observe that the Location field shows where Peachtree is stored on your computer. The default location is C:\Program Files\Peachtree\Company. Your Location field may differ. If you are restoring from a network drive, you will need to know the location of the 01-4MP.ptb file.
4. Click Browse . The Open Backup File window appears. In the Look in field, double-click on the appropriate location of the Peachtree Files-Unit 2 folder. Then, click 01-4MP.ptb to select it. (If

appropriate, select your CD drive then double-click the Peachtree Files-Unit 2 folder. Click 01-4MP.ptb to select it.)

5. Make sure the 01-4MP.ptb file is selected. (*Hint:* Starting data for the 1-4 Mastery Problem is in the Peachtree Files-Unit 2 folder.) Click Open .

6. The Select Backup File window appears. Make sure the Location field shows the correct location for the 01-4MP.ptb file; for example, X:\Peachtree Files-Unit 2\01-4MP.ptb. (Substitute the correct drive letter for X.)

7. Click Next> . The Select Company window appears. Click on the radio button next to *A New Company*. The Location field shown in this book indicates the default location where drive C is used to install Peachtree. Your Location field may differ. *Make sure that the Location field ends in* **outsport**. (If your location field does not end in "t," select An Existing Company, then click Browse . Double-click Outdoor Sport (*or*, 01-4MPXX). Your Location field shows the shortened company name outsport. Continue with step 8.)

8. Click Next> . The Restore Options window appears.

9. Make sure that the box next to Company Data is *checked*. Click Next> .

10. The Confirmation window appears. Check the From and To fields to make sure they are correct. Click Finish . When the Restore Company scale is 100% complete, your data is restored and you are returned to the menu bar.

CHANGING THE COMPANY NAME

Before you start recording transactions for the 1-4 Mastery Problem, you should look at the company information included on the 01-4MP.ptb file. Follow these steps to look at company information.

1. The Outdoor Sport menu bar should be displayed. From the menu bar, click on Maintain; Company Information. The Maintain Company Information window appears. Observe that the directory field shows where your company is stored on your computer: C:\Program Files\Peachtree\company\outsport.

2. Type **01-4MPXX** in the Company Name field.

3. When you are finished typing 01-4MPXX as the company name, click on OK . Once you have changed the Company Name, each one of your printouts will show the activity number and your initials.

Nothing has changed on your computer's hard drive. The company you restored is identified in the program folder and data folder as C:\Program Files\Peachtree\company\outsport. What you've done is change the company name so that your printouts will show the activity number and your initials. Using Maintain, Company Information to rename your company does *not* change the shortened company name.

Outdoor Sport has two departments: Backpacks and Accessories. Source documents are abbreviated as follows: debit memorandum, DM; purchase invoice, P.

Transactions:

Apr. 1 Paid cash for advertising, $95.00. C273.

1 Paid cash for rent, $1,250.00. C274.

2 Purchased accessories on account from CampWorld Supplies, $800.00. P262.

3 Paid cash on account to PackGear covering P259 for backpacks for $500.00, less 2% discount. C275.

3 Purchased backpacks on account from SierraPack, $840.00. P263.

5 Paid cash on account to CampWorld Supplies covering P261 for accessories for $645.00, less 2% discount. C276.

7 Returned backpacks to SierraPack, $88.00, from P263. DM28.

10 Purchased backpacks on account from TahoeDesigns, $388.00. P264.

11 Paid cash for administrative supplies, $82.50. C277.

14 Paid cash on account to CampWorld Supplies covering P262 for accessories; no discount. C278.

16 Returned accessories to Sequoia Sporting Goods, $132.50, from P260. DM29.

17 Purchased accessories on account from CampAll, Inc., $550.00. P265.

17 Paid cash on account to TahoeDesigns covering P264 for backpacks for $388.00, less 2% discount. C279.

18 Paid cash on account to SierraPack covering P263 for backpacks for $840.00, less DM28 for $88.00; no discount. C280.

18 Returned accessories to CampAll, Inc., $75.00, from P265. DM30.

19 Purchased backpacks on account from SierraPack, $1,120.00. P266.

21 Paid cash for administrative supplies, $62.30. C281.

23 Purchased accessories on account from Sequoia Sporting Goods, $336.00. P267.

24 Paid cash on account to CampAll, Inc. covering P265 for accessories for $550.00, less DM30 for $75.00, and less 2% discount. C282.

24 Purchased backpacks on account from PackGear, $626.40. P268.

26 Paid cash on account to SierraPack covering P266 for backpacks for $1,120.00, less 2% discount. C283.

28 Paid cash for administrative supplies, $53.00. C284

30 Paid cash to replenish the petty cash fund, $221.00: administrative supplies, $57.10; advertising, $62.50; miscellaneous, $101.40. C285.

The April 5 transaction requires two entries. One in the cash disbursements journal to make the partial payment of $645. The second entry should be in the general journal for the purchase discount.

When applying discounts to vendor payments, select the appropriate Purchases Discount account.

Instructions:

1. Journalize and post the transactions completed during April 2005 in the appropriate journal.
2. Print the purchase journal.
3. Print the cash disbursements journal.
4. Print the April 5, 2005 general journal.
5. Back up. The suggested file name is 1-4 Mastery Problem.ptb.

Journalizing and Posting Departmental Sales on Account and Sales Returns and Allowances

The instructions that follow show you how to do the following:

- Start Peachtree Complete Accounting.
- Restore starting data from the South-Western Accounting with Peachtree CD.
- Complete journal entries for April 2005.
- Print the sales journal.
- Print selected general ledger accounts.
- Print the customer ledgers.
- Complete the 2-1 Application Problem.

Before you start the 2-1 Application Problem, ask your instructor if Sequoia Sport Apparel, the company used for the 2-1 Application Problem has already been restored on your computer. The instructions that follow assume that Sequoia Sport Apparel is being used for the first time.

GETTING STARTED

Use the following instructions to start Peachtree and restore the starting data for the 2-1 Application Problem. The South-Western Accounting with Peachtree CD includes a folder called Peachtree Files-Unit 2. In the steps that follow you will restore the 02-1AP.ptb file.

1. Start Peachtree. From the startup menu, select Close .
2. The menu bar shows three options: Files; Options; and Help. Click File; Restore.
3. The Restore Wizard - Select Backup File window appears. Observe that the Location field shows where Peachtree is stored on your computer. The default location is C:\Program Files\Peachtree\Company. Your Location field may differ. If you are restoring from a network drive, you will need to know the location of the 02-1AP.ptb file.

4. Click **Browse**. The Open Backup File window appears. In the Look in field, double-click on the appropriate location of the Peachtree Files-Unit 2 folder. Then, click 02-1AP.ptb to select it. (If appropriate, select your CD drive then double-click the Peachtree Files-Unit 2 folder. Click 02-1AP.ptb to select it.)

5. Make sure the 02-1AP.ptb file is selected. (*Hint:* Starting data for the 2-1 Application Problem is in the Peachtree Files-Unit 2 folder.) Click **Open**.

6. The Select Backup File window appears. Make sure the Location field shows the correct location for the 02-1AP.ptb file; for example, X:\Peachtree Files-Unit 2\02-1AP.ptb. (Substitute the correct drive letter for X.)

7. Click **Next >**. The Select Company window appears. Click on the radio button next to *A New Company*. The Location field shown in this book indicates the default location where drive C is used to install Peachtree. Your Location field may differ. *Make sure that the Location field ends in* **seqspoap**. (If your location field does not end in "p" select An Existing Company, then click **Browse**. Double-click Sequoia Sport Apparel (*or*, 02-1APXX). Your Location field shows the shortened company name seqspoap. Continue with step 8.)

8. Click **Next >**. The Restore Options window appears.

9. Make sure that the box next to Company Data is *checked*. Click **Next >**.

10. The Confirmation window appears. Check the From and To fields to make sure they are correct. Click **Finish**. When the Restore Company scale is 100% complete, your data is restored and you are returned to the menu bar.

CHANGING THE COMPANY NAME

Before you start recording transactions for the 2-1 Application Problem, you should look at the company information included on the 02-1AP.ptb file. Follow these steps to look at company information.

1. The Sequoia Sport Apparel menu bar should be displayed. From the menu bar, click on Maintain; Company Information. The Maintain Company Information window appears. Observe that the directory field shows where your company is stored on your computer: C:\Program Files\Peachtree\company\seqspoap.

2. Type **02-1APXX** in the Company Name field.

3. When you are finished typing 02-1APXX as the company name, click on **OK**. Once you have changed the Company Name, each one of your printouts will show the activity number and your initials.

Nothing has changed on your computer's hard drive. The company you restored is identified in the program folder and data folder as C:\Program Files\Peachtree\company\seqspoap. What you've done is change the company name so that your printouts will show the activity number and your initials. Using Maintain, Company Information to rename your company does *not* change the shortened company name.

Transactions:

Sequoia Sport Apparel has two departments: Clothing and Shoes. Source documents are abbreviated as follows: credit memorandum, CM; sales invoice, S.

The customer ledgers is included on the 02-1AP.ptb file. To see the account balances, display the customer ledgers (Reports; Accounts Receivable, Preview, Customer Ledgers).

Customer Ledgers

Sequoia Sport Apparel
Customer Ledgers
For the Period From Apr 1, 2005 to Apr 30, 2005

Filter Criteria includes: Report order is by ID. Report is printed in Detail Format.

Customer ID Customer	Date	Trans No	Type	Debit Amt	Credit Amt	Balance
110 Andersen Vocational Center	4/1/05	Balance Fwd				425.00
120 Elias Carrasco	4/1/05	Balance Fwd				472.50
130 Sridhar Duggirala	4/1/05	Balance Fwd				199.25
140 Dean Fujiwara		No Activity				0.00
150 Tianshu Jian	4/1/05	Balance Fwd				373.00
160 Gail Mahr		No Activity				0.00
170 Jeffrey O'Connell	4/1/05	Balance Fwd				189.00
180 Thuc Quan		No Activity				0.00

The accounts receivable account in the general ledger shows the balance of the customer accounts: $425 + 472.50 + 199.25 + 373 + 189 = $1,658.75.

Display the general ledger's accounts receivable account (Reports; General Ledger, Preview, From 1205 to 1205). Observe that the accounts receivable balance agrees with the total accounts balances in the customer ledger.

General Ledger Account No. 1205, Accounts Receivable

Sequoia Sport Apparel
General Ledger
For the Period From Apr 1, 2005 to Apr 30, 2005
Filter Criteria includes: 1) IDs from 1205 to 1205. Report order is by ID. Report is printed with Truncated Transaction Descriptions and in Detail Format.

Account ID Account Description	Date	Reference	Jrnl	Trans Description	Debit Amt	Credit Amt	Balance
1205	4/1/05			Beginning Balance			
Accounts Receivable	4/1/05	BEGBAL	GEN		1,658.75		
				Current Period Cha	1,658.75		1,658.75
	4/30/05			**Ending Balance**			**1,658.75**

Transactions:

April	1	Sold shoes on account to Sridhar Duggirala, $85.00, plus sales tax. S63.
	2	Sold clothing on account to Thuc Quan, $150.00, plus sales tax. S64.
	5	Granted credit to Sridhar Duggirala for shoes returned, $85.00, plus sales tax from S63. CM12.
	5	Sold shoes on account to Dean Fujiwara, $60.00, plus sales tax. S65.
	5	Sold shoes on account to Gail Mahr, $180.00, plus sales tax. S66.
	7.	Sold clothing on account to Thuc Quan, $230.00, plus sales tax. S67.
	10	Granted credit to Gail Mahr for shoes returned, $100.00, plus sales tax from S66. CM13.
	12	Sold clothing on account to Jeffrey O'Connell, $350.00, plus sales tax. S68.
	15	Granted credit to Thuc Quan for clothing returned, $140.00, plus sales tax from S67. CM14.
	17	Sold shoes on account to Sridhar Duggirala, $46.00, plus sales tax. S69.
	19	Sold clothing on account to the Andersen Vocational Center, $242.00. No sales tax. S70.
	24	Granted credit to Jeffrey O'Connell for clothing returned, $120.00, plus sales tax from S68. CM15.
	27	Sold clothing on account to Elias Carrasco, $98.00, plus sales tax. S71.
	30	Sold shoes on account to Tianshu Jian, $124.00, plus sales tax. S72.

Instructions:

1. Journalize and post the transactions completed during April 2005 in the sales journal. (For sales returns, refer to the 10-4 Mastery Problem, Sales Returns: Credit Memos, page 84.)

2. Print the sales journal.

3. Print the following general ledger accounts: accounts receivable, sales tax payable, sales-clothing, sales returns and allowances-clothing, sales-shoes, sales returns and allowances-shoes.

4. Print the customer ledgers.

5. Back up. The suggested file name is 2-1 Application Problem.ptb.

Journalizing and Posting Departmental Cash Receipts

The instructions that follow show you how to do the following:

- Start Peachtree Complete Accounting.
- Restore starting data from the South-Western Accounting with Peachtree CD.
- Complete journal entries for April 2005.
- Print the cash receipts journal.
- Print selected general ledger accounts.
- Print the customer ledgers.
- Complete the 2-2 Application Problem.

Before you start the 2-2 Application Problem, ask your instructor if Colonial Furnishings, the company used for the 2-2 Application Problem has already been restored on your computer. The instructions that follow assume that Colonial Furnishings is being used for the first time.

GETTING STARTED

Use the following instructions to start Peachtree and restore the starting data for the 2-2 Application Problem. The South-Western Accounting with Peachtree CD includes a folder called Peachtree Files-Unit 2. In the steps that follow you will restore the 02-2AP.ptb file.

1. Start Peachtree. From the startup menu, select Close.
2. The menu bar shows three options: Files; Options; and Help. Click File; Restore.
3. The Restore Wizard - Select Backup File window appears. Observe that the Location field shows where Peachtree is stored on your computer. The default location is C:\Program Files\Peachtree\Company. Your Location field may differ. If you are restoring from a network drive, you will need to know the location of the 02-2AP.ptb file.

4. Click [Browse]. The Open Backup File window appears. In the Look in field, double-click on the appropriate location of the Peachtree Files-Unit 2 folder. Then, click 02-2AP.ptb to select it. (If appropriate, select your CD drive then double-click the Peachtree Files-Unit 2 folder. Click 02-2AP.ptb to select it.)

5. Make sure the 02-2AP.ptb file is selected. (*Hint:* Starting data for the 2-2 Application Problem is in the Peachtree Files-Unit 2 folder.) Click [Open].

6. The Select Backup File window appears. Make sure the Location field shows the correct location for the 02-2AP.ptb file; for example, X:\Peachtree Files-Unit 2\02-2AP.ptb. (Substitute the correct drive letter for X.)

7. Click [Next >]. The Select Company window appears. Click on the radio button next to *A New Company*. The Location field shown in this book indicates the default location where drive C is used to install Peachtree. Your Location field may differ. *Make sure that the Location field ends in* **colfurni**. (If your location field does not end in "i" select An Existing Company, then click [Browse]. Double-click Colonial Furnishings (*or*, 02-2APXX). Your Location field shows the shortened company name colfurni Continue with step 8.)

8. Click [Next >]. The Restore Options window appears.

9. Make sure that the box next to Company Data is *checked*. Click [Next >].

10. The Confirmation window appears. Check the From and To fields to make sure they are correct. Click [Finish]. When the Restore Company scale is 100% complete, your data is restored and you are returned to the menu bar.

CHANGING THE COMPANY NAME

Before you start recording transactions for the 2-2 Application Problem, you should look at the company information included on the 02-2AP.ptb file. Follow these steps to look at company information.

1. The Colonial Furnishings menu bar should be displayed. From the menu bar, click on Maintain; Company Information. The Maintain Company Information window appears. Observe that the directory field shows where your company is stored on your computer: C:\Program Files\Peachtree\company\colfurni.

2. Type **02-2APXX** in the Company Name field.

3. When you are finished typing 02-2APXX as the company name, click on [OK]. Once you have changed the Company Name, each one of your printouts will show the activity number and your initials.

Nothing has changed on your computer's hard drive. The company you restored is identified in the program folder and data folder as C:\Program Files\Peachtree\company\colfurni. What you've done is change the company name so that your printouts will show the activity number and your initials. Using Maintain, Company Information to rename your company does *not* change the shortened company name.

Transactions:

Colonial Furnishings has two departments: Tables and Chairs. Display the customer ledger. This data is included on the 02-2AP.ptb file.

Customer Ledgers

Colonial Furnishings
Customer Ledgers
For the Period From Jun 1, 2005 to Jun 30, 2005

Filter Criteria includes: Report order is by ID. Report is printed in Detail Format.

Customer ID Customer	Date	Trans No	Type	Debit Amt	Credit Amt	Balance
110 Amy Cannon	6/1/05	Balance Fwd				823.70
120 Wayne Miller	6/1/05	Balance Fwd				200.00
130 Joe Ricardo	6/1/05	Balance Fwd				1,059.90
140 David Ring	6/1/05	Balance Fwd				451.50
150 Dawn Sanzone	6/1/05	Balance Fwd				525.00
160 Bob Witt	6/1/05	Balance Fwd				481.10

The accounts receivable account in the general ledger shows the balance of the customer accounts: $823.70 + 200 + 1,059.90 + 451.50 + 525 + 481.10 = $3,541.20.

Display the general ledger's accounts receivable account. (Observe that the accounts receivable balance agrees with the total of the account balances in the customer ledger.)

General Ledger Account No. 1205, Accounts Receivable

Colonial Furnishings
General Ledger
For the Period From Jun 1, 2005 to Jun 30, 2005

Filter Criteria includes: 1) IDs from 1205 to 1205. Report order is by ID. Report is printed with Truncated Transaction Descriptions and in Detail Format.

Account ID Account Description	Date	Reference	Jrnl	Trans Description	Debit Amt	Credit Amt	Balance
1205 Accounts Receivable	6/1/05 6/1/05	BEGBAL	GEN	Beginning Balance	3,541.20		
				Current Period Cha	3,541.20		3,541.20
	6/30/05			**Ending Balance**			**3,541.20**

June	1	Received cash on account from Wayne Miller for chairs purchased May 25 on S147 for $157.50, less discount. R110.
	2	Received cash on account from Amy Cannon for two tables purchased May 26 on S148 for $388.50, less discount. R111.
	6	Received cash on account from Bob Witt for chairs purchased on account for $210.00, no discount. R112.
	6	Recorded cash and credit card sales for the week: tables, $6,240.00; chairs, $5,060.00; plus sales tax. TS66.
	11	Received cash on account from Dawn Sanzone for a table purchased June 1 on S149 for $525.00, less discount. R113.
	13	Recorded cash and credit card sales for the week: tables, $5,640.00; chairs, $3,570.00; plus sales tax. TS67.
	17	Received cash on account from Amy Cannon for a table purchased on June 9 on S150 for $336.00, less discount. R114.
	18	Received cash on account from David Ring for a table purchased on June 9 on S151 for $451.50, less discount. R115.
	20	Recorded cash and credit card sales for the week: tables, $7,110.00; chairs, $4,850.00; plus sales tax. TS68.
	24	Received cash on account from Joe Ricardo for eight chairs and a table purchased June 15 on S152 for $892.50 ($420.00 for the chairs and $472.50 for the table), less CM42 for two chairs ($100.00 plus $5.00 sales tax), less discount. R116.
	27	Recorded cash and credit card sales for the week: tables, $6,890.00; chairs, $5,150.00; plus sales tax. TS69.
	30	Recorded cash and credit card sales for the period June 28–30: tables, $3,200.00; chairs, $2,980.00; plus sales tax. TS70.

Instructions:

An illustration of the June 1 transaction is shown below.

Date		*Description of Transaction*
June	1	Received cash on account from Wayne Miller for chairs purchased May 25 on S147 for $157.50, less discount, R110. (The June 1 transaction is a partial payment of Mr. Miller's account. Observe that you use the Apply to Invoice tab first, then record the sales discount on the Apply to Revenues tab.)

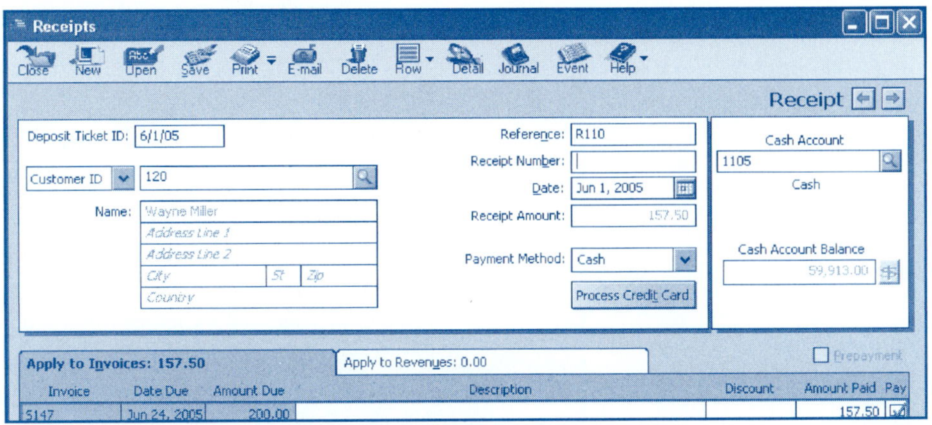

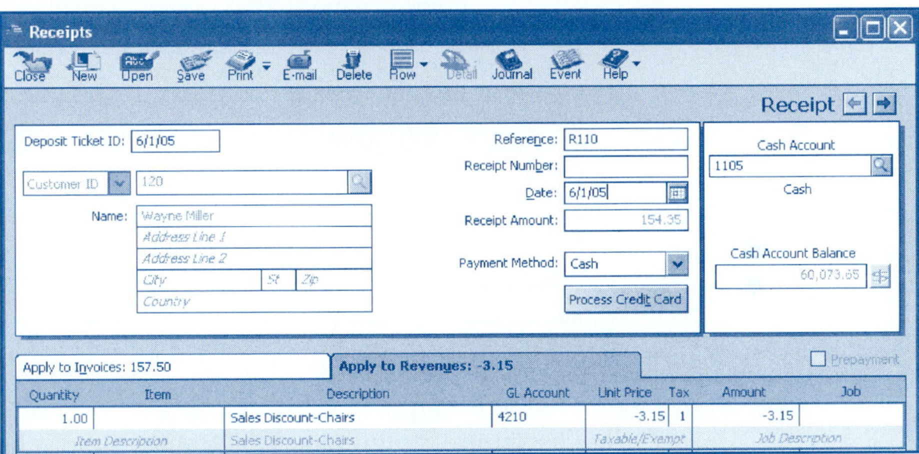

1. Journalize and post the transactions completed during June 2005 in the cash receipts journal. Colonial Furnishings offers credit terms of 2/10, n/30. The sales tax rate is 5%; assume sales tax is paid on all cash and credit cards sales. Source documents are abbreviated as follows: receipt, R; terminal summary, TS.

Each time you use the Receipts task, make sure the Cash Account field shows Account No. 1105, Cash.

The June 11th transaction, "Received cash on account from Dawn Sanzone for the table purchased June 1 on S149 for $525.00, less discount, R113," is a full payment on her account. In this case, use the Apply to Invoices tab to record *both* the discount and payment.

Full payment on account is also received on June 18th from David Ring.

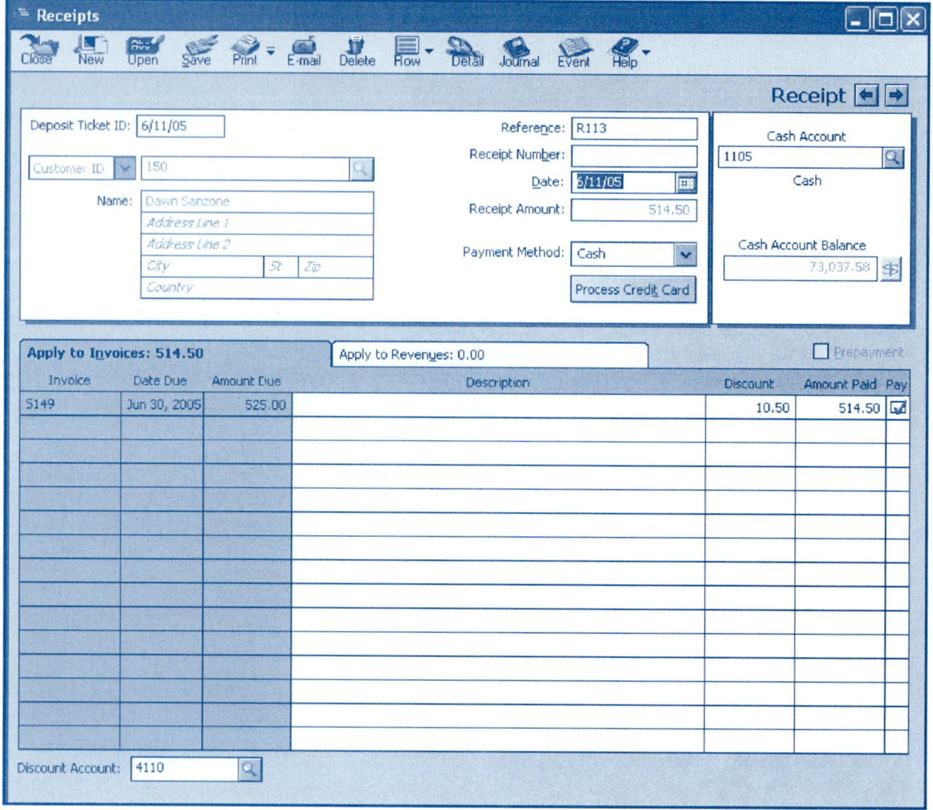

On the Receipts window, make sure you select the appropriate Discount Account—for this transaction make sure Account No. 4110, Sales Discount-Tables is selected.

For detailed steps refer to the 10-4 Mastery Problem, Peachtree's Cash Receipts Journal, pages 80–82.

2. Print the cash receipts journal.

3. Print the following general ledger accounts: cash; accounts receivable, sales tax payable, sales-tables, sales discount-tables, sales-chairs, sales discount-chairs.

4. Print the customer ledgers.

5. Back up. The suggested file name is 2-2 Application Problem.ptb.

Journalizing Departmental Sales, Sales Returns and Allowances, and Cash Receipts

The instructions that follow show you how to do the following:

- Start Peachtree Complete Accounting.
- Restore starting data from the South-Western Accounting with Peachtree CD.
- Complete journal entries for April 2005.
- Print the sales journal and cash receipts journal.
- Complete the 2-3 Mastery Problem.

Before you start the 2-3 Mastery Problem, ask your instructor if EuroFashions, the company used for the 2-3 Mastery Problem has already been restored on your computer. The instructions that follow assume that EuroFashions is being used for the first time.

GETTING STARTED

Use the following instructions to start Peachtree and restore the starting data for the 2-3 Mastery Problem. The South-Western Accounting with Peachtree CD includes a folder called Peachtree Files-Unit 2. In the steps that follow you will restore the 02-3MP.ptb file.

1. Start Peachtree. From the startup menu, select `Close`.
2. The menu bar shows three options: Files; Options; and Help. Click File; Restore.
3. The Restore Wizard - Select Backup File window appears. Observe that the Location field shows where Peachtree is stored on your computer. The default location is C:\Program Files\Peachtree\ Company. Your Location field may differ. If you are restoring from a network drive, you will need to know the location of the 02-3MP.ptb file.
4. Click `Browse`. The Open Backup File window appears. In the Look in field, double-click on the appropriate location of the Peachtree Files-Unit 2 folder. Then, click 02-3MP.ptb to select it. (If

appropriate, select your CD drive then double-click the Peachtree Files-Unit 2 folder. Click 02-3MP.ptb to select it.)

5. Make sure the 02-3MP.ptb file is selected. (*Hint:* Starting data for the 2-3 Mastery Problem is in the Peachtree Files-Unit 2 folder.) Click Open .

6. The Select Backup File window appears. Make sure the Location field shows the correct location for the 02-3MP.ptb file; for example, X:\Peachtree Files-Unit 2\02-3MP.ptb. (Substitute the correct drive letter for X.)

7. Click Next > . The Select Company window appears. Click on the radio button next to *A New Company*. The Location field shown in this book indicates the default location where drive C is used to install Peachtree. Your Location field may differ. *Make sure that the Location field ends in* **eurofash**. (If your location field does not end in "h" select An Existing Company, then click Browse . Double-click EuroFashions (*or*, 02-3MPXX). Your Location field shows the shortened company name eurofash. Continue with step 8.)

8. Click Next > . The Restore Options window appears.

9. Make sure that the box next to Company Data is *checked*. Click Next > .

10. The Confirmation window appears. Check the From and To fields to make sure they are correct. Click Finish . When the Restore Company scale is 100% complete, your data is restored and you are returned to the menu bar.

CHANGING THE COMPANY NAME

Before you start recording transactions for the 2-3 Mastery Problem, you should look at the company information included on the 02-3MP.ptb file. Follow these steps to look at company information.

1. The EuroFashions menu bar should be displayed. From the menu bar, click on Maintain; Company Information. The Maintain Company Information window appears. Observe that the directory field shows where your company is stored on your computer: C:\Program Files\Peachtree\company\eurofash.

2. Type **02-3MPXX** in the Company Name field.

3. When you are finished typing 02-3MPXX as the company name, click on OK . Once you have changed the Company Name, each one of your printouts will show the activity number and your initials.

Nothing has changed on your computer's hard drive. The company you restored is identified in the program folder and data folder as C:\Program Files\Peachtree\company\eurofash. What you've done is change the company name so that your printouts will show the activity number and your initials. Using Maintain, Company Information to rename your company does *not* change the shortened company name.

EuroFashions has two departments: Jewelry and Watches.

Transactions:

April	1	Sold jewelry on account to Ronn Hughes, $810.00, plus sales tax. S134.

April 1   Sold jewelry on account to Ronn Hughes, $810.00, plus sales tax. S134.

3   Sold jewelry on account to Dara San, $520.00, plus sales tax. S135.

4   Received cash on account from Bill Melendez for watches purchased on March 27 covering S132 for $441.00, less discount. R83.

4   Recorded cash and credit card sales: jewelry, $2,560.00; watches, $2,130.00; plus sales tax. TS74.

6   Received cash on account from Katie Minko for jewelry purchased on March 29 on S131 for $640.50, less discount. R84.

8   Granted credit to Dara San for jewelry returned, $110.00, plus sales tax, from S135. CM28.

9   Received cash on account from Dara San for a watch purchased on April 1 for $302.40, less discount. R85.

11   Received cash on account from Ronn Hughes for jewelry purchased on April 4 on S134 for $850.50, less discount. R86.

11   Sold jewelry on account to Dan Tran, $780.00, plus sales tax. S136.

11   Recorded cash and credit card sales for the week: jewelry, $5,340.00; watches, $3,910.00; plus sales tax. TS75.

13   Received cash on account from Dara San, for jewelry purchased on S135 for $546.00, less CM28 ($110.00 plus sales tax), less discount. R87.

15   Sold two watches on account to Alana Austin, $510.00, plus sales tax. S137.

17   Sold jewelry on account to Katie Minko, $320.00, plus sales tax. S138.

18   Recorded cash and credit card sales: jewelry, $4,730.00; watches, $5,260.00; plus sales tax. TS76.

21   Received cash on account from Dan Tran, for jewelry purchased on S136 for $819.00, less discount. R88.

21   Granted credit to Alana Austin for returned watch, $150.00, plus sales tax, from S137. CM29.

25   Recorded cash and credit card sales for the week: jewelry, $3,470.00; watches, $2,681.00; plus sales tax. TS77.

28   Sold watches on account to The Hamilton Foundation, $660.00; no sales tax. S139.

30   Recorded cash and credit card sales: jewelry, $1,860.00; watches, $965.00; plus sales tax. TS78.

Instructions:

1. Journalize and post the transactions completed during April 2005 in the sales journal and cash receipts journal. EuroFashions offers credit terms of 2/10, n/30. The sales tax rate is 5%; assume sales tax is paid on all cash and credit cards sales. Source documents are abbreviated as follows: credit memorandum, CM; receipt, R; sales invoice, S; terminal summary, TS.

2. Print the sales journal.

3. Print the cash receipts journal.

4. Back up. The suggested file name is 2-3 Mastery Problem.ptb.

Calculating and Journalizing Payment of Payroll Tax Liabilities

The instructions that follow show you how to do the following:

- Start Peachtree Complete Accounting.
- Restore starting data from the South-Western Accounting with Peachtree CD.
- Complete journal entries for April 2005.
- Print the cash disbursements journal.
- Complete the 3-5 Application Problem.

Before you start the 3-5 Application Problem, ask your instructor if John's Automotive, the company used for the 3-5 Application Problem has already been restored on your computer. The instructions that follow assume that John's Automotive is being used for the first time.

GETTING STARTED

Use the following instructions to start Peachtree and restore the starting data for the 3-5 Application Problem. The South-Western Accounting with Peachtree CD includes a folder called Peachtree Files-Unit 2. In the steps that follow you will restore the 03-5AP.ptb file.

1. Start Peachtree. From the startup menu, select Close.
2. The menu bar shows three options: Files; Options; and Help. Click File; Restore.
3. The Restore Wizard - Select Backup File window appears. Observe that the Location field shows where Peachtree is stored on your computer. The default location is C:\Program Files\Peachtree\Company. Your Location field may differ. If you are restoring from a network drive, you will need to know the location of the 03-5AP.ptb file.
4. Click Browse. The Open Backup File window appears. In the Look in field, double-click on the appropriate location of the Peachtree Files-Unit 2 folder. Then, click 03-5AP.ptb to select it. (If appropriate, select your CD drive then double-click the Peachtree Files-Unit 2 folder. Click 03-5AP.ptb to select it.)

5. Make sure the 03-5AP.ptb file is selected. (*Hint:* Starting data for the 3-5 Application Problem is in the Peachtree Files-Unit 2 folder.) Click `Open`.

6. The Select Backup File window appears. Make sure the Location field shows the correct location for the 03-5AP.ptb file; for example, X:\Peachtree Files-Unit 2\03-5AP.ptb. (Substitute the correct drive letter for X.)

7. Click `Next >`. The Select Company window appears. Click on the radio button next to *A New Company*. The Location field shown in this book indicates the default location where drive C is used to install Peachtree. Your Location field may differ. *Make sure that the Location field ends in* **johautom**. (If your location field does not end in "m" select An Existing Company, then click `Browse`. Double-click John's Automotive (*or,* 03-5APXX). Your Location field shows the shortened company name johautom. Continue with step 8.)

8. Click `Next >`. The Restore Options window appears.

9. Make sure that the box next to Company Data is *checked*. Click `Next >`.

10. The Confirmation window appears. Check the From and To fields to make sure they are correct. Click `Finish`. When the Restore Company scale is 100% complete, your data is restored and you are returned to the menu bar.

CHANGING THE COMPANY NAME

Before you start recording transactions for the 3-5 Application Problem, you should look at the company information included on the 03-5AP.ptb file. Follow these steps to look at company information.

1. The John's Automotive menu bar should be displayed. From the menu bar, click on Maintain; Company Information. The Maintain Company Information window appears. Observe that the directory field shows where your company is stored on your computer: C:\Program Files\Peachtree\company\johautom.

2. Type **03-5APXX** in the Company Name field.

3. When you are finished typing 03-5APXX as the company name, click on `OK`. Once you have changed the Company Name, each one of your printouts will show the activity number and your initials.

Nothing has changed on your computer's hard drive. The company you restored is identified in the program folder and data folder as C:\Program Files\Peachtree\company\johautom. What you've done is change the company name so that your printouts will show the activity number and your initials. Using Maintain, Company

Information to rename your company does *not* change the shortened
company name.

Use the following payroll data for John's Automotive for the first quarter of 2005. Employer tax rates are social security, 6.2%; Medicare, 1.45%; federal unemployment, 0.8%; and state unemployment, 5.4%

Period	Total Earnings	Social Security Tax Withheld	Medicare Tax Withheld	Federal Income Tax Withheld
Biweekly Period Ended March 28	$ 7,742.00	$480.00	$112.26	$911.00
First Quarter	46,452.00	—	—	—

Instructions:

1. Calculate the liability for federal income tax, social security tax, and Medicare tax for the biweekly pay period ended March 28, 2005. Include both the employees' tax withheld and the employer liability for social security tax, and Medicare tax.

2. Journalize and post the payment in the cash disbursements journal. The payment is made on April 3 using Check No. 492 as the source document.

3. Calculate the federal unemployment tax liability for the first quarter.

4. Journalize and post the payment in the cash disbursements journal. The payment is made on April 30 using Check No. 515 as the source document.

5. Calculate the state unemployment tax liability for the first quarter.

6. Journalize and post the payment in the cash disbursements journal. The payment is made on April 30 using Check No. 516 as the source document.

7. Print the Cash Disbursements Journal.

8. Back up. The suggested file name is 3-5 Application Problem.ptb.

Journalizing Adjusting and Closing Entries for a Departmentalized Business

The instructions that follow show you how to do the following:

- Start Peachtree Complete Accounting.
- Restore starting data from the South-Western Accounting with Peachtree CD.
- Complete adjusting and closing entries.
- Print the general journal.
- Complete the 4-5 Application Problem.

Before you start the 4-5 Application Problem, ask your instructor if AllSports Center, the company used for the 4-5 Application Problem, has already been restored on your computer. The instructions that follow assume that AllSports Center is being used for the first time.

GETTING STARTED

Use the following instructions to start Peachtree and restore the starting data for the 4-5 Application Problem. The South-Western Accounting with Peachtree CD includes a folder called Peachtree Files-Unit 2. In the steps that follow you will restore the 04-5AP.ptb file.

1. Start Peachtree. From the startup menu, select Close .
2. The menu bar shows three options: Files; Options; and Help. Click File; Restore.
3. The Restore Wizard - Select Backup File window appears. Observe that the Location field shows where Peachtree is stored on your computer. The default location is C:\Program Files\Peachtree\ Company. Your Location field may differ. If you are restoring from a network drive, you will need to know the location of the 04-5AP.ptb file.
4. Click Browse . The Open Backup File window appears. In the Look in field, double-click on the appropriate location of the Peachtree Files-Unit 2 folder. Then, click 04-5AP.ptb to select it. (If appropriate, select your CD drive then double-click the Peachtree Files-Unit 2 folder. Click 04-5AP.ptb to select it.)

5. Make sure the 04-5AP.ptb file is selected. (*Hint:* Starting data for the 4-5 Application Problem is in the Peachtree Files-Unit 2 folder.) Click Open .

6. The Select Backup File window appears. Make sure the Location field shows the correct location for the 04-5AP.ptb file; for example, X:\Peachtree Files-Unit 2\04-5AP.ptb. (Substitute the correct drive letter for X.)

7. Click Next> . The Select Company window appears. Click on the radio button next to *A New Company*. The Location field shown in this book indicates the default location where drive C is used to install Peachtree. Your Location field may differ. *Make sure that the Location field ends in* **allcente**. (If your location field does not end in "e" select An Existing Company, then click Browse . Double-click AllSports Center (*or*, 04-5APXX). Your Location field shows the shortened company name allsport. Continue with step 8.)

8. Click Next> . The Restore Options window appears.

9. Make sure that the box next to Company Data is *checked*. Click Next> .

10. The Confirmation window appears. Check the From and To fields to make sure they are correct. Click Finish . When the Restore Company scale is 100% complete, your data is restored and you are returned to the menu bar.

CHANGING THE COMPANY NAME

Before you start recording transactions for the 4-5 Application Problem, you should look at the company information included on the 04-5AP.ptb file. Follow these steps to look at company information.

1. The AllSports Center menu bar should be displayed. From the menu bar, click on Maintain; Company Information. The Maintain Company Information window appears. Observe that the directory field shows where your company is stored on your computer: C:\Program Files\Peachtree\company\allcente.

2. Type **04-5APXX** in the Company Name field.

3. When you are finished typing 04-5APXX as the company name, click on OK . Once you have changed the Company Name, each one of your printouts will show the activity number and your initials.

Nothing has changed on your computer's hard drive. The company you restored is identified in the program folder and data folder as C:\Program Files\Peachtree\company\allsport. What you've done is change the company name so that your printouts will show the activity number and your initials. Using Maintain, Company Information to rename your company does *not* change the shortened company name.

Transactions:

Refer to the AllSports Center work sheet to complete the 4-5 Application Problem.

AllSports Center
Work Sheet
For Year Ended December 31, 20--

ACCOUNT TITLE	Trial Balance Debit	Trial Balance Credit	Adjustments Debit	Adjustments Credit	Clothing Debit	Clothing Credit	Equipment Debit	Equipment Credit	Income Statement Debit	Income Statement Credit	Balance Sheet Debit	Balance Sheet Credit
1 Cash	3821300										3821300	
2 Accounts Receivable	3693500										3693500	
3 Allow. for Uncoll. Accts.		53370		(a) 145700								199070
4 Merchandise Inventory--Clothing	8236000		(b) 659000								8895000	
5 Merchandise Inventory--Equipment	10892100			(c) 1524300							9367800	
6 Supplies--Administrative	164900			(d) 83400							81500	
7 Supplies--Clothing	248000			(e) 192500							55500	
8 Supplies--Equipment	312200			(f) 128700							183500	
9 Prepaid Insurance	840000			(g) 720000							120000	
10 Office Equipment	842600										842600	
11 Acc. Depr.--Office Equipment		315000		(h) 110000								425000
12 Store Equipment--Clothing	1458000										1458000	
13 Acc. Depr.--Store Equipment, Clothing		721400		(i) 372000								1093400
14 Store Equipment--Equipment	1201000										1201000	
15 Acc. Depr.--Store Equipment, Equipment		765000		(j) 185000								950000
16 Accounts Payable		2482300										2482300
17 Employee Income Tax Payable--Federal		125330										125330
18 Employee Income Tax Payable--State		207800										207800
19 Federal Income Tax Payable				(k) 142138								142138
20 Social Security Tax Payable		148800										148800
21 Medicare Tax Payable		34800										34800
22 Sales Tax Payable		265300										265300
23 Unemployment Tax Payable--Federal		4400										4400
24 Unemployment Tax Payable--State		15100										15100
25 Health Insurance Premiums Payable		124000										124000
26 U.S. Savings Bonds Payable		21500										21500
27 Dividends Payable		1200000										1200000
28 Capital Stock		10000000										10000000
29 Retained Earnings		6837200										6837200
30 Dividends	1200000										1200000	
31 Income Summary--Clothing				(b) 659000		659000						
32 Income Summary--Equipment			(c) 1524300				1524300					
33 Income Summary--General												
34 Sales--Clothing		24425300				24425300						
35 Sales Discount--Clothing	365400				365400							
36 Sales Returns and Allowances--Clothing	347800				347800							

(continued on next page)

	ACCOUNT TITLE	TRIAL BALANCE DEBIT	TRIAL BALANCE CREDIT	ADJUSTMENTS DEBIT	ADJUSTMENTS CREDIT	CLOTHING DEBIT	CLOTHING CREDIT	EQUIPMENT DEBIT	EQUIPMENT CREDIT	INCOME STATEMENT DEBIT	INCOME STATEMENT CREDIT	BALANCE SHEET DEBIT	BALANCE SHEET CREDIT	
37	Sales--Equipment		281495 00						281495 00					37
38	Sales Discount--Equipment	2153 00						2153 00						38
39	Sales Returns and Allowances--Equipment	5110 00						5110 00						39
40	Purchases--Clothing	102852 00				102852 00								40
41	Purchases Discount--Clothing		1765 00				1765 00							41
42	Purch. Returns and Allowances--Clothing		3581 00				3581 00							42
43	Purchases--Equipment	145277 00						145277 00						43
44	Purchases Discount--Equipment		1862 00						1862 00					44
45	Purch. Returns and Allowances--Equipment		4973 00						4973 00					45
46	Advertising Expense--Clothing	2551 00				2551 00								46
47	Depr. Exp.--Store Equipment, Clothing			(i) 3720 00		3720 00								47
48	Payroll Taxes Expense--Clothing	5192 00				5192 00								48
49	Salary Expense--Clothing	36562 00				36562 00								49
50	Supplies Expense--Clothing			(e) 1925 00		1925 00								50
51	Advertising Expense--Equipment	2590 00						2590 00						51
52	Depr. Exp.--Store Equipment, Equipment			(j) 1850 00				1850 00						52
53	Payroll Taxes Expense--Equipment	5758 00						5758 00						53
54	Salary Expense--Equipment	43926 00						43926 00						54
55	Supplies Expense--Equipment			(f) 1287 00				1287 00						55
56	Credit Card Fee Expense	2786 00								2786 00				56
57	Depr. Exp.--Office Equipment			(h) 1100 00						1100 00				57
58	Insurance Expense			(g) 7200 00						7200 00				58
59	Miscellaneous Expense	1498 00								1498 00				59
60	Payroll Taxes Expense--Administrative	2364 00								2364 00				60
61	Rent Expense	28000 00								28000 00				61
62	Salary Expense--Administrative	24845 00								24845 00				62
63	Supplies Expense--Administrative			(d) 834 00						834 00				63
64	Uncollectible Accounts Expense			(a) 1457 00						1457 00				64
65	Utilities Expense	8450 00								8450 00				65
66						159934 00	256189 00	223194 00	288330 00					66
67	Department Margin--Clothing					96255 00					96255 00			67
68	Department Margin--Equipment							65136 00			65136 00			68
69						256189 00	256189 00	288330 00	288330 00					69
70	Federal Income Tax Expense	15000 00		(k) 1421 38						16421 38				70
71		771142 00	771142 00	42627 38	42627 38					94955 38	161391 00	309197 00	242761 38	71
72	Net Income after Federal Income Tax									66435 62			66435 62	72
73										161391 00	161391 00	309197 00	309197 00	73

1. Journalize and post the adjusting entries for AllSports Center.
2. Journalize and post the closing entries for AllSports Center. Dividends declared during the current quarter were $12,000.00.
3. Print the December 31, 2005 general journal.
4. Back up. The suggested file name is 4-5 Application Problem.ptb.

Processing and Reporting Departmentalized Accounting Data

The instructions that follow show you how to do the following:

- Start Peachtree Complete Accounting.
- Restore starting data from the South-Western Accounting with Peachtree CD.
- Complete journal entries for December 2005.
- Complete adjusting entries.
- Print financial statements.
- Complete closing entries.
- Print the post-closing trial balance.
- Complete Reinforcement Activity 1.

Before you start Reinforcement Activity 1, ask your instructor if BooksPlus, Inc., the company used for Reinforcement Activity 1 has already been restored on your computer. The instructions that follow assume that BooksPlus, Inc. is being used for the first time.

GETTING STARTED

Use the following instructions to start Peachtree and restore the starting data for Reinforcement Activity 1. The South-Western Accounting with Peachtree CD includes a folder called Peachtree Files-Unit 2. In the steps that follow you will restore the RA01.ptb file.

1. Start Peachtree. From the startup menu, select Close.
2. The menu bar shows three options: Files; Options; and Help. Click File; Restore.
3. The Restore Wizard - Select Backup File window appears. Observe that the Location field shows where Peachtree is stored on your computer. The default location is C:\Program Files\Peachtree\ Company. Your Location field may differ. If you are restoring from a network drive, you will need to know the location of the RA01.ptb file.

4. Click Browse . The Open Backup File window appears. In the Look in field, double-click on the appropriate location of the Peachtree Files-Unit 2 folder. Then, click RA01.ptb to select it. (If appropriate, select your CD drive then double-click the Peachtree Files-Unit 2 folder. Click RA01.ptb to select it.)

5. Make sure the RA01.ptb file is selected. (*Hint:* BooksPlus, Inc.'s Reinforcement Activity 1 data is in the Peachtree Files-Unit 2 folder.) Click Open .

6. The Select Backup File window appears. Make sure the Location field shows the correct location for the RA01.ptb file; for example, X:\Peachtree Files-Unit 2\RA01.ptb. (Substitute the correct drive letter for X.)

7. Click Next> . The Select Company window appears. Click on the radio button next to *A New Company*. The Location field shown in this book indicates the default location where drive C is used to install Peachtree. Your Location field may differ. *Make sure that the Location field ends in* **booinc**. (If your location field does not end in "c," select An Existing Company, then click Browse . Double-click BooksPlus, Inc. (*or*, RA01XX). Your Location field shows the short-ened company name booinc. Continue with step 8.)

8. Click Next> . The Restore Options window appears.

9. Make sure that the box next to Company Data is *checked*. Click Next> .

10. The Confirmation window appears. Check the From and To fields to make sure they are correct. Click Finish . When the Restore Company scale is 100% complete, your data is restored and you are returned to the menu bar.

CHANGING THE COMPANY NAME

Before you start recording transactions for Reinforcement Activity 1, you should look at the company information included on the RA01.ptb file. Follow these steps to look at company information.

1. The BooksPlus, Inc. menu bar should be displayed. From the menu bar, click on Maintain; Company Information. The Maintain Company Information window appears. Observe that the directory field shows where your company is stored on your computer: C:\Program Files\Peachtree\company\booinc.

2. Type **RA01XX** in the Company Name field.

3. When you are finished typing RA01XX as the company name, click on OK . Once you have changed the Company Name, each one of your printouts will show the activity number and your initials.

Nothing has changed on your computer's hard drive. The company you restored is identified in the program folder and data folder as C:\Program Files\Peachtree\company\booinc. What you've done is change the company name so that your printouts will show the activity number and your initials. Using Maintain, Company Information to rename your company does *not* change the shortened company name.

BooksPlus, Inc.

BooksPlus, Inc. has two departments: Books and Magazines. BooksPlus, Inc., is open for business Monday through Saturday. A monthly rent is paid on the building. The business owns the office and store equipment.

BooksPlus sells books and magazines to individuals and schools. Cash sales and sales on account are made. The business uses a national credit card service in addition to its own company credit card.

BooksPlus's fiscal year is January 1 through December 31. During the fiscal year, a monthly interim departmental statement of gross profit is prepared.

BooksPlus uses the chart of accounts and subsidiary ledgers are shown below. Beginning balances have been recorded on the RA01.ptb file.

Preparing an Interim Departmental Statement of Gross Profit

BooksPlus prepares an interim departmental statement of gross profit each month. The following data are obtained from the accounting records at the end of November of the current year.

	Books	*Magazines*
Beginning inventory, January 1	$164,164.20	$147,840.30
Estimated beginning inventory, November 1	180,205.05	157,195.78
Net purchases January 1 to October 31	133,839.60	130,449.20
Net sales, January 1 to October 31	214,179.55	220,170.40
Net purchases for November	13,007.20	14,162.58
Net sales for November	19,480.60	20,240.30
Gross profit on operation as a percent of sales	45.0%	55.0%

Instructions:

1. Use the gross profit method of estimating an inventory to prepare an estimated merchandise inventory sheet for each department for the month ended November 2005.

2. Use a blank piece of paper or the *Working Papers* to prepare an interim departmental statement of gross profit for the month ended November 30, 2005. Calculate and record component percentages for departmental and total cost of merchandise sold and gross profit on operations. Round percentage calculations to the nearest 0.1%.

GENERAL LEDGER CHART OF ACCOUNTS

Balance Sheet Accounts		**Income Statement Accounts**	
(1000)	**ASSETS**	**(4000)**	**OPERATING REVENUE**
1100–1400 CURRENT ASSETS		4105	Sales—Books
1105	Cash	4110	Sales Discount—Books
1110	Petty Cash	4115	Sales Returns and Allowances—Books
1205	Accounts Receivable	4205	Sales—Magazines
1210	Allowance for Uncollectible Accounts	4210	Sales Discount—Magazines
1305	Merchandise Inventory—Books	4215	Sales Returns and Allowances—Magazines
1310	Merchandise Inventory—Magazines	**(5000)**	**COST OF MERCHANDISE**
1315	Supplies—Administrative	5105	Purchases—Books
1320	Supplies—Books	5110	Purchases Discount—Books
1325	Supplies—Magazines	5115	Purchases Returns and Allowances—Books
1405	Prepaid Insurance	5205	Purchases—Magazines
1500–1600 PLANT ASSETS		5210	Purchases Discount—Magazines
1505	Display Equipment—Books	5215	Purchases Returns and Allowances—Magazines
1510	Accumulated Depreciation—Display Equipment, Books	**(6000)**	**DIRECT EXPENSES**
1515	Display Equipment—Magazines	6100	DIRECT EXPENSES—BOOKS
1520	Accumulated Depreciation—Display Equipment, Magazines	6105	Advertising Expense—Books
1605	Office Equipment	6110	Depreciation Expense—Display Equipment, Books
1610	Accumulated Depreciation—Office Equipment	6115	Payroll Taxes Expense—Books
(2000)	**LIABILITIES**	6120	Salary Expense—Books
2105	Accounts Payable	6125	Supplies Expense—Books
2205	Employee Income Tax Payable—Federal	**(6200)**	DIRECT EXPENSES—MAGAZINES
2210	Employee Income Tax Payable—State	6205	Advertising Expense—Magazines
2215	Federal Income Tax Payable	6210	Depreciation Expense—Display Equipment, Magazines
2220	Social Security Tax Payable	6215	Payroll Taxes Expense—Magazines
2225	Medicare Tax Payable	6220	Salary Expense—Magazines
2230	Sales Tax Payable	6225	Supplies Expense—Magazines
2235	Unemployment Tax Payable—Federal	**(7000)**	**INDIRECT EXPENSES**
2240	Unemployment Tax Payable—State	7105	Credit Card Fee Expense
2245	Health Insurance Premiums Payable	7110	Depreciation Expense—Office Equipment
2305	Dividends Payable	7115	Insurance Expense
(3000)	**STOCKHOLDERS' EQUITY**	7120	Miscellaneous Expense
3105	Capital Stock	7125	Payroll Taxes Expense—Administrative
3110	Retained Earnings	7130	Rent Expense
3115	Dividends	7135	Salary Expense—Administrative
3205	Income Summary—Books	7140	Supplies Expense—Administrative
3210	Income Summary—Magazines	7145	Uncollectible Accounts Expense
3215	Income Summary—General	**(8000)**	**INCOME TAX**
		8105	Federal Income Tax Expense

SUBSIDIARY LEDGERS CHARTS OF ACCOUNTS

Accounts Receivable Ledger		**Accounts Payable Ledger**	
110	Marcella Amco	210	A-1 Publishing
120	Matthew Barasso	220	CBG Distributors
130	Tanya Dockman	230	Grandway Products
140	Brian Fadstad	240	H & B Books
150	Gilmore Public Schools	250	Maryland Books & Magazines
160	Belinda Judd	260	Oliver Books, Inc.
170	Janelle Kamschorr	270	Strup Publishers, Inc.
180	Donald Lindgren		
190	Renville Public Schools		

Recording Transactions

Instructions:

1. Use the appropriate journal to journalize and post the following transactions completed during December 2005. Calculate and record sales tax on all sales and sales returns and allowances. The sales tax rate is 5.0%. No sales tax is charged on sales to schools.

BooksPlus offers its customers terms of 2/10, n/30. All of the vendors from which merchandise is purchased on account offer terms of 2/10, n/30. Source documents are abbreviated as follows: check, C; credit memorandum, CM; debit memorandum, DM; memorandum, M; purchase invoice, P; receipt, R; sales income, S; terminal summary, TS.

BooksPlus purchases magazines and books from the same vendor. Make sure you select the appropriate Purchases *before* journalizing and posting vendor transactions.

The same is true of customers. Sales of books *and* magazines are made to the same customer. Make sure you select the appropriate Sales account *before* journalizing and posting customer transactions.

Remember to select the appropriate purchase discount account for vendor payments, and the appropriate sales discount account for customer receipts.

Dec.	1	Paid cash for monthly payroll, $7,899.83 (total payroll: books, $4,522.20; magazines, $4,310.40; administrative, $2,630.25, less deductions: employee income tax-federal, $1,204.00; employee income tax—state, $538.11; Social Security tax, $710.70; Medicare tax, $166.21; health insurance, $944.00). C340.
	1	Recorded employer payroll taxes, $924.26, for the monthly pay period ended November 30. Taxes owed are: Social Security tax, $710.70; Medicare tax, $166.21; federal unemployment tax, $6.11; state unemployment tax, $41.24. Payroll taxes are distributed among the departments as: books, $367.04; magazines, $356.00; and administrative, $201.22. M40.
	1	Paid cash for rent, $1,200.00. C341.
	2	Paid cash for supplies, $135.00. C342.
	2	Purchased books on account from Oliver Books, Inc., $1,933.00. P115.
	3	Recorded cash and credit card sales: books, $2,478.00; magazines, $2,588.50; plus sales tax. TS33.
	5	Sold books on account to Matthew Barasso, $880.00, plus sales tax. S97.
	5	Received cash on account from Tanya Dockman, $493.92, covering S92 for magazines for $504.00 ($480.00 plus sales tax), less discount. R139.
	6	Paid cash on account to CBG Distributors, $2,185.50, covering P111 for books for $2,230.10, less discount. C343.
	7	Paid cash on account to H & B Books, $5,321.55, covering P112 for books for $5,430.15, less discount. C344.
	7	Returned books to Oliver Books, Inc., $300.00, from P115. DM59.
	8	Received cash on account from Gilmore Public Schools, $6115.40, covering S94 for magazines for $6,240.20, less discount. R140.

8	Received cash on account from Belinda Judd, $257.25, covering S95 for books for $262.50 ($250.00 plus sales tax), less discount. R141.
8	Received cash on account from Renville Public Schools, $9,389.87, covering S96 for books for $9,581.50, less discount. R142.
8	Paid cash on account to Maryland Books & Magazines, $554.09, covering P113 for magazines for $565.40, less discount. C345.
9	Paid cash on account to Oliver Books, Inc., $4,821.80, covering P114 for books for $4,920.20, less discount. C346.
9	Granted credit to Matthew Barasso for books returned, $100.00, plus sales tax, from S97. CM33.
10	Recorded cash and credit card sales: books, $4,946.50; magazines, $3,650.00; plus sales tax. TS34.
12	Paid cash on account to Oliver Books, Inc., $1,600.34, covering P115 for books for $1,933.00, less DM59, and less discount. C347.
13	Sold magazines on account to Marcella Amco, $450.00, plus sales tax. S98.
15	Paid cash for liability for federal employee income tax, $1,240.00; social security tax, $1,286.11; Medicare tax, $300.78; total, $2,826.89. C348.
15	Paid cash for quarterly federal income tax estimate, $1,200.00. C349. (Debit Federal Income Tax Expense; credit Cash.)
15	Received cash on account from Matthew Barasso, $802.62, covering S97 for books for $924.00 ($880.00 plus sales tax), less CM33, less discount. R143.
17	Recorded cash and credit card sales: books, $3,820.60; magazines, $3,240.50; plus sales tax. TS35.
22	Sold magazines on account to Renville Public Schools, $4,750.00; no sales tax. S99.
22	Purchased magazines on account from Strup Publishers, Inc., $1,647.00. P116.
22	Purchased magazines on account from A-1 Publishing, $1,278.50. P117.
23	Sold books on account to Brian Fadstad, $1,720.00, plus sales tax, S100.
23	Sold magazines on account to Janelle Kamschorr, $920.00, plus sales tax. S101.
23	Received cash on account from Marcella Amco, $463.05, covering S98 for magazines for $472.50 ($450.00 plus sales tax), less discount. R144.
24	Purchased books on account from CBG Distributors, $1,500.00. P118.
24	Paid cash for advertising for the magazine department, $500. C351.
24	Recorded cash and credit card sales: books, $4,160.10; magazines, $3,420.50; plus sales tax. TS36.

26	Sold magazines on account to Donald Lindgren, $540.00, plus sales tax. S102.
26	Returned magazines to A-1 Publishing, $265.00, from P117. DM60.
27	Purchased books on account from Maryland Books & Magazines, $2,440.50. P119.
27	Purchased magazines on account from Grandway Products, $3,157.99. P120.
28	Sold books on account to Donald Lindgren, $650.00, plus sales tax. S103.
30	Received bank statement showing December bank service charge, $11.40 (debit Miscellaneous Expense). M41.
30	Recorded credit card fee expense for December, $354.20. M42.
31	Granted credit to Renville Public Schools for magazines returned, $1,500.00, from S99. CM34.
31	Sold books on account to Gilmore Public Schools, $6,200.00; no sales tax. S104.
31	Paid cash to replenish petty cash fund, $415.00: supplies for the books department, $145.00; advertising—books, $160.00; miscellaneous, $110.00. C350.
31	Recorded cash and credit card sales: books, $3,580.40; magazines, $2,480.00; plus sales tax. TS37.

2. Print the sales journal, cash receipts journal, purchase journal, cash disbursements journal, and general journal. (*Hint*: The general journal will show December 1 beginning balances.)

3. Print the vendor ledgers and customer ledgers.

4. Print the unadjusted trial balance.

5. Back up your data. The suggested file name is Reinforcement Activity 1.unadjusted.ptb.

End of Fiscal Period Work

6. Journalize and post the adjusting entries in the general journal using the following information.

Adjustment Information, December 31

Uncollectible accounts expense estimated as 1.0% of sales on account.
Sales on account for year, $241,257.00.

Merchandise inventory—Books	$174,469.25
Merchandise inventory—Magazines	151,439.85
Supplies used—Books	940.00
Supplies used—Magazines	1,080.00
Supplies used—Administrative	706.00
Insurance Expired	880.00
Annual depreciation expense—Display Equipment, Books	870.00
Annual depreciation expense—Display Equipment, Magazines	940.00
Annual depreciation expense—Office Equipment	1,260.00
Federal income tax expense for the year	5,013.75

7. Print the adjusted trial balance.

8. Use a blank piece of paper or the *Working Papers* to prepare departmental margin statements for BooksPlus's Book Department and Magazine Department. Calculate and record component percentages for each item on the statements. Round percentage calculations to the nearest 0.1%.

9. Print the Income Statement. Calculate and record component percentages for each item on the statements. Round percentage calculations to the nearest 0.1%. (*Hint:* Peachtree's income statement reports revenue, cost of sales accounts, and expenses. Merchandise Inventory accounts, which are assets, is *not* reported on Peachtree's income statement.)

10. Print the balance sheet.

11. Use the Capital section of Peachtree's balance sheet to prepare a Statement of Stockholders' Equity. Use the following additional information.

January 1 balance of capital stock account (3,000 shares issued for $100.00 per share)	$300,000.00
No additional capital stock issued.	
January 1 balance of retained earnings account	97,525.70

12. Print the statement of retained earnings.

13. Back up. The suggested file name is Reinforcement Activity 1.adjusted.ptb.

14. Journalize and post the closing entries.

15. Print the December 31, 2005 general journal.

16. Print the general ledger.

17. Print the post-closing trial balance.

18. Back up. The suggested file name is Reinforcement Activity 1.closed.ptb.

Keeping Perpetual Inventory Records

The instructions that follow show you how to do the following:

- Start Peachtree Complete Accounting.
- Restore starting data from the South-Western Accounting with Peachtree CD.
- Journalize and post Purchase Journal and Sales Journal transactions.
- Print the Purchase Journal and Sales Journal.
- Print an Item Costing Report.
- Complete the 6-1 Application Problem.

Before you start the 6-1 Application Problem, ask your instructor if Bowman Lawn and Garden, the company used for the 6-1 Application Problem, has already been restored on your computer. The instructions that follow assume that Bowman Lawn and Garden is being used for the first time.

GETTING STARTED

Use the following instructions to start Peachtree and restore the starting data for Bowman Lawn and Garden. The South-Western Accounting with Peachtree CD includes a folder called Peachtree Files-Unit 2. In the steps that follow you will restore the 06-1A.ptb file.

1. Start Peachtree. From the startup menu, select `Close`.
2. The menu bar shows three options: Files; Options; and Help. Click File; Restore.
3. The Restore Wizard - Select Backup File window appears. Observe that the Location field shows where Peachtree is stored on your computer. The default location is C:\Program Files\Peachtree\Company. Your Location field may differ. If you are restoring from a network drive, you will need to know the location of the 06-1AP.ptb file.
4. Click `Browse`. The Open Backup File window appears. In the Look in field, double-click on the appropriate location of the Peachtree Files-Unit 2 folder. Then, click 06-1AP.ptb to select it. (If appropriate, select your CD drive then double-click the Peachtree Files-Unit 2 folder. Click 06-1AP.ptb to select it.)

5. Make sure the Peachtree Files-Unit 2 folder and 06-1AP.ptb file is selected. (*Hint:* Starting data for the 6-1 Application Problem is in the Peachtree Files-Unit 2 folder.) Click Open .

6. The Select Backup File window appears. Make sure the Location field shows the correct location for the 06-1AP.ptb file; for example, X:\Peachtree Files-Unit 2\06-1AP.ptb. (Substitute the correct drive letter for X.)

7. Click Next> . The Select Company window appears. Click on the radio button next to *A New Company*. The Location field shown in this book indicates the default location where drive C is used to install Peachtree. Your Location field may differ. *Make sure that the Location field ends in* **bowlawan**. (If your location field does not end in "n," select An Existing Company, then click Browse . Double-click Bowman Lawn and Garden (*or*, 06-1APXX). Your Location field shows the shortened company name bowlawan. Continue with step 8.)

8. Click Next> . The Restore Options window appears.

9. Make sure that the box next to Company Data is *checked*. Click Next> .

10. The Confirmation window appears. Check the From and To fields to make sure they are correct. Click Finish . When the Restore Company scale is 100% complete, your data is restored and you are returned to the menu bar.

CHANGING THE COMPANY NAME

Before you start recording transactions for 6-1 Application Problem, you should look at the company information included on the 06-1AP.ptb file. Follow these steps to look at company information.

1. The Bowman Lawn and Garden menu bar should be displayed. From the menu bar, click on Maintain; Company Information. The Maintain Company Information window appears. Observe that the directory field shows where your company is stored on your computer: C:\Program Files\Peachtree\company\bowlawan.

2. Type **06-1APXX** in the Company Name field.

3. When you are finished typing 06-1APXX as the company name, click on OK . Once you have changed the Company Name, each one of your printouts will show the problem number and your initials.

Nothing has changed on your computer's hard drive. The company you restored is identified in the program folder and data folder as C:\Program Files\Peachtree\company\bowlawan. What you've done is changed the company name so that your printouts will show the problem number and your initials. Using Maintain, Company Information to rename your company does *not* change the shortened company name.

Instructions:

Bowman Lawn and Garden sells lawn and garden equipment to a variety of customers. For many years the business used a periodic inventory system. However, it switched to a perpetual merchandise inventory system two years ago. The perpetual system gives the company better control of its inventory.

1. The following inventory records have been entered in Peachtree. Your Peachtree Problem File, 06-1AP.ptb contains this information.

Lawn mower:

Stock number	R263
Reorder	60
Minimum	15
Location	Bin 41
Number on hand, April 1	32

Hedge trimmer:

Stock number,	J184
Reorder	35
Minimum	8
Location	Bin 49
Number on hand April 1	17

2. Record the following transactions using Peachtree's Sales Journal (Sales/Invoicing task) and Purchase Journal (Purchases/Receive Inventory task).

April	2	Sold 9 lawn mowers to Rogers Lawn and Garden, S211.
	3	Sold 5 hedge trimmers to Besotral, Inc., S212
	6	Lawn Haven bought 6 lawn mowers and 6 hedge trimmers, S213.
	10	Received 35 hedge trimmers from Hughes Manufacturing, P742.
	11	Gilbert Co. bought 10 hedge trimmers, S214.
	15	Five more lawn mowers were sold to Rogers Lawn and Garden, S215.
	16	Lawn King Manufacturing shipped 60 lawn mowers, P743.
	19	Sold 30 lawn mowers to Christie's Landscaping, S216.
	20	Home Beautiful bought 20 lawn mowers and 15 hedge trimmers, S217.
	24	Twelve more lawn mowers were sold to Lawn Haven, S218.
	25	Received 60 lawn mowers from Lawn King Manufacturing, P744.
	28	Sold 10 hedge trimmers to Green, Inc., S219.
	29	Hughes Manufacturing shipped 35 hedge trimmers, P745.
	30	Sold 7 lawn mowers to Movin' Mowers, S220.

3. Journalize and post the April transactions in Peachtree's Sales Journal and Purchase Journal. (*Hint:* After entering the quantity sold or purchased, remember to select the appropriate inventory item for each sale and purchase.)

4. Print the Purchase Journal.

5. Print the Sales Journal.

6. Print the Item Costing Report. (*Hint:* This is an inventory report.)

7. Back up. The suggested file name is 6-1 Application Problem.ptb.

Journalizing Entries to Write Off Uncollectible Accounts – Direct Write Off Method

The instructions that follow show you how to do the following:

- Start Peachtree Complete Accounting.
- Restore starting data from the South-Western Accounting with Peachtree CD.
- Journalize and post entries related to Uncollectible Accounts Receivable
- Print a Sales Journal and a Cash Receipts Journal.
- Complete the 7-1 Application Problem.

Before you start the 7-1 Application Problem, ask your instructor if Stallworth, the company used for the 7-1 Application Problem, has already been restored on your computer. The instructions that follow assume that Stallworth is being used for the first time.

GETTING STARTED

Use the following instructions to start Peachtree and restore the starting data for Stallworth. The South-Western Accounting with Peachtree CD includes a folder called Peachtree Files-Unit 2. In the steps that follow you will restore the 07-1AP.ptb file.

1. Start Peachtree. From the startup menu, select **Close**.
2. The menu bar shows three options: Files; Options; and Help. Click File; Restore.
3. The Restore Wizard - Select Backup File window appears. Observe that the Location field shows where Peachtree is stored on your computer. The default location is C:\Program Files\Peachtree\ Company. Your Location field may differ. If you are restoring from a network drive, you will need to know the location of the 07-1AP.ptb file.
4. Click **Browse**. The Open Backup File window appears. In the Look in field, double-click on the appropriate location of the Peachtree

Files-Unit 2 folder. Then, click 07-1AP.ptb to select it. (If appropriate, select your CD drive then double-click the Peachtree Files-Unit 2 folder. Click 07-1AP.ptb to select it.)

5. Make sure the Peachtree Files-Unit 2 folder and the 07-1AP.ptb file is selected. (*Hint:* Starting data for the 7-1 Application Problem is in the Peachtree Files-Unit 2 folder.) Click ▭ Open ▭.

6. The Select Backup File window appears. Make sure the Location field shows the correct location for the 07-1AP.ptb file; for example, X:\Peachtree Files-Unit 2\07-1AP.ptb. (Substitute the correct drive letter for X.)

7. Click ▭ Next > ▭. The Select Company window appears. Click on the radio button next to *A New Company*. The Location field shown in this book indicates the default location where drive C is used to install Peachtree. Your Location field may differ. *Make sure that the Location field ends in* **stallwor**. (If your location field does not end in "r," select An Existing Company, then click ▭ Browse ▭. Double-click Stallworth (*or*, 07-1APXX). Your Location field shows the shortened company name stallwor. Continue with step 8.)

8. Click ▭ Next > ▭. The Restore Options window appears.

9. Make sure that the box next to Company Data is *checked*. Click ▭ Next > ▭.

10. The Confirmation window appears. Check the From and To fields to make sure they are correct. Click ▭ Finish ▭. When the Restore Company scale is 100% complete, your data is restored and you are returned to the menu bar.

CHANGING THE COMPANY NAME

Before you start recording transactions for the 7-1 Application Problem, you should look at the company information included on the 07-1AP.ptb file. Follow these steps to look at company information.

1. The Stallworth menu bar should be displayed. From the menu bar, click on Maintain; Company Information. The Maintain Company Information window appears. Observe that the directory field shows where your company is stored on your computer: C:\Program Files\Peachtree\company\stallwor.

2. Type **07-1APXX** in the Company Name field.

3. When you are finished typing 07-1APXX as the company name, click on ▭ OK ▭. Once you have changed the Company Name, each one of your printouts will show the problem number and your initials.

Nothing has changed on your computer's hard drive. The company you restored is identified in the program folder and data folder as C:\Program Files\Peachtree\company\stallwor. What you've done is changed the company name so that your printouts will show the problem number and your initials. Using Maintain, Company Information to rename your company does *not* change the shortened company name.

Instructions:

Stallworth uses the direct write off method of recording uncollectible accounts expense.

1. Journalize and post the following transactions completed during the 2005. Source documents are abbreviated as follows: memorandum, M; receipt, R.

Transactions:

Feb.	16	Wrote off William Rose's past due account as uncollectible, $215.64. M18.
Mar.	23	Received cash in full payment of Emma Peden's account, previously written off as uncollectible, $175.00. M43 and R215.
May	7	Wrote of Tom Ming's past due account uncollectible. $187.32. M61.
Aug.	10	Received cash in full payment of Williams Rose's account, previously written off as uncollectible, $215.64. M78 and R341.

2. Print the Cash Receipts Journal (February 16 – August 10, 2005).

3. Print the Sales Journal (March 23 – August 10, 2005).

4. Back up. The suggested file name is 7-1 Application Problem.ptb.

Journalizing Entries to Write Off Uncollectible Accounts and Collect Written-off Accounts—Allowance Method

The instructions that follow show you how to do the following:

- Start Peachtree Complete Accounting.
- Restore starting data from the South-Western Accounting with Peachtree CD.
- Journalize and post entries related to Uncollectible Accounts Receivable.
- Print a Sales Journal and a Cash Receipts Journal.
- Complete the 7-4 Application Problem.

Before you start the 7-4 Application Problem, ask your instructor if McCafferty, Inc., the company used for the 7-4 Application Problem, has already been restored on your computer. The instructions that follow assume that McCafferty, Inc. is being used for the first time.

GETTING STARTED

Use the following instructions to start Peachtree and restore the starting data for McCafferty, Inc.. The South-Western Accounting with Peachtree CD includes a folder called Peachtree Files-Unit 2. In the steps that follow you will restore the 07-4A.ptb file.

1. Start Peachtree. From the startup menu, select Close.
2. The menu bar shows three options: Files; Options; and Help. Click File; Restore.
3. The Restore Wizard - Select Backup File window appears. Observe that the Location field shows where Peachtree is stored on your computer. The default location is C:\Program Files\Peachtree\Company. Your Location field may differ. If you are restoring from a network drive, you will need to know the location of the 07-4AP.ptb file.

4. Click Browse . The Open Backup File window appears. In the Look in field, double-click on the appropriate location of the Peachtree Files-Unit 2 folder. Then, click 07-4AP.ptb to select it. (If appropriate, select your CD drive then double-click the Peachtree Files-Unit 2 folder. Click 07-4AP.ptb to select it.)

5. Make sure the Peachtree Files-Unit 2 folder and the 07-4AP.ptb file is selected. (*Hint:* Starting data for the 7-4 Application Problem is in the Peachtree Files-Unit 2 folder.) Click Open .

6. The Select Backup File window appears. Make sure the Location field shows the correct location for the 07-4AP.ptb file; for example, X:\Peachtree Files-Unit 2\07-4AP.ptb. (Substitute the correct drive letter for X.)

7. Click Next> . The Select Company window appears. Click on the radio button next to *A New Company*. The Location field shown in this book indicates the default location where drive C is used to install Peachtree. Your Location field may differ. *Make sure that the Location field ends in* **mccinc**. (If your location field does not end in "c, select An Existing Company, then click Browse . Double-click McCafferty, Inc. (*or*, 07-4APXX). Your Location field shows the shortened company name mccinc. Continue with step 8.)

8. Click Next> . The Restore Options window appears.

9. Make sure that the box next to Company Data is *checked*. Click Next> .

10. The Confirmation window appears. Check the From and To fields to make sure they are correct. Click Finish . When the Restore Company scale is 100% complete, your data is restored and you are returned to the menu bar.

CHANGING THE COMPANY NAME

Before you start recording transactions for 7-4AP Application Problem, you should look at the company information included on the 07-4AP.ptb file. Follow these steps to look at company information.

1. The McCafferty, Inc. menu bar should be displayed. From the menu bar, click on Maintain; Company Information. The Maintain Company Information window appears. Observe that the directory field shows where your company is stored on your computer: C:\Program Files\Peachtree\company\mccinc.

2. Type **07-4APXX** in the Company Name field.

3. When you are finished typing 07-4APXX as the company name, click on OK . Once you have changed the Company Name, each one of your printouts will show the problem number and your initials.

Nothing has changed on your computer's hard drive. The company you restored is identified in the program folder and data folder as C:\Program Files\Peachtree\company\mccinc. What you've done is changed the company name so that your printouts will show the problem number and your initials. Using Maintain, Company Information to rename your company does *not* change the shortened company name.

Instructions:

McCafferty, Inc. uses the allowance method for recording uncollectible accounts expense.

1. The following inventory records have been entered in Peachtree. Your Peachtree Problem File, 07-4AP.ptb contains this information.
2. Record the following transactions using Peachtree's Sales Journal (Sales/Invoicing task) and Cash Receipts Journal (Receipts task).

Transactions:

Feb.	14	Wrote off Peggy King's past due account as uncollectible, $357.00. M16.
Apr.	25	Wrote off Mel Kober's past due account as uncollectible, $84.98. M34.
May	12	Received cash in full payment of Carolyn Kelly's account, previously written off as uncollectible, $74.00. M43 and R264.
Aug.	2	Wrote off Lynn Hartman's past due account as uncollectible, $74.93. M71.
Oct.	6	Received cash in full payment of Peggy King's account, previously written off as uncollectible $357.00. M92 and R484.

Journalize and post these transactions in Peachtree's Sales Journal and Cash Receipts Journal.

1. Print the Cash Receipts Journal (February 14–October 6, 2005).
2. Print the Sales Journal (May 12 –October 6, 2005).
3. Back up. The suggested file name is 7-4 Application Problem.ptb.

Recording Entries for Plant Assets

The instructions that follow show you how to do the following:

- Start Peachtree Complete Accounting.
- Restore starting data from the South-Western Accounting with Peachtree CD.
- Journalize and post entries for Plant Assets.
- Print the General Journal, Cash Receipts Journal and the Cash Disbursements Journal.
- Complete the 8-11 Mastery Problem.

Before you start the 8-11 Mastery Problem, ask your instructor if Western, Inc. the company used for the 8-11 Mastery Problem, has already been restored on your computer. The instructions that follow assume that Western, Inc. is being used for the first time.

GETTING STARTED

Use the following instructions to start Peachtree and restore the starting data for Western, Inc. The South-Western Accounting with Peachtree CD includes a folder called Peachtree Files. In the steps that follow you will restore the 08-11MP.ptb file.

1. Start Peachtree. From the startup menu, select Close .
2. The menu bar shows three options: Files; Options; and Help. Click File; Restore.
3. The Restore Wizard - Select Backup File window appears. Observe that the Location field shows where Peachtree is stored on your computer. The default location is C:\Program Files\Peachtree\Company. Your Location field may differ. If you are restoring from a network drive, you will need to know the location of the 08-11MP.ptb file.
4. Click Browse . The Open Backup File window appears. In the Look in field, double-click on the appropriate location of the Peachtree Files-Unit 2 folder. Then, click 08-11MP.ptb to select it. (If appropriate, select your CD drive then double-click the Peachtree Files-Unit 2 folder. Click 08-11MP.ptb to select it.)

5. Make sure the Peachtree Files-Unit 2 folder and the 08-11MP.ptb file is selected. (*Hint:* Starting data for the 8-11 Mastery Problem is in the Peachtree Files-Unit 2 folder.) Click Open.

6. The Select Backup File window appears. Make sure the Location field shows the correct location for the 08-11MP.ptb file; for example, X:\Peachtree Files-Unit 2\08-11MP.ptb. (Substitute the correct drive letter for X.)

7. Click Next>. The Select Company window appears. Click on the radio button next to *A New Company*. The Location field shown in this book indicates the default location where drive C is used to install Peachtree. Your Location field may differ. *Make sure that the Location field ends in* **wesinc**. (If your location field does not end in "c," select An Existing Company, then click Browse. Double-click Western, Inc. (*or,* 08-11MPXX). Your Location field shows the shortened company name wesinc. Continue with step 8.)

8. Click Next>. The Restore Options window appears.

9. Make sure that the box next to Company Data is *checked*. Click Next>.

10. The Confirmation window appears. Check the From and To fields to make sure they are correct. Click Finish. When the Restore Company scale is 100% complete, your data is restored and you are returned to the menu bar.

CHANGING THE COMPANY NAME

Before you start recording transactions for 8-11 Mastery Problem, you should look at the company information included on the 08-11MP.ptb file. Follow these steps to look at company information.

1. The menu bar should be displayed. From the menu bar, click on Maintain; Company Information. The Maintain Company Information window appears. Observe that the directory field shows where your company is stored on your computer: C:\Program Files\Peachtree\company\wesinc.

2. Type **08-11MPXX** in the Company Name field.

3. When you are finished typing 08-11MPXX as the company name, click on OK. Once you have changed the Company Name, each one of your printouts will show the problem number and your initials.

Nothing has changed on your computer's hard drive. The company you restored is identified in the program folder and data folder as C:\Program Files\Peachtree\company\wesinc. What you've done is changed the company name so that your printouts will show the problem number and your initials. Using Maintain, Company Information to rename your company does *not* change the shortened company name.

Instructions:

Western, Inc. uses the straight-line method of calculating depreciation expense. Western uses one plant asset account, Office Equipment, account no. 1230. Beginning account balances have been entered in Peachtree. Your Peachtree Problem File, 08-11MP.ptb contains this information.

1. Journalize and post the January 2 through March 29, 2005 transactions using Peachtree's General Journal or Cash Disbursements Journal. Source documents are abbreviated as follows: check, C; memorandum, M; receipt, R.

Transactions:

Jan.	2	Paid cash for new computer, plant asset no. 172, $1900: estimated salvage value, $400.00; estimated useful life, five years; serial no. SD345J267. C122.
Jan.	2	Discarded desk, serial no. D3481, plant asset no. 167. M47.
Mar.	29	Discarded table, serial no. T3929, plant asset no. 168. M52.

2. Refer to the Receipts window shown below to record the March 30 and June 29, 2005 transactions.

Mar.	30	Received cash from sale of word processor, $100.00: serial no. TM48194H32, plant asset no. 170. M54 and R191.
Jun.	29	Received cash from sale of filing cabinet, $150.00: serial no. FC125, plant asset no. 169. M62 and R224.

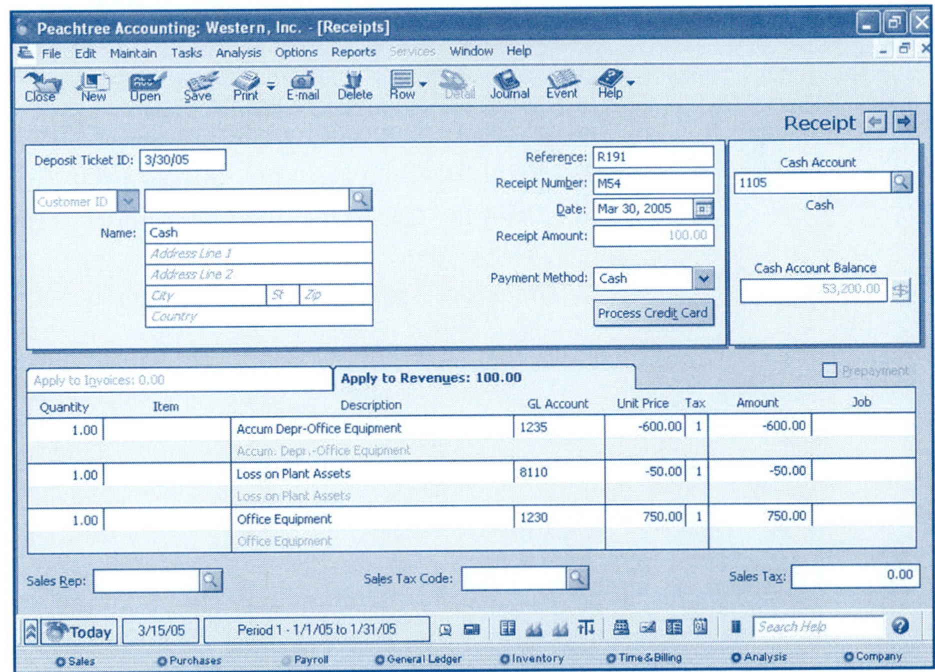

Jul.   2   Paid cash, $500.00, plus old copying machine, serial no. C56M203, plant asset no. 171, for new copying machine: estimated salvage value of new machine, $100.00; estimated useful life of new machine, five years; serial no., C35194, plant asset no. 173. M70 and C239.

3. Refer to the Payments window shown below to complete the July 2 transaction.

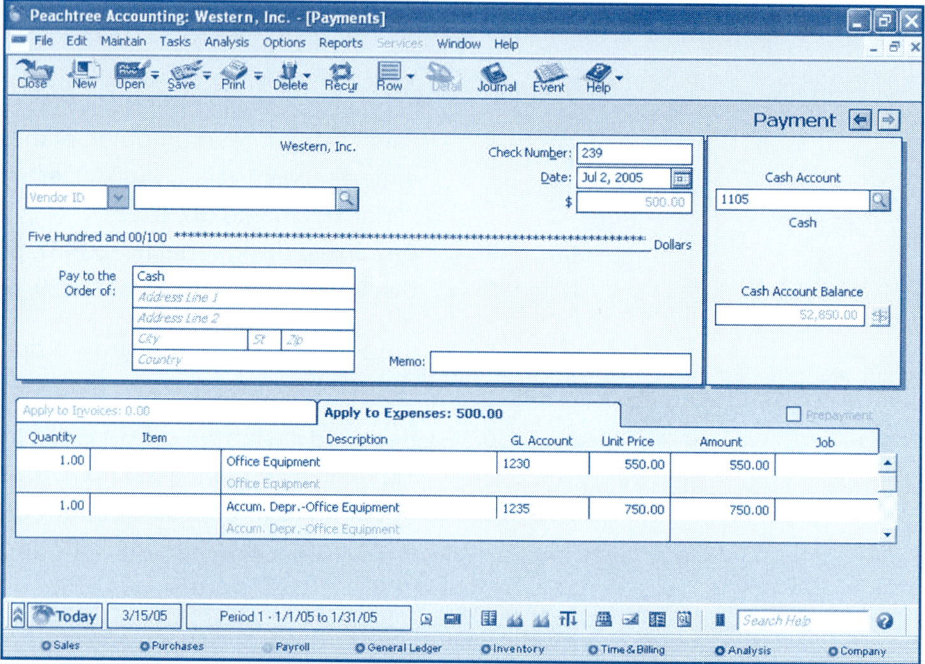

4. Print the General Journal (January 2 through July 2, 2005).

5. Print the Cash Receipts Journal (March 30 through June 29, 2005).

6. Print the Cash Disbursements Journal (January 2 through July 2, 2005).

7. Back up. The suggested file name is 8-11 Mastery Problem.ptb.

Recording Entries for Plant Assets

The instructions that follow show you how to do the following:

- Start Peachtree Complete Accounting.
- Restore starting data from the South-Western Accounting with Peachtree CD.
- Journalize and post entries for Plant Assets.
- Print the General Journal and the Cash Disbursements Journal.
- Complete the 8-12 Challenge Problem.

Before you start the 8-12 Challenge Problem, ask your instructor if McNeilley, Inc., the company used for the 8-12 Challenge Problem, has already been restored on your computer. The instructions that follow assume that McNeilley, Inc. is being used for the first time.

GETTING STARTED

Use the following instructions to start Peachtree and restore the starting data for McNeilley, Inc. The South-Western Accounting with Peachtree CD includes a folder called Peachtree Files-Unit 2. There are two Peachtree data files for the 8-12 Challenge Problem: 08-12CP_2005.ptb and 08-12CP_2007.ptb. In the steps that follow you will restore the 08-12CP_2005.ptb file.

1. Start Peachtree. From the startup menu, select Close.
2. The menu bar shows three options: Files; Options; and Help. Click File; Restore.
3. The Restore Wizard - Select Backup File window appears. Observe that the Location field shows where Peachtree is stored on your computer. The default location is C:\Program Files\Peachtree\Company. Your Location field may differ. If you are restoring from a network drive, you will need to know the location of the 08-12CP_2005.ptb file.
4. Click Browse. The Open Backup File window appears. In the Look in field, double-click on the appropriate location of the Peachtree Files-Unit 2 folder. Then, click 08-12CP_2005.ptb to select it. (If appropriate, select your CD drive then double-click the Peachtree Files-Unit 2 folder. Click 08-12CP_2005.ptb to select it.)

5. Make sure the Peachtree Files-Unit 2 folder and the 08-12CP_2005.ptb file is selected. (*Hint:* Starting data for the 8-12 Challenge Problem is in the Peachtree Files-Unit 2 folder.) Click [Open].

6. The Select Backup File window appears. Make sure the Location field shows the correct location for the 08-12CP_2005.ptb file; for example, X:\Peachtree Files-Unit 2\08-12CP_2005.ptb. (Substitute the correct drive letter for X.)

7. Click [Next >]. The Select Company window appears. Click on the radio button next to *A New Company*. The Location field shown in this book indicates the default location where drive C is used to install Peachtree. Your Location field may differ. *Make sure that the Location field ends* **mcninc**. (If your location field does not end in "c, select An Existing Company, then click [Browse]. Double-click McNeilley, Inc. (*or,* 08-12CP_2005XX). Your Location field shows the shortened company name mcninc. Continue with step 8.)

8. Click [Next >]. The Restore Options window appears.

9. Make sure that the box next to Company Data is *checked*. Click [Next >].

10. The Confirmation window appears. Check the From and To fields to make sure they are correct. Click [Finish]. When the Restore Company scale is 100% complete, your data is restored and you are returned to the menu bar.

CHANGING THE COMPANY NAME

Before you start recording transactions for the 8-12 Challenge Problem, you should look at the company information included on the 08-12CP_2005.ptb file. Follow these steps to look at company information.

1. The McNeilley, Inc. menu bar should be displayed. From the menu bar, click on Maintain; Company Information. The Maintain Company Information window appears. Observe that the directory field shows where your company is stored on your computer: C:\Program Files\Peachtree\company\mcninc.

2. Type **08-12CP_2005XX** in the Company Name field.

3. When you are finished typing 08-12CP_2005XX as the company name, click on [OK]. Once you have changed the Company Name, each one of your printouts will show the problem number and your initials.

Nothing has changed on your computer's hard drive. The company you restored is identified in the program folder and data folder as C:\Program Files\Peachtree\company\mcninc. What you've done is changed the company name so that your printouts will show the problem number and your initials. Using Maintain, Company Information to rename your company does *not* change the shortened company name.

Instructions:

McNeilley, Inc. uses the straight-line method to calculate depreciation expense. McNeilley, Inc. uses two plant asset accounts, Office

Equipment and Delivery Equipment. Observe that the transactions are shown for 2005 and 2007.

Transactions for 2005:

Jan.	1	Paid cash for new office word processor, plant asset no. 1, $600.00 estimated salvage value, $100.00; estimated useful life, eight years; serial no. T45M3409, C130.
Mar.	1	Paid cash for office desk, plant asset no. 2, $700.00: estimated salvage value, $10.00; estimated useful life, five years; no serial no. D345. C190.
Jun.	30	Paid cash for office chair, plant asset no. 3, $125.00; estimated salvage value, $10.00; estimated useful life, five years; no serial no. C200.
Jul.	1	Paid cash for delivery truck, plant asset no. 4, $10,000.00: estimated salvage value, $1,000.00; estimated useful life, five years; serial no. T45X32LD54. C220.

Transactions for 2007:

Jan.	2	Paid cash, $400.00, plus old word processor, serial no. T45M3409, for new word processor: estimated salvage value of new word processor, $100.00; estimated useful life of new word processor, plant asset no. 5, five years; new word processor serial no. T64M4391. M50 and C300.
Jul.	1	Discarded office chair bought on June 30, 20X1. M66.
Sep.	1	Paid cash, $5,500.00, plus old delivery truck, serial no. 345X32LD54, for new delivery truck: estimated salvage value of new truck, $2,200.00; estimated useful life of new truck, plant asset no. 6, five years; new truck serial no. 432XY30LE25. M70 and C310.

1. Journalize and post the 2005 transactions in the Cash Disbursements Journal.
2. Print the Cash Disbursements Journal from January 1, 2005 to July 1, 2005.
3. Back up. The suggested file name is 8-12 Challenge Problem_2005.ptb.
4. Restore the 08-12CP_2007.ptb file.
5. Change the company name to 08-12CP_2007XX.
6. Journalize and post the 2007 transactions in the Cash Disbursements Journal and General Journal.
7. Print the Cash Disbursements Journal from January 2 to September 1, 2007.
8. Print the General Journal from July 1, 2007 to September 1, 2007.
9. Back up. The suggested file name is 8-12 Challenge Problem_2007.ptb.

Journalizing Notes Payable Transactions

The instructions that follow show you how to do the following:

- Start Peachtree Complete Accounting.
- Restore starting data from the South-Western Accounting with Peachtree CD.
- Journalize and post notes payable transactions.
- Print a Cash Receipts Journal and Cash Disbursements Journal.
- Complete the 9-1 Application Problem.

Before you start the 9-1 Application Problem, ask your instructor if Raecker, Inc., the company used for the 9-1 Application Problem, has already been restored on your computer. The instructions that follow assume that Raecker, Inc., is being used for the first time.

GETTING STARTED

Use the following instructions to start Peachtree and restore the starting data for Raecker, Inc. The South-Western Accounting with Peachtree CD includes a folder called Peachtree Files-Unit 2. In the steps that follow you will restore the 09-1AP.ptb file.

1. Start Peachtree. From the startup menu, select [Close].

2. The menu bar shows three options: Files; Options; and Help. Click File; Restore.

3. The Restore Wizard - Select Backup File window appears. Observe that the Location field shows where Peachtree is stored on your computer. The default location is C:\Program Files\Peachtree\Company. Your Location field may differ. If you are restoring from a network drive, you will need to know the location of the 09-1AP.ptb file.

4. Click [Browse]. The Open Backup File window appears. In the Look in field, double-click on the appropriate location of the Peachtree Files-Unit 2 folder. Then, click 09-1AP.ptb to select it. (If appropriate, select your CD drive then double-click the Peachtree Files-Unit 2 folder. Click 09-1AP.ptb to select it.)

5. Make sure the Peachtree Files-Unit 2 folder and the 09-1AP.ptb file is selected. (*Hint:* Starting data for the 9-1 Application Problem is in the Peachtree Files-Unit 2 folder.) Click Open .

6. The Select Backup File window appears. Make sure the Location field shows the correct location for the 09-1AP.ptb file; for example, X:\Peachtree Files-Unit 2\09-1AP.ptb. (Substitute the correct drive letter for X.)

7. Click Next> . The Select Company window appears. Click on the radio button next to *A New Company*. The Location field shown in this book indicates the default location where drive C is used to install Peachtree. Your Location field may differ. *Make sure that the Location field ends in* **raeinc**. (If your location field does not end in "c, select An Existing Company, then click Browse . Double-click Raecker, Inc. (*or,* 09-1APXX). Your Location field shows the shortened company name raeinc. Continue with step 8.)

8. Click Next> . The Restore Options window appears.

9. Make sure that the box next to Company Data is *checked*. Click Next> .

10. The Confirmation window appears. Check the From and To fields to make sure they are correct. Click Finish . When the Restore Company scale is 100% complete, your data is restored and you are returned to the menu bar.

CHANGING THE COMPANY NAME

Before you start recording transactions for 9-1 Application Problem, you should look at the company information included on the 09-1AP.ptb file. Follow these steps to look at company information.

1. The Raeinc menu bar should be displayed. From the menu bar, click on Maintain; Company Information. The Maintain Company Information window appears. Observe that the directory field shows where your company is stored on your computer: C:\Program Files\Peachtree\company\raeinc.

2. Type **09-1APXX** in the Company Name field.

3. When you are finished typing 09-1APXX as the company name, click on OK . Once you have changed the Company Name, each one of your printouts will show the problem number and your initials.

Nothing has changed on your computer's hard drive. The company you restored is identified in the program folder and data folder as C:\Program Files\Peachtree\company\raeinc. What you've done is changed the company name so that your printouts will show the problem number and your initials. Using Maintain, Company Information to rename your company does *not* change the shortened company name.

Raecker, Inc., completed the following transactions during 2005. Source documents are abbreviated as follows: check, C; receipt, R.

Transactions:

Aug.	1	Signed a 90-day, 11% note with City National Bank for $1,100.00, R143.
Sep.	12	Signed a 60-day, 12% note with First American Bank for $1,200.00. R176.
Oct.	21	Signed a 60-day, 10% note with Commercial State Bank for $800.00. R203.

1. Journalize and post the transactions in the cash receipts journal.

2. Use a blank piece of paper or the *Working Papers* to calculate the maturity dates for each note.

3. Use a blank piece of paper or the *Working Papers* to calculate the total amount of interest due at maturity for each note.

4. Journalize and post the following transactions in the cash disbursements journal. Use the maturity dates and the interest amounts calculated in tuje preceding steps.

> Paid cash for the maturity value of the City National Bank note, C245.
>
> Paid cash for the maturity value of the First American Bank note, C352.
>
> Paid cash for the maturity value of Commercial State Bank note, C459.

5. Print the Cash Receipts Journal (August 1 through October 21, 2005).

6. Print the Cash Disbursements Journal (October 30 through December 20, 2005).

7. Back up. The suggested file name is 9-1 Application Problem.ptb.

Journalizing Adjusting and Reversing Entries for Prepaid Expenses Intially Recorded as Expenses and for Accrued Expenses

The instructions that follow show you how to do the following:

- Start Peachtree Complete Accounting.
- Restore starting data from the South-Western Accounting with Peachtree CD.
- Journalize and post transactions.
- Print the General Journal, the Cash Receipts Journal and the Cash Disbursements Journal
- Complete the 9-4 Mastery Problem.

Before you start the 9-4 Mastery Problem, ask your instructor if Sass, Inc. the company used for the 9-4 Mastery Problem, has already been restored on your computer. The instructions that follow assume that Sass, Inc. is being used for the first time.

GETTING STARTED

Use the following instructions to start Peachtree and restore the starting data for Sass, Inc. The South-Western Accounting with Peachtree CD includes a folder called Peachtree Files-Unit 2. In the steps that follow you will restore the 09-4MP.ptb file.

1. Start Peachtree. From the startup menu, select Close .
2. The menu bar shows three options: Files; Options; and Help. Click File; Restore.
3. The Restore Wizard - Select Backup File window appears. Observe that the Location field shows where Peachtree is stored on your computer. The default location is C:\Program Files\Peachtree\Company. Your Location field may differ. If you are restoring from a network drive, you will need to know the location of the 09-4MP.ptb file.
4. Click Browse . The Open Backup File window appears. In the Look in field, double-click on the appropriate location of the Peachtree

Files-Unit 2 folder. Then, click 09-4MP.ptb to select it. (If appropriate, select your CD drive then double-click the Peachtree Files-Unit 2 folder. Click 09-4MP.ptb to select it.)

5. Make sure the Peachtree Files-Unit 2 folder and the 09-4MP.ptb file is selected. (*Hint:* Starting data for the 9-4 Mastery Problem is in the Peachtree Files-Unit 2 folder.) Click Open .

6. The Select Backup File window appears. Make sure the Location field shows the correct location for the 09-4MP.ptb file; for example, X:\Peachtree Files-Unit 2\09-4MP.ptb. (Substitute the correct drive letter for X.)

7. Click Next> . The Select Company window appears. Click on the radio button next to *A New Company*. The Location field shown in this book indicates the default location where drive C is used to install Peachtree. Your Location field may differ. *Make sure that the Location field ends in* **sasinc**. (If your location field does not end in "c," select An Existing Company, then click Browse . Double-click Sass, Inc. (*or,* 09-4MPXX). Your Location field shows the shortened company name sasinc. Continue with step 8.)

8. Click Next> . The Restore Options window appears.

9. Make sure that the box next to Company Data is *checked*. Click Next> .

10. The Confirmation window appears. Check the From and To fields to make sure they are correct. Click Finish . When the Restore Company scale is 100% complete, your data is restored and you are returned to the menu bar.

CHANGING THE COMPANY NAME

Before you start recording transactions for 9-4 Mastery Problem, you should look at the company information included on the 09-4MP.ptb file. Follow these steps to look at company information.

1. The Sass, Inc. menu bar should be displayed. From the menu bar, click on Maintain; Company Information. The Maintain Company Information window appears. Observe that the directory field shows where your company is stored on your computer: C:\Program Files\Peachtree\company\sasinc.

2. Type **09-4MPXX** in the Company Name field.

3. When you are finished typing 09-4MPXX as the company name, click on OK . Once you have changed the Company Name, each one of your printouts will show the problem number and your initials.

Nothing has changed on your computer's hard drive. The company you restored is identified in the program folder and data folder as C:\Program Files\Peachtree\company\sasinc. What you've done is changed the company name so that your printouts will show the problem number and your initials. Using Maintain, Company Information to rename your company does *not* change the shortened company name.

Sass, Inc., completed the following transactions during 2005. Sass initially records prepaid expenses as expenses. Source documents are abbreviated as follows: check, C; receipt, R.

Transactions:

Jul.	1	Signed a 60-day, 12% note with Southern Bank for $700.00. R123.
Oct.	10	Signed a 45-day, 10% note with American Bank for $1,500.00. R149.
Nov.	1	Signed a 90-day, 11% note with Commercial Bank for $1,000.00. R152.

1. Journalize and post the transactions in the cash receipts journal.
2. Use a blank piece of paper or the *Working Papers* to calculate the maturity dates for each note.
3. Journalize and post the following transactions in the cash disbursements journal. Use the maturity dates calculated in the prior step.

> Paid cash for the maturity value of the Southern Bank note. C105.
> Paid cash for the maturity value of the American Bank note. C195.

4. Sass, Inc., has the following general ledger balances on December 31, 2005 before adjusting entries are recorded.

Supplies Expense – Administrative	$400.00
Supplies Expense – Sales	600.00
Insurance Expense	900.00

Use the following information to journalize and post adjusting entries for prepaid expenses and accrued expenses on December 31, 2005. The estimated federal income tax is $800.00.

Administrative Supplies Inventory	$200.00
Sales Supplies Inventory	300.00
Value of Prepaid Insurance	350.00

Payroll and Employee Payroll Taxes	
Salaries – Administrative	$350.00
Salaries – Sales	415.00
Federal Income Tax Withheld	120.00
Social Security Tax Withheld	49.73
Medicare Tax Withheld	11.47

Employer Payroll Taxes	
Social Security Tax	$49.73
Medicare Tax	11.47
Federal Unemployment Tax	6.12
State Unemployment Tax	41.31

3. Print the Cash Receipts Journal (July 1 to November 1, 2005).

4. Print the Cash Disbursements Journal (August 30 to November 24, 2005).

5. Journalize and post the appropriate reversing entries on January 1, 2006.

6. Print the General Journal (December 31, 2005 through January 1, 2006).

7. Back up. The suggested file name is 9-4 Mastery Problem.ptb.

Journalizing Transactions for Notes Receivable

The instructions that follow show you how to do the following:

- Start Peachtree Complete Accounting.
- Restore starting data from the South-Western Accounting with Peachtree CD.
- Journalize and post Notes Receivable transactions.
- Print the Cash Receipts Journal and the Sales Journal.
- Complete the 10-1 Application Problem.

Before you start the 10-1 Application Problem, ask your instructor if Bellingham, Inc., the company used for the 10-1 Application Problem, has already been restored on your computer. The instructions that follow assume that Bellingham, Inc. is being used for the first time.

GETTING STARTED

Use the following instructions to start Peachtree and restore the starting data for Bellingham, Inc. The South-Western Accounting with Peachtree CD includes a folder called Peachtree Files-Unit 2. In the steps that follow you will restore the 10-1AP.ptb file.

1. Start Peachtree. From the startup menu, select Close .
2. The menu bar shows three options: Files; Options; and Help. Click File; Restore.
3. The Restore Wizard - Select Backup File window appears. Observe that the Location field shows where Peachtree is stored on your computer. The default location is C:\Program Files\Peachtree\Company. Your Location field may differ. If you are restoring from a network drive, you will need to know the location of the 10-1AP.ptb file.
4. Click Browse . The Open Backup File window appears. In the Look in field, double-click on the appropriate location of the Peachtree Files-Unit 2 folder. Then, click 10-1AP.ptb to select it. (If appropriate, select your CD drive then double-click the Peachtree Files-Unit 2 folder. Click 10-1AP.ptb to select it.)

5. Make sure the Peachtree Files-Unit 2 folder and the 10-1AP.ptb file is selected. (*Hint:* Starting data for the 10-1 Application Problem is in the Peachtree Files-Unit 2 folder.) Click [Open].

6. The Select Backup File window appears. Make sure the Location field shows the correct location for the 10-1AP.ptb file; for example, X:\Peachtree Files-Unit 2\10-1AP.ptb. (Substitute the correct drive letter for X.)

7. Click [Next >]. The Select Company window appears. Click on the radio button next to *A New Company*. The Location field shown in this book indicates the default location where drive C is used to install Peachtree. Your Location field may differ. *Make sure that the Location field ends in* **belinc**. (If your location field does not end in "c," select An Existing Company, then click [Browse]. Double-click Bellingham (*or,* 10-1APXX). Your Location field shows the shortened company name belinc. Continue with step 8.)

8. Click [Next >]. The Restore Options window appears.

9. Make sure that the box next to Company Data is *checked*. Click [Next >].

10. The Confirmation window appears. Check the From and To fields to make sure they are correct. Click [Finish]. When the Restore Company scale is 100% complete, your data is restored and you are returned to the menu bar.

CHANGING THE COMPANY NAME

Before you start recording transactions for the 10-1 Application Problem, you should look at the company information included on the 10-1AP.ptb file. Follow these steps to look at company information.

1. The Bellingham, Inc. menu bar should be displayed. From the menu bar, click on Maintain; Company Information. The Maintain Company Information window appears. Observe that the directory field shows where your company is stored on your computer: C:\Program Files\Peachtree\company\belinc.

2. Type **10-1APXX** in the Company Name field.

3. When you are finished typing 10-1APXX as the company name, click on [OK]. Once you have changed the Company Name, each one of your printouts will show the problem number and your initials.

Nothing has changed on your computer's hard drive. The company you restored is identified in the program folder and data folder as C:\Program Files\Peachtree\company\belinc. What you've done is changed the company name so that your printouts will show the problem number and your initials. Using Maintain, Company Information to rename your company does *not* change the shortened company name.

Bellingham, Inc., completed the following transactions during the year.

Transactions:

Aug.	1	Bellingham agreed to an extension of time on James Huber's account by accepting a 60-day, 10% note from him, $200.00. NR1.
Aug.	1	Accepted a 60-day, 12% note from Frank Otto for a sale on account, $300.00. NR2.
Sep.	30	The 60-day, 10% note from James Huber (NR1) was dishonored; $200.00 plus interest. M12.
Sep.	30	Accepted a 60-day, 10% note from Melissa Carr for an extension of time on her account, $500.00. NR3.
Sep.	30	Received cash for the maturity value of NR2, $300.00 plus interest. R10.
Nov.	30	Principal, $500.00, plus interest was received for the maturity value of NR3. R32.
Dec.	1	James Huber sent a check for dishonored NR1, $203.33 plus additional interest. R33.

1. Journalize and post the August 1 through December 1, 2005 transactions using the Cash Receipts Journal or Sales Journal.
2. Print the Cash Receipts Journal (August 1 through December 1, 2005).
3. Print the Sales Journal (September 30 through September 30, 2005).
4. Back up. The suggested file name is 10-1 Application Problem.ptb.

Journalizing Notes Receivable, Unearned Revenue, and Accrued Revenue Initially Recorded as Revenue Transactions

The instructions that follow show you how to do the following:

- Start Peachtree Complete Accounting.
- Restore starting data from the South-Western Accounting with Peachtree CD.
- Journalize and post Notes Receivable transactions.
- Print the Cash Receipts Journal, Sales Journal, and the General Journal.
- Journalize and post adjusting entries.
- Journalize and post reversing entries.
- Complete the 10-4 Mastery Problem.

Before you start the 10-4 Mastery Problem, ask your instructor if Marier, Inc., the company used for the 10-4 Mastery Problem, has already been restored on your computer. The instructions that follow assume that Marier, Inc. is being used for the first time.

GETTING STARTED

Use the following instructions to start Peachtree and restore the starting data for Marier, Inc. The South-Western Accounting with Peachtree CD includes a folder called Peachtree Files-Unit 2. In the steps that follow you will restore the 010-4MP.ptb file.

1. Start Peachtree. From the startup menu, select Close .
2. The menu bar shows three options: Files; Options; and Help. Click File; Restore.
3. The Restore Wizard - Select Backup File window appears. Observe that the Location field shows where Peachtree is stored on your computer. The default location is C:\Program Files\Peachtree\ Company. Your Location field may differ. If you are restoring from a network drive, you will need to know the location of the 10-4MP.ptb file.

4. Click Browse . The Open Backup File window appears. In the Look in field, double-click on the appropriate location of the Peachtree Files-Unit 2 folder. Then, click 10-4MP.ptb to select it. (If appropriate, select your CD drive then double-click the Peachtree Files-Unit 2 folder. Click 10-4MP.ptb to select it.)

5. Make sure the Peachtree Files-Unit 2 folder and the10-4MP.ptb file is selected. (*Hint:* Starting data for the 10-4 Mastery Problem is in the Peachtree Files-Unit 2 folder.) Click Open .

6. The Select Backup File window appears. Make sure the Location field shows the correct location for the 10-4MP.ptb file; for example, X:\Peachtree Files-Unit 2\10-4MP.ptb. (Substitute the correct drive letter for X.)

7. Click Next> . The Select Company window appears. Click on the radio button next to *A New Company*. The Location field shown in this book indicates the default location where drive C is used to install Peachtree. Your Location field may differ. *Make sure that the Location field ends in* **marinc**. (If your location field does not end in "c," select An Existing Company, then click Browse . Double-click Marier, Inc. (*or*, 10-4MPXX). Your Location field shows the shortened company name marinc. Continue with step 8.)

8. Click Next> . The Restore Options window appears.

9. Make sure that the box next to Company Data is *checked*. Click Next> .

10. The Confirmation window appears. Check the From and To fields to make sure they are correct. Click Finish . When the Restore Company scale is 100% complete, your data is restored and you are returned to the menu bar.

CHANGING THE COMPANY NAME

Before you start recording transactions for 10-4 Mastery Problem, you should look at the company information included on the 10-4MP.ptb file. Follow these steps to look at company information.

1. The Marier, Inc. menu bar should be displayed. From the menu bar, click on Maintain; Company Information. The Maintain Company Information window appears. Observe that the directory field shows where your company is stored on your computer: C:\Program Files\Peachtree\company\marinc.

2. Type **10-4MPXX** in the Company Name field.

3. When you are finished typing 10-4MPXX as the company name, click on OK . Once you have changed the Company Name, each one of your printouts will show the problem number and your initials.

Nothing has changed on your computer's hard drive. The company you restored is identified in the program folder and data folder as C:\Program Files\Peachtree\company\marinc. What you've done is changed the company name so that your printouts will show the problem number and your initials. Using Maintain, Company Information to rename your company does *not* change the shortened company name.

Instructions:

Marier, Inc., completed the following transactions during 2005. Marier initially records prepaid and unearned items as revenue

Transactions:

Jul.	1	Accepted a 90 day, 10% note from Timothy Johnson for a sale on account, $500.00. NR12.
Jul.	5	Accepted a 90-day, 12% note from Gerald Krammer for an extension of time on his account, $600.00. NR13.
Sep.	29	Timothy Johnson dishonored NR12, a 90-day, 10% note, $500.00 plus interest. M32.
Oct.	3	Received cash for the maturity value of NR13, $600.00 plus interest. R65.
Nov.	1	Received cash for November through January rent, $500.00 per month, in advance from Centuria, Inc., $1500.00. R70.
Dec.	1	Received cash from Timothy Johnson for dishonored NR12, $512.50 plus additional interest. R81.
Dec.	4	Accepted a 90-day, 12% note from Jackie Webb for sale on account, $900.00. NR14.

1. Journalize and post the August 1 through December 1 transactions using Peachtree's Cash Receipts Journal and Sales Journal.
2. Print the Cash Receipts Journal (July 1 through December 4, 2005).
3. Print the Sales Journal (September 20 through September 20, 2005).
4. Journalize and post the necessary adjusting entries.
5. Journalize the reversing entries on January 1, 2006.
6. Print the December 31, 2005 through January 1, 2006 general journal.
7. Back up. The suggested file name is 10-4 Mastery Problem.ptb.

Journalizing Transactions for Declaring and Paying Dividends

The instructions that follow show you how to do the following:

- Start Peachtree Complete Accounting.
- Restore starting data from the South-Western Accounting with Peachtree CD.
- Journalize and post transactions for declaring and paying dividends.
- Print the General Journal and the Cash Disbursements Journal.
- Complete the 11-4 Application Problem.

Before you start the 11-4 Application Problem, ask your instructor if PlasticTech, Inc., the company used for the 11-4 Application Problem, has already been restored on your computer. The instructions that follow assume that PlasticTech, Inc. is being used for the first time.

GETTING STARTED

Use the following instructions to start Peachtree and restore the starting data for PlasticTech, Inc. The South-Western Accounting with Peachtree CD includes a folder called Peachtree Files-Unit 2. In the steps that follow you will restore the 011-4AP.ptb file.

1. Start Peachtree. From the startup menu, select Close .
2. The menu bar shows three options: Files; Options; and Help. Click File; Restore.
3. The Restore Wizard - Select Backup File window appears. Observe that the Location field shows where Peachtree is stored on your computer. The default location is C:\Program Files\Peachtree\Company. Your Location field may differ. If you are restoring from a network drive, you will need to know the location of the 11-4AP.ptb file.
4. Click Browse . The Open Backup File window appears. In the Look in field, double-click on the appropriate location of the Peachtree Files-Unit 2 folder. Then, click 11-4AP.ptb to select it. (If appropriate, select your CD drive then double-click the Peachtree Files-Unit 2 folder. Click 11-4AP.ptb to select it.)

5. Make sure the Peachtree Files-Unit 2 folder and the 11-4AP.ptb file is selected. (*Hint:* Starting data for the 11-4 Application Problem is in the Peachtree Files-Unit 2 folder.) Click Open .

6. The Select Backup File window appears. Make sure the Location field shows the correct location for the 11-4AP.ptb file; for example, X:\Peachtree Files-Unit 2\11-4AP.ptb. (Substitute the correct drive letter for X.)

7. Click Next> . The Select Company window appears. Click on the radio button next to *A New Company*. The Location field shown in this book indicates the default location where drive C is used to install Peachtree. Your Location field may differ. *Make sure that the Location field ends in* **plainc**. (If your location field does not end in "c," select An Existing Company, then click Browse . Double-click Plastic Tech, Inc. (*or*, 11-4APXX). Your Location field shows the shortened company name plainc. Continue with step 8.)

8. Click Next> . The Restore Options window appears.

9. Make sure that the box next to Company Data is *checked*. Click Next> .

10. The Confirmation window appears. Check the From and To fields to make sure they are correct. Click Finish . When the Restore Company scale is 100% complete, your data is restored and you are returned to the menu bar.

CHANGING THE COMPANY NAME

Before you start recording transactions for 11-4 Application Problem, you should look at the company information included on the 11-4AP.ptb file. Follow these steps to look at company information.

1. PlasticTech, Inc. menu bar should be displayed. From the menu bar, click on Maintain; Company Information. The Maintain Company Information window appears. Observe that the directory field shows where your company is stored on your computer: C:\Program Files\Peachtree\company\plainc.

2. Type **11-4APXX** in the Company Name field.

3. When you are finished typing 11-4APXX as the company name, click on OK . Once you have changed the Company Name, each one of your printouts will show the problem number and your initials.

Nothing has changed on your computer's hard drive. The company you restored is identified in the program folder and data folder as C:\Program Files\Peachtree\company\plainc. What you've done is changed the company name so that your printouts will show the problem number and your initials. Using Maintain, Company Information to rename your company does *not* change the shortened company name.

PlasticTech, Inc. completed the following transactions during 2005.

Transactions:

Aug. 12   Plastic Tech's board of directors declared an annual dividend of $180,000.00. Preferred stock issued is $500,000.00 of 10%, $100.00 par-value preferred stock. Common stock issued is $1,000,000.00 of $1,000.00 stated-value common stock. Date of payment is November 15. M65.

Nov. 15   Paid $180,000.00 cash for annual dividend declared August 12. C139.

1. Journalize and post the August 12 and November 12 transactions using Peachtree's General Journal and Cash Disbursements Journal.

2. Print the General Journal (August 12 through August 12, 2005).

3. Print the Cash Disbursements Journal (November 15 through November 15, 2005).

4. Back up. The suggested file name is 11-4 Application Problem.ptb.

Journalizing Transactions for Starting a Corporation, Declaring and Paying Dividends, and Preparing a Balance Sheet

The instructions that follow show you how to do the following:

- Start Peachtree Complete Accounting.
- Restore starting data from the South-Western Accounting with Peachtree CD.
- Journalize and post the transaction for starting a corporation
- Journalize and post transactions for declaring and paying dividends.
- Print the Cash Receipts Journal, Cash Disbursements Journal.
- Print the Balance Sheet.
- Print the General Journal.
- Complete the 11-5 Mastery Problem.

Before you start the 11-5 Mastery Problem, ask your instructor if SkyPark, Inc., the company used for the 11-5 Mastery Problem, has already been restored on your computer. The instructions that follow assume that SkyPark, Inc. is being used for the first time.

GETTING STARTED

Use the following instructions to start Peachtree and restore the starting data for SkyPark, Inc. The South-Western Accounting with Peachtree CD includes a folder called Peachtree Files-Unit 2. In the steps that follow you will restore the 011-5MP.ptb file.

1. Start Peachtree. From the startup menu, select Close .

2. The menu bar shows three options: Files; Options; and Help. Click File; Restore.

3. The Restore Wizard - Select Backup File window appears. Observe that the Location field shows where Peachtree is stored on your computer. The default location is C:\Program Files\Peachtree\Company. Your Location field may differ. If you are restoring from a network drive, you will need to know the location of the 11-5MP.ptb file.

4. Click [Browse]. The Open Backup File window appears. In the Look in field, double-click on the appropriate location of the Peachtree Files-Unit 2 folder. Then, click 11-5MP.ptb to select it. (If appropriate, select your CD drive then double-click the Peachtree Files-Unit 2 folder.) Click 11-5MP.ptb to select it.

5. Make sure the Peachtree Files-Unit 2 folder and the 11-5MP.ptb file is selected. (*Hint:* Starting data for the 11-5 Mastery Problem is in the Peachtree Files-Unit 2 folder.) Click [Open].

6. The Select Backup File window appears. Make sure the Location field shows the correct location for the 11-5MP.ptb file; for example, X:\Peachtree Files-Unit 2\11-5MP.ptb. (Substitute the correct drive letter for X.)

7. Click [Next >]. The Select Company window appears. Click on the radio button next to *A New Company*. The Location field shown in this book indicates the default location where drive C is used to install Peachtree. Your Location field may differ. *Make sure that the Location field ends in* **skyinc**. (If your location field does not end in "c," select An Existing Company, then click [Browse]. Double-click SkyPark, Inc. (*or*, 11-5MPXX). Your Location field shows the shortened company name skyinc. Continue with step 8.)

8. Click [Next >]. The Restore Options window appears.

9. Make sure that the box next to Company Data is *checked*. Click [Next >].

10. The Confirmation window appears. Check the From and To fields to make sure they are correct. Click [Finish]. When the Restore Company scale is 100% complete, your data is restored and you are returned to the menu bar.

CHANGING THE COMPANY NAME

Before you start recording transactions for 11-5 Mastery Problem, you should look at the company information included on the 11-5MP.ptb file. Follow these steps to look at company information.

1. SkyPark, Inc. menu bar should be displayed. From the menu bar, click on Maintain; Company Information. The Maintain Company Information window appears. Observe that the directory field shows where your company is stored on your computer: C:\Program Files\Peachtree\company\skyinc

2. Type **11-5MPXX** in the Company Name field.

3. When you are finished typing 11-5MPXX as the company name, click on [OK]. Once you have changed the Company Name, each one of your printouts will show the problem number and your initials.

Nothing has changed on your computer's hard drive. The company you restored is identified in the program folder and data folder as C:\Program Files\Peachtree\company\skyinc. What you've done is

changed the company name so that your printouts will show the problem number and your initials. Using Maintain, Company Information
to rename your company does *not* change the shortened company
name.

Instructions:

SkyPark, Inc. received its charter on August 1, 2005. The corporation is
authorized to issue 150,000 shares of $5.00 stated-value common stock
and 50,000 shares of 10%, $100.00 par-value preferred stock.

Transactions:

Aug.	4	Ten incorporators pay cash for 50,000 shares of $5.00 stated-value common stock, $250,000.00. R1-10.
Aug.	4	Dan O'Brien was reimbursed for organizations costs, $6,500.00. C1.
Aug.	6	Diane Scalacci subscribed to purchase 500 shares of $5.00 stated-value common stock, $2,500.00. M1.
Aug.	21	McCabe Daniels subscribed to purchase 3,000 shares of $5.00 stated-value common stock, $15,000.00. M2.
Sep.	16	Diane Scolacci made full payment on stock subscription, $2,500.00. R11.
Sep.	16	Issued Stock Certificate No. 11 to Diane Scalacci for 500 shares. M3.
Oct.	1	McCabe Daniels made a partial payment on stock subscription, $7,500.00. R12.
Oct.	15	Kay Mehta subscribed to purchase 6,000 shares of $5.00 stated-value common stock, $30,000.00. M4.
Nov.	1	McCabe Daniels made final payment on stock subscription, $7,500.00. R13.
Nov.	1	Issued Stock Certificate No. 12 to McCabe Daniels for 3,000 shares. M5.

1. Journalize and post the August 4 through November 1, 2005 transactions using Peachtree's General Journal, Cash Receipts Journal,
   and Cash Disbursements Journal.

2. Print the Cash Receipts Journal (August 4 through November 11,
   2005).

3. Print the Cash Disbursements Journal (August 4 through August 4,
   2005).

4. Print the Balance Sheet (as of December 31, 2005). To print the
   Balance Sheet (as of December 31, 2005). Click Reports; Financial
   Statements. Then, highlight <Standard> Balance Sheet and click
   [Print]. On the <Standard> Balance Sheet window, click the down-
   arrow in the Time Frame field, then select Range. Click the From
   field and select Period 8, (8/1/05), then click the To field and select
   Period 12 (12/31/05). Make the selections to print.

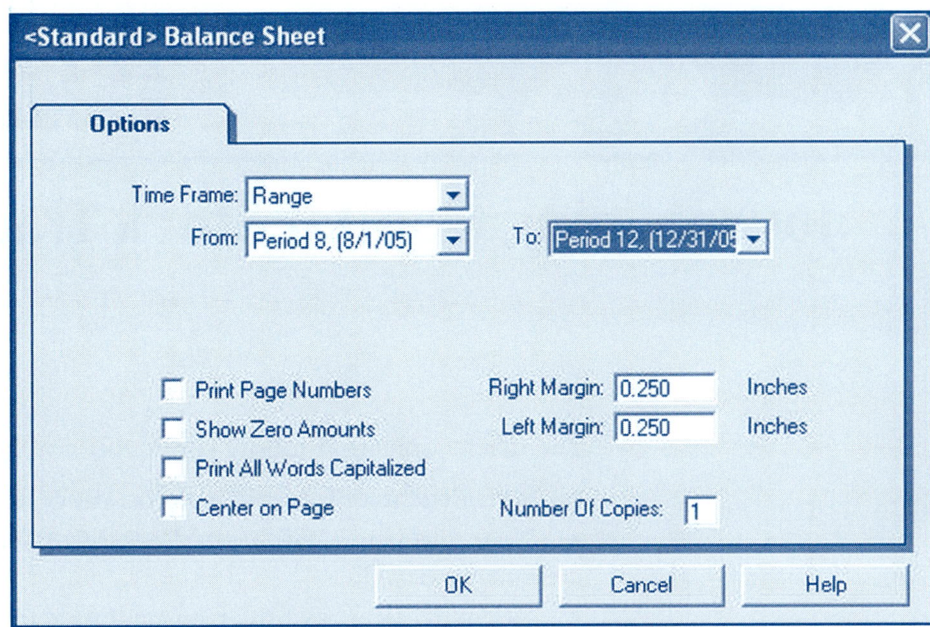

5. Back up. The suggested file name is 11-5 Mastery Problem_12-31-05.ptb.

6. Record this transactions for 2006:

Nov 15   SkyPark's board of directors declared an annual dividend of $40,000.00. Preferred stock issued is $100,000.00 of 10%, $100.00 par-value preferred stock. Common stock issued is $400,000.00 of $5.00 stated-value common stock. Date of payment is January 15. M206.

7. Print the General Journal from (August 6, 2005 through November 15, 2006).

8. Back up. The suggested file name is 11-5 Mastery Problem.ptb.

9. Use a blank piece of paper or the *Working Papers* to complete the following journal entry for the third year (2007). In Peachtree you can journalize and post entries for two years, *not* three.

Jan 15   Paid cash for annual dividend declared November 15, $40,000.00. C339.

Journalizing Capital Stock Transactions

The instructions that follow show you how to do the following:

- Start Peachtree Complete Accounting.
- Restore starting data from the South-Western Accounting with Peachtree CD.
- Journalize and post the transactions related to the issuance of stock.
- Print the Cash Receipts Journal and the General Journal
- Complete the 12-1 Application Problem.

Before you start the 12-1 Application Problem, ask your instructor if PC Design, Inc., the company used for the 12-1 Application Problem, has already been restored on your computer. The instructions that follow assume that PC Design, Inc. is being used for the first time.

GETTING STARTED

Use the following instructions to start Peachtree and restore the starting data for PC Design, Inc. The South-Western Accounting with Peachtree CD includes a folder called Peachtree Files-Unit 2. In the steps that follow you will restore the 12-1AP.ptb file.

1. Start Peachtree. From the startup menu, select [Close].
2. The menu bar shows three options: Files; Options; and Help. Click File; Restore.
3. The Restore Wizard - Select Backup File window appears. Observe that the Location field shows where Peachtree is stored on your computer. The default location is C:\Program Files\Peachtree\Company. Your Location field may differ. If you are restoring from a network drive, you will need to know the location of the 12-1AP.ptb file.
4. Click [Browse]. The Open Backup File window appears. In the Look in field, double-click on the appropriate location of the Peachtree Files-Unit 2 folder. Then, click 12-1AP.ptb to select it. (If appropriate, select your CD drive then double-click the Peachtree Files-Unit 2 folder. Click 12-1AP.ptb to select it.)

5. Make sure the Peachtree Files-Unit 2 folder and the 12-1AP.ptb file is selected. (*Hint:* Starting data for the 12-1 Application Problem is in the Peachtree Files-Unit 2 folder.) Click [Open].

6. The Select Backup File window appears. Make sure the Location field shows the correct location for the 12-1AP.ptb file; for example, X:\Peachtree Files-Unit 2\12-1AP.ptb. (Substitute the correct drive letter for X.)

7. Click [Next >]. The Select Company window appears. Click on the radio button next to *A New Company*. The Location field shown in this book indicates the default location where drive C is used to install Peachtree. Your Location field may differ. *Make sure that the Location field ends in* **pcdesinc**. (If your location field does not end in "c," select An Existing Company, then click [Browse]. Double-click PC Design, Inc. (*or*, 12-1APXX). Your Location field shows the shortened company name pcdesinc. Continue with step 8.)

8. Click [Next >]. The Restore Options window appears.

9. Make sure that the box next to Company Data is *checked*. Click [Next >].

10. The Confirmation window appears. Check the From and To fields to make sure they are correct. Click [Finish]. When the Restore Company scale is 100% complete, your data is restored and you are returned to the menu bar.

CHANGING THE COMPANY NAME

Before you start recording transactions for the 12-1 Application Problem, you should look at the company information included on the 12-1AP.ptb file. Follow these steps to look at company information.

1. PC Design, Inc. menu bar should be displayed. From the menu bar, click on Maintain; Company Information. The Maintain Company Information window appears. Observe that the directory field shows where your company is stored on your computer: C:\Program Files\Peachtree\company\pcdesinc

2. Type **12-1APXX** in the Company Name field.

3. When you are finished typing 12-1APXX as the company name, click on [OK]. Once you have changed the Company Name, each one of your printouts will show the problem number and your initials.

Nothing has changed on your computer's hard drive. The company you restored is identified in the program folder and data folder as C:\Program Files\Peachtree\company\pcdesinc. What you've done is changed the company name so that your printouts will show the problem number and your initials. Using Maintain, Company Information to rename your company does *not* change the shortened company name.

PC Design, Inc. is authorized to issue 200,000 shares of $5.00 stated-value common stock and 50,000 shares of 12%, $100.00 par value preferred stock. PC Design has 25,000 shares of common stock outstanding.

Transactions:

Feb. 8   Andre Cashman sent a check for 5,000 shares of $5.00 stated value common stock at $5.00 per share, $25,000.00. R398.

Feb. 26   Jason Gutta exchanged a parcel of land at an agreed value of $30,000.00 for 300 shares of $100.00 par value preferred stock. M67.

Apr. 15   Jacquelyn Parker sent a $40,000.00 check for 400 shares of $100.00 par value preferred stock at $100.00 pweer share. R518.

Aug. 25   Received a $48,000.00 check from Lynn Kruschke for 500 shares of $100.00 par value preferred stock at $96.00 per share. R601

Dec. 11   Received cash from Behrooz Behzadi for 200 shares of $100.00 par value preferred stock at $102.00 per share, $20,400.00. R698.

1. Journalize and post the February 8 through December 11 transactions using Peachtree's Cash Receipts Journal and General Journal.
2. Print the Cash Receipts Journal (February 8 through December 11, 2005).
3. Print the General Journal (February 26 through February 26, 2005).
4. Back up the 12-1 Application Problem.ptb.

Journalizing Stock and Bond Transactions

The instructions that follow show you how to do the following:

- Start Peachtree Complete Accounting.
- Restore starting data from the South-Western Accounting with Peachtree CD.
- Journalize and post transactions related to the issuance of bonds
- Journalize and post a transaction related to the purchase of stock.
- Print the Cash Receipts Journal and the Cash Disbursements Journal
- Complete the 12-4 Mastery Problem.

Before you start the 12-4 Mastery Problem, ask your instructor if Sentry VideoLink, Inc., the company used for the 12-4 Mastery Problem, has already been restored on your computer. The instructions that follow assume that Sentry VideoLink, Inc. is being used for the first time.

GETTING STARTED

Use the following instructions to start Peachtree and restore the starting data for Sentry VideoLink, Inc. The South-Western Accounting with Peachtree CD includes a folder called Peachtree Files-Unit 2. In the steps that follow you will restore the 12-4MP.ptb file.

1. Start Peachtree. From the startup menu, select Close .
2. The menu bar shows three options: Files; Options; and Help. Click File; Restore.
3. The Restore Wizard - Select Backup File window appears. Observe that the Location field shows where Peachtree is stored on your computer. The default location is C:\Program Files\Peachtree\ Company. Your Location field may differ. If you are restoring from a network drive, you will need to know the location of the 12-4MP.ptb file.
4. Click Browse . The Open Backup File window appears. In the Look in field, double-click on the appropriate location of the Peachtree Files-Unit 2 folder. Then, click 12-4MP.ptb to select it. (If

appropriate, select your CD drive then double-click the Peachtree Files-Unit 2 folder. Click 12-4MP.ptb to select it.)

5. Make sure the Peachtree Files-Unit 2 folder and the 12-4MP.ptb file is selected. (*Hint:* Starting data for the 12-4 Mastery Problem is in the Peachtree Files-Unit 2 folder.) Click Open .

6. The Select Backup File window appears. Make sure the Location field shows the correct location for the 12-4MP.ptb file; for example, X:\Peachtree Files-Unit 2\12-4MP.ptb. (Substitute the correct drive letter for X.)

7. Click Next > . The Select Company window appears. Click on the radio button next to *A New Company*. The Location field shown in this book indicates the default location where drive C is used to install Peachtree. Your Location field may differ. *Make sure that the Location field ends in* **senvidin**. (If your location field does not end in "n," select An Existing Company, then click Browse . Double-click Sentry VideoLink, Inc. (*or,* 12-4MPXX). Your Location field shows the shortened company name senvidin. Continue with step 8.)

8. Click Next > . The Restore Options window appears.

9. Make sure that the box next to Company Data is *checked*. Click Next > .

10. The Confirmation window appears. Check the From and To fields to make sure they are correct. Click Finish . When the Restore Company scale is 100% complete, your data is restored and you are returned to the menu bar.

CHANGING THE COMPANY NAME

Before you start recording transactions for the 12-4 Mastery Problem, you should look at the company information included on the 12-4MP.ptb file. Follow these steps to look at company information.

1. The Sentry VideoLink, Inc. menu bar should be displayed. From the menu bar, click on Maintain; Company Information. The Maintain Company Information window appears. Observe that the directory field shows where your company is stored on your computer: C:\Program Files\Peachtree\company\senvidin

2. Type **12-4MPXX** in the Company Name field.

3. When you are finished typing 12-4MPXX as the company name, click on OK . Once you have changed the Company Name, each one of your printouts will show the problem number and your initials.

Nothing has changed on your computer's hard drive. The company you restored is identified in the program folder and data folder as C:\Program Files\Peachtree\company\senvidin. What you've done is changed the company name so that your printouts will show the problem number and your initials. Using Maintain, Company Information to rename your company does *not* change the shortened company name.

On January 1, 2005 Sentry VideoLink, Inc., received cash, $50,000.00, for a bond issue. The bond agreement provides that Sentry VideoLink is to increase a bond sinking fund by $5,000.00 every six months for the next five years.

Transactions:

Jan.	1	Received cash for the face value of a 5-year, 12%, $1,000.00 par value bond issue, $50,000.00. R198.
Jan.	12	Received cash from Stuart Peterson for 1,000 shares of $10.00 stated value common stock of $10.00 per share. $R210.
Feb.	21	Paid cash to Ruben Mendoza for 900 shares of $10.00 stated value common stock at $12.00 per share. C97.
Feb.	28	Received cash from Tai Banh for 500 shares of treasury stock at $12.00 per share. Treasury stock was bought on February 21 at $12.00 per share. R215.
Mar.	13	Received cash from Rebecca Munson for 200 shares of $10.00 stated value common stock at $15.00 per share. R220.
Mar.	22	Paid cash to Dermot Concannon for 2,000 shares of $10.00 stated value common stock at $16.00 per share. C138.
Apr.	8	Received cash for Rachel Kaplan for 100 shares of $100.00 par value preferred stock at $101.00 per share. R226.
Apr.	15	Received cash from Blake Kenefick for 300 shares of treasury stock at $18.00 per share. Treasury stock was bought on February 21 at $12.00 per share. R231.
May	15	Received cash from Paige Anderson for 800 shares of $100.00 pare value preferred stock at $97.50 per share. R232.
Jul.	1	Paid cash to bond trustee for semiannual interest on bond issue, $3,000.00. C200.
Jul.	1	Paid cash to bond trustee for semiannual deposit to bond sinking fund, $5,000.00. C201.
Jul.	14	Received delivery equipment from Travis Kimball at an agreed on value of $20,000.00 for 200 shares of $100.00 par value preferred stock. M148.
Jul.	23	Received cash from Brad Manning for 300 shares of treasury stock at $14.00 per share. Treasury stock consisted of 100 shares bought on February 21 at $12.00 per share and 200 shares bought on March 22 at $16.00 per share. R353.

Use the 2006 for the next two entries:

Jan.	1	Paid cash to bond trustee for semiannual interest on bond issue, $3000.00. C504.
Jan.	1	Paid cash to bond trustee for semiannual deposit to bond sinking fund, $4,600.00, and recorded interest earned on bond sinking fund, $400.00. C505.

1. Journalize and post the following transactions using Peachtree's Cash Receipts Journal, Cash Disbursements Journal and General Journal.
2. Print the Cash Receipts Journal (January 1 through July 23, 2005).
3. Print the General Journal (July 14 through July 14, 2005).
4. Print the Cash Disbursements Journal (February 21 through January 1, 2006).
5. Back up. The suggested file name is 12-4 Mastery Problem.ptb.
6. Use a blank piece of paper or in the *Working Papers* to complete the following transaction. Date the transaction January 1, 2010.

Jan.   1   Received notice from bond trustee that bond issue was retired using bond sinking fund, $50,000.00. M491.

Completing End-of-Fiscal-Period Work for a Corporation

The instructions that follow show you how to do the following:

- Start Peachtree Complete Accounting.
- Restore starting data from the South-Western Accounting with Peachtree CD.
- Complete adjusting entries.
- Print the required financial statements.
- Complete the 13-5 Mastery Problem.

Before you start the 13-5 Mastery Problem, ask your instructor if Lander, Inc., the company used for the 13-5 Mastery Problem, has already been restored on your computer. The instructions that follow assume that Lander, Inc. is being used for the first time.

GETTING STARTED

Use the following instructions to start Peachtree and restore the starting data for Lander, Inc. The South-Western Accounting with Peachtree CD includes a folder called Peachtree Files-Unit 2. In the steps that follow you will restore the 13-5MP.ptb file.

1. Start Peachtree. From the startup menu, select `Close`.
2. The menu bar shows three options: Files; Options; and Help. Click File; Restore.
3. The Restore Wizard - Select Backup File window appears. Observe that the Location field shows where Peachtree is stored on your computer. The default location is C:\Program Files\Peachtree\Company. Your Location field may differ. If you are restoring from a network drive, you will need to know the location of the 13-5MP.ptb file.
4. Click `Browse`. The Open Backup File window appears. In the Look in field, double-click on the appropriate location of the Peachtree Files-Unit 2 folder. Then, click 13-5MP.ptb to select it. (If appropriate, select your CD drive then double-click the Peachtree Files-Unit 2 folder. Click 13-5MP.ptb to select it.)

5. Make sure the Peachtree Files-Unit 2 folder and the 13-5MP.ptb file is selected. (*Hint:* Starting data for the 13-5 Mastery Problem is in the Peachtree Files-Unit 2 folder.) Click Open .

6. The Select Backup File window appears. Make sure the Location field shows the correct location for the 13-5MP.ptb file; for example, X:\Peachtree Files-Unit 2\13-5MP.ptb. (Substitute the correct drive letter for X.)

7. Click Next> . The Select Company window appears. Click on the radio button next to *A New Company*. The Location field shown in this book indicates the default location where drive C is used to install Peachtree. Your Location field may differ. *Make sure that the Location field ends in* **laninc**. (If your location field does not end in "c," select An Existing Company, then click Browse . Double-click Lander, Inc. (*or*, 13-5MPXX). Your Location field shows the shortened company name laninc. Continue with step 8.)

8. Click Next> . The Restore Options window appears.

9. Make sure that the box next to Company Data is *checked*. Click Next> .

10. The Confirmation window appears. Check the From and To fields to make sure they are correct. Click Finish . When the Restore Company scale is 100% complete, your data is restored and you are returned to the menu bar.

CHANGING THE COMPANY NAME

Before you start recording transactions for 13-5 Mastery Problem, you should look at the company information included on the 13-5MP.ptb file. Follow these steps to look at company information.

1. The Lander, Inc. menu bar should be displayed. From the menu bar, click on Maintain; Company Information. The Maintain Company Information window appears. Observe that the directory field shows where your company is stored on your computer: C:\Program Files\Peachtree\company\laninc

2. Type **13-5MPXX** in the Company Name field.

3. When you are finished typing 13-5MPXX as the company name, click on OK . Once you have changed the Company Name, each one of your printouts will show the problem number and your initials.

Nothing has changed on your computer's hard drive. The company you restored is identified in the program folder and data folder as C:\Program Files\Peachtree\company\laninc. What you've done is changed the company name so that your printouts will show the problem number and your initials. Using Maintain, Company Information to rename your company does *not* change the shortened company name.

The general ledger account titles and balances for Lander, Inc., are included on the 13-5MP.ptb file. Follow these instruction to print Peachtree's general ledger trial balance to see the starting balances for Lander, Inc.

1. Print the General Ledger Trial Balance and compare with the one shown below. This trial balance is included on the 13-5MP.ptb file.

Lander, Inc.
General Ledger Trial Balance
As of Dec 31, 2005

Filter Criteria includes: Report order is by ID. Report is printed in Detail Format.

Account ID	Account Description	Debit Amt	Credit Amt
1105	Cash	42,560.24	
1110	Petty Cash	500.00	
1112	Notes Receivable	21,561.77	
1115	Accounts Receivable	56,058.86	
1120	Allow. Uncoll. Accounts		156.18
1125	Merchandise Inventory	87,146.53	
1130	Supplies-Sales	17,088.54	
1135	Supplies-Administrative	10,485.59	
1140	Prepaid Insurance	6,871.77	
1145	Bond Sinking Fund	7,000.00	
1205	Store Equipment	67,974.77	
1210	Accum. Depr.-Store Equip		8,035.91
1215	Building	48,000.00	
1220	Accum. Deprec.-Building		5,328.00
1225	Office Equipment	53,010.02	
1230	Accum. Depr.-Office Equip		2,208.96
1235	Land	104,285.03	
1240	Organization Costs	300.00	
2100	Notes Payable		520.59
2105	Accounts Payable		10,468.53
2108	Emp. Income Tax Payable		416.47
2125	Social Security Tax Payabl		204.15
2128	Medicare Tax Payable		47.11
2130	Sales Tax Payable		728.82
2135	Unemploy. Tax Pay.-Feder		83.09
2140	Unemploy. Tax Pay.-State		561.92
2145	Health Ins. Prem. Payable		156.18
2150	Dividends Payable		14,922.80
2152	Bonds Payable		70,000.00
3105	Capital Stock-Common		184,000.00
3107	Pd. Cap. Exc. St. Val.-Com		30,000.00
3108	Capital Stock-Preferred		72,000.00
3109	Pd. Cap. Exc. Par-Pref.		1,800.00
3110	Disc. Sale Pref. Stock	3,000.00	
3111	Treasury Stock	1,200.00	
3112	Pd. Cap. Sale Tr. Stock		240.00
3115	Retained Earnings		22,645.60
3120	Dividends-Common	7,722.80	
3122	Dividends-Preferred	7,200.00	
4105	Sales		376,735.50
4110	Sales Discount	593.47	
4115	Sales Returns & Allow.	890.21	
5105	Purchases	155,655.99	
5110	Purchases Discount		2,646.15
5115	Purch. Returns & Allow.		933.94
6105	Advertising Expense	3,956.47	
6110	Credit Card Fee Expense	4,477.06	
6120	Miscellaneous Exp.-Sales	6,975.89	
6125	Salary Expense-Sales	34,150.61	
6215	Miscellaneous Expense-Ad	6,518.24	
6220	Payroll Taxes Expense	4,710.44	
6222	Property Tax Expense	2,300.00	
6225	Salary Expense-Admin.	9,110.30	
6245	Utilities Expense	9,318.54	
7105	Interest Income		208.24
8105	Interest Expense	4,425.00	
9105	Federal Income Tax Expen	20,000.00	
	Total:	**805,048.14**	**805,048.14**

2. Journalize and post adjusting entries in the general journal using the following information.

Adjustment Information, December 31, 2005

Accrued Interest Income	$277.18
Uncollectible Accounts Expense (estimated as 1.0% of sales on account)	213,411.00
Merchandise Inventory	86,676.38
Sales Supplies Inventory	9,808.79
Administrative Supplies Inventory	3,620.75
Value of Prepaid Insurance	2,363.94
Prepaid Interest	3.12
Annual Depreciation Expense—Store Equipment	9,746.00
Annual Depreciation Expense—Building	2,400.00
Annual Depreciation Expense—Office Equipment	2,185.95
Organization Expense	75.00
Accrued Interest Expense	7,004.34
Accrued Salaries-Sales	375.65
Accrued Payroll Taxes—Social Security tax	89.55
Accrued Payroll Taxes—Medicare	20.67
Accrued Payroll Taxes—Federal Unemployment Tax	1.27
Accrued Payroll Taxes—State Unemployment Tax	8.59
Federal Income Taxes are based on the tax rate table in this chapter	20,000.00

3. Print the December 31, 2005 Income Statement.

4. On a blank piece of paper or in the *Working Papers*, calculate and record the following component percentages: (a) cost of merchandise sold, (b) gross profit on operations, (c) total selling expenses, (d) total administrative expenses, (e) total operating expenses, (f) income from operations, (g) net addition or deduction resulting from other revenue and expenses, (h) net income before federal income tax, (i) federal income tax expense, and (j) net income after federal income tax. Round percentage calculations to the nearest 0.1%.

5. On a blank piece of paper or in the *Working Papers*, use the Income Statement analysis completed in Step 4 to analyze Lander's income statement by determining whether component percentages are within acceptable levels. If any component percentage is not within an acceptable level, suggest steps that the company should take.

6. On a blank piece of paper or in the *Working Papers*, calculate earnings per share. Round the calculation to the nearest cent. Lander has 18.400 shares of $10.00 stated-value common stock issued and 720 shores of $100.00 par-value preferred stock issued. Treasury stock consists of 90 shares of common stock. The dividend rate on preferred stock is 10%.

7. Print the Balance Sheet. Use the Capital section of Peachtree's balance sheet to prepare a Statement of Stockholders' Equity. Use a blank piece of paper or the *Working Papers* to prepare a Statement of Stockholders' Equity for December 31, 2005. Use the following additional information.

	January 1 Balance	Issued During the Year	December 31 Balance
Common Stock:			
No. of Shares	8,000	400	18,400
Amount	$180,000.00	$ 4,000.00	$184,000.00
Preferred Stock:			
No. of Shares	600	120	720
Amount	$ 60,000.00	$12,000.00	$ 72,000.00

8. On a blank piece of paper or in the *Working Papers*, calculate the following items based on information on the statement of stockholders' equity: (a) equity per share of stock and (b) price-earnings ratio. The market price of common stock on December 31, 2005 is $30.00.

9. Calculate the following items based on information from the balance sheet.

   a) Accounts receivable turnover ratio. Net sales on account were $213,441.00. Accounts receivable and allowance for doubtful accounts on January 1 were $49,435.32 and $2,146.40, respectively.

   b) Rate earned on average stockholders' equity. Total stockholders' equity on January 1 was $290,485.60.

   c) Rate earned on average total assets. Total assets on January 1 were $392,691.70.

10. Back up. The suggested filename is 13-5 Mastery Problem_Adjusted.ptb.

11. Journalize and post the closing entries.

12. Print the post-closing trial balance.

13. Back up. The suggested filename is 13-5 Mastery Problem_Closed.ptb.

14. Journalize and post the reversing entries.

15. Print the December 31, 2005 through January 1, 2006 General Journal.

16. The suggested filename is 13-5 Mastery Problem_Reversed.ptb.

Processing and Reporting Accounting Data for a Corporation

The instructions that follow show you how to do the following:

- Start Peachtree Complete Accounting.
- Restore starting data from the South-Western Accounting with Peachtree CD.
- Complete journal entries for December 2005.
- Complete adjusting, closing, and reversing entries.
- Print the required financial statements.
- Complete Reinforcement Activity 2.

Before you start Reinforcement Activity 2, ask your instructor if Whitehurst, Inc., the company used for Reinforcement Activity 2 has already been restored on your computer. The instructions that follow assume that Whitehurst, Inc. is being used for the first time.

GETTING STARTED

Use the following instructions to start Peachtree and restore the starting data for Reinforcement Activity 2. The South-Western Accounting with Peachtree CD includes a folder called Peachtree Files-Unit 2. In the steps that follow you will restore the RA02.ptb file.

1. Start Peachtree. From the startup menu, select Close .
2. The menu bar shows three options: Files; Options; and Help. Click File; Restore.
3. The Restore Wizard - Select Backup File window appears. Observe that the Location field shows where Peachtree is stored on your computer. The default location is C:\Program Files\Peachtree\Company. Your Location field may differ. If you are restoring from a network drive, you will need to know the location of the RA02.ptb file.
4. Click Browse . The Open Backup File window appears. In the Look in field, double-click on the appropriate location of the Peachtree Files-Unit 2 folder. Then, click RA02.ptb to select it. (If

appropriate, select your CD drive then double-click the Peachtree Files-Unit 2 folder. Click RA02.ptb to select it.)

5. Make sure the RA02.ptb file is selected. (*Hint:* Whitehurst, Inc.'s Reinforcement Activity 2 data is in the Peachtree Files-Unit 2 folder.) Click Open.

6. The Select Backup File window appears. Make sure the Location field shows the correct location for the RA02.ptb file; for example, X:\Peachtree Files-Unit 2\RA02.ptb. (Substitute the correct drive letter for X.)

7. Click Next>. The Select Company window appears. Click on the radio button next to *A New Company*. The Location field shown in this book indicates the default location where drive C is used to install Peachtree. Your Location field may differ. *Make sure that the Location field ends in* **whiinc**. (If your location field does not end in "c," select An Existing Company, then click Browse. Double-click Whitehurst, Inc. (*or*, RA02XX). Your Location field shows the shortened company name whiinc. Continue with step 8.)

8. Click Next>. The Restore Options window appears.

9. Make sure that the box next to Company Data is *checked*. Click Next>.

10. The Confirmation window appears. Check the From and To fields to make sure they are correct. Click Finish. When the Restore Company scale is 100% complete, your data is restored and you are returned to the menu bar.

CHANGING THE COMPANY NAME

Before you start recording transactions for Reinforcement Activity 2, you should look at the company information included on the RA02.ptb file. Follow these steps to look at company information.

1. The Whitehurst, Inc. menu bar should be displayed. From the menu bar, click on Maintain; Company Information. The Maintain Company Information window appears. Observe that the directory field shows where your company is stored on your computer: C:\Program Files\Peachtree\company\whiinc.

2. Type **RA02XX** in the Company Name field.

3. When you are finished typing RA02XX as the company name, click on OK. Once you have changed the Company Name, each one of your printouts will show the activity number and your initials.

Nothing has changed on your computer's hard drive. The company you restored is identified in the program folder and data folder as C:\Program Files\Peachtree\company\whiinc. What you've done is change the company name so that your printouts will show the activity number and your initials. Using Maintain, Company Information to rename your company does *not* change the shortened company name.

Whitehurst, Inc.

The accounting activities are for Whitehurst, Inc., a merchandising business organized as a corporation. Whitehurst sells plumbing and related products to building contractors, homeowners, and other consumers. Whitehurst's fiscal year is from January 1 through December 31, 2005.

Part A: Journalizing Transactions

In Part A of this reinforcement activity, selected transactions for Whitehurst, Inc., completed during December 2005 are journalized and posted. Whitehurst uses the chart of accounts shown below. The journals used by Whitehurst are the Sales Journal, Cash Receipts Journal, Cash Disbursements Journal, and General Journal.

GENERAL LEDGER CHART OF ACCOUNTS

Balance Sheet Accounts

(1000)	ASSETS
1100	CURRENT ASSETS
1105	Cash
1110	Petty Cash
1115	Notes Receivable
1120	Interest Receivable
1125	Accounts Receivable
1130	Allowance for Uncollectible Accounts
1135	Subscriptions Receivable
1140	Merchandise Inventory
1145	Supplies—Sales
1150	Supplies—Administrative
1155	Prepaid Insurance
1160	Prepaid Interest
1200	LONG-TERM INVESTMENT
1205	Bond Sinking Fund
1300	PLANT ASSETS
1305	Store Equipment
1310	Accumulated Depreciation—Store Equipment
1315	Building
1320	Accumulated Depreciation—Building
1325	Office Equipment
1330	Accumulated Depreciation—Office Equipment
1335	Land
1400	INTANGIBLE ASSET
1405	Organization Costs
(2000)	LIABILITIES
2100	CURRENT LIABILITIES
2105	Notes Payable
2110	Interest Payable
2115	Accounts Payable
2120	Employee Income Tax Payable
2125	Federal Income Tax Payable
2130	Social Security Tax Payable
2133	Medicare Tax Payable
2135	Salaries Payable
2140	Sales Tax Payable
2145	Unearned Rent
2150	Unemployment Tax Payable—Federal
2155	Unemployment Tax Payable—State
2160	Health Insurance Premiums Payable
2165	Dividends Payable
2200	LONG-TERM LIABILITY
2205	Bonds Payable
(3000)	STOCKHOLDERS' EQUITY
3105	Capital Stock—Common
3110	Stock Subscribed—Common
3115	Paid-in Capital in Excess of Stated Value—Common

3120	Capital Stock—Preferred
3125	Stock Subscribed—Preferred
3130	Paid-in Capital in Excess of Par Value—Preferred
3135	Treasury Stock
3140	Paid-in Capital from Sale of Treasury Stock
3145	Retained Earnings
3150	Dividends—Common
3155	Dividends—Preferred
3160	Income Summary

Income Statement Accounts

(4000)	OPERATING REVENUE
4105	Sales
4110	Sales Discount
4115	Sales Returns and Allowances
(5000)	COST OF MERCHANDISE
5105	Purchases
5110	Purchases Discount
5115	Purchases Returns and Allowances
(6000)	OPERATING EXPENSES
6100	Selling Expenses
6105	Advertising Expense
6110	Credit Card Fee Expense
6115	Depreciation Expense—Store Equipment
6120	Miscellaneous Expense—Sales
6125	Salary Expense—Sales
6130	Supplies Expense—Sales
6200	ADMINISTRATIVE EXPENSES
6205	Depreciation Expense—Building
6210	Depreciation Expense—Office Equipment
6215	Insurance Expense
6220	Miscellaneous Expense—Administrative
6225	Payroll Taxes Expense
6230	Property Tax Expense
6235	Salary Expense—Administrative
6240	Supplies Expense—Administrative
6245	Uncollectible Accounts Expense
6250	Utilities Expense
(7000)	OTHER REVENUE
7105	Gain on Plant Assets
7110	Interest Income
7115	Rent Income
(8000)	OTHER EXPENSES
8105	Interest Expense
8110	Loss on Plant Assets
8115	Organization Expense
(9000)	INCOME TAX
9105	Federal Income Tax Expense

Recording Transactions

Instructions:

1. Journalize and post the following transactions completed during December 2005.

Dec.	1	Whitehurst's board of directors declared an annual dividend of $15,820.00. Preferred stock issued is $40,400.00 of 10%, $100.00 par-value preferred stock. Common stock issued is $11,780.00 of $10.00 stated-value common stock. Date of payment is December 30. M316.
	1	Wrote off Susan Vine's past-due account as uncollectible, $427.50. M317.
	1	Received cash for three months' rent in advance from Woodcrest, Inc., $2,400.00. R126.
	1	Discarded a store fixture: original cost, $1,050.00; total accumulated depreciation through December 31 of last year, $840.00; additional depreciation to be recorded through December 1 of the current year, $210.00. M318.
	1	Received a subscription from Delmar Adams for 30 shares of $100.00 par-value preferred stock, $3,000.00. M319.
	2	Paid cash for office equipment, $2,650.00. C476.
	4	Patrick Carson dishonored NR4, a 30-day, 10% note, maturity value due today: principal, $150.00; interest, $1.25; total, $151.25. M320.
	4	Discarded an office table: original cost, $250.00; total accumulated depreciation through December 31 of last year, $150.00; additional depreciation to be recorded through December 4 of the current year, $50.00. M321.
	4	Received a 60-day, 10% note from Leigh Calhoun for an extension of time on her account, $500.00. NR5.
	5	Issued a 6-month, 10% note, $10,000.00. NP6.
	5	Paid cash to bond trustee for annual interest on bond issue, $24,000.00. C482.
	5	Paid cash to bond trustee for annual deposit to bond sinking fund, $18,400.00, and recorded interest earned on bond sinking fund, $1,600.00. C487.
	6	Received cash from Leslie Johns for 700 shares of $10.00 stated-value common stock at $11.00 per share, $7,700.00. R134.
	7	Received cash for the maturity value of NR1, principal, $150.00, plus interest, $2.47; total, $152.47. R136.
	11	Received cash from sale of office equipment, $70.00: original cost, $700.00; total accumulated depreciation through December 31 of last year, $500.00; additional depreciation to be recorded through December 11 of the current year, $100.00. M322 and R138.
	11	Paid cash to Marlin Pratt for 60 shares of $10.00 stated-value common stock at $9.00 per share, $540.00. C502.

12	Paid cash for the maturity value of NP4: principal, $300.00, plus interest, $6.00; total, $306.00. C503.
13	Received cash from Robert Shull for 200 shares of $10.00 stated-value common stock at $10.00 per share, $2,000.00. R140.
14	Received cash for the maturity value of NR2: principal, $247.50, plus interest; $4.07; total $251.57. R141.
16	Paid cash for the maturity value of NP3: principal, $1,000.00, plus interest, $16.44; total, $1,016.44. C509.
19	Received office equipment from Valerie DeLong at an agreed value of $1,000.00 for 10 shares of $100.00 par-value preferred stock. M323.
20	Received cash in full payment of Susan Vine's account, previously written off as uncollectible, $427.50. M324 and R143.
21	Paid cash, $2,000.00, plus an office microcomputer, for a new microcomputer: original cost of old microcomputer, $3,500.00; total accumulated depreciation through December 31 of last year, $2,100.00; additional depreciation to be recorded through December 21 of the current year, $700.00. M325 and C515.
27	Discounted at 12% a 60-day non-interest-bearing note, $5,000.00; proceeds, $4,900.00; interest, $100.00. NP7.
28	Received cash from James Dier for 10 shares of treasury stock at $13.00 per share, $130.00. Treasury stock was bought on December 11 at $9.00 per share. R146.
29	Received cash from sale of an old cash register used in sales, $800.00: original cost, $1,600.00; total accumulated depreciation through December 31 of last year, $896.00; additional depreciation to be recorded through December 29 of the current year, $144.00. M326 and R147.
29	Received cash from Patrick Carson for dishonored NR4: principal, $151.25, plus additional interest, $1.05; total, $152.30. R148.
29	Received cash from Delmar Adams in payment of stock subscription, $3,000.00. R149.
29	Issued Stock Certificate No. 14 to Delmar Adams for 30 shares of $100.00 par-value preferred stock, $3,000.00. M327.
30	Paid cash for annual dividend declared December 1, $15,820.00. C519.

2. Print the unadjusted trial balance. (If you completed a worksheet in the *Working Papers* for this assignment, compare Peachtree general ledger trial balance to the worksheet's Trial Balance columns.)

3. Back up your data. The suggested file name is Reinforcement Activity 2.Part A.ptb.

Part B: End of Fiscal Period Work

1. Journalize and post the adjusting entries in the general journal using the following information.

Accrued interest income	$ 95.70
Uncollectible accounts expense estimated as 0.1% of net sales on account.	
Net sales on account for year, $343,472.60.	
Merchandise inventory	206,618.63
Sales supplies inventory	1,456.06
Administrative supplies inventory	730.00
Value of prepaid insurance	970.00
Prepaid interest	93.33
Annual depreciation expense—store equipment	8,300.00
Annual depreciation expense—building	1,500.00
Annual depreciation expense—office equipment	1,150.00
Organization expense	300.00
Accrued interest expense	2,025.00
Accrued salaries—sales	3,232.04
Accrued salaries—administrative	716.50
Accrued payroll taxes—Social Security tax	256.65
Accrued payroll taxes—Medicare tax	59.23
Accrued payroll taxes—federal unemployment tax	15.79
Accrued payroll taxes—state unemployment tax	106.58
Rent received in advance and still unearned	1,200.00

Federal income tax expense for the year is calculated at the following rates:
   15% of net income before taxes, zero to $50,000.00.
   Plus 25% of net income before taxes, $50,000.00 to $75,000.00.
   Plus 34% of net income before taxes, $75,000.00 to $100,000.00.
   Plus 39% of net income before taxes, $100,000.00 to $335,000.00.
   Plus 34% of the net income before taxes over $335,000.00.

2. Print the December 31, 2005 Income Statement. (*Hint:* Peachtree's income statement reports revenue. cost of sales, and expense accounts. If you prepared an income statement for the *Working Papers* which included beginning and ending inventory, observe that Peachtree's net income amount differs. Peachtree does *not* include merchandise inventory, which is an asset account, on its income statement. Observe that Peachtree's income statement includes Gain on Plant Assets, Interest Income and Rent Income in the Revenue section, *not* in a separate Other Revenue section, which may be the case on a manually prepared income statement.)

3. On a blank piece of paper or in the *Working Papers*, calculate and record the following component percentages. (a) Cost of merchandise sold. (b) Gross profit on operations. (c) Total selling expenses. (d) Total administrative expenses. (e) Total operating expenses. (c) Total selling expenses. (d) Total administrative expenses. (e) Total operating expenses. (f) Income from operations. (g) Net additional or deduction resulting from other revenue and expenses. (h) Net income before federal income tax. (i) Federal Income tax expense.

(j) Net income after federal income tax. Round percentage calculations to the nearest 0.1%.

4. On a blank piece of paper or in the *Working Papers*, analyze Whitehurst's income statement by determining if component percentages are within acceptable levels. If any component percentage is not within an acceptable level, suggest steps that the company should take.

5. On a blank piece of paper or in the *Working Papers*, calculate earnings per share. Round the calculation to the nearest cent. Whitehurst has 12,680 shares of $10.00 stated value common stock issued and 444 shares of 10% $100.00 par-value preferred stock issued. Treasury stock consists of 560 shares of common stock.

6. On a blank piece of paper or in the *Working Papers*, calculate the following items based on information on the statement of stockholders' equity. (a) Equity per share of stock. (b) Price-earnings ratio. The market price of common stock on December 31, 2005 is $13.50.

7. Print the December 31, 2005 Balance Sheet. Use the Capital section of Peachtree's balance sheet to prepare a Statement of Stockholders' Equity. Use a blank piece of paper or the *Working Papers* to prepare a Statement of Stockholders' Equity for December 31, 2005. Use the following additional information. The January 1 balance of Retained Earnings was $26,759.39.

	January 1 Balance	Issued During the Year	December 31 Balance
Common Stock:			
No. of shares	11,780	900	12,680
Amount	$117,800.00	$9,000.00	$126,800.00
Preferred Stock:			
No. of shares	404	40	444
Amount	$ 40,400.00	$4,000.00	$ 44,400.00

The January 1 balance of Retained Earnings was $26,759.39.

8. Calculate the following items based on information from the balance sheet.

   a) Accounts receivable turnover ratio. Accounts receivable and uncollectible accounts on January 1 were $36,785.45 and $698.35, respectively.

   b) Rate earned on average stockholders' equity. Total stockholders' equity on January 1 was $186,459.39.

   c) Rate earned on average total assets. Total assets on January 1 were $458,204.24.

9. Print the sales journal, cash receipts journal, and cash disbursements journal.

10. Back up. The suggested filename is Reinforcement Activity 2_Part B Adjusted.ptb.

11. Journalize and post the closing entries.

12. Back up. The suggested filename is Reinforcement Activity 2_Part B Closed.ptb.

13. Journalize and post the January 1, 2006 reversing entries.

14. Print the December 1, 2005 to January 1, 2006 General Journal. (December 1 beginning balances are reported.)

15. The suggested filename is Reinforcement Activity 2_Part B Reversed.ptb.

Journalizing Cost Accounting Transactions for a Manufacturing Company

The instructions that follow show you how to do the following:

- Start Peachtree Complete Accounting.
- Restore starting data from the South-Western Accounting with Peachtree CD.
- Complete journal entries for August 2005.
- Print the purchase journal and cash payments journal.
- Complete the 20-1 Application Problem.

Before you start the 20-1 Application Problem, ask your instructor if Perry, Inc., the company used for the 20-1 Application Problem has already been restored on your computer. The instructions that follow assume that Perry, Inc. is being used for the first time.

GETTING STARTED

Use the following instructions to start Peachtree and restore the starting data for the 20-1 Application Problem. The South-Western Accounting with Peachtree CD includes a folder called Peachtree Files-Unit 2. In the steps that follow you will restore the 20-1AP.ptb file.

1. Start Peachtree. From the startup menu, select Close .
2. The menu bar shows three options: Files; Options; and Help. Click File; Restore.
3. The Restore Wizard - Select Backup File window appears. Observe that the Location field shows where Peachtree is stored on your computer. The default location is C:\Program Files\Peachtree\Company. Your Location field may differ. If you are restoring from a network drive, you will need to know the location of the 20-1AP.ptb file.
4. Click Browse . The Open Backup File window appears. In the Look in field, double-click on the appropriate location of the Peachtree Files-Unit 2 folder. Then, click 20-1AP.ptb to select it. (If appropriate, select your CD drive then double-click the Peachtree Files-Unit 2 folder. Click 20-1AP.ptb to select it.)

5. Make sure the 20-1AP.ptb file is selected. (*Hint:* Starting data for the 20-1 Application Problem is in the Peachtree Files-Unit 2 folder.) Click Open.

6. The Select Backup File window appears. Make sure the Location field shows the correct location for the 20-1AP.ptb file; for example, X:\Peachtree Files-Unit 2\20-1AP.ptb. (Substitute the correct drive letter for X.)

7. Click Next>. The Select Company window appears. Click on the radio button next to *A New Company*. The Location field shown in this book indicates the default location where drive C is used to install Peachtree. Your Location field may differ. *Make sure that the Location field ends in* **perinc**. (If your location field does not end in "c," select An Existing Company, then click Browse. Double-click Perry, Inc. (*or*, 20-1APXX). Your Location field shows the shortened company name perinc. Continue with step 8.)

8. Click Next>. The Restore Options window appears.

9. Make sure that the box next to Company Data is *checked*. Click Next>.

10. The Confirmation window appears. Check the From and To fields to make sure they are correct. Click Finish. When the Restore Company scale is 100% complete, your data is restored and you are returned to the menu bar.

CHANGING THE COMPANY NAME

Before you start recording transactions for the 20-1 Application Problem, you should look at the company information included on the 20-1AP.ptb file. Follow these steps to look at company information.

1. The Perry, Inc. menu bar should be displayed. From the menu bar, click on Maintain; Company Information. The Maintain Company Information window appears. Observe that the directory field shows where your company is stored on your computer: C:\Program Files\Peachtree\company\perinc.

2. Type **20-1APXX** in the Company Name field.

3. When you are finished typing 20-1APXX as the company name, click on OK. Once you have changed the Company Name, each one of your printouts will show the activity number and your initials.

Nothing has changed on your computer's hard drive. The company you restored is identified in the program folder and data folder as C:\Program Files\Peachtree\company\perinc. What you've done is change the company name so that your printouts will show the activity number and your initials. Using Maintain, Company Information to rename your company does *not* change the shortened company name.

Perry, Inc. completed the following factory cost transactions during August 2005.

Aug. 4   Purchased $6,152.80 of material from Sharon Company on account. PO47.

7   Paid cash for machinery used for production, $3,458.00. C651

15   Bought supplies for use in the factory by paying $583.83 cash. C658.

21   Had machinery repaired. Made cash payment of $1,123.00 to repairer. C667. (Miscellaneous Expense-Factory)

24   Purchased materials on account from Hubbard Company, $3,510.72. P048. Monthly factory payroll was paid in cash, $7,599.32 (direct labor, $7,200.00, and indirect labor, $1,920.00; less deductions: employee income tax, $823.00; Social security tax, $566.87; Medicare tax, $130.81). C679.

Instructions:

1. Journalize and post the August 2005 transactions in the Purchase Journal and the Cash Payments Journal. (For Peachtree, substitute the Materials Purchases Journal with the Purchase Journal. Observe, when you use the Purchases/Receive Inventory task that Account No. 1125, Materials, is automatically debited; Account No. 2105, Accounts Payable/Vendor account is automatically credited.)

2. Print the purchase journal.

3. Print the cash disbursements journal.

4. Back up. The suggested file name is 20-1 Application Problem.ptb.

Journalizing Entries that Summarize Cost Records at the End of a Fiscal Period; Preparing Financial Statements

The instructions that follow show you how to do the following:

- Start Peachtree Complete Accounting.
- Restore starting data from the South-Western Accounting with Peachtree CD.
- Print the unadjusted trial balance.
- Complete adjusting entries.
- Print the income statement and balance sheet.
- Complete the 20-5 Challenge Problem

Before you start the 20-5 Challenge Problem, ask your instructor if Cozart Company, the company used for the 20-5 Challenge Problem has already been restored on your computer. The instructions that follow assume that Cozart Company is being used for the first time.

GETTING STARTED

Use the following instructions to start Peachtree and restore the starting data for the 20-5 Challenge Problem. The South-Western Accounting with Peachtree CD includes a folder called Peachtree Files-Unit 2. In the steps that follow you will restore the 20-5CP.ptb file.

1. Start Peachtree. From the startup menu, select Close.
2. The menu bar shows three options: Files; Options; and Help. Click File; Restore.
3. The Restore Wizard - Select Backup File window appears. Observe that the Location field shows where Peachtree is stored on your computer. The default location is C:\Program Files\Peachtree\Company. Your Location field may differ. If you are restoring from a network drive, you will need to know the location of the 20-5CP.ptb file.

4. Click Browse . The Open Backup File window appears. In the Look
   in field, double-click on the appropriate location of the Peachtree
   Files-Unit 2 folder. Then, click 20-5CP.ptb to select it. (If appropriate, select your CD drive then double-click the Peachtree Files-
   Unit 2 folder. Click 20-5CP.ptb to select it.)

5. Make sure the 20-5CP.ptb file is selected. (*Hint:* Starting data for the
   20-5 Challenge Problem is in the Peachtree Files-Unit 2 folder.) Click
   Open .

6. The Select Backup File window appears. Make sure the Location
   field shows the correct location for the 20-5CP.ptb file; for example,
   X:\Peachtree Files-Unit 2\20-5CP.ptb. (Substitute the correct drive
   letter for X.)

7. Click Next> . The Select Company window appears. Click on the
   radio button next to *A New Company*. The Location field shown in
   this book indicates the default location where drive C is used to
   install Peachtree. Your Location field may differ. *Make sure that the
   Location field ends in* **cozcompa**. (If your location field does not end
   in "a," select An Existing Company, then click Browse . Double-click
   Cozart Company (*or*, 20-5CPXX). Your Location field shows the
   shortened company name cozcompa. Continue with step 8.)

8. Click Next> . The Restore Options window appears.

9. Make sure that the box next to Company Data is *checked*. Click
   Next> .

10. The Confirmation window appears. Check the From and To fields
    to make sure they are correct. Click Finish . When the Restore
    Company scale is 100% complete, your data is restored and you
    are returned to the menu bar.

CHANGING THE COMPANY NAME

Before you start recording transactions for the 20-5 Challenge Problem,
you should look at the company information included on the 20-
5CP.ptb file. Follow these steps to look at company information.

1. The Cozart Company menu bar should be displayed. From the
   menu bar, click on Maintain; Company Information. The Maintain
   Company Information window appears. Observe that the directory
   field shows where your company is stored on your computer:
   C:\Program Files\Peachtree\company\cozcompa.

2. Type **20-5CPXX** in the Company Name field.

3. When you are finished typing 20-5CPXX as the company name, click
   on OK . Once you have changed the Company Name, each one of
   your printouts will show the activity number and your initials.

Nothing has changed on your computer's hard drive. The company
you restored is identified in the program folder and data folder as
C:\Program Files\Peachtree\company\cozcompa. What you've done
is change the company name so that your printouts will show the
activity number and your initials. Using Maintain, Company

Information to rename your company does *not* change the shortened company name.

Instructions:

1. Display the unadjusted trial balance.

Cozart Company
General Ledger Trial Balance
As of Jul 31, 2005

Filter Criteria includes: Report order is by ID. Report is printed in Detail Format.

Account ID	Account Description	Debit Amt	Credit Amt
1105	Cash	63,061.56	
1110	Petty Cash	375.00	
1115	Accounts Receivable	115,300.30	
1120	Allowance for Uncoll. Accounts		2,819.65
1125	Materials	44,112.28	
1130	Work in Process	37,860.00	
1135	Finished Goods	67,216.45	
1140	Supplies-Factory	2,474.55	
1145	Supplies-Sales	3,107.03	
1150	Supplies-Administrative	794.20	
1155	Prepaid Insurance	1,422.23	
1205	Factory Equipment	103,005.00	
1210	Accum. Deprec.-Factory Equip		28,116.00
1215	Office Equipment	8,613.00	
1220	Accum. Depr.-Office Equipment		2,769.30
1225	Store Equipment	7,771.50	
1230	Accum. Depr.-Store Equipment		2,884.56
1235	Building	237,600.00	
1240	Accum. Depr.-Building		23,760.00
1245	Land	99,445.89	
2105	Accounts Payable		16,535.86
2110	Employee Income Tax Payable		9,890.72
2120	Social Security Tax Payable		11,688.85
2125	Medicare Tax Payable		2,697.43
2130	Unemploy. Tax Pay.-Federal		1,078.80
2135	Unemploy. Tax Pay.-State		7,281.90
2205	Mortgage Payable		56,250.00
3105	Capital Stock		450,000.00
3110	Retained Earnings		145,960.58
3120	Income Summary		191.83
4105	Sales		183,580.00
5105	Cost of Good Sold	112,176.83	
6105	Advertising Expense	2,416.05	
6110	Delivery Expense	5,842.24	
6120	Miscellaneous Expense-Sales	1,500.33	
6125	Salary Expense-Sales	11,604.38	
6215	Miscellaneous Expense-Admin	1,561.41	
6220	Payroll Taxes Expense-Admin	2,529.95	
6225	Property Tax Expense-Admin	92.59	
6230	Salary Expense-Administrative	15,309.90	
7105	Gain on Plant Assets		155.93
8105	Interest Expense	468.74	
	Total:	**945,661.41**	**945,661.41**

2. Cozart's general ledger accounts and their balances on July 31, 2005 are shown on Peachtree's general ledger trial balance. These are the starting balances for the 20-5 Challenge Problem. Using the adjustment Information for July 31, journalize and post the adjusting entries. Type a., b., c., d., e., f. g. in the General Journal Entry window's Reference field.

Adjustment Information, July 31

Uncollectible Accounts Expense Estimated as 1.0% of Total Sales on Account.

Sales on Account for Year	$76,275.00
Sales Supplies Inventory	1,762.50
Administrative Supplies Inventory	520.74
Value of Prepaid Administrative Insurance	1,383.30
Monthly Depreciation Expense—Office Equipment	68.51
Monthly Depreciation Expense—Store Equipment	61.88
Federal Income Tax Expense Estimated for the Month	7,807.00

3. Add the following cost of sales account, Account No. 5555, Overapplied Overhead. Record an additional adjusting entry:

   h. Debit the income summary account for its balance; credit over-applied overhead.

4. Print the July 31, 2005 general journal.

5. Print the July 31, 2005 income statement. (Remember, Peachtree's income statement does *not* show Overapplied Overhead of $191.83. This amount is shown as the income summary balance on the unadjusted trial balance.)

6. On a blank piece of paper, calculate and record the following component percentages: (a) net cost of goods sold, (b) gross profit on operations, (c) total operation expenses, (d) income from operations, (e) net additional or deduction resulting from other revenue and expenses, (f) net income before federal income tax, (g) federal income tax expense, and (h) net income after federal income tax. Round percentage calculations to the nearest 0.1%.

7. Print the July 31, 2005 balance sheet.

8. Back up. The suggested file name is 20-5 Challenge Problem.ptb.

Forming a Partnership

The instructions that follow show you how to do the following:

- Start Peachtree Complete Accounting.
- Restore starting data from the South-Western Accounting with Peachtree CD.
- Change the accounting period to Period 6, June 1 to June 30, 2005.
- Complete journal entries for June 2005.
- Print the cash receipts journal.
- Complete the 21-1 Application Problem.

Before you start the 21-1 Application Problem, ask your instructor if Carmen's Crafts, the company used for the 21-1 Application Problem has already been restored on your computer. The instructions that follow assume that Carmen's Crafts is being used for the first time.

GETTING STARTED

Use the following instructions to start Peachtree and restore the starting data for the 21-1 Application Problem. The South-Western Accounting with Peachtree CD includes a folder called Peachtree Files-Unit 2. In the steps that follow you will restore the 21-1AP.ptb file.

1. Start Peachtree. From the startup menu, select Close.
2. The menu bar shows three options: Files; Options; and Help. Click File; Restore.
3. The Restore Wizard - Select Backup File window appears. Observe that the Location field shows where Peachtree is stored on your computer. The default location is C:\Program Files\Peachtree\Company. Your Location field may differ. If you are restoring from a network drive, you will need to know the location of the 21-1AP.ptb file.
4. Click Browse. The Open Backup File window appears. In the Look in field, double-click on the appropriate location of the PPeachtree Files-Unit 2 folder. Then, click 21-1AP.ptb to select it. (If appropriate, select your CD drive then double-click the Peachtree Files-Unit 2 folder. Click 21-1AP.ptb to select it.)

5. Make sure the 21-1AP.ptb file is selected. (*Hint:* Starting data for the 21-1 Application Problem is in the Peachtree Files-Unit 2 folder.) Click Open .

6. The Select Backup File window appears. Make sure the Location field shows the correct location for the 21-1AP.ptb file; for example, X:\Peachtree Files-Unit 2\21-1AP.ptb. (Substitute the correct drive letter for X.)

7. Click Next> . The Select Company window appears. Click on the radio button next to *A New Company*. The Location field shown in this book indicates the default location where drive C is used to install Peachtree. Your Location field may differ. *Make sure that the Location field ends in* **carcraft**. (If your location field does not end in "t," select An Existing Company, then click Browse . Double-click Carmen's Crafts (*or*, 21-1APXX). Your Location field shows the shortened company name carcraft. Continue with step 8.)

8. Click Next> . The Restore Options window appears.

9. Make sure that the box next to Company Data is *checked*. Click Next> .

10. The Confirmation window appears. Check the From and To fields to make sure they are correct. Click Finish . When the Restore Company scale is 100% complete, your data is restored and you are returned to the menu bar.

CHANGING THE COMPANY NAME

Before you start recording transactions for the 21-1 Application Problem, you should look at the company information included on the 21-1AP.ptb file. Follow these steps to look at company information.

1. The Carmen's Crafts menu bar should be displayed. From the menu bar, click on Maintain; Company Information. The Maintain Company Information window appears. Observe that the directory field shows where your company is stored on your computer: C:\Program Files\Peachtree\company\carcraft.

2. Type **21-1APXX** in the Company Name field.

3. When you are finished typing 21-1APXX as the company name, click on OK . Once you have changed the Company Name, each one of your printouts will show the activity number and your initials.

Nothing has changed on your computer's hard drive. The company you restored is identified in the program folder and data folder as C:\Program Files\Peachtree\company\carcraft. What you've done is change the company name so that your printouts will show the activity number and your initials. Using Maintain, Company Information to rename your company does *not* change the shortened company name.

Carmen Estrada and Paula Jeter agree to form a partnership on June 1, 2005. The partnership assumes the assets and liabilities of Carmen's existing business. Paula invests cash equal to Carmen's investment. Partners share equally in all changes in equity. The May 31 balance sheet for Carmen's existing business is as follows.

Instructions:

1. Display the May 31, 2005 balance sheet and compare it to the one shown.

Carmen's Crafts
Balance Sheet
May 31, 2005

ASSETS

Current Assets		
Cash	$ 14,532.00	
Accounts Receivable	3,746.47	
Allow. for Uncoll. Accts.	(74.92)	
Merchandise Inventory	26,298.34	
Supples	670.59	
Total Current Assets		45,172.48
Property and Equipment		
Equipment	9,481.12	
Total Property and Equipment		9,481.12
Other Assets		
Total Other Assets		0.00
Total Assets		$ 54,653.60

LIABILITIES AND CAPITAL

Current Liabilities		
Accounts Payable	$ 8,653.60	
Total Current Liabilities		8,653.60
Long-Term Liabilities		
Total Long-Term Liabilities		0.00
Total Liabilities		8,653.60
Capital		
Carmen Estrada, Capital	46,000.00	
Net Income	0.00	
Total Capital		46,000.00
Total Liabilities & Capital		$ 54,653.60

June 1   Received cash from partner, Paula Jeter, as an initial investment, $46,000.00. R1.

1   Accepted assets and liabilities of Carmen Estrada's existing business as an initial investment, $46,000.00. R2.

Instructions:

1. Add the following accounts:

Account No.	Description	Account Type
3115	Paula Jeter, Capital	Equity-doesn't close
3116	Paula Jeter, Drawing	Equity-gets closed

2. Change accounting period to Period 6, Jun 01 to Jun 30, 2005.
3. Journalize and post the transactions using the cash receipts journal. Source documents are abbreviated as follows: memorandum, M; receipt, R.
4. Print the cash receipts journal.
5. Back up. The suggested file name is 21-1 Application Problem.ptb.

21-6 MASTERY PROBLEM

Forming and Expanding Partnership

The instructions that follow show you how to do the following:

- Start Peachtree Complete Accounting.
- Restore starting data from the South-Western Accounting with Peachtree CD.
- Change the accounting period to Period 7, July 1 to July 31, 2005.
- Complete journal entries for July 2005.
- Print the cash receipts journal and general journal.
- Complete the 21-6 Mastery Problem.

Before you start the 21-6 Mastery Problem, ask your instructor if Hatfield Financial Services, the company used for the 21-6 Mastery Problem has already been restored on your computer. The instructions that follow assume that Hatfield Financial Services is being used for the first time.

GETTING STARTED

Use the following instructions to start Peachtree and restore the starting data for the 21-6 Mastery Problem. The South-Western Accounting with Peachtree CD includes a folder called Peachtree Files-Unit 2. In the steps that follow you will restore the 21-6MP.ptb file.

1. Start Peachtree. From the startup menu, select [Close].
2. The menu bar shows three options: Files; Options; and Help. Click File; Restore.
3. The Restore Wizard - Select Backup File window appears. Observe that the Location field shows where Peachtree is stored on your computer. The default location is C:\Program Files\Peachtree\Company. Your Location field may differ. If you are restoring from a network drive, you will need to know the location of the 21-6MP.ptb file.
4. Click [Browse]. The Open Backup File window appears. In the Look in field, double-click on the appropriate location of the Peachtree Files-Unit 2 folder. Then, click 21-6MP.ptb to select it. (If appropriate, select your CD drive then double-click the Peachtree Files-Unit 2 folder. Click 21-6MP.ptb to select it.)

5. Make sure the 21-6MP.ptb file is selected. (*Hint:* Starting data for the 21-6 Mastery Problem is in the Peachtree Files-Unit 2 folder.) Click Open.

6. The Select Backup File window appears. Make sure the Location field shows the correct location for the 21-6MP.ptb file; for example, X:\Peachtree Files-Unit 2\21-6MP.ptb. (Substitute the correct drive letter for X.)

7. Click Next>. The Select Company window appears. Click on the radio button next to *A New Company*. The Location field shown in this book indicates the default location where drive C is used to install Peachtree. Your Location field may differ. *Make sure that the Location field ends in* **hatfinse**. (If your location field does not end in "e," select An Existing Company, then click Browse. Double-click Hatfield Financial Services (*or*, 21-6MPXX). Your Location field shows the shortened company name hatfinse. Continue with step 8.)

8. Click Next>. The Restore Options window appears.

9. Make sure that the box next to Company Data is *checked*. Click Next>.

10. The Confirmation window appears. Check the From and To fields to make sure they are correct. Click Finish. When the Restore Company scale is 100% complete, your data is restored and you are returned to the menu bar.

CHANGING THE COMPANY NAME

Before you start recording transactions for the 21-6 Mastery Problem, you should look at the company information included on the 21-6MP.ptb file. Follow these steps to look at company information.

1. The Hatfield Financial Services menu bar should be displayed. From the menu bar, click on Maintain; Company Information. The Maintain Company Information window appears. Observe that the directory field shows where your company is stored on your computer: C:\Program Files\Peachtree\company\hatfinse.

2. Type **21-6MPXX** in the Company Name field.

3. When you are finished typing 21-6MPXX as the company name, click on OK. Once you have changed the Company Name, each one of your printouts will show the activity number and your initials.

Nothing has changed on your computer's hard drive. The company you restored is identified in the program folder and data folder as C:\Program Files\Peachtree\company\hatfinse. What you've done is change the company name so that your printouts will show the activity number and your initials. Using Maintain, Company Information to rename your company does *not* change the shortened company name.

1. Display the June 30, 2005 balance sheet and compare it to the one shown.

Hatfield Financial Services
Balance Sheet
June 30, 2005

ASSETS

Current Assets		
Cash	$ 4,291.23	
Accounts Receivable	3,303.60	
Allow. for Uncoll. Accts.	(35.79)	
Supplies	290.19	
Total Current Assets		7,849.23
Property and Equipment		
Equipment	4,378.14	
Total Property and Equipment		4,378.14
Other Assets		
Total Other Assets		0.00
Total Assets		$ 12,227.37

LIABILITIES AND CAPITAL

Current Liabilities		
Accounts Payable	$ 227.37	
Total Current Liabilities		227.37
Long-Term Liabilities		
Total Long-Term Liabilities		0.00
Total Liabilities		227.37
Capital		
Roy Hatfield, Capital	12,000.00	
Net Income	0.00	
Total Capital		12,000.00
Total Liabilities & Capital		$ 12,227.37

Transactions:

On July 1, 2005, Roy Hatfield and Michelle Allen form a partnership. The partners share equally in all changes in equity. The partnership assumes the assets and liabilities of Roy's existing business. Michelle invests cash equal to Roy's investment.

July	1	Received cash from partner, Michelle Allen, as an initial investment, $12,000.00. R1.
	1	Accepted assets and liabilities of Roy Hatfield's existing business as an initial investment, $12,000.00. R2.
Aug.	1	Journalized personal sale to new partner, Frank Boyd, $8,000.00, distributed as follows: from Michelle Allen, $4,000.00; from Roy Hatfield, $4,000. M8.
Oct.	1	Received cash from new partner, Danita McGrew, for a one-fourth equity in the business, $8,000.00. R80.
	20	Received cash from new partner, Donna Wells, for a one-fifth equity in the business, $7,000.00. Existing equity is redistributed as follows: from Michelle Allen, $200.00; from Roy Hatfield, $200.00; from Frank Boyd, $200.00; from Danita McGrew, $200.00. R92 and M18.
Dec.	5	Received cash from new partner, Pearl Morgan, for a one-sixth equity in the business, $8,200.00. Goodwill, $2,000.00, is distributed as follows: Roy Hatfied, $400.00; Michelle Allen, $400.00; Frank Boy7d, $400.00; Danita McGrew, $400.00; Donna Wells, $400.00. R118 and M24.

Instructions:

1. Add the following accounts:

Account No.	Description	Account Type
3107	Michelle Allen, Capital	Equity-doesn't close
3108	Michelle Allen, Drawing	Equity-gets closed
3109	Frank Boyd, Capital	Equity-doesn't close
3110	Frank Boyd, Drawing	Equity-gets closed
3111	Danita McGrew, Capital	Equity-doesn't close
3112	Danita McGrew, Drawing	Equity-gets closed
3113	Donna Wells, Capital	Equity-doesn't close
3114	Donna Wells, Drawing	Equity-gets closed
3115	Pearl Morgan, Capital	Equity-doesn't close
3116	Pearl Morgan, Drawing	Equity-gets closed

2. Change accounting period to Period 7, Jul 01 to Jul 31, 2005.

3. Journalize and post the July 1 through December 5, 2005 transactions using the cash receipts journal and general journal. (*Hint:* You do *not* need to change accounting periods for August through December transactions.)

4. Print the July 1 through December 5 cash receipts journal.

5. Print the August 1 through December 5 general journal.

6. Back up. The suggested file name is 21-6 Mastery Problem.ptb.

Forming and Expanding Partnership

The instructions that follow show you how to do the following:

- Start Peachtree Complete Accounting.
- Restore starting data from the South-Western Accounting with Peachtree CD.
- Complete adjusting entries.
- Print an income statement.
- Complete closing entries.
- Print the December 31, 2005 general journal.
- Print a balance sheet.
- Complete the 22-5 Mastery Problem.

Before you start the 22-5 Mastery Problem, ask your instructor if J & L Service, the company used for the 22-5 Mastery Problem has already been restored on your computer. The instructions that follow assume that J & L Service is being used for the first time.

GETTING STARTED

Use the following instructions to start Peachtree and restore the starting data for the 22-5 Mastery Problem. The South-Western Accounting with Peachtree CD includes a folder called Peachtree Files-Unit 2. In the steps that follow you will restore the 22-5MP.ptb file.

1. Start Peachtree. From the startup menu, select `Close`.
2. The menu bar shows three options: Files; Options; and Help. Click File; Restore.
3. The Restore Wizard - Select Backup File window appears. Observe that the Location field shows where Peachtree is stored on your computer. The default location is C:\Program Files\Peachtree\ Company. Your Location field may differ. If you are restoring from a network drive, you will need to know the location of the 22-5MP.ptb file.
4. Click `Browse`. The Open Backup File window appears. In the Look in field, double-click on the appropriate location of the Peachtree Files-Unit 2 folder. Then, click 22-5MP.ptb to select it. (If appropriate, select your CD drive then double-click the Peachtree Files-Unit 2 folder. Click 22-5MP.ptb to select it.)

5. Make sure the 22-5MP.ptb file is selected. (*Hint:* Starting data for the 22-5 Mastery Problem is in the Peachtree Files-Unit 2 folder.) Click Open.

6. The Select Backup File window appears. Make sure the Location field shows the correct location for the 22-5MP.ptb file; for example, X:\Peachtree Files-Unit 2\22-5MP.ptb. (Substitute the correct drive letter for X.)

7. Click Next>. The Select Company window appears. Click on the radio button next to *A New Company*. The Location field shown in this book indicates the default location where drive C is used to install Peachtree. Your Location field may differ. *Make sure that the Location field ends in* **jlservic**. (If your location field does not end in "c," select An Existing Company, then click Browse. Double-click J & L Service (*or*, 22-5MPXX). Your Location field shows the shortened company name jlservic. Continue with step 8.)

8. Click Next>. The Restore Options window appears.

9. Make sure that the box next to Company Data is *checked*. Click Next>.

10. The Confirmation window appears. Check the From and To fields to make sure they are correct. Click Finish. When the Restore Company scale is 100% complete, your data is restored and you are returned to the menu bar.

CHANGING THE COMPANY NAME

Before you start recording transactions for the 22-5 Mastery Problem, you should look at the company information included on the 22-5MP.ptb file. Follow these steps to look at company information.

1. The J & L Service menu bar should be displayed. From the menu bar, click on Maintain; Company Information. The Maintain Company Information window appears. Observe that the directory field shows where your company is stored on your computer: C:\Program Files\Peachtree\company\jlservic.

2. Type **22-5MPXX** in the Company Name field.

3. When you are finished typing 22-5MPXX as the company name, click on OK. Once you have changed the Company Name, each one of your printouts will show the activity number and your initials.

Nothing has changed on your computer's hard drive. The company you restored is identified in the program folder and data folder as C:\Program Files\Peachtree\company\jlservic. What you've done is change the company name so that your printouts will show the activity number and your initials. Using Maintain, Company Information to rename your company does *not* change the shortened company name.

Instructions:

Sarah Saxon and Jane Rolf are partners in a business called J & L Service. The partnership's work sheet for the year ended December 31, 2005 is shown below.

J & L Service
Work Sheet
For Year Ended December 31, 20--

	ACCOUNT TITLE	TRIAL BALANCE DEBIT	TRIAL BALANCE CREDIT	ADJUSTMENTS DEBIT	ADJUSTMENTS CREDIT	INCOME STATEMENT DEBIT	INCOME STATEMENT CREDIT	BALANCE SHEET DEBIT	BALANCE SHEET CREDIT	
1	Cash	30165 84						30165 84		1
2	Petty Cash	300 00						300 00		2
3	Accounts Receivable	1799 38						1799 38		3
4	Allowance for Uncollectible Accounts		27 98		(a) 107 00				134 98	4
5	Supplies—Service	8403 07			(b) 6932 42			1470 65		5
6	Supplies—Office	1600 00			(c) 1280 89			319 11		6
7	Prepaid Insurance	1218 87			(d) 451 55			767 32		7
8	Equipment	13621 00						13621 00		8
9	Accum. Depr.—Equipment		2141 00		(e) 1362 00				3503 00	9
10	Truck	12000 00						12000 00		10
11	Accum. Depr.—Truck		2715 00		(f) 1600 00				4315 00	11
12	Accounts Payable		5490 32						5490 32	12
13	Sarah Saxon, Capital		15000 00						15000 00	13
14	Sarah Saxon, Drawing	8000 00						8000 00		14
15	Jane Rolf, Capital		12000 00						12000 00	15
16	Jane Rolf, Drawing	10000 00						10000 00		16
17	Income Summary									17
18	Sales		82838 26				82838 26			18
19	Advertising Expense	800 00				800 00				19
20	Depr. Expense—Equipment			(e) 1362 00		1362 00				20
21	Dept Expense—Truck			(f) 1600 00		1600 00				21
22	Insurance Expense			(d) 451 55		451 55				22
23	Miscellaneous Expense	16024 40				16024 40				23
24	Rent Expense	9600 00				9600 00				24
25	Supplies Expense—Service			(b) 6932 42		6932 42				25
26	Supplies Expense—Office			(c) 1280 89		1280 89				26
27	Truck Expense	4880 00				4880 00				27
28	Uncollectible Accounts Expense			(a) 107 00		107 00				28
29	Utilities Expense	1800 00				1800 00				29
30		120212 56	120212 56	11733 86	11733 86	44838 26	82838 26	78443 30	40443 30	30
31	Net Income					38000 00			38000 00	31
32						82838 26	82838 26	78443 30	78443 30	32

1. Journalize the adjusting entries. In the Reference field, type **Adjustment a.; Adjustment b., Adjustment c.,** etc.

2. Print an income statement. Using a blank piece of paper or the *Working Papers*, calculate and record the component percentages for total operating expenses and net income. Round percentage computations to the nearest 0.1%.

3. Using a blank piece of paper or the *Working Papers,* prepare a distribution of net income statement. Each partner is to receive 10% interest on January 1 equity. The January 1 equity is Sarah, $15,000.00 and Jane, $12,000.00. Also, partners' salaries are Sarah, $10,000.00 and Jane, $15,000.00. The partners share remaining met income, net loss, or deficit equally.

4. Using a blank piece of paper or the *Working Papers,* prepare a statement of owners' equity. (*Hint:* Before completing step 6's closing entries, view Peachtree's balance sheet. Refer to this balance sheet to complete the statement of owners' equity.)

5. Back up. The suggested file name is 22-5 Mastery Problem.adjusted.ptb.

6. Journalize and post the closing entries. In the Reference field, type **Closing entries**.

7. Print a December 31, 2005 general journal.

8. Print a balance sheet.

9. Back up. The The suggested file name is 22-5 Mastery Problem.closed.ptb.

Completing End-of-Fiscal Period Work for a Partnership

The instructions that follow show you how to do the following:

- Start Peachtree Complete Accounting.
- Restore starting data from the South-Western Accounting with Peachtree CD.
- Complete adjusting entries.
- Print an income statement and balance sheet.
- Prepare an owners' equity statement.
- Complete the 22-6 Challenge Problem.

Before you start the 22-6 Challenge Problem, ask your instructor if D & E Sales, the company used for the 22-6 Challenge Problem has already been restored on your computer. The instructions that follow assume that D & E Sales is being used for the first time.

GETTING STARTED

Use the following instructions to start Peachtree and restore the starting data for the 22-6 Challenge Problem. The South-Western Accounting with Peachtree CD includes a folder called Peachtree Files-Unit 2. In the steps that follow you will restore the 22-6CP.ptb file.

1. Start Peachtree. From the startup menu, select Close.
2. The menu bar shows three options: Files; Options; and Help. Click File; Restore.
3. The Restore Wizard - Select Backup File window appears. Observe that the Location field shows where Peachtree is stored on your computer. The default location is C:\Program Files\Peachtree\Company. Your Location field may differ. If you are restoring from a network drive, you will need to know the location of the 22-6CP.ptb file.
4. Click Browse. The Open Backup File window appears. In the Look in field, double-click on the appropriate location of the Peachtree Files-Unit 2 folder. Then, click 22-6CP.ptb to select it. (If

appropriate, select your CD drive then double-click the Peachtree Files-Unit 2 folder. Click 22-6CP.ptb to select it.)

5. Make sure the 22-6CP.ptb file is selected. (*Hint:* Starting data for the 22-6 Challenge Problem is in the Peachtree Files-Unit 2 folder.) Click Open.

6. The Select Backup File window appears. Make sure the Location field shows the correct location for the 22-6CP.ptb file; for example, X:\Peachtree Files-Unit 2\22-6CP.ptb. (Substitute the correct drive letter for X.)

7. Click Next>. The Select Company window appears. Click on the radio button next to *A New Company*. The Location field shown in this book indicates the default location where drive C is used to install Peachtree. Your Location field may differ. *Make sure that the Location field ends in* **desales**. (If your location field does not end in "s" select An Existing Company, then click Browse. Double-click D & E Sales (*or*, 22-6CPXX). Your Location field shows the shortened company name desales. Continue with step 8.)

8. Click Next>. The Restore Options window appears.

9. Make sure that the box next to Company Data is *checked*. Click Next>.

10. The Confirmation window appears. Check the From and To fields to make sure they are correct. Click Finish. When the Restore Company scale is 100% complete, your data is restored and you are returned to the menu bar.

CHANGING THE COMPANY NAME

Before you start recording transactions for the 22-6 Challenge Problem, you should look at the company information included on the 22-6CP.ptb file. Follow these steps to look at company information.

1. The D & E Sales menu bar should be displayed. From the menu bar, click on Maintain; Company Information. The Maintain Company Information window appears. Observe that the directory field shows where your company is stored on your computer: C:\Program Files\Peachtree\company\desales.

2. Type **22-6CPXX** in the Company Name field.

3. When you are finished typing 22-6CPXX as the company name, click on OK. Once you have changed the Company Name, each one of your printouts will show the activity number and your initials.

Nothing has changed on your computer's hard drive. The company you restored is identified in the program folder and data folder as C:\Program Files\Peachtree\company\desales. What you've done is change the company name so that your printouts will show the activity number and your initials. Using Maintain, Company Information to rename your company does *not* change the shortened company name.

Transactions:

The D & E Sales uses a general fund for all financial transactions. Expenditures are recorded by type of expenditure and by department. The four categories of expenditures are personnel, supplies, other charges, and capital outlays. Departments are: General Government, Public Safety, Public Works, and Recreations. The partnership's work sheet for the year ended December 31 is shown below.

D & E Sales

Work Sheet

For Year Ended December 31, 20--

	ACCOUNT TITLE	TRIAL BALANCE DEBIT	TRIAL BALANCE CREDIT	ADJUSTMENTS DEBIT	ADJUSTMENTS CREDIT	INCOME STATEMENT DEBIT	INCOME STATEMENT CREDIT	BALANCE SHEET DEBIT	BALANCE SHEET CREDIT	
1	Cash	6 806 99						6 806 99		1
2	Petty Cash	400 00						400 00		2
3	Accounts Receivable	560 36						560 36		3
4	Allowance for Uncollectible Accounts		12 33		(a) 34 52				46 85	4
5	Merchandise Inventory	12 646 40			(b) 354 69			12 291 71		5
6	Supplies—Sales	1 285 46			(c) 629 88			655 58		6
7	Supplies—Office	914 94			(d) 411 72			503 22		7
8	Prepaid Insurance	1 260 72			(e) 642 97			617 75		8
9	Equipment	11 597 00						11 597 00		9
10	Accum. Depr.—Equipment		2 331 00		(f) 1 159 70				3 490 70	10
11	Truck	7 340 00						7 340 00		11
12	Accum. Depr.—Truck		1 512 04		(g) 734 00				2 246 04	12
13	Accounts Payable		4 839 02						4 839 02	13
14	Theresa Doron, Capital		24 250 00						24 250 00	14
15	Theresa Doron, Drawing	6 000 00						6 000 00		15
16	Roy Eden, Capital		21 500 00						21 500 00	16
17	Roy Eden, Drawing	5 000 00						5 000 00		17
18	Income Summary			(b) 354 69		354 69				18
19	Sales		44 176 74				44 176 74			19
20	Purchases	28 869 38				28 869 38				20
21	Purchases Returns and Allowances		317 56				317 56			21
22	Advertising Expense	750 00				750 00				22
23	Depr. Expense—Equipment			(f) 1 159 70		1 159 70				23
24	Depr. Expense—Truck			(g) 734 00		734 00				24
25	Insurance Expense			(e) 642 97		642 97				25
26	Miscellaneous Expense	928 00				928 00				26
27	Rent Expense	8 400 00				8 400 00				27
28	Supplies Expense—Sales			(c) 629 88		629 88				28
29	Supplies Expense—Office			(d) 411 72		411 72				29
30	Truck Expense	5 227 94				5 227 94				30
31	Uncollectible Accounts Expense			(a) 34 52		34 52				31
32	Utilities Expense	951 50				951 50				32
33		98 938 69	98 938 69	3 967 48	3 967 48	49 094 30	44 494 30	51 772 61	56 372 61	33
34	Net Loss						460 00	460 00		34
35						49 094 30	49 094 30	56 372 61	56 372 61	35

Instructions:

1. Journalize the adjusting entries. In the Reference field, type **Adjustment a.**; **Adjustment b.**, **Adjustment c.**, etc.

2. Print an income statement. Using a blank piece of paper or the *Working Papers*, calculate and record the component percentages for total operating expenses and net income. Round percentage computations to the nearest 0.1%. If there is a net loss, use a minus sign with the component percentage. (*Hint:* Remember Peachtree's income statement shows revenues, cost of sales, and expenses.)

3. Using a blank piece of paper or the *Working Papers*, prepare a distribution of net income statement. Each partner is to receive 10% interest on January 1 equity. The January 1 equity is Theresa, $24,250.00 and Roy, $21,500.00. Also, partners' salaries are Theresa, $12,000.00 and Roy, $10,000.00. The remaining net income, net loss, or deficit is shared as follows: Theresa, 55%; Roy, 45%.

4. Print a balance sheet.

5. Print the December 31, 2005 general journal.

6. Use a blank piece of paper or the *Working Papers* to prepare an owner's equity statement. (*Hint:* Refer to Peachtree's balance sheet.)

7. Back up. The suggested file name is 22-6 Challenge Problem.ptb.

Journalizing Governmental Encumbrances, Expenditures, and Other Transactions

The instructions that follow show you how to do the following:

- Start Peachtree Complete Accounting.
- Restore starting data from the South-Western Accounting with Peachtree CD.
- Complete journal entries.
- Complete the 23-3 Application Problem.

Before you start the 23-3 Application Problem, ask your instructor if the Town of Templeton, the company used for the 23-3 Application Problem has already been restored on your computer. The instructions that follow assume that the Town of Templeton is being used for the first time.

GETTING STARTED

Use the following instructions to start Peachtree and restore the starting data for the 23-3 Application Problem. The South-Western Accounting with Peachtree CD includes a folder called Peachtree Files-Unit 2. In the steps that follow you will restore the 23-3AP.ptb file.

1. Start Peachtree. From the startup menu, select `Close`.
2. The menu bar shows three options: Files; Options; and Help. Click File; Restore.
3. The Restore Wizard - Select Backup File window appears. Observe that the Location field shows where Peachtree is stored on your computer. The default location is C:\Program Files\Peachtree\Company. Your Location field may differ. If you are restoring from a network drive, you will need to know the location of the 23-3AP.ptb file.
4. Click `Browse`. The Open Backup File window appears. In the Look in field, double-click on the appropriate location of the Peachtree Files-Unit 2 folder. Then, click 23-3AP.ptb to select it. (If appropriate, select your CD drive then double-click the Peachtree Files-Unit 2 folder. Click 23-3AP.ptb to select it.)

5. Make sure the 23-3AP.ptb file is selected. (*Hint:* Starting data for the 23-3 Application Problem is in the Peachtree Files-Unit 2 folder.) Click Open.

6. The Select Backup File window appears. Make sure the Location field shows the correct location for the 23-3AP.ptb file; for example, X:\Peachtree Files-Unit 2\23-3AP.ptb. (Substitute the correct drive letter for X.)

7. Click Next >. The Select Company window appears. Click on the radio button next to *A New Company*. The Location field shown in this book indicates the default location where drive C is used to install Peachtree. Your Location field may differ. *Make sure that the Location field ends in* **towoftem**. (If your location field does not end in "m," select An Existing Company, then click Browse. Double-click Town of Templeton (*or,* 23-3APXX). Your Location field shows the shortened company name towoftem. Continue with step 8.)

8. Click Next >. The Restore Options window appears.

9. Make sure that the box next to Company Data is *checked*. Click Next >.

10. The Confirmation window appears. Check the From and To fields to make sure they are correct. Click Finish. When the Restore Company scale is 100% complete, your data is restored and you are returned to the menu bar.

CHANGING THE COMPANY NAME

Before you start recording transactions for the 23-3 Application Problem, you should look at the company information included on the 23-3AP.ptb file. Follow these steps to look at company information.

1. The Town of Templeton menu bar should be displayed. From the menu bar, click on Maintain; Company Information. The Maintain Company Information window appears. Observe that the directory field shows where your company is stored on your computer: C:\Program Files\Peachtree\company\towoftem.

2. Type **23-3APXX** in the Company Name field.

3. When you are finished typing 23-3APXX as the company name, click on OK. Once you have changed the Company Name, each one of your printouts will show the activity number and your initials.

Nothing has changed on your computer's hard drive. The company you restored is identified in the program folder and data folder as C:\Program Files\Peachtree\company\towoftem. What you've done is change the company name so that your printouts will show the activity number and your initials. Using Maintain, Company Information to rename your company does *not* change the shortened company name.

The Town of Templeton uses a general fund for all financial transactions. Expenditures are recorded by type of expenditure and by department. The four categories of expenditures are personnel, supplies, other charges, and capital outlays. Departments are: General Government, Public Safety, Public Works, and Recreations.

Transactions:

Jan.	11	Paid cash for supplies in public works department, $205.00. C244.
	15	Encumbered estimated amount for supplies in public safety department, $235.00. M33.
Jan.	16	Issued a one-month, 10% note, $150,000.00. NP6.
	28	Paid cash for public safety department supplies, $232.00, encumbered January 15 per M33. M40 and C258.
Feb.	5	Paid cash for calculator for general government department, $255.00. C267. (Capital Outlays)
	16	Paid cash for the maturity value of NP6: principal, $150,000.00, plus interest, $1,250.00; total, $151,250.00. C279.
	28	Encumbered estimated amount for supplies in public works department, $276.00. M49.
Mar.	15	Paid cash for a 3-month, 8% certificate of deposit, $200,000.00. C296.
	18	Paid cash for public works department supplies, $278.00, encumbered February 28 per M49. M58 and C315.
	21	Paid cash for consultant's services in recreation department, $360.00. C322. (Personnel)
June	15	Received cash for the maturity value of certificate of deposit due today: principal, $200,000.00, plus interest, $4,000.00; total, $204,000.00. R184.

Instructions:

1. Journalize and post the January 11 through June 15 transactions. Use the appropriate journal.
2. Print the January 11 through March 21, 2005 cash disbursements journal.
3. Print the January 16 through June 15, 2005 cash receipts journal.
4. Print the January 15 through March 18, 2005 general journal.
5. Back up. The suggested file name is 23-3 Application Problem.ptb.

Journalizing Governmental Transactions

The instructions that follow show you how to do the following:

- Start Peachtree Complete Accounting.
- Restore starting data from the South-Western Accounting with Peachtree CD.
- Complete journal entries.
- Complete the 23-4 Mastery Problem.

Before you start the 23-4 Mastery Problem, ask your instructor if the Town of Ingalls, the company used for the 23-4 Mastery Problem has already been restored on your computer. The instructions that follow assume that the Town of Ingalls is being used for the first time.

GETTING STARTED

Use the following instructions to start Peachtree and restore the starting data for the 23-4 Mastery Problem. The South-Western Accounting with Peachtree CD includes a folder called Peachtree Files-Unit 2. In the steps that follow you will restore the 23-4MP.ptb file.

1. Start Peachtree. From the startup menu, select Close.
2. The menu bar shows three options: Files; Options; and Help. Click File; Restore.
3. The Restore Wizard - Select Backup File window appears. Observe that the Location field shows where Peachtree is stored on your computer. The default location is C:\Program Files\Peachtree\Company. Your Location field may differ. If you are restoring from a network drive, you will need to know the location of the 23-4MP.ptb file.
4. Click Browse. The Open Backup File window appears. In the Look in field, double-click on the appropriate location of the Peachtree Files-Unit 2 folder. Then, click 23-4MP.ptb to select it. (If appropriate, select your CD drive then double-click the Peachtree Files-Unit 2 folder. Click 23-4MP.ptb to select it.)
5. Make sure the 23-4MP.ptb file is selected. (*Hint:* Starting data for the 23-4 Mastery Problem is in the Peachtree Files-Unit 2 folder.) Click Open.

6. The Select Backup File window appears. Make sure the Location field shows the correct location for the 23-4MP.ptb file; for example, X:\Peachtree Files-Unit 2\23-4MP.ptb. (Substitute the correct drive letter for X.)

7. Click [Next >]. The Select Company window appears. Click on the radio button next to *A New Company*. The Location field shown in this book indicates the default location where drive C is used to install Peachtree. Your Location field may differ. *Make sure that the Location field ends in* **towofing**. (If your location field does not end in "g," select An Existing Company, then click [Browse]. Double-click Town of Ingalls (*or*, 23-4MPXX). Your Location field shows the shortened company name towofing. Continue with step 8.)

8. Click [Next >]. The Restore Options window appears.

9. Make sure that the box next to Company Data is *checked*. Click [Next >].

10. The Confirmation window appears. Check the From and To fields to make sure they are correct. Click [Finish]. When the Restore Company scale is 100% complete, your data is restored and you are returned to the menu bar.

CHANGING THE COMPANY NAME

Before you start recording transactions for the 23-4 Mastery Problem, you should look at the company information included on the 23-4MP.ptb file. Follow these steps to look at company information.

1. The Town of Ingalls menu bar should be displayed. From the menu bar, click on Maintain; Company Information. The Maintain Company Information window appears. Observe that the directory field shows where your company is stored on your computer: C:\Program Files\Peachtree\company\towofing.

2. Type **23-4MPXX** in the Company Name field.

3. When you are finished typing 23-4MPXX as the company name, click on [OK]. Once you have changed the Company Name, each one of your printouts will show the activity number and your initials.

Nothing has changed on your computer's hard drive. The company you restored is identified in the program folder and data folder as C:\Program Files\Peachtree\company\towofing. What you've done is change the company name so that your printouts will show the activity number and your initials. Using Maintain, Company Information to rename your company does *not* change the shortened company name.

Transactions:

The Town of Ingalls uses a general fund for all financial transactions. Expenditures are recorded by type of expenditure and by department. The four categories of expenditures are personnel, supplies, other charges, and capital outlays. Departments are: General Government, Public Safety, Public Works, and Recreations.

Jan.	2	Recorded current year's approved operating budget: estimated revenues, $1,270,000.00; appropriations, $1,224,000.00; budgetary fund balance, $46,000.00. M42.
	2	Recorded current year's property tax levy: taxes receivable—current, $1,220,000.00; allowance for uncollectible taxes—current, $12,200.00; property tax revenue, $1,207,800.00. M43.
	9	Received cash for current taxes receivable, $57,300.00. R105.
	11	Paid cash for gas utility service in general government department, $234.00. C168.
	12	Issued a 2-month, 9% note, $200,000.00. NP7.
	16	Encumbered estimated amount for supplies in public works department, $165.00. M54.
	20	Received cash from traffic fines, $225.00. R111. (Other Revenue)
	30	Paid cash for lawn mower for public works department, $450.00. (Capital Outlays) C182.
Feb.	6	Paid cash for public works department supplies, $170.00, encumbered January 16 per M54. M58 and C190.
	24	Encumbered estimated amount for supplies in recreation department, $133.00. M69.
Mar.	1	Recorded reclassification of current taxes receivable to delinquent status, $51,400.00, and the accompanying allowance for uncollectible accounts, $12,200.00. M76.
	12	Paid cash for the maturity value of NP7: principal, $200,000.00, plus interest, $3,000.00; total, $203,000.00. C222.
	20	Paid cash for a 3-month, 8% certificate of deposit, $400,000.00. C234.
	22	Paid cash for recreation department supplies, $131.00, encumbered February 24 per M69. M88 and C241.
Apr.	10	Received cash for delinquent taxes receivable, $21,000.00. R355.
	25	Paid cash for consultant's services in recreation department, $500.00. C266. (Personnel)
June	20	Received cash for the maturity value of certificate of deposit due today: principal, $400,000.00, plus interest, $8,000.00; total, $408,000.00. R497.

Instructions:

1. Journalize and post the January 2 through June 20 transactions. Use the appropriate journal.
2. Print the January 11 through April 25, 2005 cash disbursements journal.
3. Print the January 9 through June 20, 2005 cash receipts journal.
4. Print the January 2 through March 22, 2005 general journal.
5. Back up. The suggested file name is 23-4 Mastery Problem.ptb.

Completing the End-of-Fiscal-Period Work for a Governmental Organization

The instructions that follow show you how to do the following:

- Start Peachtree Complete Accounting.
- Restore starting data from the South-Western Accounting with Peachtree CD.
- Complete adjusting entries.
- Complete closing entries.
- Complete the 24-4 Mastery Problem.

Before you start the 24-4 Mastery Problem, ask your instructor if the Town of Duluth, the company used for the 24-4 Mastery Problem has already been restored on your computer. The instructions that follow assume that the Town of Duluth is being used for the first time.

GETTING STARTED

Use the following instructions to start Peachtree and restore the starting data for the 24-4 Mastery Problem. The South-Western Accounting with Peachtree CD includes a folder called Peachtree Files-Unit 2. In the steps that follow you will restore the 24-4MP.ptb file.

1. Start Peachtree. From the startup menu, select Close .
2. The menu bar shows three options: Files; Options; and Help. Click File; Restore.
3. The Restore Wizard - Select Backup File window appears. Observe that the Location field shows where Peachtree is stored on your computer. The default location is C:\Program Files\Peachtree\Company. Your Location field may differ. If you are restoring from a network drive, you will need to know the location of the 24-4MP.ptb file.
4. Click Browse . The Open Backup File window appears. In the Look in field, double-click on the appropriate location of the Peachtree Files-Unit 2 folder. Then, click 24-4MP.ptb to select it. (If appropriate, select your CD drive then double-click the Peachtree Files-Unit 2 folder. Click 24-4MP.ptb to select it.)

5. Make sure the 24-4MP.ptb file is selected. (*Hint:* Starting data for the 24-4 Mastery Problem is in the Peachtree Files-Unit 2 folder.) Click Open.

6. The Select Backup File window appears. Make sure the Location field shows the correct location for the 24-4MP.ptb file; for example, X:\Peachtree Files-Unit 2\24-4MP.ptb. (Substitute the correct drive letter for X.)

7. Click Next >. The Select Company window appears. Click on the radio button next to *A New Company*. The Location field shown in this book indicates the default location where drive C is used to install Peachtree. Your Location field may differ. *Make sure that the Location field ends in* **towofdul**. (If your location field does not end in "l," select An Existing Company, then click Browse. Double-click Town of Duluth (*or*, 24-4MPXX). Your Location field shows the shortened company name towofdul. Continue with step 8.)

8. Click Next >. The Restore Options window appears.

9. Make sure that the box next to Company Data is *checked*. Click Next >.

10. The Confirmation window appears. Check the From and To fields to make sure they are correct. Click Finish. When the Restore Company scale is 100% complete, your data is restored and you are returned to the menu bar.

CHANGING THE COMPANY NAME

Before you start recording transactions for the 24-4 Mastery Problem, you should look at the company information included on the 24-4MP.ptb file. Follow these steps to look at company information.

1. The Town of Duluth menu bar should be displayed. From the menu bar, click on Maintain; Company Information. The Maintain Company Information window appears. Observe that the directory field shows where your company is stored on your computer: C:\Program Files\Peachtree\company\towofdul.

2. Type **24-4MPXX** in the Company Name field.

3. When you are finished typing 24-4MPXX as the company name, click on OK. Once you have changed the Company Name, each one of your printouts will show the activity number and your initials.

Nothing has changed on your computer's hard drive. The company you restored is identified in the program folder and data folder as C:\Program Files\Peachtree\company\towofdul. What you've done is change the company name so that your printouts will show the activity number and your initials. Using Maintain, Company Information to rename your company does *not* change the shortened company name.

The Town of Duluth uses a general fund. The trial balance for December 31, 2005 is shown below. The December 31 adjustment information is shown on the next page.

1. Display Peachtree's general ledger trial balance. Compare it to the one shown below. If you are using the *Working Papers,* this trial balance is the same as the one shown on the 24-4 Mastery Problem's worksheet.

Town of Duluth
General Ledger Trial Balance
As of Dec 31, 2005

Filter Criteria includes: Report order is by ID. Report is printed in Detail Format.

Account ID	Account Description	Debit Amt	Credit Amt
1010	Cash	103,390.00	
1040	Taxes Receivable-Delinquent	10,430.00	
1050	Allow. Uncoll. Taxes-Delinq.		6,940.00
2010	Accounts Payable		29,340.00
3010	Unreserved Fund Balance		35,550.00
3020	Reserve for Encumbrances-CY		1,870.00
4010	Property Tax Revenue		1,265,000.00
4020	Interest Revenue		6,680.00
4030	Other Revenue		8,120.00
5110	Expenditure-Personnel, Gen Gov	211,640.00	
5120	Expenditure-Supplies, Gen Gov	10,490.00	
5130	Expenditure-Oth Chrg, Gen Gov	106,550.00	
5140	Expenditure-Cap Out, Gen Gov	12,300.00	
5210	Expenditure-Personnel, Pub Saf	397,540.00	
5220	Expenditure-Supplies, Pub Saf	18,620.00	
5230	Expenditure-Oth Chr, Pub Saf	144,150.00	
5240	Expenditure-Cap Out, Pub Saf	72,300.00	
5310	Expenditure-Personnel, Pub Wrk	92,200.00	
5320	Expenditure-Supplies, Pub Wrk	5,250.00	
5330	Expenditure-Oth Chr, Pub Wrk	44,750.00	
5340	Expenditure-Cap Out, Pub Wrk	39,600.00	
5410	Expenditure-Personnel, Recreat	48,220.00	
5420	Expenditure-Supplies, Recreat	1,850.00	
5430	Expenditure-Oth Chr, Recreat	23,480.00	
5440	Expenditure-Cap Out, Recreat	8,870.00	
6010	Estimated Revenues	1,280,000.00	
6020	Appropriations		1,240,000.00
6030	Budgetary Fund Balance		40,000.00
6120	Encumbrance-Supplies, Gen Gov	1,870.00	
	Total:	**2,633,500.00**	**2,633,500.00**

Town of Duluth
Annual Operating Budget—General Fund
For Year Ended December 31, 20--

ESTIMATED REVENUES

Property Tax	$1,265,000.00	
Interest	7,250.00	
Other	7,750.00	
Total Estimated Revenues		$1,280,000.00

ESTIMATED EXPENDITURES AND BUDGETARY FUND BALANCE

General Government:		
Personnel	$ 211,750.00	
Supplies	11,360.00	
Other Charges	106,700.00	
Capital Outlays	12,390.00	
Total General Government		$ 342,200.00
Public Safety:		
Personnel	$ 397,590.00	
Supplies	18,900.00	
Other Charges	144,290.00	
Capital Outlays	72,320.00	
Total Public Safety		633,100.00
Public Works:		
Personnel	$ 92,270.00	
Supplies	5,280.00	
Other Charges	44,770.00	
Capital Outlays	39,680.00	
Total Public Works		182,000.00
Recreation:		
Personnel	$ 48,220.00	
Supplies	1,880.00	
Other Charges	23,690.00	
Capital Outlays	8,910.00	
Total Recreation		82,700.00
Total Estimated Expenditures		$1,240,000.00
Budgetary Fund Balance		40,000.00
Total Estimated Expenditures and Budgetary Fund Balance		$1,280,000.00

2. Using a blank piece of paper or the *Working Papers*, prepare a statement of revenues, expenditures, and changes in fund balance—budget and actual for the year ended December 31, 2005. The unreserved fun balance on January 1 was $35,550.00.

3. Analyze the December 31 adjustment information. Journalize and post the adjusting entries.

Adjustment Information, December 31

Supplies Inventory	$2,900.00
Interest Revenue Due but not Collected	2,350.00

An estimated 20% of the interest revenue due will not be collected.

The reserve for encumbrances for the current year is reclassified to prior year status.

4. Journalize the closing entries.
5. Print the December 31, 2005 general journal.
6. Print a balance sheet.
7. Back up. The suggested file name is 24-4 Mastery Problem.ptb.

Completing the End-of-Fiscal-Period Work for a Governmental Organization

The instructions that follow show you how to do the following:

- Start Peachtree Complete Accounting.
- Restore starting data from the South-Western Accounting with Peachtree CD.
- Complete adjusting entries.
- Complete closing entries.
- Complete the 24-5 Challenge Problem.

Before you start the 24-5 Challenge Problem, ask your instructor if the Town of Plymouth, the company used for the 24-5 Challenge Problem has already been restored on your computer. The instructions that follow assume that the Town of Plymouth is being used for the first time.

GETTING STARTED

Use the following instructions to start Peachtree and restore the starting data for the 24-5 Challenge Problem. The South-Western Accounting with Peachtree CD includes a folder called Peachtree Files-Unit 2. In the steps that follow you will restore the 24-5CP.ptb file.

1. Start Peachtree. From the startup menu, select Close.
2. The menu bar shows three options: Files; Options; and Help. Click File; Restore.
3. The Restore Wizard - Select Backup File window appears. Observe that the Location field shows where Peachtree is stored on your computer. The default location is C:\Program Files\Peachtree\Company. Your Location field may differ. If you are restoring from a network drive, you will need to know the location of the 24-5CP.ptb file.
4. Click Browse. The Open Backup File window appears. In the Look in field, double-click on the appropriate location of the Peachtree Files-Unit 2 folder. Then, click 24-5CP.ptb to select it. (If appropriate, select your CD drive then double-click the Peachtree Files-Unit 2 folder. Click 24-5CP.ptb to select it.)

5. Make sure the 24-5CP.ptb file is selected. (*Hint:* Starting data for the 24-5 Challenge Problem is in the Peachtree Files-Unit 2 folder.) Click ⬚ Open .

6. The Select Backup File window appears. Make sure the Location field shows the correct location for the 24-5CP.ptb file; for example, X:\Peachtree Files-Unit 2\24-5CP.ptb. (Substitute the correct drive letter for X.)

7. Click ⬚ Next > . The Select Company window appears. Click on the radio button next to *A New Company*. The Location field shown in this book indicates the default location where drive C is used to install Peachtree. Your Location field may differ. *Make sure that the Location field ends in* **towofply**. (If your location field does not end in "y," select An Existing Company, then click ⬚ Browse . Double-click Town of Plymouth (*or*, 24-5CPXX). Your Location field shows the shortened company name towofply. Continue with step 8.)

8. Click ⬚ Next > . The Restore Options window appears.

9. Make sure that the box next to Company Data is *checked*. Click ⬚ Next > .

10. The Confirmation window appears. Check the From and To fields to make sure they are correct. Click ⬚ Finish . When the Restore Company scale is 100% complete, your data is restored and you are returned to the menu bar.

CHANGING THE COMPANY NAME

Before you start recording transactions for the 24-5 Challenge Problem, you should look at the company information included on the 24-5CP.ptb file. Follow these steps to look at company information.

1. The Town of Plymouth menu bar should be displayed. From the menu bar, click on Maintain; Company Information. The Maintain Company Information window appears. Observe that the directory field shows where your company is stored on your computer: C:\Program Files\Peachtree\company\towofply.

2. Type **24-5CPXX** in the Company Name field.

3. When you are finished typing 24-5CPXX as the company name, click on ⬚ OK . Once you have changed the Company Name, each one of your printouts will show the activity number and your initials.

Nothing has changed on your computer's hard drive. The company you restored is identified in the program folder and data folder as C:\Program Files\Peachtree\company\towofply. What you've done is change the company name so that your printouts will show the activity number and your initials. Using Maintain, Company Information to rename your company does *not* change the shortened company name.

Instructions:

The Town of Plymouth uses a general fund. The trial balance for December 31, 2005 is shown below. The adjustment information for December 31 is shown on the next page.

1. Display Peachtree's general ledger trial balance. Compare it to the one shown below. If you are using the *Working Papers,* this trial balance is the same as the one shown on the 24-5 Challenge Problem's worksheet.

Town of Plymouth
General Ledger Trial Balance
As of Dec 31, 2005

Filter Criteria includes: Report order is by ID. Report is printed in Detail Format.

Account ID	Account Description	Debit Amt	Credit Amt
1010	Cash	56,148.00	
1040	Taxes Receivable-Delinquent	28,074.00	
1050	Allow. Uncoll. Taxes-Delinq.		11,225.00
2010	Accounts Payable		35,816.00
3010	Unreserved Fund Balance		63,450.00
3020	Reserve for Encumbrances-CY		1,076.00
4010	Property Tax Revenue		1,455,900.00
4020	Interest Revenue		9,885.00
4030	Other Revenue		15,973.00
5110	Expenditure-Personnel, Gen Gov	260,520.00	
5120	Expenditure-Supplies, Gen Gov	14,394.00	
5130	Expenditure-Oth Chrg, Gen Gov	129,975.00	
5140	Expenditure-Cap Out, Gen Gov	15,168.00	
5210	Expenditure-Personnel, Pub Saf	483,590.00	
5220	Expenditure-Supplies, Pub Saf	21,973.00	
5230	Expenditure-Oth Chr, Pub Saf	175,843.00	
5240	Expenditure-Cap Out, Pub Saf	85,745.00	
5310	Expenditure-Personnel, Pub Wrk	113,225.00	
5320	Expenditure-Supplies, Pub Wrk	6,687.00	
5330	Expenditure-Oth Chr, Pub Wrk	52,684.00	
5340	Expenditure-Cap Out, Pub Wrk	48,820.00	
5410	Expenditure-Personnel, Recreat	56,855.00	
5420	Expenditure-Supplies, Recreat	2,678.00	
5430	Expenditure-Oth Chr, Recreat	28,910.00	
5440	Expenditure-Cap Out, Recreat	10,960.00	
6010	Estimated Revenues	1,485,840.00	
6020	Appropriations		1,511,160.00
6030	Budgetary Fund Balance	25,320.00	
6110	Encumbrance-Personnel, Gen Gov	1,076.00	
	Total:	**3,104,485.00**	**3,104,485.00**

Town of Plymouth
Annual Operating Budget—General Fund
For Year Ended December 31, 20--

ESTIMATED REVENUES AND BUDGETARY FUND BALANCE

Property Tax	$1,455,900.00	
Interest	13,360.00	
Other	16,580.00	
Total Estimated Revenues		$1,485,840.00
Budgetary Fund Balance		25,320.00
Estimated Revenues and Budgetary Fund Balance		$1,511,160.00

ESTIMATED EXPENDITURES

General Government:		
Personnel	$ 260,480.00	
Supplies	14,280.00	
Other Charges	130,240.00	
Capital Outlays	15,130.00	
Total General Government		$ 420,130.00
Public Safety:		
Personnel	$ 484,610.00	
Supplies	23,080.00	
Other Charges	176,920.00	
Capital Outlays	84,920.00	
Total Public Safety		769,530.00
Public Works:		
Personnel	$ 113,300.00	
Supplies	6,660.00	
Other Charges	53,120.00	
Capital Outlays	48,875.00	
Total Public Works		221,955.00
Recreation:		
Personnel	$ 56,855.00	
Supplies	2,790.00	
Other Charges	28,925.00	
Capital Outlays	10,975.00	
Total Recreation		99,545.00
Total Estimated Expenditures		$1,511,160.00

2. Using a blank piece of paper or the *Working Papers,* prepare a statement of revenues, expenditures, and changes in fund balance—budget and actual for the year ended December 31, 2005. The unreserved fun balance on January 1 was $63,450.00.

3. Analyze the December 31 adjustment information. Journalize and post the adjusting entries.

Adjustment Information, December 31

Supplies Inventory	$3,382.00
Interest Revenue Due but not Collected	6,080.00

An estimated 20% of the interest revenue due will not be collected.

The reserve for encumbrances for the current year is reclassified to prior year status.

4. Journalize the closing entries.
5. Print the December 31, 2005 general journal.
6. Print a balance sheet.
7. Back up. The suggested file name is 24-5 Challenge Problem.ptb.